Feasts

ARCHAEOLOGICAL AND

ETHNOGRAPHIC PERSPECTIVES

ON FOOD, POLITICS, AND POWER

Edited by Michael Dietler and Brian Hayden

SMITHSONIAN INSTITUTION PRESS

WASHINGTON AND LONDON

© 2001 by the Smithsonian Institution
All rights reserved

COPY EDITOR: Peter Donovan
PRODUCTION EDITOR: Duke Johns
DESIGNER: Amber Frid-Jimenez

Library of Congress Cataloging-in-Publication Data
Feasts : archaeological and ethnographic perspectives on food, politics, and power / edited by
Michael Dietler, Brian Hayden.
    p.   cm.
    Includes bibliographical references and index.
    ISBN 1-56098-861-4 (alk. paper) — ISBN 1-56098-840-1 (paper : alk. paper)
    1. Festivals—Congresses. Fasts and feasts—Congresses. I. Dietler, Michael.
II. Hayden, Brian.
    GT3930.F4   2001
    394.26—dc21   00-061932

British Library Cataloguing-in-Publication Data available

Manufactured in the United States of America

08 07 06 05 04 03 02 01   5 4 3 2 1

♾ The paper used in this publication meets the minimum requirements of the American
National Standard for Information Sciences—Permanence of Paper for Printed Library
Materials ANSI Z39.48-1984.

For permission to reproduce illustrations appearing in this book, please correspond directly
with the owners of the works, as listed in the individual captions. The Smithsonian Institution
Press does not retain reproduction rights for these illustrations individually, or maintain a file
of addresses for photo sources.

Contents

Illustrations

Tables

Contributors

Linda A. Brown, Department of Anthropology, University of Colorado, Boulder

Michael J. Clarke, Department of Archaeology, Simon Fraser University

Warren R. DeBoer, Department of Anthropology, Queens College, City University of New York

Michael Dietler, Department of Anthropology, University of Chicago

Brian Hayden, Department of Archaeology, Simon Fraser University

Ingrid Herbich, Department of Anthropology, University of Chicago

Laura Lee Junker, Department of Anthropology, Western Michigan University

Lucretia S. Kelly, Department of Anthropology, Washington University, St. Louis

Patrick V. Kirch, Department of Anthropology, University of California, Berkeley

Vernon James Knight, Department of Anthropology, University of Alabama

James R. Perodie, Department of Archaeology, Simon Fraser University

William L. Rathje, Department of Anthropology, University of Arizona

Denise Schmandt-Besserat, Center for Middle Eastern Studies, University of Texas at Austin

Polly Wiessner, Department of Anthropology, University of Utah

Douglas C. Wilson, National Park Service, Vancouver, Washington

1

DIGESTING THE FEAST: GOOD TO EAT, GOOD TO DRINK, GOOD TO THINK

AN INTRODUCTION

Michael Dietler and Brian Hayden

With apologies to Lévi-Strauss for yet another usurping of his famous dictum, a central argument of this volume is surely that feasts are "good to think." Indeed, these chapters collectively indicate the appropriateness of this statement in two crucial senses. In the first place, they convincingly demonstrate that thinking about feasts can, and should, provide an important point of departure for understanding culture and social life in both past and present societies. In particular, the time is long overdue for feasts to be taken seriously by archaeologists as a significant—perhaps a central—social practice. Secondly, however, these chapters also show that transforming feasts from something considered as epiphenomenal trivia worthy of little more than bemused speculation into a subject of recognized importance and analytical utility is by no means a straightforward proposition. We need to think seriously and critically about what feasts are, how they operate, and how we can detect and interpret them. Otherwise, they risk becoming one more ill-digested archaeological interpretive fad.

One of the main stimuli for undertaking this book, and for convening the symposium that generated it, was that both of the editors came to the conclusion over a decade ago that feasts are an extremely significant aspect of social life on a worldwide scale, and that understanding them is crucial for apprehending and comprehending many social and cultural processes in ancient societies. However, we arrived at this mutual conclusion by quite different routes and from very different theoretical dispositions.

As will be evident from our respective chapters and prior publications on the subject, Hayden's perspective (see Chapter 2) is firmly grounded in a cultural-ecology orientation. Furthermore, he was originally led to explore this line of research largely by his interest in the evolutionary implications of feasting in the transformation of sociopolitical structures in hunter-gatherer societies of the Pacific Northwest and Paleolithic Europe. Dietler's perspective (see Chapter 3), on the other hand, grew out of the domain of social theory often referred to by the ecologically inclined as "culturalist"—that is, a perspective that takes culture seriously as a historical agent as well as a historical product—although, because of its determinist implications, this label is one that few scholars would actually apply to themselves. Hence, Dietler's perspective actually has a strong social orientation, with roots in practice theory and political economy (in a nutshell, there is a central concern with the intricate relationship between culture and power). Moreover, he was induced to investigate feasting as a result of archaeological and ethnographic research among agrarian societies in Europe and Africa.

This very fact of arriving at a conjuncture of interest and understanding from such strikingly different directions strengthened our convictions that, despite our continuing dialogue of disagreement over a number of issues (see below, and Chapters 2 and 3), we had stumbled upon something of genuine and general significance.

One of the more disconcerting conclusions that we also agreed upon, however, was that feasting was both severely undertheorized in the existing literature and lacked systematic empirical documentation of a kind that would be useful for archaeological interpretation. This is not to claim that feasting has been completely ignored in the earlier archaeological and anthropological literature, or that significant insights have not been forthcoming (e.g., see Friedman 1984; Friedman and Rowlands 1978). However, these earlier works generally included analyses of feasts as peripheral observations: they did not generate a systematic theoretical exploration of the subject and they failed to engender a sustained archaeological pursuit of their implications. Hence, we sought to convene a group of other scholars who have recently begun to pursue similar issues in a wide variety of both ethnographic and archaeological contexts in order to forge a better, if still provisional, understanding of the nature of the feast as a social institution and cultural practice. As the chapters in this volume attest, these scholars also exhibit a healthy diversity of theoretical orientations and ideas about how to understand feasts. Consequently, this brief introductory essay is less an attempt to force these chapters into a strained synthetic summary than it is a selective highlighting of a few key themes that indicate the current state of research and suggest future directions.

CATEGORIES AND DEFINITIONS

Perhaps the most obvious question that needs to be addressed at this point is, "Are we all talking about the same thing when we use the word *feast*?" Obviously, we are not really talking about a "thing" at all, but about a category used to describe collectively a diverse set of cultural practices. Hence, equally important to ask is the related question, "Is this a useful analytical category?" In other words, it is clear that we all use the rubric *feast* to cover a wide range of cultural practices. Are we agreed on the criteria by which we selectively lump these practices together and exclude others, and does the resulting category have enough coherence and specificity to be useful? We believe the answer to both questions is "yes," with a few stipulations.

Each paper provides at least a general working definition of feasts. These definitions show some variability in both the details (such as the requisite social distance of the participants and size of the gathering) and the ways they are phrased; and some are more explicit than others. However, common to all of these is the idea that feasts are events essentially constituted by the communal consumption of food and/or drink. Most authors are also explicit in differentiating such food-consumption events from both everyday domestic meals and from the simple exchange of food without communal consumption. These are important distinctions to maintain if the category is to have analytical utility. To the extent that one begins to conflate feasts with the general exchange of food or with the other kinds of transactions for which feasts may serve as a context, one precludes both understanding feasts as a specific social practice and understanding the important semiotic and functional relationships between feasts and these other kinds of practices.

Dietler (Chapter 3) also argues that it is crucial to recognize and understand feasting as a particular form of *ritual* activity. This is what distinguishes feasts from daily meals, gives them their peculiar power in articulating social relations and action, and makes them analytically approachable by building upon an existing body of theoretical work. The dramaturgical effects usually associated with feasting (e.g., singing, dancing, inebriation, oratorical displays) underline the ritual nature of these events. They help to create the experience of "condensed meaning" (Cohen 1979) and render feasts such ideal stages for other important social transactions, such as prestations of valuables, making alliances, and, as Wiessner (Chapter 4) demonstrates, the construction of value.

In contrast, Hayden (Chapter 2) uses a somewhat broader definition, simply stipulating that any unusual occasion accompanied by an unusual shared meal should be considered a feast. Moreover, in his view, ritual aspects may or may not be identifiable archaeologically and may not even be overtly manifest in some ethnographic cases. Other authors propose yet other minor variations for the definition of feasts. However, despite these differences, there is still a very large degree of agreement on identifying many kinds of shared meals as feasts when confronted with empirical cases in ethnographic contexts.

Given these stipulations, it seems clear that "feasts" is a category that has sufficient specificity to be analytically powerful yet brings within its scope a significant range of important practices around the world and through time. Hence "feasts" is a productive category. It is "good to think."

Within the domain of practices that we designate as feasts, there are many possible ways to categorize the range of differences and similarities. This fact explains the considerable diversity of classificatory schemes brought to bear on the subject by the authors in this volume. While some readers may find the lack of a uniform classification troubling or disappointing, we would suggest that this diversity need not worry us and is, in fact, a good thing—especially at this stage of theoretical development. Classifications are, after all, simply tools of analysis. Different ones will be appropriate for different purposes. The criteria for selecting them should be simply the effectiveness they demonstrate in achieving the goals for which they were designed, the interest of those goals, and, of course, the logical consistency of the classifications. As research progresses in this relatively novel field, our various ways of characterizing and understanding feasts will undoubtedly improve. But this does not mean that we will move toward the development of a single typology of feasts. In our view that would be counterproductive: in the social sciences, classificatory reification is generally the enemy of understanding.

Hayden (Chapter 2) has expressed the hope that eventually we may develop an archaeological classification of feasts based on material remains. Others (e.g., Dietler, Chapter 3) are less sanguine about this prospect, believing that the culturally constituted nature of feasts mandates that archaeological interpretation will always require the construction of a richly textured and culturally specific contextual argument grounded in a theoretical understanding of the complexities of feasting in comparative ethnographic perspective—in other words, a version of what Hayden calls "triangulation." The difficulties of distinguishing on a priori grounds between, for example, the permutations of ritual practices that are used to mark feasts off from everyday meals, and those that are used to mark off social classes in "diacritical" feasts (see Dietler, Chapter 3) suggest that uniform typologies of material signatures may not help us much beyond the mere identification of the existence of feasting.

Whatever the eventual resolution of this discussion, what is clear is that moving beyond the basic identification of presence toward understanding what kinds of feasts were being mounted, what kinds of ritual work were being undertaken, and what the social ramifications were, requires complex and nuanced forms of recursive argumentation. However, even if a handy interpretive formula may ultimately be unattainable for archaeologists (as well as for cultural anthropologists and historians), this does not mean that we cannot develop a much better understanding of the material dimension of feasting. Indeed, at present, the lack of precise information on this issue is one of the biggest impediments to the archaeological investigation of feasting and the evaluation of the relative plausibility of different archaeological interpretations. For the most part, archaeologists do not yet know precisely what to look for. The exemplary archaeological studies by Junker (Chapter 10), Knight (Chapter 11), Kelly (Chapter 12), Brown (Chapter 13), and Schmandt-Besserat (Chapter 14) in this volume point the way toward profitable strategies for interrogating the archaeological record for this kind of information (see also, for example, Blitz 1993; Clark and Blake 1994; Dietler 1990, 1996, 1999b; Gardeisen 1999; Moore 1989; Morris 1979; Murray 1995). But much more primary ethnographic research focusing specifically on feasting, of the kind undertaken by Clarke (Chapter 5), Hayden (Chapter 2), and Dietler and Herbich (Chapters 3 and 9), is urgently needed. Moreover, this work should be undertaken by scholars already familiar with the problems of detecting feasts in archaeological contexts. Again, it is the synergistic dialectical conversation between these domains that will propel the development of theory and method for both.

As a final note on classification, a brief word about the classificatory structure of this volume is also in order. Part One assembles considerations of feasting based upon ethnographic and historical data, either through comparative analysis or individual case studies. These chapters use these rich sources of information about social life to develop a fuller understanding of feasting practices and they discuss the material implications of the analyses they undertake. Several of these chapters are explicitly concerned with developing new theoretical approaches to feasting, and all offer at least implicit theoretical insights. Moreover, all have as a major goal assessing and aiding the possibilities for archaeological interpretation of feasts, although, given the limitations of space, they do not actually involve the application of such insights to specific archaeological cases.

Thus, Hayden (Chapter 2) examines feasting from a cross-cultural and ecological perspective toward the development of a general framework for the archaeological detection and interpretation of feasts. Dietler (Chapter 3) uses the Luo and other African cases to argue for the inherently political role of feasts and to develop a general theoretical analysis of the complex relationship between feasts, commensality, and power. Wiessner (Chapter 4) provides a rich ethnohistorical analysis of the role of feasts in religious cults and strategies of New Guinea big-men for promoting their self-interests and transforming conceptions of value. Clarke (Chapter 5) shows how feasts are used by the Akha tribes of Thailand to establish socioeconomic safety networks. Kirch (Chapter 6) uses a comparison of three Polynesian cases to demonstrate how the magnitude of, and facilities associated with, feasting increase with increasing size and complexity of the polities. Perodie (Chapter 7) documents the range of feasting on the Northwest Coast of North America and illustrates what advantages accrued to hosts. DeBoer (Chapter 8) provides an important example of Amazonian feasting with its unique girl's initiation features and competitive male boasting, and reflects upon long-term historical transformations and continuities. Finally, Dietler and Herbich (Chapter 9) use a comparative examination of the political-economic dynamics of work feasts among the Samia of Africa and other societies to propose a general theoretical model for the crucial role of feasts in labor mobilization and exploitation.

Part Two contains chapters that move in the opposite interpretive direction. That is, they attempt to grapple with the detection of feasting in the material record and to then make plausible inferences about the social life and culture of the people who were producing and participating in those feasts. These creatively ingenious studies illustrate both the difficulties and potential of this domain of inquiry, as well as the necessity of a recursive dialectical conversation between ethnographically derived theory and archaeological data. At first glance, it may appear curious that Wilson and Rathje's (Chapter 15) study of garbage in present-day Tucson should be classed together with these latter chapters; but, in fact, the logic of this interpretive exercise is thoroughly archaeological. The samples of refuse were obtained by means other than excavation, but these material items are then used to reason inferentially back to an interpretation of the practices that produced them based upon an understanding of the general social context (but without direct observation of those specific practices). Hence, they provide a good heuristic test of the possibilities for understanding feasting through material remains in a social and cultural context with which many readers will have some familiarity.

Other chapters in this section offer a range of more obviously archaeological case studies. Junker (Chapter 10) provides a regional analysis of the economic and political role of feasts in the very dynamic cultural environment of the Philippines during the second millennium A.D. Knight (Chapter 11) explores the important role of feasting in the creation and use of the first platform mounds among the Woodland cultures of the southeastern United States during the first millennium A.D., while Kelly (Chapter 12) documents large-scale feasting at the largest Mississippian sites during the early stages of the succeeding millennium. Brown (Chapter 13) presents an analysis of new evidence for the use of special feasting structures for lineage feasts in non-elite Maya contexts around A.D. 600. Finally, moving to the ancient Near East, Schmandt-Besserat (Chapter 14) explores the use of feasts by Sumerian elites to collect surpluses.

It is worth emphasizing that, despite the impressive diversity of geographical and temporal contexts represented by the chapters in this section, the intention was clearly not to provide a comprehensive global coverage of feasting in prehistory. Hence, the absence of studies from certain regions should by no means be taken as an indication that the editors judged that feasting was not an important feature of the ancient social landscape in those areas or that the potential for the archaeological analysis of feasts is less good in those contexts. Far from it. Europe, for example, is not covered in this volume even though feasting is now increasingly recognized to have been a practice of major importance implicated in various kinds of social change throughout the region and despite the fact that one of the editors has previously undertaken several studies of feasting in different European archaeological contexts (Dietler 1990, 1996, 1999a, 1999b; see also Murray 1995; Schmitt Pantel 1992; Sherratt 1991). The intention of Part Two was simply to provide a selected set of fresh cases demonstrating cutting-edge possibilities for the identification and interpretation of feasts in a diverse, rather than exhaustive, range of archaeological contexts.

FEASTS AND FEASTING

Another important question to pose is whether one legitimately can discuss *feasting* in archaeological contexts without actually being able to identify specific *feasts*. In other words, can one detect the traces of a practice, or process, without necessarily being able to identify its constituent events? We would strongly suggest that one can. Indeed, archaeologists should have no inherent methodological objection to this kind of procedure. We do it all the time for other processes, such as trade or agriculture, for which specific events are usually very difficult, if not impossible, to identify. We feel quite confident in assuming the existence of trade, for example, on the basis of general regional patterns reflecting the results of its operation, without ever being able to point to a particular place where exchanges actually took place. We would suggest that the same is true of feasting. The requirements are that we have a good theoretical understanding of the social roles of feasting and their permutations, and that we know what the relevant diagnostic criteria are and how to look for them in regional archaeological data. Archaeologists know quite well how to sniff out trade and characterize its quantitative and qualitative dimensions through the use of, for example, petrographic, chemical, and stylistic analysis of ceramics found in contexts of consumption. But they are generally not yet familiar with the ways that one can detect and characterize feasting *as a process*. Hence, they are less alert to the possibilities and more skeptical of the endeavor unless one can produce a Pompeiiesque example of a feast.

Junker's (Chapter 10) analysis of feasting in the Philippines is of great interest precisely because it is an excellent example of how the analysis of feasting as a process can be convincingly and profitably done through sensitive examination of things like regional patterns of ceramic import consumption. A similar case has been made for different regional patterns of feasting in Iron Age Europe (Dietler 1990, 1996) with the subsequent identification of an actual feast event (Dietler 1999b; Gardeisen 1999). What such studies demand is a careful contextual analysis of patterns of consumption. That is, not merely looking at the distribution of ceramic types or wares over the landscape, but undertaking an analysis of the quantitative, context-specific distribution of specific forms and the patterns of association where they are found. It involves asking, for example, whether certain kinds of tableware are found in all or only some graves or settlements in a region, in all or only some domestic or ceremonial contexts on those settlements, associated with what other kinds and sizes of ceramic cooking vessels and in what relative quantities in each of those contexts, associated with what kinds of faunal remains, and so on. It also requires looking at transformations of these patterns over time. Such analysis can be very revealing not only of the existence of feasting, but, more importantly, of its forms and historical significance. Of course, as Schmandt-Besserat (Chapter 14) has nicely demonstrated with her Near Eastern study, the possibilities for understanding regional feasting practices are greatly enhanced by the presence of contemporary pictorial and textual representations (see also, for example, Arsenault 1992; Joffe 1998; Schmitt Pantel 1992). But a great deal is possible even in the absence of these latter kinds of data.

Hayden (Chapter 2) provides a summary of the many kinds of material evidence that can potentially be used for dealing with feasting archaeologically, but virtually all the contributions to this volume address this issue in one way or another. One of the interesting features to emerge from this discussion is that feasting actually has an advantage over trade as a subject of archaeological investigation in that it offers much better possibilities for being able to identify at least some specific feasting events. This is true, in part, because feasting activities by their very nature produce copious amounts of distinctive refuse at the locations where they occur, and feasting locations are often associated with notable ritual structures. In contrast, specific trade activity areas are more difficult to identify, and the *act* of exchange produces little if any distinctive refuse. Ironically, because feasts often provide the context for exchange events, the advantages of detecting feasting in the archaeological record may even help us to better understand trade. Methods for accomplishing this are still being worked out, but the contributions by Brown (Chapter 13), Kelly (Chapter 12), and Knight (Chapter 11) all offer exemplary case studies showing how the presence of feast events can be teased out of various permutations of spatial, faunal, and artifactual data. As these chapters also ably demonstrate, the mere identification of the existence of feasts at individual archaeological sites is not the ultimate goal of such research. Rather, we want to know what they mean in terms of the societies that produced them—and this requires situating them within broader regional patterns.

Part of the potential visibility of feasts derives from the fact that, to reiterate once again, they are ritual (or, as Hayden would qualify it, "ritualized") events. This means that they are commonly a central element of life-crisis ceremonies such as initiations, weddings, and burials, of which at least the latter have a good chance of being preserved as single-event archaeological sites. More broadly, it means that the same kinds of elucidation (e.g., qualitative and quantitative differences in food consumed, spatial segregation, architectonic elaboration for dramaturgical effect, etc.) that may be used, often in combination, to symbolically mark feasts off from daily meals as ritual events may also make them stand out in the archaeological record—if we know how to look for them. That, of course, will require that we become sensitized to their existence and importance, and that we develop the theoretical competence to deal with their operation in a more sophisticated manner. This task is a large and complex one, but a task in which we can already see considerable productive strides being made.

One of the encouraging signs to emerge out of the studies in this volume is the frequent association of feasting with spatial differentiation or architectonic elaboration that may be readily recognizable. This is certainly the case in Brown's (Chapter 13) study of non-elite feasting at Cerén in El Salvador, Kelly's (Chapter 12) study of Cahokia, Knight's (Chapter 11) analysis of platform mounds, two out of three of Kirch's (Chapter 6) Polynesian cases, and the potlatches reported by Perodie (Chapter 7), to name a few prominent examples. It is important to emphasize that not only were these structures specially constructed sites *for* feasting, but they were most probably constructed *through* feasting. That is, the more marked the architectonic elaboration, the more such features represent the congealed labor of work feasts and are, in effect, an advertisement of the feasts that went into their construction (see Dietler and Herbich, Chapter 9). In other cases (e.g., Clarke's Akha example, Kirch's Tikopia example, the Luo feasts in the homestead reported by Dietler, Chapter 3), where there is less architectonic elaboration or smaller feasts are held in or near domestic contexts, the detection of feasting sites may be considerably more difficult. However, under extraordinary conditions it may still be possible to recognize feasts in domestic contexts through analysis of permutations of faunal and artifactual remains (e.g., Clarke, Chapter 5; Dietler 1999b; Gardeisen 1999). Evidence for the presence of alcohol may be another usefully widespread diagnostic sign of feasts. In most small-scale societies, and particularly with pre-distillation forms of alcohol, drinking is not a part of daily meals—it is something reserved for, and indexical of, feasts (see Dietler 1990 and Chapter 3). As Wilson and Rathje's (Chapter 15) study shows, even in present-day Tucson there is a strong association between alcohol and feasts.

FEASTS AND GENDER

One of the topics that we would suggest still needs much more explicit treatment and fuller elaboration is the gender relations that underlie, and are reproduced and transformed through, feasts. Of course, these are by no means uniform. But one can already begin to discern a few significant tendencies that require further research and theoretical discussion.

In the first place, feasting practices almost always act to mark and naturalize gender categories (see Dietler, Chapter 3). That is, even in societies with a strong egalitarian ethos, feasts serve to define and inculcate social categories—and gender categories are among the most common distinctions marked by these rituals. Such marking occurs through a wide variety of symbolic diacritica that may be combined in different permutations. These may include: (1) spatial segregation or positioning while eating (i.e., differences indicated by men and women eating in different locations or seated in standardized configurations: alternate seating, opposite sides of a room, inner and outer circles, etc.), (2) temporal distinctions (i.e., differences indicated by order of serving), (3) qualitative distinctions (i.e., differences in the nature of the food, drink, or serving vessels offered to men and women), (4) quantitative distinctions (i.e., differences in the amounts of food or drink served to women and men), or (5) behavioral expectations (i.e., differences in the ways women and men are expected to act during and after feasting: for example, who is permitted to act drunk, who may talk while eating, who may reach for food, who retires from the meal first, etc.). Where social classes exist, these diacritical patterns may vary between classes such that gender is marked in different ways within each class—a situation suggested, for example, in Kirch's (Chapter 6) discussion of Hawaiian royal feasting.

In addition to this aspect, however, gender considerations must also enter the analysis of feasts because feasting frequently involves a gendered asymmetry in terms of labor and benefits. That is, very often female labor largely supports a system of feasting in which men are the primary beneficiaries in the political arena. Female labor is frequently of primary importance in the domain of agricultural production and the raising of household domestic animals (such as fowl and swine), although the relative gendered contribution in this domain is highly variable (Boserup 1970; Guyer 1988). Far more common, however, is a dominant female contribution to the crucial culinary and serving labor that transforms raw food ingredients into feasts. These labor inputs are one of the main reasons why there is such a strong linkage between polygyny and male political power (see Dietler, Chapter 3; Dietler and Herbich, Chapter 9). In brief, cases where women provide the agricultural, culinary, and serving labor for male political activities are quite common (Bohannan and Bohannan 1968 provides a typical example). However, cases of the inverse pattern (where men consistently provide the agricultural, culinary, and serving labor that underwrites feasts formally hosted by women) may exist, but they are extremely rare.

These features need not be interpreted as a universal pattern of exploitation, however. In some cases there is a more balanced, or even male-dominated, pattern of labor in the production of feasts (especially in the butchering and cooking of animals), if not in the production of daily meals (e.g., the Akha case described by Clarke, Chapter 5). Moreover, women may share in the status and political benefits from their labor by being members of an influential household or lineage (in matrilineal contexts). They may also derive considerable categorical and individual status from their central role in the furnishing of hospitality (e.g., see Gero 1992; March 1998). And, in many societies, women do host their own work feasts and other feast events, although usually on a smaller scale than men. Finally, in the recent past, the common traditional female monopolization of cooking and brewing duties has frequently given them opportunities for entering the monetized market economy and gaining a source of income (e.g., through beer sales) that has enabled them to acquire considerable independence and intrafamilial power under changing socioeconomic conditions (e.g., see Colson and Scudder 1988; Netting 1964).

Hence, feasts are intimately implicated in the representation, reproduction, and transformation of gender identity and in the gendered division of feasting labor and benefits, although in complex and variable ways. Archaeologists can ill afford to ignore these features if we want to use feasting as a way of perceiving and understanding the development of sociopolitical relations in ancient societies. However, we urgently need more careful attention to such matters in ethnographic studies of feasting and the development of ethnological theory on feasts.

ECOLOGICAL MATERIALISM VERSUS CULTURE AND POWER

There is an interesting ontological tension underlying this volume that also merits a few comments. Indeed, a major part of the interest of the book is the dialogue it presents between radically different perspectives on the same set of practices. Although the most explicitly articulated contrast in ontological positions is that between the two editors alluded to earlier, the implications of this debate are apparent throughout the volume. Hayden (Chapter 2) makes a forceful case for an ecologically grounded materialist consideration of feasting, and this approach is closely echoed in several other contributions (especially Perodie, Chapter 7, and Clarke, Chapter 5). Others find this perspective less compelling and approach the subject from quite different theoretical positions (see especially Dietler, Chapter 3; Wiessner, Chapter 4; Kirch, Chapter 6; DeBoer, Chapter 8; Dietler and Herbich, Chapter 9). These perspectives need not necessarily be entirely in conflict with each other: Wiessner (Chapter 4) and Junker (Chapter 10), for example, discuss the ecological constraints on the historical development of feasting patterns within interpretive frameworks that are not ecologically deterministic and that are quite sensitive to the importance of culture and historical contingency. Moreover, a central concern with political power and the prominent role attributed to it in all the chapters provide a very significant basis for common ground. One can reach agreement on the forms and importance of political power while ultimately viewing it as either a major type of ecological behavior or as a culturally defined field of social action. It is for this reason that Hayden describes his approach as "political ecology."

However, a chapter claiming to fulfill an introductory role would be sorely remiss to the extent that it failed to reveal and explore a few of the divergences in basic ontological premises that characterize the volume. Clearly, neither of the editors undertakes this analysis from a disinterested position. Hence, *caveat lector.*

Hayden (Chapter 2) and Perodie (Chapter 7) insist that a practice as ubiquitous and enormously "expensive" as feasting must have some "practical benefits," with an understanding of practicality rooted in the perspective of Marvin Harris. They acknowledge that idiosyncratic values motivate some people to use their resources and power in nonrational, non–self-interested, nonpredictable fashions. However, they argue that in aggregate, people do tend to make decisions based on their own self-interests and the information or choices that are available. In this respect, they act in ecologically (and economically) rational terms. Idiosyncratic variations do occur but rarely are accepted, supported, or perpetuated by the communities at large for any length of time. In archaeological evolutionary terms, these idiosyncrasies become "background noise" for the basic trends that form the archaeological record. In this outlook, political power plays a major role in promoting and defending individual or factional self-interests—which is why feasting becomes so important in traditional societies that can afford to produce the necessary surpluses.

Other perspectives, including perhaps most explicitly that of Dietler (Chapter 3), strongly disagree with aspects of this ecological/materialist vision, although not all from precisely the same theoretical basis. Without wishing to refight the "Culture and Practical Reason" battle (see Sahlins 1976, 1995), Dietler feels it is important to signal the quite widespread anthropological position, in which his and several other contributions to this volume are rooted, which holds that "practicality" is not a universal principle of bottom-line materialism, but is a culturally constructed concept. To the extent that Hayden and Perodie mean by practical benefits something like the proposition that feasting involves a strong element of "strategic," self-interested political action, whether consciously acknowledged or euphemized in the shared "sincere fictions" (Bourdieu 1990) that make possible the reproduction of the system, it is probable that all of the authors would concede some common ground. What then becomes the crucial question is the culturally specific definition of appropriate goals and strategic paths. Obviously, relentless material accumulation is not a universal goal of self-interested action: in many cases it will lead to scorn, ostracism, witchcraft accusations, and an early death. In such cultural contexts, the skilled self-interested actor will play by a quite different set of rules and toward a very different end than the capitalist robber baron. As the various chapters indicate, each in its own way, the interest of the feast is not simply that it enables the accumulation of wealth or material goods, but that it is a remarkably supple ritual practice that allows the strategic reciprocal conversion of economic and symbolic capital toward a wide variety of culturally appropriate political goals. This is what accounts for the striking ubiquity and durability of the feast as an institutionalized practice in the face of dramatic social transformations, as illustrated in particularly remarkable fashion by DeBoer's (Chapter 8) Shipibo-Conibo example.

There is an additional element of the "practical benefits" argument that moves the debate beyond common ground. This is the principle expressed by Hayden (Chapter 2) that, because of its costliness and ubiquity, the feast must be a form of "adaptive behavior"—that it must have practical benefits for reproduction and individual survival. Here a number of the authors would politely disagree. In Dietler's view, this functionalist logic would necessitate drawing the same conclusion about American professional football games and rock concerts. It is hard to see the significance of either of these for the *survival* of American society at large, and both are clearly deleterious to the long-term life of the performers. Similarly, feasts can easily escalate into conditions that are dangerous both for the health of the society and for individuals involved. The Hawaiian royal pattern is a classic case in point (Kirch, Chapter 6; Sahlins 1992), as were Enga pig feasts (Wiessner, Chapter 4), the feasting customs among the Masa of Africa (Garine 1996), and Luo funeral feasts, which often impoverish families (Dietler, Chapter 3). Hence, from this point of view, the value of a concept such as "adaptive behavior" in explaining cultural practices seems highly questionable and the demonstration of a causal connection seems illusory at best.

From Hayden's perspective, on the other hand, the adaptiveness of rock concerts is not to be found so much in the present cultural context, but in the early genetic evolutionary roots of the human species where ecstatic rituals included rhythms and music that enhanced emotional bonds between individuals and groups critical for surviving severe periods of stress (Hayden 1987, 1993:159ff). Emotional aggressivity toward groups identified as enemies, whether in sports or real conflicts, may have a similar origin and may still be part of our innate emotional heritage (Hayden 1993:175–176). In more immediate terms, it is clear that, irrespective of the physical effects these events may have on the players involved, the players clearly feel that they are benefiting handsomely, which their multimillion-dollar contracts amply confirm. Hayden argues that benefits of comparable scale ought to exist for the principal players in feasts that escalate in costs far beyond the norm, such as the royal Hawaiian and Enga feasts. However, all-out competitive feasting undoubtedly entails both winners and losers who risk everything in their economic battles; and as in competitive businesses, those who are losers are typically ruined and crushed so that it is not surprising to find families impoverished by feasting where feasting becomes competitive.

Much of this disagreement turns around different views of culture. From Dietler's perspective, feasts, like many other important cultural practices, have little direct significance for "survival" (except occasionally in the negative sense when practices sometimes have deleterious unintended consequences) and the concept of "adaptation" is powerless to explain either the generation of the myriad forms that feasts take or their social significance. On the other hand, he would claim that feasts have a great deal to do with politics and power, and that much of what Hayden calls "adaptation" is simply social competition of highly variable, unpredictable, contradictory, and largely unverifiable adaptive significance for societies, social groups, and individuals, respectively. Alternatively, for Hayden and others, politics and the creation of differential power or social safety nets through feasting play critical roles in economic success, reproduction, and survival.

Within Dietler's perspective, Hayden and Perodie's dismissal of "prestige" and "status" as inconsequential psychological phenomena is also highly contentious. For Dietler, these words describe crucial aspects of the kind of symbolic capital that is a necessary condition for becoming an influential member of society.

They are the preconditions for developing the moral authority to influence group decisions, exert leadership, and wield power—or to resist the power of others. They are the essential elements of the possibility of political action. Indeed, the case can be made that, even in late-capitalist America, they are what the accumulation of economic capital is ultimately all about. From Hayden's perspective, on the other hand, "prestige" and "status" in traditional societies are simply euphemisms for economic success and political power.

Finally, from Dietler's ontological position, it is also important to envisage culture *not* as something that is destroyed by confrontation with "external realities," or that withers away or can be abandoned in the face of opportunities for self-advancement (cf. Hayden, Chapter 2)—a kind of optional, external decorative façade covering a universal bedrock core of materialist rationality. Nor is it something inherited from the past as a static bundle of traits. Rather, it is a way of perceiving and thinking about the world, and of solving the problems of daily life through the application of distinctive categorical and analogical understandings. Hence, culture is not an alternative to a universal "practicality," but rather the very way that practicality is constituted.

Ultimately, Hayden feels (somewhat more optimistically than Dietler) that some of these contentious issues may be only a matter of difference in emphasis and that more common ground may be recognized in the future. Both of us argue that some of the agendas behind the hosting of feasts are unvoiced but driven by political or other self-interested considerations. Moreover, neither approach sees cultural norms as imposing such stringent controls on human behavior that no innovation or change ever takes place. On the other hand, neither approach goes so far as to claim that cultural traditions do not impose some constraints on the behavioral and conceptual options that people must choose from. In Hayden's view, the emphasis, however, is more on people's penchant to recognize the existing constraints and to use cultural concepts as well as technology simply as tools to achieve their own self-interested goals. If suitable concepts, values, or other cultural tools are not available, highly motivated individuals typically set about trying to create them, as documented in Wiessner's Enga data (Chapter 4; see also Wiessner and Tumu 1998). Whether they succeed or not depends upon the economic costs, the effectiveness of the introduced elements, and the competing self-interests of other community members. That is where selection comes in. While there may be idiosyncratic variations among people and even communities in the short term, self-interest in the long run and for most people is ultimately characterized by basic ecological imperatives of survival, reproduction, and health.

In Dietler's view, people's very concepts of self-interest are constituted not by universal ecological imperatives, but through logics of action that are defined by both specific cultural context and the social situation of actors and which are, at the same time, inculcated and continually transformed through the practices of everyday life and ritual. Hayden acknowledges this factor, but argues that what he views as the distortion or redirection of self-interest through cultural values applies primarily to situations where the practical impacts are not extreme. He believes that, as the consequences of cultural values become increasingly detrimental to individual self-interests, people must eventually refuse to accept values that authorities promote, even under extreme threats of retribution. It is difficult to explain revolutions otherwise. In Dietler's view, this conclusion, with its classic "false consciousness" vision of culture as something that can be equated with values promoted by authorities, underlines again the fundamentally different conceptions of culture held by the editors (for a fuller discussion of this perspective on the relationship between ideology, hegemony, and culture, see Dietler 1999a).

It is important that the reader have a clear sense of the differences outlined above. This is not simply an arcane bone of friendly contention between the editors, but a crucial issue that is manifested throughout the book in often quite subtle ways. We are not, of course, suggesting that all of the chapters can be lined up on either side of a binary "great divide" defined by the terms of this debate, and we have, in fact, hesitated to speak for other authors in specifying their diverse, and often implicit, ontological premises. What we are suggesting is both that such fundamental differences are important to consider in reading the ensuing chapters and, perhaps even more importantly, that *the issue of feasts is not the product of a particular theoretical camp*, but can be approached profitably from a variety of quite different theoretical orientations. In fact, what is surprising is not that the various authors of this book have contrasting ontological positions, but that, given those positions, we are able to agree on so much. That we all see feasts as an extremely important cultural practice with characteristic social and political roles, despite our respectful divergence on fundamental theoretical matters, is, we believe, a strong endorsement of the viability of pursuing the exploration of feasting.

FEASTS AND SOCIAL CHANGE

One of the main reasons for exploring the subject of feasts was the suspicion that they have been intimately involved in processes of social change. That is, it was suspected that they were not simply epiphenomenal reflections of changes in culture and society, but central arenas of social action that have had a profound impact on the course of historical transformations. Indeed, Hayden (1990, Chapter 2) has even suggested that the origins of agriculture may be tied to the production demands generated in political feasting contests, while Dietler (1990, 1996) has shown how feasts have served as arenas for the articulation and entanglement of colonial encounters and the transformation of tastes, value, and relations of power. Many of the papers in this volume have contributed other novel and compelling arguments for the role of feasts in social change.

Wiessner's (Chapter 4) rich historical study, for example, shows how feasts among the Enga of New Guinea have acted as ritual theaters for the cultural construction and transformation of value (see also Wiessner and Tumu 1998). The dramaturgically charged presentation of the pig by big-men resulted in its incorporation into feasting and exchange networks in ways that had major consequences for the historical transformation of politics and the ecology of the region. Similarly, Junker's (Chapter 10) analysis shows how the importation of ceramics for feasts played into the competitive rivalries between chiefs in the highly unstable political landscape of the prehispanic Philippines and how feasting became a socially transformative practice through its constant realignment of alliances and patron-client networks. Dietler (Chapter 3) uses the case of the Luo of Kenya to show how feasts can serve as mechanisms for the transformation of informal power into institutionalized formal political roles, and how dependent the maintenance of authority is on the practice of feasting. Finally, Dietler and Herbich (Chapter 9) show how the work feast can become a mechanism of labor exploitation that can result in spiraling asymmetries in economic and symbolic capital and in the emergence of social stratification in egalitarian societies.

AN INVITATION TO THE FEAST

These chapters offer a compelling collective demonstration that feasts are indeed "good to think" in many ways. Moreover, they go a long way toward showing archaeologists *how* to think about feasts. Clearly, much empirical and theoretical work remains to be done in order to improve our ability to deal with the interpretive subtleties of feasting in archaeological contexts. But there is now a solid foundation upon which to build. It is no longer possible to ignore the significant role that feasts have played in the social, political, and economic domains of life around the world and throughout history. Archaeologists need to be aware of this and to develop the skills necessary to seek and interpret evidence of feasts.

But our challenge at this stage is also to not let this new awareness dissipate into yet another ill-digested vogue or an oversimplified mechanistic model of feasts to meet all occasions. The detection of some form of feasting in the archaeological record is, we would strongly emphasize, but the first of many hurdles that must be overcome before archaeologists will be able to reap the rich insights into the past that we think the in-depth study of feasting has to offer. Invocations of feasting are clearly becoming increasingly popular in the recent archaeological literature, but sometimes this appears to amount to little more than signaling the presence of feasts, as if their significance were uniform and self-explanatory. However, we emphatically reiterate that, without an adequately theorized and contextualized analysis of feasting, the mere documentation of the existence of such practices will not yield the kind of understanding of prehistoric societies and their social, political, and economic dynamics for which this domain of activity holds such heuristic promise. It is crucial to identify the specific nature of prehistoric feasts in particular cases and to explain how and why they operated in specific socioeconomic contexts that can be inferred from archaeological remains or other data. Hence, although the task is complex, we need to further develop the exploration of feasts as a powerful, versatile, and subtle analytical tool capable of providing a window of entry into the diverse array of forms of political and economic action and social relations in ancient societies. The collective effort represented in this volume provides a solid basis for optimism and further work in this quest.

REFERENCES

Arsenault, D.

    1992   Pratiques alimentaires rituelles dans la société mochica: Le contexte du festin. *Recherches Amérindiennes au Québec* 22:45–64.

Blitz, J.

    1993   Big Pots for Big Shots: Feasting and Storage in a Mississippian Community. *American Antiquity* 58:80–96.

Bohannan, P., and L. Bohannan

    1968   *Tiv Economy.* Evanston: Northwestern University Press.

Boserup, E.

    1970   *Women's Role in Economic Development.* London: Allen and Unwin.

Bourdieu, P.

    1990   *The Logic of Practice.* Stanford: Stanford University Press.

Clark, J. E., and M. Blake

    1994   The Power of Prestige: Competitive Generosity and the Emergence of Ranked Societies in Lowland Mesoamerica. In *Factional Competition and Political Development in the New World,* edited by E. Brumfield and J. Fox, pp. 17–30. Cambridge: Cambridge University Press.

Cohen, A.

    1979   Political Symbolism. *Annual Review of Anthropology* 8:87–113.

Colson, E., and T. Scudder

    1988   *For Prayer and Profit: The Ritual, Economic, and Social Importance of Beer in Gwembe District, Zambia, 1950–1982.* Stanford: Stanford University Press.

Dietler, M.

    1990   Driven by Drink: The Role of Drinking in the Political Economy and the Case of Early Iron Age France. *Journal of Anthropological Archaeology* 9:352–406.

1996   Feasts and Commensal Politics in the Political Economy: Food, Power, and Status in Prehistoric Europe. In *Food and the Status Quest: An Interdisciplinary Perspective*, edited by P. Wiessner and W. Schiefenhövel, pp. 87–125. Oxford: Berghahn Books.

1999a   Rituals of Commensality and the Politics of State Formation in the "Princely" Societies of Early Iron Age Europe. In *Les princes de la protohistoire et l'émergence de l'état*, edited by P. Ruby, pp. 135–152. Naples: Cahiers du Centre Jean Bérard, Institut Français de Naples 17—Collection de l'École Française de Rome 252.

1999b   Reflections on Lattois Society during the 4th Century B.C. In *Lattara 12: Recherches sur le quatrième siècle avant notre ère à Lattes*, edited by M. Py, pp. 663–680. Lattes: Association pour la Recherche Archéologique en Languedoc Oriental.

Friedman, J.

1984   Tribes, States, and Transformations. In *Marxist Analyses and Social Anthropology*, edited by M. Bloch, pp. 161–202. London: Tavistock.

Friedman J., and M. J. Rowlands

1978   Notes toward an Epigenetic Model of the Evolution of "Civilisation." In *The Evolution of Social Systems*, edited by J. Friedman and M. J. Rowlands, pp. 201–278. London: Duckworth.

Gardeisen, A.

1999   Découpe et consommation de viande au début du IVe siècle avant notre ère: Quelques éléments de boucherie gauloise. In *Lattara 12: Recherches sur le quatrième siècle avant notre ère à Lattes*, edited by M. Py, pp. 569–588. Lattes: Association pour la Recherche Archéologique en Languedoc Oriental.

Garine, I. de

1996   Food and the Status Quest in Five African Cultures. In *Food and the Status Quest: An Interdisciplinary Perspective*, edited by P. Wiessner and W. Schiefenhövel, pp. 193–218. Oxford: Berghahn Books.

Gero, J. M.

1992   Feasts and Females: Gender Ideology and Political Meals in the Andes. *Norwegian Archaeological Review* 25:15–30.

Guyer, J.

1988   The Multiplication of Labor: Historical Methods in the Study of Gender and Agricultural Change in Modern Africa. *Current Anthropology* 29:247–272.

Hayden, B.

1987   Alliances and Ritual Ecstasy: Human Responses to Resource Stress. *Journal for the Scientific Study of Religion* 26:81–91.

1990   Nimrods, Piscators, Pluckers, and Planters: The Emergence of Food Production. *Journal of Anthropological Archaeology* 9:31–69.

1993   *Archaeology: The Science of Once and Future Things.* New York: W. H. Freeman.

Joffe, A.

1998   Alcohol and Social Complexity in Ancient Western Asia. *Current Anthropology* 39:297–322.

March, K. S.

  1998   Hospitality, Women, and the Efficacy of Beer. In *Food and Gender: Identity and Power*, edited by C. M. Counihan and S. L. Kaplan, pp. 45–80. Amsterdam: Harwood Academic Publishers.

Moore, J. D.

  1989   Pre-Hispanic Beer in Coastal Peru: Technology and Social Context of Prehistoric Production. *American Anthropologist* 91:682–695.

Morris, C.

  1979   Maize Beer in the Economics, Politics, and Religion of the Inca Empire. In *Fermented Foods in Nutrition*, edited by C. Gastineau, W. Darby, and T. Turner, pp. 21–34. New York: Academic Press.

Murray, M.

  1995   Viereckschanzen and Feasting: Socio-Political Ritual in Iron-Age Europe. *Journal of European Archaeology* 3:125–151.

Netting, R.

  1964   Beer as a Locus of Value among the West African Kofyar. *American Anthropologist* 66:375–384.

Sahlins, M.

  1976   *Culture and Practical Reason.* Chicago: University of Chicago Press.

  1992   The Economics of Develop-man in the Pacific. *Res* 21:12–25.

  1995   *How "Natives" Think: About Captain Cook, for Example.* Chicago: University of Chicago Press.

Schmitt Pantel, P.

  1992   *La Cité au banquet: histoire des repas publics dans les cités grecques.* Collection de l'École Française de Rome, 157. Paris: De Boccard.

Sherratt, A.

  1991   Sacred and Profane Substances: The Ritual Use of Narcotics in Later Prehistoric Europe. In *Sacred and Profane: Proceedings of a Conference on Archaeology, Ritual and Religion*, edited by P. Garwood, D. Jennings, R. Skeates, and J. Toms, pp. 50–64. Oxford: Oxford University Committee for Archaeology, no. 32.

Wiessner, P., and A. Tumu

  1998   *Historical Vines: Enga Networks of Exchange, Ritual, and Warfare in Papua New Guinea.* Washington, D.C.: Smithsonian Institution Press.

Part 1

ETHNOGRAPHIC PERSPECTIVES

2

FABULOUS FEASTS

A PROLEGOMENON TO THE IMPORTANCE OF FEASTING

Brian Hayden

————————————

Everything that is not given is lost

Hindu proverb

I am always a bit uncomfortable and self-conscious when people ask me what I am studying in my research in far-off lands. I anticipate the knowing smiles and mirthful expressions when I say that I am studying *feasting*. I can see that most people think that here is someone who has found a way to use taxpayer dollars to achieve personal bliss. Well, it is a gluttonous, thankless task that most serious scholars have avoided, perhaps for fear of ridicule. But someone has to do it!

Feasting behavior has been largely ignored by archaeologists since the inception of the discipline, and by anthropologists for the last two decades. The fact that there is almost no body of archaeological interpretation involving feasts is probably in part due to the limited theoretical attention devoted to the topic in general anthropology. While there are many descriptive accounts of feasts in earlier ethnographies, few anthropologists address the theoretical importance of feasting in any specific areas (the Northwest Coast potlatch constituting a notable exception—see Suttles 1968; Piddocke 1965; Harris 1971:248, 394; Ruyle 1973). Almost no attempt has been made to examine feasting from a cross-cultural or ecological perspective (exceptions include Mauss 1924; Rappaport 1968; Suttles 1968; Dalton 1977). Perhaps occidental researchers have been biased in their views of the importance of feasting, attributing such behavior to a sybaritic self-indulgent aspect of human nature that is unworthy of serious attention. Perhaps archaeologists have simply written the study of feasting off as a frivolous type of psychological self-gratification that pleasure-loving individuals engage in, but which is not particularly important for understanding adaptive behavior, economics, social structures, or cultural change, especially given the assumed difficulty of detecting feasting in the sparse material remains of the archaeological record.

Whether these or other reasons account for the relative absence of studies on feasting in recent decades, we intend to change the perspective of the discipline. Feasting behavior in traditional societies is not simply self-indulgent, social, or gustatory gratification on the part of pleasure-seeking individuals. Rather, as the following studies demonstrate, feasting is emerging as one of the most powerful cross-cultural explanatory concepts for understanding an entire range of cultural processes and dynamics ranging from the generation and transformation of surpluses, to the emergence of social and political inequalities, to the creation of prestige technologies including specialized domesticated foods, and to the underwriting of elites in complex societies. In the past, archaeologists have studied such things as prestige technology, regional exchange, domestication, and many other material domains; but archaeologists have neglected the study of one of the most critical causal phenomena capable of tying changes in all these domains together: namely, feasting.

There are some good a priori reasons for considering feasting as being an important adaptive behavior for human beings. Cultural ecology maintains that behaviors that are (1) widespread, (2) persistent over time, and (3) expensive in terms of time, resources, and/or energy should have definite adaptive values. By adaptive value, I mean behavior that has some practical benefits for reproduction and survival rather than the psychological self-gratification, ego-grooming, pride, prestige, or status benefits that are usually assumed to explain feasting behavior. Although these psychological benefits certainly are part and parcel of feasting and may explain some of the individual motivations for hosting or attending feasts, such psychological factors do not adequately explain the magnitude of many feasts or why others besides the hosts agree to contribute time, energy, and surpluses to feasts.

From an ecological point of view, it is clear that feasting is extremely widespread, if not universal; that it is extremely persistent, probably dating back to the Upper Paleolithic (Conkey 1980), if not before; and that in many instances it requires years of preparation and surplus accumulation, extending even into future, debt-ridden years due to the deficit financing of feasts. Clearly, there is something of substantial importance transpiring in these cases, as emic statements about the importance of feasts so frequently proclaim. What are these weighty matters that archaeological and anthropological inquiries have been so silent about until now?

For the vanguard of archaeologists and anthropologists that has taken up the quest to find the underlying significance of feasting, the challenge is daunting. Yet there are many clues provided by some of the excellent descriptive ethnographies written in the 1970s and in earlier years. There are also early written records and pictorial representations of feasts (as demonstrated in Chapter 14). There are important principles of inference provided by animal ecologists concerning the observation of behavior, its context, consequences, and inferred adaptive significance. Moreover, there are ongoing possibilities of making new observations about feasting in societies that still use feasting to structure their economic, social, and political worlds. In addition, we can ask individuals in traditional societies why they host or support feasts. We hope to employ all of these avenues in trying to understand the role and significance of feasting behavior. We will monitor the specific interactions, the magnitude of the event, the cost and effort expended by hosts, the outcomes, and the material signatures of these events. We will ask probing questions of those most involved in feasts. We are confident that important conclusions will result.

At the outset, I suggest that it is useful to make several important distinctions in analyzing feasts. *Form* versus *symbolical content* is one distinction. By *form*, I refer to the overall nature of the behavior that we are trying to explain, whether large-scale feasts, the construction of massive architecture, or the manufacture of costly items that are meant to create spectator reactions of awe. By *content*, I refer to the specific symbolical meaning emically attributed to a specific behavior or to the creation of a particular object. Such content could be the particular meaning attributed to the presentation of a particular kind of food, pretexts for holding feasts (e.g., to please an ancestor), the meaning of spiral decorations, or any number of other symbolical meanings. Previous studies of feasting have often become bogged down in the myriad, culture-specific, indigenous symbols of feasting behavior. Perhaps this is why there have been few attempts at cross-cultural or ecological understanding of feasting behavior. I suggest that our first task is to understand the reason for the emergence of a particular behavioral *form*, like competitive feasting or the building of megaliths. If we can resolve these issues, then it may be of interest to go on and attempt to disentangle the problems related to symbolical meanings. Many of the articles in this volume, in fact, focus primarily on questions of form and function rather than symbolic content of feasting.

Five key chapters directly address the basic issues of the underlying functions of feasts. The analysis by Michael Clarke on the creation of political and social safety nets via feasting among the Akha (Chapter 5) is an important ethnoarchaeological foundation study of feasting. Equally important are Laura Junker's analysis of how feasting was used in Philippine chiefdoms to create political and military alliances to control lucrative trade (Chapter 10), Michael Dietler's analysis of African feasting in order to centralize political and economic power (Chapter 3), and Michael Dietler and Ingrid Herbich's documentation of how work feasts can increase socioeconomic inequalities (Chapter 9). Polly Wiessner (Chapter 4) adds an important dimension by looking at sacred feasts in New Guinea meant to promote solidarity and support for secular feasts where self-interest is pursued in a much less restrained fashion. Then in a refreshing reexamination of the potlatch, James Perodie also examines the diverse underlying motives for feasting on the Northwest Coast (Chapter 7).

ECOLOGY AND FEASTING

To broaden the context for understanding feasting behavior from an ecological viewpoint, I propose that it is worth considering feasting as one component, albeit a major component, of what I like to refer to as "social technology." Social technology can be defined as the creation and maintenance of social relationships that are predicated on securing access to resources, labor, or security (see Keesing 1975:122 for a general discussion how social factors are related to ecology). Other facets of social technology certainly include many aspects of kinship (real and fictive), ritual (Hayden 1987), gift giving, and language. Indeed, since all these behaviors can have the same ultimate goal, such as establishing subsistence or defensive alliances (e.g., Wiessner 1982; Dalton 1977), it is far from coincidental that they all tend to occur and be used together in the same contexts, although the relative emphasis may vary from one instance to another. Development of such an elaborate social technology (rather than material technology, communication, or intellectual abilities) is perhaps the most distinctive aspect of human nature that sets us apart from the rest of the animal kingdom. Feasts, unlike kinship and language, have clear archaeological consequences, which I will enumerate shortly. Cultural and behavioral ecologists have been remarkably resistant to examining the adaptive value of feasting and other social technological behaviors, choosing instead to examine optimal foraging choices of resources and monitoring cost benefits of resource exploitation. Perhaps they have adhered too closely to the ecological model established by mainstream biological ecologists.

Most ecologists tend to emphasize the fact that human beings are animals like many others in the world and that human behavior, too, should conform to ecological models. They are probably correct in thinking that differences in language ability and intelligence by themselves do not necessarily change the fundamental nature of ecological adaptations. Yet, there *is* a critical difference between the behavior of other animals and human behavior in more complex cultural systems that *does* create a vast gulf between humans and animals. This difference has an extraordinarily profound effect on how people use resources and on which ecological models can be applied to human behavior. This difference is simply: *the ability of humans to transform food surpluses into other kinds of useful or desirable goods and services.* Because of the distinctive dynamics of human behavior in this domain, I refer to its study as "political ecology."

Other animals and insects, such as squirrels and bees, may harvest and store food surpluses; however, no other animals transform those surpluses into usable nonfood items or services that have real consequences for survival (Hayden 1994,1998). For other animals, the value of food resources is ultimately limited by individual or group metabolic needs. In contrast, humans invest surplus food and labor, with a remarkable ability to expand consumption constraints. Feasting and gift giving are probably the principal means for transforming surpluses in order to improve chances of survival and reproduction. Feasting is, above all, concerned with surpluses, their production, use, transformation, control, and distribution. We use feasts to display our success whereas other animals use antlers, plumage, calls, colors, or manes (Zahavi and Zahavi 1997). In fact, numerous anecdotal accounts, as well as several more systematic studies (e.g., Blanton and Taylor 1995; Izikowitz 1951:341, 354; Stanish 1994; Cowgill 1996; Blackburn 1976:242; Friedman 1975; Friedman and Rowlands 1977:208–214—see also Wiessner's Chapter 4) indicate that *the drive to achieve advantages through feasting* is probably the single most important impetus behind the intensified production of surpluses beyond household needs for survival. The transformation of surpluses is a unique human ability, but one not without rudimentary origins in other primates, as exemplified by food sharing for favors. *Transformation of surpluses created an entirely new ecological dynamic* that has been consuming world resources at a geometrically increasing rate since the advent of transegalitarian feasting and prestige technologies (Hayden 1998).

NEW APPROACHES TO FEASTING BEHAVIOR
DEFINITIONS
Given this new approach to the study of feasting, what specific questions need to be asked? At the outset, we need an operational definition of feasting. There are also a number of important issues that need to be resolved. Perhaps the most

difficult issue is how to meaningfully categorize the extensive variety of feasts recorded ethnographically. We should determine which of these types may have had practical benefits and what those benefits are likely to have been. Understanding how different types of feasts are related to social, economic, and political dynamics of traditional communities constitutes yet another major theoretical undertaking. Finally, understanding how different types of feasts can be recognized archaeologically is an area that is critical for prehistorians but largely unexplored. These are the major themes of this book. I would suggest that if we are ever to get beyond the detailed, myopic view of many social anthropologists who see the trees well enough but who have little idea about the forest, it is essential to take a cross-cultural and comparative perspective.

To begin with definitions, I would like to propose that a feast be defined as *any sharing between two or more people of special foods* (i.e., foods not generally served at daily meals) *in a meal for a special purpose or occasion*. As Dietler (1996:89) has pointed out, there is usually a highly ritualized component to feasting as well; however, it is conceivable that in some cases the ritualized content may be fairly minimal (as at some dinner parties in contemporary societies). Daily family meals can also be highly ritualized (including prayers or the saying of grace) but would not constitute feasts. The definition that I use above explicitly excludes gift exchanges without meals; it excludes food offerings to spirits on the part of individuals or groups who do not themselves eat or drink; it excludes communion-style consumption in churches; it excludes sacrifices in which there is no consumption of food or special drink; and it excludes group meals shared for mechanical convenience, as in cafeteria-style meals that are part of workshops, rituals, or other events. Other slightly different definitions of feasts are presented by Michael Dietler, Polly Wiessner, Michael Clarke, Laura Junker, and Linda Brown (Chapters (3, 4, 5, 10, and 13). However, in archaeological operational terms, the use of foods in a nondomestic pattern is a recurring central feature (Chapters 5, 10–13 by Clarke, Junker, Knight, Kelly, and Brown).

The term *adaptive value* simply indicates behavior that generates some practical benefit for survival, reproduction, health, or standard of living.

PURPOSES

Probably the most contentious issue in the study of feasts is why feasts are held. Do hosts really expect to gain practical benefits from every feast that they hold? If they deny such motives, or are not conscious of them, is it possible to still impute an adaptive value to such feasting behavior? Have the original or barely conscious practical purposes been lost sight of amidst the fog of ideology and symbolism that is usually generated by the aggrandizer-promoters of feasts? Have religion and ritual obscured the real relationships of power vested in the elites, as Marx argued, or become the shared "sincere fictions" of entire communities, as Bourdieu (1990) suggests? To take an example from Western culture, how would most people explain the lavish dinners and exchanging of presents at Christmas? Many, if not most people would explain these feasts in symbolical (content) religious terms, as celebrations of the birth of Christ. And this is precisely the kind of explanation that is most common in the ethnographic descriptions of feasting (as funerals necessary for the safe journey of the dead's soul, etc.). Yet, few social scientists today would hesitate to attribute a more basic, underlying, explanation to Christmas feasts as essentially highly ritualized events that are meant to create social solidarity and cooperative bonds between family members and close social affiliates.

In order to reach such conclusions, it is not necessary to depend on emic rationales, pretexts, or ideology to explain why specific types of feasting occur. However, it would be foolish to entirely ignore what practitioners, especially insightful practitioners, have to say about these matters as well. Questions about the symbolical content of feasts and about the formal functions of feasts represent very different levels of inquiry. In my fieldwork, I have always found that people in traditional societies can easily articulate answers concerning symbolic content, but rarely seem to comprehend questions about formal aspects of feasts or other behavior such as why funeral feasts are so large and expensive. Thus, a judicious combination of empirical observation and emic commentary is probably the optimal avenue of inquiry. Empirical observation of behavior, contexts, materials, and outcomes has been the standard for interpreting animal behavior and much human behavior for well over a century. It can also be successfully used in the study of feasting especially if we ever hope to deal with formal questions of function. Although archaeologists must rely heavily on ethnologists and ethnoarchaeologists to understand the basic nature of feasting behavior (as well as all other basic forms of human behavior), once its material correlates have been established, archaeologists are in an important position to delineate the evolution of such behavior, and understand the conditions under which it emerged and diversified into specific types of feasts. The studies in this volume by Junker, Dietler, Clarke, and Perodie constitute ample evidence of the utility of this formal ethnographic approach.

PRACTICAL BENEFITS

Given our present state of knowledge about feasting, what are the most obvious or important practical benefits that can be proposed to account for the substantial time and resources expended in some feasts? There are nine basic types of practical benefits that I would suggest occur most commonly. Feasting can:

1. mobilize labor;
2. create cooperative relationships within groups or conversely, exclude different groups;

3. create cooperative alliances between social groups (including political support between households);
4. invest surpluses and generate profits;
5. attract desirable mates, labor, allies, or wealth exchanges by advertising the
   success of the group;
6. create political power (control over resources and labor) through the creation of a network of reciprocal debts;
7. extract surplus produce from the general populace for elite use;
8. solicit favors;
9. compensate for transgressions.

Except for work feasts, penalty feasts, and solicitation feasts, all other benefits
of feasting revolve around *the creation or maintenance of important social relationships*. These relationships may be important for different reasons (defense, marriage, wealth accumulation, and so on—Dalton 1977:202–204), but establishing
desirable social relationships constitutes the bottom line for many feasts. This is
an extremely important feature of some feasts that has far-reaching implications
for the transformation of technology and culture. Notably, in order to create a favorable disposition among guests, hosts generally try to demonstrate the special-
ness and importance of the guests by presenting them with special foods, drinks,
gifts, or ritual displays as indications of how much the hosts value their guests.
The more important the relationship is, the more effort, time, and resources
should be involved in giving an impressive feast. In potlatch-type alliance feasts,
Dalton (1977:207) stresses that feasts are made as lavish as possible to demonstrate
the wealth and power of the hosts, and therefore the desirability of hosts as allies.
Trying to impress one's guests, for whatever reason, means obtaining and preparing labor-intensive foods, drinks, serving vessels, prestige items, and ritual
items—an extremely dynamic and powerful engine for the generation of cultural
and technological change (Hayden 1998).

The above benefits of feasting, are, of course, not meant to exclude competitive attempts to diminish rivals. However, I view such competitive feasting as subsumed under strategies to obtain political power, including displays of success
(which may only make sense in competitive contexts). It should also be noted
that there is probably a major difference between the practical benefits (listed
above) to the hosts as a group versus the practical benefits to the promoter and
organizer of feasts who, in the most active cases, is usually a Triple A personality
(aggressive, aggrandizive, and accumulative) out to maximize his own self-
interest, wealth, and political power (see Hayden 1995). Not all lineage heads who
are responsible for organizing lineage feasts and maintaining alliances advantageous for their lineage promote their own self-interest over their lineage's inter-

est. But demographic characteristics ensure that some lineage heads, clan heads, and community heads will be aggressive aggrandizers, and they will be the most notable ones with the most impact on cultural change. These aggressive aggrandizers promote the benefits of feasting to the community or their support group and try to get as many people to produce as much surplus as possible. The aggrandizers then assume as much control over the use of surpluses for their own benefit as possible. These aggrandizers attempt to set the agendas, they manipulate war, peace, and alliances, and they create cults and secret societies to further their own self-centered goals (Chapters 4 and 7; also Hayden 1995).

While many indigenous informants and social anthropologists emphasize psychological reasons that people give feasts, I would like to argue that concepts such as "status" and "prestige," as usually used in Western society, really hold little explanatory value on their own. If they are to be entertained as causal motivations for holding large costly feasts, they should be scrutinized carefully. I have three objections to these concepts. First, they posit some inherent (and in many accounts, economically self-destructive) drive for psychological approval from others. Such desires for approval, or at least acceptance, certainly exist in many people, but the variability and distribution of their intensity has never been documented, nor has the emergence of these emotions been convincingly tied to any cultural or biological evolutionary theory that I am aware of. Thus, one wonders what their selective advantage might have been, and why such traits should have become widespread in human populations as posited by proponents of these views.

Secondly, admitting that some people do have strong psychological penchants for seeking approval from others, the magnitude of expenses involved in some feasts (with supposedly no other benefit than achieving approval from others) seems out of line with the ego-gratification received. Indeed, in some societies such as the Akha, hosts are unusually obsequious and display little satisfaction or pride as noted by Clarke (Chapter 5). Nor does it seem realistic that the desire for approval would *generally* outweigh desires for personal gain or turn most rational beings into economic lemmings. Moreover, it is highly unlikely that the prestige or status resulting from giving gifts or feasts would be long-lived, just as gift giving, by itself, in contemporary society is a tenuous means of establishing influence or prestige. Compulsive gift-givers are just as likely to be ridiculed as fools behind their backs, as they are to be revered for their gifts. In order for gift giving to have longer lasting effects, it must be backed up by other features, such as the creation of agreed upon or de facto contractual debts—an aspect of traditional feasting that Laura Junker strongly emphasizes in her chapter, as do Mauss (1924), Dalton (1977:205, 207), Gosden (1989), Lightfoot and Feinman (1982:66), and others.

Thirdly, given the variability in human genetic and personal developmental histories, it is certainly possible that there will always be a few people who feel compelled to accumulate large amounts of wealth in order to be able to dispense it simply in the hopes of acquiring honor or prestige—especially perhaps under conditions of cultural collapse (e.g., see Dalton 1977:207 on changes in the pot-latch). The laws of chance dictate that such idiosyncratic individuals will emerge from time to time. However, I contend that such personality types are rare and that the vast majority of individuals in all cultures have, and always will follow their own practical self-interests in the long run. It is doubtful that trying to es-tablish cultural traditions and institutions that are costly to individuals solely on the basis of a purported widespread desire for honor, status, or prestige would be successful or long-lasting without some real practical benefits to back up psycho-logical benefits or other ideological pretexts (e.g., pacifying the ancestors, or courting the favor of the gods).

Thus, it seems unlikely that Western concepts of status, prestige, honor, or ap-proval from others by themselves play a dominant role in the institutionalized hosting of feasts involving large numbers of people and major expenditures of time, energy, and resources. However, it must be emphasized that all of these are Western sociocultural analytical concepts. English terms may only be the closest approximations to indigenous terms with significantly different connotations. So-cial anthropologists have often taken these translations at face value. However, I am convinced that a careful reading of the texts and the implications of *status* or *prestige* clearly indicate that traditional usage of these terms carries a very differ-ent meaning from the Western translations. In brief, my impression is that while the Western terms *status* and *prestige* carry connotations of psychological gratifi-cation stemming from the approval of others, equivalent terms in transegalitar-ian societies generally carry a different set of connotations relating more to economic success, political success and power, reliability in honoring debts, and the ability to organize people for a variety of purposes. Citing Voss (1987:131), Laura Junker makes the point explicitly: in the Philippines, the prestige came from the creation of social debts through feasting. Dalton (1977:207) also clearly views the lavishness of feasts as statements of wealth and power and success. Similarly, Friedman and Rowlands point out that the surpluses used to host feasts result in prestige, but a "prestige whose cultural content is very different than in our own society" (1977:207). The status gained is "the 'social value' attributed to the ability . . . to produce such wealth." In Chapter 4, Polly Wiessner provides additional observations along these lines. She suggests that prestige accrued to those who brought benefits to the group; however this "prestige" was really a li-cense for aggrandizers to produce wealth, marry many women, and retain ser-vants. In summary, I would argue that a more appropriate translation of *status* and *prestige* in contemporary terms might be "credit rating."

The antithesis of the status that ambitious people seek, especially in transegalitarian societies, is embodied by people who are systematically reviled as "lazy," "moochers," "dead skin," or "rubbish men" (see Chapter 7; also Yan 1996:103). The vilification of such people is a recurring theme, if not an obsession, of elites in many transegalitarian cultures. The consequences of being considered a moocher or rubbish man are that one's credit rating is low or nonexistent for loans, reciprocal gifts, reciprocal feasts, and other events because such people are unreliable and unproductive. In many cases, these people cannot marry because of these liabilities. They are the people who do not support aggrandizers' strategies for generating surpluses. The worst fear of aggrandizers is to have to default on feasting and other debts. This precipitates their fall to the status of rubbish man, a person to whom no one will lend wealth or only at exorbitant rates, a person who has essentially declared bankruptcy. They have no "status."

These are only my impressions gleaned from the ethnographies and others' analyses in passing. While a full exegesis of "status" and "prestige" in transegalitarian societies would be extremely enlightening, I am not prepared to undertake such a task here. Nevertheless, it is perhaps worth noting that a strong argument can probably be made for this new meaning of *status* (i.e., as success recognition) as having an adaptive value. Evolutionarily, it should be adaptive to imitate individuals who display clearly successful behavior, as it should also be adaptive to reproduce with such individuals. In fact, the biological world is replete with examples of species where individuals compete with each other to display their superior biological success, sometimes even to their own detriment, as in the case of elaborate moose or elk antlers (Beardsley 1993; Zahavi and Zahavi 1997). Displays of success are vitally important for attracting desirable mates and supporters or coworkers, both in the biological realm and in the cultural realm. Feasts constitute one of the most prominent venues for displaying success among humans, and "status" is the verbal symbolic expression of that success.

The standard response of more sociocultural anthropologists at this juncture in the dialogue is to invoke the power of cultural traditions, norms, values, and beliefs in curtailing people's own practical self-interests and promoting the giveaway of wealth for more etheric goals such as recognition and approval by others. While cultural norms may urge some people to take on costly social roles without providing practical benefits, and while this may occur in some cases over the short term, my experience in tribal villages indicates that even in the most "tradition-bound" cultures such as the Maya, the Akha, and the Western Desert Aborigines, when self-interest no longer accords with cultural traditions, then the cultural traditions wither and die, provided other options are viable. As Lewis-Williams notes: "Cosmological, social, religious and iconographic frameworks are not immutable givens. They are reproduced through complex processes and forms of representations and are therefore *always open to negotiation"* (1997:827—emphasis added).

Similarly Blitz (1993a:23) argues that individuals do not merely react to the social idiom of ritual but continually create, alter, reinterpret, or manipulate its information content with dramatic results. Indeed, if this were not the case, we would be in dire straits in trying to explain how and why cultures change. We would be thrown back to relying on diffusion or similar explanations. In fact, Marxism, Cultural Materialism, Post-Processualism, Ecology, Darwinism, and Processualism all share a commitment to viewing individual actors as the locus of change and as rationally pursuing their own self-interests as a fundamental tenet of understanding the workings of culture.

There is no more dramatic demonstration of the relatively weak hold that cultural traditions have over people's behavior than the occurrence of nonconformists and revolutionaries. In the tribal cultures where I have worked, I have always been impressed at the large percentage of individuals who simply did not buy into the traditional value system and who would be generally classified as agnostic or atheistic in contemporary terms. For example, in the very traditional Maya Highland villages where I worked, about 10 percent of the household heads interviewed would have to be classified as a-religious or agnostic, while another 10–20 percent of households had changed their beliefs and affiliation from traditional community cults to more charismatic forms of Christianity. Izikowitz (1951:321) makes similar observations for Southeast Asian tribal societies. It seems that in all cultures, there are probably significant proportions of independent thinkers who evaluate situations on their own merits irrespective of handed-down traditional wisdom or promulgated ideologies. It is the individual who is the locus of cultural selection (Harris 1979:61). Cultural values or ideas do not fetter individual actions to the point of acting against important self-interests—real consequences from other community members do. It is the freethinkers who pioneer creative new thoughts and new behaviors, and who serve as models for possible new cultural, social, political, and economic configurations. If this were not the case, there would be no unions or revolutions, and little cultural change.

To illustrate the relative roles of ideology versus practical benefits, it is useful to consider the parable of the shopping cart. Before 1970, supermarket storeowners appealed tirelessly to the traditional cultural values of customers (neatness, courtesy, reciprocity, etc.) to return their shopping carts to the store rather than leaving them in parking lots. However, appeal to these supposedly strong cultural norms had little effect on people's actual behavior *until* store owners began adding a practical consequence to the return of shopping carts—the investment of 25 cents to obtain a cart, redeemable upon the return of the cart to its proper storage location. The change in behavior was dramatic. Even stronger cultural values were involved in trying to prevent people from polluting and littering, all to little avail until substantial fines and bottle/can deposits were established. The moral of these parables is, as Marvin Harris (1979:59, 270–277) long ago argued, that while cultural values certainly do exist and are used to back up or justify actual behavioral choices, practical consequences play a much more dominant role in behavioral choices.

In terms of feasting, one of the most powerful enforcing criteria is the acceptance of a contractual debt when one accepts an invitation to a feast intended to create social bonds or reciprocal obligations. Debt relationships also prolong and maintain the "status" associated with gift giving because the "superior" status is active as long as the gift has not been repaid. And it usually takes one or more years for many gifts to be repaid. Moreover, overdue unpaid debts entail socioeconomic rupture between social groups (Dalton 1977:205, 207), engendering additional weighty consequences. But gifts and debts generally constitute immediate advantages. The ulterior and adaptive advantages have been noted above (alliances, attraction of mates and labor, investments, profits, performing work, and political control through debts). It is certainly necessary to acknowledge the full range of idiosyncratic behaviors, but it is also necessary to carefully differentiate these from the behavior of the majority of people, upon which major traditions and institutions are based, including feasting.

A number of the chapters in this volume carefully document the dynamics, benefits, and strategies of feasting using ethnographic and historical data. Laura Junker provides a broad overview of the role of feasts in acquiring political and economic power in Southeast Asia, and Michael Clarke focuses on the use of feasts to establish economic and social security networks in tribal Thailand. Polly Wiessner examines how big-men manipulate group solidarity and values through feasts for their own benefit in New Guinea. Both James Perodie and Michael Dietler document the broad range of practical benefits that feasts provided on the historic Northwest Coast (Perodie) and sub-Saharan Africa (Dietler). In an innovative analysis of Sumerian data, Denise Schmandt-Besserat also demonstrates how feasting was used by early state elites to underwrite early Mesopotamian state economies.

VARIETIES OF FEASTS

Having discussed the raison d'être of feasts, it is now possible to deal with the question of how to classify feasts, for not all feasts are the same. Indeed, there is a wide range of different typologies of feasts. It is possible to classify feasts by:

1. symbolical content;
2. inferred functions (types of practical benefits);

3. size;

4. goals of creating social bonds vs. achievement of more immediate, limited objectives;

5. the use of prestige materials or other archaeological indicators;

6. participating, or core, social units;

7. horizontal vs. vertical social relationships between guest and host;

8. the kind of reciprocity involved;

9. the degree of obligation (social necessity vs. self-initiated hosting);

10. seasonal or calendrical occurrences vs. life or economic conditions.

Yan (1996:44ff) discusses classification in regard to the parallel phenomenon of gift giving. The traditional ethnographic approach has been to classify feasts according to their emically stated purposes, based on the specific symbolical pretexts for holding feasts: harvest feasts, ancestral feasts, marriage feasts, funeral feasts, puberty feasts, and others. For the understanding of feasting as a behavioral form (in contrast to the symbolical content of feasting), emic classifications are clearly the least useful type of classification, although some do tend to have specific functions and can be classed within one or more specific functional types of feast (e.g., community harvest feasts as solidarity and/or promotional feasts).

All of the other approaches have much more utility for archaeologists, and in fact, many of these other classificatory approaches are used by authors in this volume. Michael Clarke uses the range of social groups involved, James Perodie uses reciprocity expectations, and Michael Dietler uses a political function classification. Polly Wiessner uses a secular versus sacred distinction with differing patterns of refuse and special structures. My own preference is to adopt a functional approach as an intermediary step to generating an archaeological classification based on material remains. Unfortunately, because of the complexity of feasting behavior, there are seldom feasts with pure functions, and in some cases the same emic pretext for a feast (e.g., a funeral feast) may have quite different functions in different households (e.g., in a poor versus a rich household). In order to deal with such distinctions, it is either necessary to add a great deal more detail to our descriptions and analyses of feasts or to create more subcategories of functional or traditional emic categories of feasts. However, I am hopeful that this kind of confusion will largely disappear when we pass to archaeological classifications of feasts. The endeavor to create such a useful archaeological typology is still in its earliest stages and is one of the principal reasons why we have assembled this volume.

Of the ten approaches to classification just listed, the following are probably the most common or have the most potential for use by prehistorians.

1. *Emic*: Emic feast types are theoretically almost limitless, since the kinds of pretexts that might be used for holding feasts are only constrained by human creativity. People are constantly trying out new pretexts for holding feasts or giving socially binding gifts (Yan 1996:60). However, it seems that people everywhere find some pretexts for holding feasts much more compelling than others. Thus, there are some extremely common recurrent emic types. These include feasts for marriages, funerals, children's maturation events, plantings, harvests, work, status, new houses, making war and making peace, rituals, ancestor worship, and noteworthy celestial or seasonal events. In Chapter 3, Dietler provides a discussion of why such emotionally, theatrically, and ritually charged contexts are especially appropriate for feasting events.

2. *Functional*: In terms of practical purposes or social functions, there is a fairly narrow range of important proximate benefits likely to be derived from hosting feasts. These benefits can be grouped into two main divisions: creating cooperation, alliance, or social distinctions on the one hand versus economic benefits on the other hand (Fig. 2.1). Feasts in the first division include those meant to create cooperative in-group relationships or distinctiveness between groups (Michael Dietler's diacritical feasts); feasts to create alliances between groups; feasts to create political support; and feasts to attract desirable mates and labor via advertising. The division of feasts having to do with proximate economic benefits includes feasts held to accomplish some task, investment feasts (including high-cost maturation events), competitive feasts, solicitation feasts, and feasts given in lieu of punishment. It may be possible that another basic category is common in which emergency situations (due to climate, disease, or other catastrophes) make people willing to surrender surpluses to charismatic leaders who promise relief if a large enough feast or ritual can be held. It probably makes most sense to view these situations as being manipulated purely for the benefit of those organizing the feasts who try to expropriate the surpluses of others. They therefore might be termed "exploitative" or "calamity" feasts. I have argued that despot aggrandizers often intentionally create disputes between villages precisely in order to create a climate of crisis and impending calamity that the despots manipulate for their own advantage, largely via the need for alliance and compensation feasts (Hayden 1995). Although some of the details of Michael Dietler's terms and functional classification of feasts (Chapter 3) may differ from the ones I use, we use many of the same basic distinctions.

I feel that it is important to attempt to distinguish between different functional types of feasts because the consequences for the material cul-

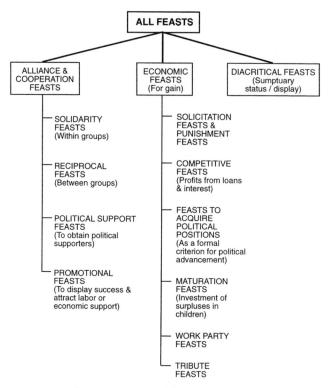

Figure 2.1. A schematic diagram of the most important divisions in the types of feasts discussed in this chapter.

ture expressions should be quite different and because *the consequences for community dynamics and impacts on technological changes should be very different*. For instance, solidarity feasts, no matter what their size, should entail minimal departures from standard daily foods or material items, whereas competitive and promotional feasts should represent major departures with consequent pressures to develop and change both food and material technologies.

3. *Size*: Feasts vary enormously in size from the minimum of a two-person (dyadic) solicitation or friendship (solidarity) dinner to intercommunity events involving hundreds or thousands of people. Clearly the smaller types of feasts will be difficult to identify archaeologically unless the remains of special foods or special serving/preparation vessels are present. Even then, it may be difficult to determine whether such remains are from small special meals or whether they were part of larger, more lavish spe-

cial feasts. However, one might expect some differences to occur with increasing sizes of feasts. In general, perhaps the more people involved, the more specialized and numerous food items, food preparation facilities (hearths, roasting pits, kitchens), food preparation and serving vessels, and architectural structures will be. Thus, irrespective of function or emic purpose, one useful way of classifying feasts for archaeological purposes may be by sheer scale. While this approach enables us to make some sense of the archaeological data, I would argue that it might obscure some important potential distinctions that might be made with a bit more diligent enquiry.

4. *Social bonds vs. limited goals*: Many limited-goal feasts (Yan 1996) probably leave minimally distinctive material remains. Work feasts, solicitation feasts, punishment feasts, crisis feasts, and similar events are either relatively small, and/or are unlikely to involve particularly special foods or vessels. In these cases, we need to develop better criterion for distinguishing such feasts from normal eating. However, Michael Dietler (personal communication) has observed some work feasts where lavish food and prestige wares were used in order to attract more and better-quality labor. Thus, limited-goal types of feasts may be either minimally distinctive from normal meals except for size and perhaps location, or they may be hard to distinguish from other feast types. There may be some useful distinctions for archaeologists in this approach to classification, but the issue needs to be explored in greater depth and more empirical data are sorely needed.

5. *Social units*: One way of adding meaning to size classifications of feasts is by examining the social units involved in feasts, as suggested by Michael Clarke. Social units range from individual families, to lineages, to clans, to communities, and extend to regions. While there are some distinctions that can be made at each level, the higher levels tend to include lower levels (e.g., lineages include individual families), and thus, each level of social unit tends to be associated with a specific size range (number of participants) of feasting. This is a productive way of analyzing feasts for archaeological purposes, although within each social group it may still be desirable to try to distinguish feasts held for different purposes, especially solidarity versus promotional or competitive feasts.

6. *Material-based (archaeological) classifications*: In my estimation, it would be ideal if we could develop an archaeological classification of feasts that exactly matched ethnographically known or inferred functions of feasts. However, at this juncture it seems highly unlikely that such a high degree of specificity will soon be attainable using archaeological remains. Instead, the archaeologically attainable is more likely to involve various combina-

tions of material indicators, creating new distinctions between feasting events that will be significant for understanding how past cultures functioned and changed. Initially, it is probably most useful simply to list the kinds of material remains that can be used to identify feasting events from the past (see Table 2.1). Various values and combinations of these same

TABLE 2.1
Archaeological Signatures of Feasts

Food	Rare or labor-intensive plant or animal species (especially condiments, spices, and domestic animals)
	Special "recreational" foods (e.g., tobacco, opium, cannabis, and alcohol)
	Quantity of food items
	Evidence of waste of food items (e.g., deposition of articulated joints, unprocessed bone)
Preparation vessels	Unusual types (e.g., for beer-making, chili-grinding, perhaps initial appearance of cooking pots)
	Unusual large sizes
	Unusual numbers
Serving vessels	Unusual quality or materials (e.g., first occurrence of pottery or highly decorated or specially finished pottery, large gourds, stone bowls)
	Unusual size of serving vessels
	Unusual numbers of serving vessels
Food-preparation facilities	Unusual size of facilities (e.g., large roasting pits or hearths)
	Unusual number of facilities (e.g., several hearths in a row)
	Unusual location or construction of facilities
Special food-disposal features	Bone dumps
	Special refuse fires containing feasting items
	Feasting middens
Feasting facilities	Special structures (temporary vs. permanent) for highest-ranking guests and hosts, or for large numbers of people
	Special display facilities, scaffolds, poles, or other features
Special locations	Mortuary or remote locations that are clearly not habitation sites (e.g., in front of Megalithic tombs, at henge monuments, inside caves)
	Loci associated with nuclear households, residential corporate households, large feasting middens or central community spaces
Associated prestige items	Presence or absence, and relative abundance of prestige items typically used in different types of feasts (e.g., ritual display items, feathers, shell jewelry)
	The destruction of wealth or prestige items (via intentional breakage or burial)

TABLE 2.1 continued

Ritualized items of etiquette	Smoking or other narcotic paraphernalia
	Ritualized vessels for consumption of alcohol, chocolate, kava, or other prestige drinks
Paraphernalia for public rituals	Dance masks or costume elements
Existence of aggrandizers	Wealthy burials; social or site hierarchies; large residences with high storage per capita
Recordkeeping devices	The presence or absence and frequency of tally sticks, counting tokens, or symbolic pictograms
Pictorial and written records of feasts	
Food-storage facilities	Stables, storage pits, granaries
Resource characteristics	Abundance, intensified exploitation, invulnerability to overexploitation

factors should be useful in trying to distinguish different types of feasting events, no matter which classification approach one adopts.

Undoubtedly, more types of observations can be added to the list in Table 2.1. However, even at this early stage of theory development, archaeologists probably have more variables to work with than might be initially assumed in their quest to deal with past feasting behavior. Many chapters in this volume focus on a number of specific material indicators of feasts. Warren DeBoer discusses the unusual size and decoration of feasting vessels in the Amazon as does Laura Junker for the prehispanic Philippines, Linda Brown for the Maya, and Michael Clarke for the Hill Tribes of Thailand. DeBoer also provides a good, albeit somewhat unusual example of specialized ritual paraphernalia used in overall feast contexts, as does Linda Brown for prehistoric rural Maya feasting. Almost all chapters deal with unusual foods consumed in feasts. The dominant role of animals in feasting is emphasized by Knight for early Moundbuilders, Lucretia Kelly at Cahokia, Junker for the early Philippine chiefdoms, and Clarke for contemporary Thai Hill Tribes. Large game such as deer, and large domestic animals feature most prominently in all these contexts, leading to interesting models involving the role of feasting in the domestication of animals. Brown makes similar observations for the Maya but is also able to document the use of special plant foods such as achiote. Similarly, the special nature of feasting refuse is documented in many of these chapters (e.g., Kelly, Knight, Wiessner), and is the special focus of Wilson and Rathje's analysis of contemporary industrial garbage.

A number of papers focus on the emergence of specialized structures related to feasting activities. Linda Brown identifies a rural Maya feasting and ritual structure, possibly related to lineage ancestor worship. James Knight argues that the early platform mounds of the southeastern United States constitute specialized feasting structures with scaffolds, while Patrick Kirch documents the spectacular elaborations of special feasting structures and food-preparation facilities in increasingly complex levels of Polynesian chiefdoms. In the case of the southeastern platform mounds and the simpler Polynesian structures, these may be the first examples of specialized public architecture that occur in the regional culture sequences, and I think it is worth asking whether the initial appearance of specialized public structures in many more, or perhaps all, regional cultural sequences may be related to feasting activities. Finally, in an impressive tour de force centered on Sumerian remains, Denise Schmandt-Besserat reminds us that there is a great deal to be gleaned from pictorial representations and early written texts, not only concerning the existence of feasting, but its dynamics as well.

In order to determine how these various types of observations might fit together in a provisional archaeological classification, it would probably be useful to see what material patterning can be gleaned from a brief overview of feasting in several different types of cultures. I will consider this topic next.

THE EVOLUTION OF FEASTING: GENERALIZED HUNTER/GATHERERS

There is little information available on feasting among generalized hunter/gatherers. Whether this is because it is absent or rare as Polly Wiessner suggests (1996, personal communication), or because it may have a different character, or because it has simply not been reported in the ethnographic literature is unclear. Sharp (1994) argues that all Chipewyan meals are solidarity-enhancing events by their very nature and that no special meals are used for those purposes. On the other hand, among other groups there are *a few* indications that large game kills and ritual gatherings were sometimes accompanied by festive meals (Sandal 1966; Richardson and Ianzelo 1974). Whether these were special meals or simply logistically convenient ways of organizing meals for a gathering of people is unclear. In the existing literature, there are few indications that most ritual meals had any special connotation or involved any special foods or preparations, although large quantities of meat with high fat content seem to have been highly valued by many groups.

There are also occasional statements that special cuts of meat were, or could be, reserved for men's consumption at special ritual locations (Woodburn 1966). This is perhaps the closest approximation that exists to the feasts documented for more complex types of societies. I am unaware of feasting accounts involving interband visiting and alliance brokering, or the kinds of meals that may have been served at such events. Nevertheless, is difficult to imagine that no special gastronomic hospitality would be displayed for potential or continuing allies in other bands, even if only on a dyadic partnership basis. Such alliances could have been sought for many reasons, including defense, refuges in times of starvation, marriage, and rituals (Wiessner 1977, 1982).

Even if it is demonstrated that some kinds of alliance and solidarity feasts do occur among generalized hunter/gatherers, they may differ in character from solidarity and alliance feasts in more complex societies. This would be because of three important factors:

1) Feasting as we are most familiar with it among more complex groups is largely predicated on the accumulation, storage, and use of surpluses. Most generalized hunter/gatherers do not accumulate or store surpluses, and they have few if any mechanisms for dealing with, or transforming surpluses (Wiessner 1982, 1996). Hunter/gatherers certainly do invite their allies to partake of unusually desirable and abundant resource occurrences when hosts have far more food in their territory than they can use (Flood 1980). But in these instances, all families have a glut of the same abundant foods, and there is really no reason for any sharing between families.

2) In addition, there are few ways in which generalized hunter/gatherers can create special foods by intensifying labor to procure or process foods. There is little need for developing more intensified ways of processing foods (collecting and grinding cereal grains may be one exception). Moreover, the specialized technology needed for more intensified preparations would only be cumbersome for highly nomadic groups. Similarly, it is difficult to predict when most specialty (and even routinely used) species might be found or procured because almost by definition these will be rare or difficult to get, and all such food procurement is on a probabilistic or encounter basis. As Richard Lee (1979:243) documented, even the !Kung only kill about 28 medium or large game animals per year per band. The yearly average per hunter is only 0.6. Moreover, storage is not practiced. Thus, it would be difficult to plan a feast for any particular time and be confident of actually being able to procure or serve specialty foods such as big game meat. Trying to return such food gifts in any reciprocal fashion would similarly become almost impossible because of lack of predictability and storage capabilities.

3) There is also an extremely strong egalitarian and sharing ethic that characterizes most, if not all, generalized hunter/gatherers and which is clearly adaptive for survival (Winterhalder 1996; Wiessner 1996). Given such a strong ethic, the idea of someone "giving" a feast seems at odds with the rest of the dominant and adaptive cultural values. The sharing of food is simply expected, if not demanded, in *all* social, ritual, and other contexts. There are certainly "host" groups and "visitor" groups, however these distinctions may not go beyond the control over access to resources or the active versus passive roles that each group might

play in rituals. The idea of a "host" who gives a feast based on his stockpiling of foods or gifts, and his control over family and other labor, simply seems to be antithetical to the rest of generalized hunter/gatherer existence. These factors may account for the relatively ordinary, perhaps even mechanical, sharing of food between hunter/gatherer social units.

In addition to these factors, the best-documented example of specialty foods being consumed (the hind leg of large animals consumed at men's ritual sites— Woodburn 1966) seems to represent consumption at remote and obscure ritual locations, removed from normal living sites. It is questionable as to whether such locations would be very visible archaeologically, whether they would be recorded in any archaeological surveys, or whether they could meaningfully be distinguished from transit encampments on the basis of their artifactual or feature contents.

Thus, if feasting did exist at the generalized hunter/gatherer level, it is not certain that the foods involved were significantly different from daily seasonal fare, that there would be any clear host or guest relationship, or that the remains could be identified archaeologically. While feasting certainly plays a pivotal role in establishing alliances among more complex cultures, it may be that for generalized hunter/gatherers, the forging and maintenance of alliances were dealt with by alternative social techniques such as marriage, the negotiating of kinship relationships and classes, gift giving, and participation in ritual cults (Hayden 1987). A great deal more basic research is required dealing with generalized hunter/gatherers before a clear picture of feasting at this important base level emerges.

TRANSEGALITARIAN HUNTER/GATHERERS AND HORTICULTURALISTS

With the emergence of transegalitarian societies (those between chiefdoms and true egalitarian societies), the full range of feasting that has been previously discussed becomes established. A range of other developments characterizes transegalitarian societies. These developments include the production of reliable surpluses, storage of food and valuables, private ownership of resources and products, the transformation of surpluses into prestige items, economically based competition, and the establishment of contractual debts. It is probably these features that also make feasting a viable means of transforming surplus food into other desirable currencies such as establishing alliances in order to reduce the risk of starvation, attack, and other problems of existence. In fact, there appears to be a major shift in the types of risk-reducing strategies used by generalized hunter/gatherers versus transegalitarian hunter/gatherers. Generalized hunter/gatherers place by far the greatest emphasis on sharing and alliance formation via kinship and rituals (Wiessner 1982; Hayden 1987). Complex hunter/gatherers, in contrast, put much more emphasis on food storage, raiding, wealth accumulation, and the creation of alliances via the consumption or giving away of economic surpluses in feasting. All transegalitarian societies use these new capacities for surplus production, storage, wealth accumulation, and economically based competition to create many types of feasts. Some of the most interesting types are alliance feasts between families, lineages, clans, or communities.

Another type of transegalitarian feast is the promotional feast that advertises the economic, social, and political success of a social group and the desirability of becoming affiliated with such groups either via marriage, wealth exchanges, political support, or by adoption. Typically, the construction of a new house, the installation of major new wealth items, the death of an administrator and installation of a new administrator, and marriages or maturation events, are all viewed as prime opportunities to display success.

Profit and investment feasts probably also emerge where the transegalitarian surplus base is ample enough. These include work feasts, reciprocal food and wealth exchange feasts, high-expense maturation feasts, and competitive feasts where there is a contractual debt to return the amount received plus a substantial increment or interest. Similarly, manipulative, or calamity, feasts probably only occur in transegalitarian and more complex societies.

Another key component of the new feasting types that emerge with transegalitarian societies is the presence of specialized witnesses or recordkeepers. Their function is to ensure that none of the contractual debts are forgotten or neglected, and to ensure that the full value of elevated individuals is a matter of public record. Because the amounts in these transactions can be staggering at times, we frequently find examples of simple recording devices or counters being employed, whether in the form of notched sticks, engraved bones or stones, knotted cords, or clay tokens (Schmandt-Besserat 1986; Wilson and Towne 1978; Lewis 1969:214). In fact, given these ethnographic occurrences and the transegalitarian nature of European Upper Paleolithic art, it is worth wondering if some of the numerous cases of "periodic notation" on bone and stone such as those reported by Marshack (1997) might not be feasting and debt tallies. Typically, too, the counting systems of ethnographic transegalitarian societies reach into the hundreds and thousands, far beyond the 1–20 numeration limit of most generalized hunter/gatherers.

It is worth emphasizing again, that feasts are simply one of a number of social strategies used to achieve specific goals. It should come as no surprise to find that the different techniques and strategies used to achieve these goals are often intermixed in order to ensure that the desired effect is actually achieved. Thus, the reaffirmation of kinship ties, the giving of gifts (the return of which is obligatory if social rupture and hostilities are to be avoided—Dalton 1977:205, 207), and especially ritual all tend to play important subsidiary roles in feasts, while feasting often plays an important supporting role in events where kinship or ritual is the central focus.

CHIEFDOMS AND EARLY STATES

There are undoubtedly additional permutations and developments of feasting events that take place with the emergence of chiefdom and state-level societies. Chiefdoms, especially, are probably much more variable in both organizational and feasting characteristics than I had initially assumed (Hayden 1995:64). On the basis of Laura Junker's data, for instance, it seems that an important distinction should be made between the sociopolitical dynamics of territory-based versus labor-based chiefdoms. Other distinctions, especially those related to the population size of chiefdoms, are also undoubtedly important. However, the complexities of the issue (not the least of which is how to distinguish between complex transegalitarian societies and chiefdoms—see Miller and Boxberger 1994) require more detailed consideration than is possible here. Nevertheless, it is clear that major changes in feasting behavior take place with the transition from transegalitarian to stratified societies. We may not be able to identify all these changes or provide coherent explanations for them at this point, but it does seem that changes in the scale and function of feasts broach new dimensions in many chiefdoms and early states such as discussed by Kelly, Kirch, Junker, Dietler, and Schmandt-Besserat. In particular the pretext of feasting seems to be manipulated by chiefs and elites in early states in order to collect surpluses from the populace (alluded to by Pat Kirch [1984:263] and dealt with in more detail by Laura Junker, Michael Dietler, and Denise Schmandt-Besserat in this volume and by Urry [1993] for New Zealand). The feasts held at Mesoamerican ballcourts and documented by Fox (1996), may well have served a similar function. This change appears to coincide with the holding of feasts on previously unheard-of scales of size, generating enormous amounts of specialized feasting refuse. The spectacular 65,000-cubic-meter Bronze Age feasting midden at East Chisenbury near Stonehenge is probably only the first of this type of deposit to be recognized (McOmish 1996). This is a prime candidate for remains of chiefly level tribute feasts. The feasting refuse that fills ditches surrounding British causewayed enclosures probably represents earlier versions of tribute feasts among smaller chiefdoms. For now, however, I will limit my discussion to transegalitarian feasting, with which I am most familiar.

ARCHAEOLOGICAL CONSTELLATIONS OF FEASTING TRAITS

Here, I would like to examine some broad distinctions in feasting that might be identifiable in the archaeological record. Several basic questions need to be addressed. First, is it possible to identify feasting events in the archaeological record? Considering the criteria in Table 2.1, the answer is clearly, *yes*. Second, is it possible to identify the level of involvement of specific households in feasting? The answer is *yes*. Third, is it possible to distinguish meaningful types of feasts? Again the answer is *yes*.

We can affirm without hesitation that it is certainly possible to identify at least some feasts in the archaeological record. There are many instances of feasting documented in prehistory, especially in the European Neolithic where abundant food remains of specialized nature have been found in front of, or in, megalithic tombs and associated with causewayed enclosures or other ring-ditch monuments (Bradley 1984; Hedges 1984). There are many other examples documented in this volume. The earliest clear evidence in world prehistory is documented at Hallan Cemi (Rosenberg and Davis 1992).

In terms of cultural evolution, it is probable that feasting was taking place at some Upper Paleolithic transegalitarian, faunally rich and diversified aggregation sites such as Altamira, Cueto de la Mina (Conkey 1980), or Enlene (personal observation). If so, it should come as no surprise that good examples of feasting also occur in relatively affluent Epipaleolithic transegalitarian sites such as Hallan Cemi (Rosenberg and Davis 1992) and some Natufian sites (Byrd 1989:78–80). However, in most of these cases, feasting has been documented because of its unusually large scale and sometimes special location. Large-scale occurrences are not particularly difficult to identify as feasts. The real question of importance is whether the existence of smaller-scale feasts can be detected, and whether different kinds of feasts at several scales of size can be distinguished. There is also the possibility that some feasting loci were kept meticulously clean as important sacred areas, as with kivas. Identifying special structures related to feasting when there are no food remains may pose considerable challenges. However, initially, we will concentrate on situations with clearer feasting indications.

Intermediate size feasting (with about 10–50 people) rarely seems to leave the kinds of features, structural remains, or abundant refuse that facilitates the identification of precise feasting locations (unless intermediate-size feasts are held at special locations such as megalithic tombs). Thus, let us turn to the second question: whether households engaged in such feasting can be identified, for it is in the household assemblage that the existence of intermediate-size feasts should be the most apparent archaeologically. Work by Michael Clarke (Chapter 2) and John Blitz (1993a, 1993b) clearly indicate that it is possible to identify households involved in feasting (Fig. 2.2). It is probably even possible to identify the relative frequency and size of feasts on the basis of the proportionate number of serving and food-preparation vessels as well as their absolute size. The larger the preparation and serving vessels, the larger should be the number of regular feast participants.

Figure 2.2. Storage of oversized food-preparation vessels and extra serving vessels used for feasting in the household of a Yao village headman. The occurrence of large sizes and high frequencies of serving or preparation vessels clearly identifies this household as involved in major feasting activities.

On the basis of ethnographic observations among the Maya and the Akha, it appears that, in general, only households that *regularly* host feasts of a certain size acquire vessels and containers appropriate for that size feast. For infrequent feasts of unusual size, the food-preparation and serving needs of particular households are generally met by borrowing the required materials. Of course, care must be taken to differentiate food-preparation and serving vessels from storage vessels, but this should not present a major problem in most cases. In some cases, the fine quality or decoration of serving vessels makes it abundantly clear that certain wares were primarily used in feasting contexts, for example the Peten Polychromes of the Maya, the Kamares ware of Crete (Day and Wilson 1998). In other cases, the contexts and distributions of certain wares, for example the Neolithic Grooved ware of the British Isles (Sherratt 1991:55) or European beakers indicate feasting functions. In any event, let us assume for now that the identification of feasting vessels can be reliably carried out for specific archaeological households or communities and that the ceramic tradition is relatively developed. Where there are *both* daily ceramics and feasting ceramics for large gatherings, we would expect to find histograms of the sizes of individual types of preparation and serving vessels to exhibit some degree of bimodality or even trimodality (e.g., Clarke's data in Chapter 5, Fig. 5.5; also Blitz 1993b:fig. 4). The difference in size between the modes (as well as the amplitude of the modes) should reflect the relative size of the feasting groups and the frequency or intensity of feasting for the household, corporate residence, community, or other sampling unit. Households that did not host significant numbers of intermediate or high-level feasts would be expected to have unimodal size distributions of vessel types. However, it must be kept in mind that in early or initial ceramic assemblages, *all* ceramic vessels may have been used for feast preparation and serving (Hayden 1995b; Clark and Gosser 1995). Such situations might be characterized by unimodal vessel-size distributions as well.

Where domesticated animals are used for feasting, the absolute and proportionate frequencies of various sized and aged animals represented in the refuse associated with a particular household can also be used to gauge the frequency and size of various kinds of feasts, either feasts hosted by the household (perhaps where cranial and low-utility bones predominate) or feasts at which the household members were guests (where bone remains from high-utility cuts predominate, although reciprocal feasting would probably lead to a mixture of high- and low-utility bones). Theoretically, the larger the maximum-sized animal, the larger the feast should be. This relationship seems to be generally backed up by empirical observations (e.g., Michael Clarke's data). The degree of bone reduction versus waste is probably also related to the size of the feasts, with much less waste occurring in small or intermediate feasts. At individual households and corporate residences, the occurrence of outside hearths or roasting pits may also be indicative of the hosting of unusually large feasts (Figs. 2.3–2.5). Small and intermediate-sized feasts are generally prepared over normal household hearths. By far the most common, if not exclusive use of domestic animals in transegalitarian societies is for feasting (Keswani 1994; Blanton and Taylor 1995; Hayden 1990). On the basis of ethnographic observations among the Akha by Michael Clarke, both food vessels and food wastes occurring in the toft zones of individual households appear to reflect real frequencies and sizes of feasting involvement. Thus, even without the occurrence of special facilities or obvious feasting middens, it should be possible to identify feasting involvement at the household level using a number of indicators.

The third question, that of determining the purpose of feasts, is the least explored, but perhaps the most interesting. At the outset, we may iterate the possibility that generalized hunter/gatherers may not host any feasts in the usual

Figure 2.3. For large feasts such as this Hmong funeral, multiple outside hearths are the typical solution to preparing large-scale meals. One hearth not being used occurs in the foreground; two others in use occur behind it. Note also the very large size of food-preparation and serving vessels on the hearths, on the ground, and on the table.

sense, or that if they do, their feasts probably most closely resemble what I would call solidarity feasts. In many (but perhaps not all) solidarity feasts, there seems to be minimal attempt at expending large amounts of resources or consuming special foods; there is little ostentatious display, and all participants often make equal contributions. Thus, these feasts should be minimally differentiated from daily meals, and may only differ from them in terms of size. These characteristics seem consistent with what we currently know about generalized hunter/gatherer communal meals.

At the transegalitarian level, there are several heuristic principles that can be proposed for differentiating feasting functions, all of which require far closer scrutiny with empirical data, refinement, and reevaluation. We can begin, first,

Figure 2.4. The multiple outside hearths made for a Ta Oi marriage feast in Vietnam. Note the location only a few meters from the rear of the longhouse where about 100 guests were served.

by postulating that solidarity feasts will often be the least materially distinctive as just discussed.

Second, there is probably a relationship between the quantity and quality and cost of prestige / display items on the one hand, and the degree of promotion and competition involved in the feasts on the other hand, whether at the interlineage level or at the intercommunity level. Among transegalitarian societies, there frequently seems to be only a loose fit between household feasting activity and household wealth or political power in a community. As Michael Clarke argues in his analysis of the Akha, this is because multifamily socioeconomic and political alliances (usually based on kinship), rather than nuclear families, appear to be the most important units of competition in most transegalitarian communities. By themselves, single households simply appear to be too vulnerable to vicissitudes of economic, social, and political life and stand little chance of winning any competitive struggles against multifamily alliances such as strong lineages. This is clearly documented in Condominas (1977:86–87, 95, 100, 123, 139, 151, 156) where

Figure 2.5. A closeup of the food-preparation area in Figure 2.4 showing several hearths in use and the large food-preparation vessels.

poor or politically isolated families could be disenfranchised or even enslaved or killed for minor transgressions or disputes with the more powerful. Thus, individual households generally seek alliances with the strongest lineage (or other) network open to them, and it is in their interests to see that the lineage is strengthened as much as possible. Therefore, they make substantial contributions to all lineage marriage, funeral, house building, and other feasts, and they participate in the many lineage solidarity feasts.

In terms of feasting, this results in the major promotional and competitive loci occurring at lineage or community levels rather than at the nuclear household level. The fact that individual households may exhibit elaborate feasting paraphernalia but not necessarily be the most wealthy or the most powerful household in the lineage or clan or community (although this is often the case) can distress some archaeologists. Yet, from an archaeological perspective, such concordance of material with economic, social, and political roles of individual households is not of critical importance, since we know all too well that varying strategies and individual idiosyncrasies create a great deal of variability at the individual-household level (Hayden and Cannon 1984). What is of the utmost importance is the fact that such materials as the foods and paraphernalia associated with different levels and types of feasting exist at all, and then that these items are differentially distributed among the social units within a given community and that the magnitude of these differences can be monitored. It is the existence of the overall feasting system and the magnitude of differentiation within the system that is of the greatest archaeological importance, not necessarily the correct identification of each household's status within the community or the system or within a specific lineage. However, to obtain a precise estimate of such differentiation within a community, excavations and analysis of individual household assemblages is essential.

A third potential principle for interpreting transegalitarian feasts is based on an initial perusal of the literature indicating that the purposeful destruction of *high-cost wealth* items (versus personal use) items via breakage, burning, permanent burial (in offerings or graves), or submersion in deep water, may only occur in the context of competitive feasts. Thus, the occurrence of destroyed wealth, as exemplified by the burned Liangzu burial offerings in China (Xuanpei 1992), the bronze wealth objects dropped in British rivers or bogs (Bradley 1990), the highly valued Northwest Coast coppers dropped into the sea, and many other examples, can probably be used to distinguish simple promotional and/or alliance feasting from the more elaborate competitive feasting forms. The presence, frequency, and relative cost of major wealth items may also be a measure of the degree of surpluses and competitiveness involved in feasting.

A possible fourth principle is related to specialized structures. Though large feasts can be for purposes of community solidarity, lineage or community promotion, or community competition, it seems unlikely that special structures for feast-related activities characterize this entire range or scale of functions. Rather, it seems possible that special structures, especially if they are permanent rather than erected only for single events, may reflect more institutionalized competitive or promotional (or perhaps even alliance) feasting for the highest-ranking administrators of large groups such as lineages, clans, or communities (Fig. 2.6). Exactly how lineage feasting and ritual structures operated in this context is not entirely clear from the ethnographies that I have seen, but I suspect that they are constructed primarily as promotional adjuncts to lineage feasts and rituals. On the other hand, the specialized Kepele cult structures that Wiessner documents in Chapter 4 for New Guinea indicate that such relationships are probably complex and require much more investigation.

If these and similar principles can be established as reliable material guides for understanding past feasting behavior, it may be possible to classify archaeological

Figure 2.6. A Vietnamese lineage shrine used for lineage feasts. Only high-ranking lineage men use the interior of this structure for feasting and rituals. Women, children, and low-ranking lineage members eat their meals outside the structure.

feasting events into a number of broad categories. Four such categories might consist of:

1. MINIMALLY DISTINCTIVE FEASTS

There are no archaeological examples of minimally distinctive feasts proposed in this volume. However, ethnographically, at least at some levels, solidarity feasts are minimally distinctive. Most generalized hunter/gatherer feasts are probably minimally distinctive as well. In these cases, only the size of the food-preparation and serving materials may differ from daily meals, as well perhaps as some food species of minimally higher value (chickens, ducks, rabbits, small pigs). There are many small-scale (less than 10 people) household and moderate-sized (about 10–50 people) lineage solidarity feasts of this type, as well as dyadic friendship feasts, solicitation feasts, and possibly punishment feasts—for which data are sparse. Given the single event and unforeseen nature of punishment feasts, as well as the likely desire of the giver to minimize costs, little special food-preparation or serving paraphernalia would be expected to be used for punishment feasts, except through borrowing. Even moderate-size lineage solidarity feasts probably occur as a rule within normal residences, without special paraphernalia other than perhaps slightly larger ordinary preparation and serving vessels.

Where surpluses are limited, alliance feasts between lineages, clans, or communities may also be minimally distinctive in that prestige items might rarely be used for display or for serving, although animals of greater value could be killed to accommodate the larger numbers expected in such circumstances. Another instance where animals of unusual value might be used as part of solidarity feasts is the large-scale community meal in which all interested households make contributions to obtain an unusually large domestic animal such as a large pig or bull. The animal can be killed at a central location, but the meat is often divided up according to individual household financial contributions. In Southeast Asia, household members take the meat back to their houses for cooking and consumption with no village-wide communal meal, although considerable visiting often occurs. Animal horns or mandibles from such communal events are usually saved and placed in prominent locations such as the village priest's or headman's house in order to display the community's ability to sponsor such events (Figs. 2.7 and 2.8). As far as I know, beyond this simple corporate display, prestige items are not associated with such solidarity feasts.

Small- and medium-sized work feasts probably share most of the material characteristics of solidarity feasts. As with community feasts, many hosts probably seek to minimize costs and might not use prestige serving vessels to feed workers, especially if they draw mainly on kinship ties to recruit workers. Like some community solidarity feasts, work feasts sometimes take place in unusual locations (forests or springs). On the other hand, Michael Dietler (personal communication) has observed that as the number or required skill of workers increases beyond the near kin group, greater material inducements must be provided to attract the required number or expertise of workers. Therefore, unusually high-quality foods and serving vessels may be used, and other types of entertainment or treats may be provided. This level of work feast might better be classed with promotional feasts in terms of material patterning.

2. PROMOTIONAL/ALLIANCE FEASTS

Although individual families sponsor marriage, funeral, ancestral, and new house feasts, these are generally lineage or clan affairs in which the success of the social group at large is on display (see Michael Clarke's analysis of Akha feasting). There are, of course, important lineage or clan *solidarity* aspects to these events as well. However, to the extent that advertising group success (to attract mates and desirable labor) is important in these feasts, and to the extent that surpluses are available, prestige items for promotional display (including serving vessels) should increase in frequency and cost. Large-scale food-preparation facilities,

Figure 2.7 (top). Water-buffalo horns from feasts are frequently displayed on the houses of the sponsoring individuals. Here, an Akha village head has placed horns from community feasts on the walls of his house as a display of community prosperity. In other groups, such as Torajan communities in Sulawesi, horns are displayed on houses to indicate household or lineage wealth. Figure 2.8 (bottom). Pig mandibles are also conserved after smaller feasts and used to display household, lineage, and sometimes community feasting activities, as in this Akha administrator's house.

preparation vessels, serving vessels, and perhaps even temporary architecture typically characterize these feasts. Such feasts also tend to be typified by a variety of associated ritual paraphernalia used to indicate that participants use and understand the same feasting conventions and recognize the contractual nature of debts incurred by accepting invitations to feasts. Such paraphernalia includes items such as pipes and the ritual sharing of tobacco smoking, special vessels for the consumption of alcoholic or other drinks like chocolate, kava or coffee (e.g., Dietler 1990), and other ritualized narcotic paraphernalia. Community alliance and promotional feasts are probably indistinguishable from lineage- or clan-sponsored promotional feasts in terms of size and material signatures although locations may shift from individual family or corporate residences to central spaces or facilities of communities. Specialized structures may be associated with some levels of this type of feasting. Large household-sponsored work feasts, household or lineage investment feasts, (such as maturation feasts for children in wealthy families), as well as diacritical feasts as discussed in Chapter 3 and Dietler (1996), may be archaeologically indistinguishable from promotional feasts, except perhaps for size. Several of the archaeological examples in this volume probably represent promotional and alliance feasting, in particular, the Maya lineage feasting and ritual structure documented by Brown and the Woodland platform mounds described by Knight. By further examining these archaeological cultures in more detail, it may be possible to further refine this gross level of interpretation in specific cases. The feasting documented at Cahokia by Kelly and in the Philippines by Junker may also incorporate promotional and alliance feasting components, however their scale and the inclusion of costly prestige wares associated with chiefs seem to indicate other feasting components such as tribute or competitive feasting.

3. COMPETITIVE FEASTS

These feasts have all the material characteristics of promotional feasts but have even more and more costly prestige items, more prestige serving vessels, sometimes intentionally destroyed high-value wealth items, and possibly more elaborate, permanent, specialized structures for feasting-related activities. Junker's Philippine feasts likely included competitive feasts, given the importance of Chinese porcelain wares (Chapter 10).

There is bound to be blurring between the above divisions, especially as surpluses become abundant, which may lead to the incorporation of displays of success in feasts that are fundamentally predicated on promoting solidarity within a social group. In fact, it is rare to find a "pure" feast in terms of function. As noted, even the remains from community solidarity feasts are often displayed in the form of bull horns displayed in the community as a sign that the community was successful enough to sponsor one or more large-scale feasts. However, there are real foci in both the intended purpose of feasts as well as in the material patterning associated with different types of feasts. I am convinced that ignoring these functional foci will only impede our understanding of feasts and our ability to make sense of the archaeological remains of feasts.

4. TRIBUTE FEASTS

These feasts probably characterize chiefdom and early state levels of organization. They may be far larger than any other type of feast. They are held at regular, calendrical intervals and should be as inclusive as possible within a given polity. It seems unlikely that wealth distribution would be common since the goal of these feasts is to amass as much surplus as possible, and to sequester as large a proportion of it as possible for elite use. These types of feasts probably generate a large amount of food refuse due to the large-scale consumption of most surplus food by the populace in order to motivate them to support the elites and tribute feasts. Tribute feasts are likely to be intimately tied to rituals honoring polity deities and in many cases are associated with monumental structures and spaces associated with those deities. Schmandt-Besserat makes a convincing case for tribute feasts in Sumer (Chapter 14), and similar events may be represented by Kelly's Cahokian feasts (Chapter 12), the large British Neolithic and Bronze Age feasting middens previously mentioned (McOmish 1996), and large-scale feasting remains at Incan sites (Morris 1988).

PRINCIPLES AND CONCLUSIONS

The major points that I wish to make about feasting can be summarized as follows:

1. The high cost of some feasts, their widespread occurrence, and their persistence over time indicate that feasts are probably adaptive in an evolutionary and cultural ecological sense.

2. Feasts are techniques for *transforming surpluses* into socially, economically, and politically useful currencies that can be used to further individual and group self-interest and survival. This appears to be one of the most unique and distinctive capabilities that distinguish humans from the rest of the animal world.

3. In transegalitarian societies, clear adaptive advantages can be established via feasts that give households and lineages advantages in warfare, acquiring mates, help in emergencies and catastrophes, and in political control over resources and people. Feasting frequently operates by establishing long-term social ties and debts although immediate benefits are often ob-

tained through work feasts. Feasts can also be used for financial investment, to manipulate people, and perhaps for other purposes.

4. Feasting is probably the main dynamic factor behind the development of
   prestige technologies, especially the development of food production and
   the domestication of plants and animals.

5. Feasting in transegalitarian and other complex types of societies is predicated on the production and use of economic surpluses. Thus, the presence and magnitude of storage facilities should be related to the type and
   intensity of feasting. The greater the surpluses, the greater should be the
   cost and frequency of prestige items, prestige foods, prestige serving vessels, and possibly feasting architecture. Also, the greater the surpluses, the
   greater the expected promotional and competitive nature of the feasts.

6. Feasting is probably not a prominent part of generalized hunter/gatherer
   behavior.

7. The larger the feast and the larger the surpluses, the greater the waste of
   food and goods is expected to be, culminating in the intentional destruction of wealth in competitive feasts. This seems supported by both ethnographic studies and studies of modern material culture such as that of
   Wilson and Rathje in this volume.

8. Feasting may also be strongly implicated in the emergence of the first spe-
   cial-function architectural structures in transegalitarian communities.

9. As in most archaeological inquiries, single lines of evidence for inferring
   behavior or social organization are tenuous at best, given the idiosyncrasies of people, history, preservation, sampling, excavation, processing,
   and interpretation. However, it should be apparent from the foregoing and
   the many contributions in this volume, that in studying feasting, we are
   not restricted to a single line of evidence. Rather, there are many different
   types of data, both theoretical and empirical, that we can use to document
   and investigate the prehistoric occurrence of feasting (Table 2.1). I strongly
   endorse the use of as many lines of evidence as can be marshaled in studying feasting. Sociologists call this approach "triangulation," and it is a good
   metaphor. It is also essential to continuously reexamine and reassess the
   logic and perhaps premature generalizations that we are developing in trying to grapple with this relatively complex but potentially fruitful topic.

In conclusion, it is worth reiterating that our theoretical and comparative understanding of feasting is abysmal, but we are taking active measures to remedy
this situation. The chapters in this volume provide eloquent testimony of the advances that are possible. Nevertheless, the corpus of existing empirical observations on material culture related to feasting is depressing. Traditional social

anthropology and ethnography have not been of great service to archaeologists in this respect. It seems that the future development and validation of accurate and reliable principles related to feasting must be undertaken by ethnoarchaeologists or sympathetic ethnographers. There is a great deal of literature on the topic in ethnographies, but most of it has debilitating gaps that render it of minimal value for archaeological purposes. For instance, despite the great wealth of descriptions on New Guinea feasts, there are no published plans of feasting structures or even any indication of the locations of feasting or food-preparation facilities such as roasting pits for feasts. Polly Wiessner provides some of the first illustrations in this volume. The task for ethnoarchaeologists and ethnographers is enormous, but it is not too late to launch such an undertaking. The gathering of minds represented in this volume is ample testimony to the interest and potential relevance that the future study of feasting holds for us all.

ACKNOWLEDGMENTS

My sincerest gratitude is extended to Ralana Maneeprasert and Chantaboon Sutthi (former Director) of the Tribal Research Institute in Chiang Mai, Thailand, as well as to Professor Chang Quoc Vuong, Director of the Vietnamese Culture and Ecology Program at Hanoi National University. Their unselfish sharing of knowledge and help in visiting traditional Hill Tribe communities was invaluable in opening my eyes to the realities of Hill Tribe culture and feasting. Funding for these investigations was provided by the Social Science and Humanities Research Council of Canada.

REFERENCES

Beardsley, Tim
    1993   Honest Advertising. *Scientific American* 268 (5): 24–27.

Blackburn, Thomas
    1976   Ceremonial Integration and Social Interaction in Aboriginal California. In *Native Californians: A Theoretical Retrospective*, edited by Lowell Bean and Thomas Blackburn, pp. 225–243. Socorro, N.M.: Ballena Press.

Blanton, Richard, and Jody Taylor
    1995   Patterns of Exchange and the Social Production of Pigs in Highland New Guinea. *Journal of Archaeological Research* 3:113–145.

Blitz, John
    1993a   Big Pots for Big Shots: Feasting and Storage in a Mississippian Community. *American Antiquity* 58:80–96.
    1993b   *Ancient Chiefdoms of the Tombigbee.* Tuscaloosa: University of Alabama Press.

Bourdieu, P.
    1990   *The Logic of Practice.* Stanford: Stanford University Press.

Bradley, Richard
    1990   *The Passage of Arms.* Cambridge: Cambridge University Press.

Byrd, Brian
  1989   *The Natufian Encampment*. Jutland Archaeological Society Publication XXIII:1. Denmark: Aarhus University Press.
Clark, John, and Denis Gosser
  1995   Reinventing Mesoamerica's First Pottery. In *The Emergence of Pottery*, edited by W. Barnett and J. Hoopes, pp. 209–221. Washington, D.C.: Smithsonian Institution Press.
Condominas, Georges
  1977   *We Have Eaten the Forest*. New York: Hill and Wang.
Conkey, Margaret
  1980   The Identification of Prehistoric Hunter/Gatherer Aggregation Sites: The Case of Altimira. *Current Anthropology* 21:609–630.
Cowgill, George
  1996   Population, Human Nature, Knowing Actors, and Explaining the Onset of Complexity. In *Debating Complexity*, edited by D. Meyer, P. Dawson, and D. Hanna, pp. 16–22. Calgary: University of Calgary Archaeology Association.
Dalton, George
  1977   Aboriginal Economies in Stateless Societies. In *Exchange Systems in Prehistory*, edited by T. Earle and J. Ericson, pp. 191–212. New York: Academic Press.
Dat, Peter M., and David E. Wilson
  1990   Consuming Power: Kamares Ware in Protopalatial Knossos. *Antiquity* 72:350–358.
Dietler, Michael
  1990   Driven by Drink: The Role of Drinking in the Political Economy and the Case of Early Iron Age France. *Journal of Anthropological Archaeology* 9:352–406.
  1996   Feasts and Commensal Politics in the Political Economy: Food, Power, and Status in Prehistoric Europe. In *Food and the Status Quest*, edited by P. Wiessner and W. Schiefenhövel, pp. 87–125. Oxford: Berghahn Books.
Flood, Josephine
  1980   *The Moth Hunters: Aboriginal Prehistory of the Australian Alps*. Canberra: Australian Institute of Aboriginal Studies.
Fox, J. G.
  1996   Paying with Power: Ballcourts and Political Ritual in Southern Mesoamerica. *Current Anthropology* 37:483–509.
Friedman, J.
  1975   Tribes, States, and Transformations. In *Marxist Analyses and Social Anthropology*, edited by M. Bloch, pp. 161–202. London: Malaby Press.
Friedman, J., and J. Rowlands
  1977   Notes toward an Epigenetic Model of the Evolution of "Civilization." In *The Evolution of Social Systems*, edited by J. Friedman and M. J. Rowlands, pp. 201–276. London: Duckworth.

Gosden, Chris

    1989   Debt, Production, and Prehistory. *Journal of Anthropological Archaeology* 8:355–387.

Harris, Marvin

    1971   *Culture, Man, and Nature.* New York: Crowell.

    1979   *Cultural Materialism.* New York: Random House.

Hayden, Brian

    1987   Alliances and Ritual Ecstasy: Human Responses to Resource Stress. *Journal for the Scientific Study of Religion* 26 (1): 81–91.

    1994   Competition, Labor, and Complex Hunter-Gatherers. In *Key Issues in Hunter-Gatherer Research.*, edited by Ernest Burch Jr., pp. 223–239. Oxford: Berg Publishers.

    1995a   Pathways to Power: Principles for Creating Socioeconomic Inequalities. In *Foundations of Social Inequality*, edited by T. Douglas Price and Gary Feinman, pp. 15–85. New York: Plenum Press.

    1995b   The Emergence of Prestige Technologies and Pottery. In *The Emergence of Pottery*, edited by William Barnett and J. Hoopes, pp. 257–265. Washington, D.C.: Smithsonian Institution Press.

    1998   Practical and Prestige Technologies: The Evolution of Material Systems. *Journal of Archaeological Method and Theory* 5:1–55.

Hedges, John

    1984   *Tomb of the Eagles.* London: John Murray.

Izikowitz, Karl

    1951   *Lamet: Hill Peasants in French Indochina.* Uppsala: Goteborg.

Keesing, Roger

    1975   *Kin Groups and Social Structure.* New York: Holt, Rinehart and Winston.

Keswani, Priscilla

    1994   The Social Context of Animal Husbandry in Early Agricultural Societies. *Journal of Anthropological Archaeology* 13:255–277.

Kirch, Patrick

    1984   *The Evolution of the Polynesian Chiefdoms.* Cambridge: Cambridge University Press.

Lee, Richard

    1979   *The !Kung San.* Cambridge: Cambridge University Press.

Lewis, Paul

    1969   Ethnographic Notes on the Akhas of Burma. Human Relations Area Files, New Haven.

Lewis-Williams, J. D.

    1997   Agency, Art, and Altered Consciousness. *Antiquity* 71:810–830.

Lightfoot, Kent, and Gary Feinman

    1982   Social Differentiation and Leadership Development in Early Pithouse Villages in the Mogollon Region of the American Southwest. *American Antiquity* 47:64–85.

Marshack, Alexander
  1997   Paleolithic Image Making and Symboling in Europe and the Middle East: A
          Comparative Review. In *Beyond Art: Pleistocene Image and Symbol*, edited by M.
          Conkey, O. Soffer, D. Stratmann, and N. Jablonski, pp. 53–91. Memoirs of the
          California Academy of Sciences, No. 23.
Mauss, Marcel
  1954
  [1924] *The Gift*. New York: Free Press.
McOmish, David
  1996   East Chisenbury: Ritual and Rubbish at the British Bronze Age–Iron Age
          Transition. *Antiquity* 70:68–76.
Miller, Bruce, and Daniel Boxberger
  1994   Creating Chiefdoms: The Puget Sound Case. *Ethnohistory* 41 (2): 267–294.
Morris, Craig
  1988   A City Fit for an Inka. *Archaeology* 41:43–49.
Piddocke, Stuart
  1965   The Potlatch System of the Southern Kwakiutl: A New Perspective. *South-
          western Journal of Anthropology* 21:244–264.
Rappaport, Roy
  1968   *Pigs for the Ancestors*. New Haven: Yale University Press.
Richardson, B., and T. Ianzelo
  1974   *Our Hunters of Mistassini* (film). National Film Board, Ottawa.
Rosenberg, Michael, and Michael Davis
  1992   Hallan Cemi Tepesi, an Early Aceramic Neolithic Site in Eastern Anatolia.
          Anatolica 18:1–18.
Ruyle, Eugene
  1973   Slavery, Surplus, and Stratification on the Northwest Coast: The Ethnoener-
          getics of an Incipient Stratification System. *Current Anthropology* 14:603–617.
Sandal, Roger
  1966   *Walbiri Ritual at Ngama* (film). Canberra: Australian Institute of Aboriginal
          Studies.
Schmandt-Besserat, Denise
  1986   An Ancient Token System: The Precursor to Numerals and Writing. *Archae-
          ology* 39 (6): 32–39.
Sharp, Henry S.
  1994   Inverted Sacrifice. In *Circumpolar Religion and Ecology: An Anthropology of the
          North*, edited by Takashi Irimoto and Takako Yamada, pp. 253–271. Tokyo:
          University of Tokyo Press.
Sherratt, Andrew
  1991   Sacrifice and Profane Substances: The Ritual Use of Narcotics in Later Ne-
          olithic Europe. In *Sacred and Profane*, edited by Paul Garwood, D. Jennings, R.
          Skeates, and J. Toms, pp. 50–64. Oxford: Oxford University Committee for Ar-
          chaeology.

Stanish, Charles

　1994　The Hydraulic Hypothesis Revisited: Lake Titicaca Basin Raised Fields in Theoretical Perspective. *Latin American Antiquity* 5:312–332.

Suttles, Wayne

　1968　Coping with Abundance. In *Man the Hunter*, edited by R. Lee and I. Devore, pp. 56–68. Chicago: Aldine.

Urry, Katherine

　1993　Te Hakari: Feasting in Maori Society and Its Archaeological Implications. Master of Arts Thesis, Department of Anthropology, University of Auckland.

Voss, Joachim

　1987　The Politics of Pork and Rituals of Rice: Redistributive Feasting and Commodity Circulation in Northern Luzon, the Philippines. In *Beyond the New Economic Anthropology*, edited by J. Clammer, pp. 121–141. New York: St. Martin's Press.

Wiessner, Polly

　1977　Hxaro: A Regional System of Reciprocity for Reducing Risk among the Kung San. Ph.D. Dissertation, Department of Anthropology, University of Michigan, Ann Arbor.

　1982　Beyond Willow Smoke and Dogs' Tails. *American Antiquity* 47:171–178.

　1996　Leveling the Hunter: Constraints on the Status Quest in Foraging Societies. In *Food and the Status Quest*, edited by P. Wiessner and Wulf Schiefenhövel, pp. 171–192. Oxford: Berghahn Books.

Wilson, N., and A. Towne

　1978　Nisenan. In *Handbook of North American Indians, Vol. 8, California*, edited by R. Heizer, pp. 387–397. Washington, D.C.: Smithsonian Institution.

Winterhalder, Bruce

　1996　Social Foraging and the Behavioral Ecology of Intragroup Resource Transfers. *Evolutionary Anthropology* 5 (2): 46–57.

Woodburn, James

　1966　*The Hadza* (film). London: London School of Economics.

Yan, Xuang

　1996　*The Flow of Gifts*. Stanford: Stanford University Press.

Zahavi, Amotz, and Avishag Zahavi

　1997　*The Handicap Principle*. Oxford: Oxford University Press.

3

THEORIZING THE FEAST

RITUALS OF CONSUMPTION, COMMENSAL POLITICS, AND POWER IN AFRICAN CONTEXTS

Michael Dietler

"Feast" is an analytical rubric used to describe forms of ritual activity that involve the communal consumption of food and drink. Rituals of this kind play many important social, economic, and political roles in the lives of peoples around the world. As the chapters in this volume attest, recognition of this fact has been growing rapidly among archaeologists recently, along with the fertile insights that feasts may offer in understanding social relations and processes in ancient societies. I would suggest that one of the reasons that a focus on feasting is, in fact, crucial to archaeology is that it constitutes part of a central domain of social action that has been largely absent from archaeological analysis to date, much to our detriment. Discussions of the transformation of political systems, for example, have tended rather crudely to link broad evolutionary processes to general structural typologies without considering the intervening kinds of social practices by which people actually negotiate relationships, pursue economic and political goals, compete for power, and reproduce and contest ideological representations of social order and authority. Hence, there has been a general failure to deal effectively with issues of agency and to understand the ways in which practice transforms structure.

In my view, it is essential for archaeologists to come to grips with the arenas of social action in which, and the sets of practices by which, the micropolitics of daily life are played out. This is the only way we will move beyond mechanistic typological reductionism in understanding historical transformations of various relations of power and in addressing such perennial issues as the development of social stratification and political centralization. For example, it is undoubtedly important to nuance our understanding of complex political structures with taxonomic distinctions, such as that between hierarchy and heterarchy raised by Crumley (1987); but it is equally important to attempt to understand the practices by which individuals create, maintain, and contest positions of power and authority within systems structured in these ways and, in the pursuit of their conflicting interests, transform the structures of the systems themselves. Put in simpler terms, we need to think seriously and realistically about political life as it is lived and experienced if we are to fill our analytical categories with meaningful content and advance beyond mechanistic structural correlations, vague pronouncements about overdetermined social processes, and sweeping evolutionist teleologies.

FEASTS, POLITICS, AND ARCHAEOLOGY

There has been much written recently about the need to develop a practice-oriented approach in archaeology, but rather few coherent suggestions or effective demonstrations of how this can be accomplished. This is one of the principal attractions of a focus on feasts. Although as yet curiously underacknowledged, the "commensal politics" of feasting is a domain of political action that is both extremely important on a worldwide scale and potentially accessible to archaeological analysis (Dietler 1990, 1996, 1999a; Hayden 1990, 1996). Indeed, I would contend both that feasts are inherently political and that they constitute a fundamental instrument and theater of political relations. In making this statement, let me explicitly emphasize that I manifestly do not mean to make the naive reductionist argument that feasts are *only* about power; nor do I mean that they are the only significant domain of political action. Far from it. But they are commonly an important arena for the representation and manipulation of political relations, and it behooves us to explore critically this dimension of such a widespread cultural institution. However, before we are able to fully exploit this promising avenue of analysis, we need not only a greater range of empirical information about the diagnostic characteristics of feasts, but, most crucially, a more developed theoretical understanding of the nature of feasts as a distinctive kind of ritual practice. Ultimately, it is only through the latter that we will be able to comprehend and exploit the former. This is by no means a simple or straightforward proposition: it requires detailed, careful, and subtle analytical exploration and argumentation.

As noted above, I define feasts explicitly as a form of public ritual activity centered around the communal consumption of food and drink. Let me immediately anticipate a common misunderstanding of this definition by some archaeologists and make clear that identifying feasts as ritual activity does not mean that they are necessarily highly elaborate ceremonies. A ritual act can be as simple as making the sign of the cross upon entering a church, pouring a few drops of beer on the threshold of a house as a libation, or throwing a small wine and cheese reception for a visiting anthropologist who has just presented a colloquium lecture. Moreover, as the last example suggests, rituals need not necessarily be "sacred" in character (Moore and Myerhoff 1985). The defining criterion of rituals is that they are in some way symbolically differentiated from everyday activities in terms of forms of action or purpose: in Kertzer's (1988:9) phrase, they are "action wrapped in a web of symbolism." More will be said about this later. For the moment, let me simply assert that, as with other types of ritual, feasts provide an arena for both the highly condensed symbolic representation and the active manipulation of social relations. Moreover, as a particular form of ritual in which food and drink constitute the medium of expression and commensal consumption constitutes the basic symbolic idiom, feasts have some distinctive properties (which, again, will be discussed in more detail later).[1]

In earlier publications, I used comparative ethnographic data to develop a theoretical discussion of several major political dimensions of feasting ritual, with distinctions based upon a consideration of the conjuncture of the different political roles played by feasts and the nature of their symbolic action. These different modes of commensal politics were labeled "entrepreneurial," "patron-role," and "diacritical" feasts, and I used different contexts in prehistoric Europe to illustrate how the application of this perspective can aid archaeological understanding of ancient societies (see Dietler 1990, 1996, 1998, 1999a, 1999b). In this chapter I use a variety of ethnographic evidence from African agrarian societies to emend and further elucidate these theoretical constructs and explore their utility for archaeological interpretation.[2]

I focus upon Africa for several reasons. The most obvious reason is that I have firsthand experience of it from having spent several years conducting ethnographic research there.[3] More important than mere personal familiarity, how-

ever, is the fact that Africa is the ethnographic terrain that really gave birth to political anthropology as a field (Amselle 1998:58; Moore 1994). Because so much research during the colonial era was pragmatically driven from an early date by
attempts to understand the operation of politics in both myriad stateless societies
and the large centralized kingdoms that were encountered (e.g., Fortes and
Evans-Pritchard 1940; Middleton and Tait 1958), the African literature is unusually
rich in comparative observations on, and insights into, structures of power and the
operation of politics in daily life. Moreover, despite the obvious cautious source
criticism necessary in negotiating much of the earlier structural-functionalist
political work, Africanists have remained at the vanguard of political analysis and
the theoretical exploration of power. Hence, Africa does offer an especially
promising context for investigating the political dimension of feasting.

But there is more. Africa is also of interest because it has frequently been singled out by scholars as presenting some intriguingly distinctive characteristics in
the realm of food and politics. This is, after all, the continent that was designated
by Goody (1982) as the prototypic land without "cuisine." His book *Cooking, Cuisine, and Class* was largely dedicated to explaining why African societies, even the
highly stratified kingdoms, had not developed the kind of markedly differentiated culinary practices that characterize Europe and China. I hasten to add that
one should be wary of Goody's rather sweeping regional generalizations, but
they do point to some interesting theoretical issues that are important for understanding the archaeological interpretation of feasting. Likewise, several scholars
have recently suggested both that the nature of power in Africa differs fundamentally from that in "the West" (in that it is centered more around consumption than around "transformation," that is, the capacity to consume rather than
the ability to get people to do things: Schatzberg 1993:446), and that it is inseparably associated with metaphors of food and its consumption (see Bayart 1993;
Lentz 1998; Schatzberg 1993). Again, Lentz (1998) quite rightly cautions against
accepting such broad generalizations and reifications, pointing out the tremendous diversity of political practices, strategies, and moral philosophies of power
in Africa. But, whether one ultimately accepts these arguments for African excep-
tionalism or not, what such examples indicate is that African societies do furnish
a challenging context in which to examine and refine theoretical constructs concerning feasting and politics derived from broader surveys of ethnographic data.

FEASTS AND THE POLITICAL ECONOMY

Before undertaking a more detailed analysis of the micropolitical dimensions of
feasting ritual, or what may be labeled "commensal politics," I will begin with the
general observation that in Africa, as elsewhere, feasts serve a wide variety of important structural roles in the broader political economy. They create and main-

tain social relations that bind people together in various intersecting groups and networks on a wide range of scales, from the local household cluster to the regional political community. For example, they are extremely important in establishing sentiments of friendship, kinship, and community solidarity, as well as in cementing bonds between affine groups and political links between leaders of various kinds. In this sense, they may be seen to perform, at a variety of scales, the classic integrative function of creating *communitas*, which was identified by earlier functionalist analysts of ritual (see especially Turner 1969). Unfortunately, the relatively limited considerations of feasting by archaeologists have tended not to penetrate much beyond this level until quite recently. As later discussion will demonstrate, a more productive political analysis of feasting must also explore the complex contradictory processes and tensions simultaneously operating in feasting ritual. However, it is important to acknowledge this integrative function which, among other things, enables feasts to act frequently as the nodal contexts that articulate regional exchange systems: commensal hospitality establishes relationships between exchange partners, affines, or political leaders and provides the social ambiance for the exchange of valuables, bridewealth, and other goods that circulate through a region. Feasts may also provide the main context for the arbitration of disputes, the passing of legal judgments, and the public acting out of sanctions (ridicule, mimicry, ostracism, etc.) that maintain social control within a community. In the important religious sphere, feasts also serve to provide links to the gods or ancestors that can also be used to define the structure of relations between social groups or categories within a region or community. They also provide a crucial mechanism for the process of labor mobilization that underlies the political economy and they serve to articulate conversions between spheres of exchange (see Chapter 9).

Examples of these features are ubiquitous in the anthropological and historical literature on Africa. But, important as these features are, a proper analysis of feasting must move beyond functional consideration of such general structural roles to examine the dynamic nature of feasts as privileged ritual sites of political and economic practice, to show in detail how and why they work, and to demonstrate how feasts are implicated in social change.

FEASTS AS RITUAL, RITUAL AS POLITICS

As noted earlier, feasts are defined as public ritual events of communal food and drink consumption. This means that they differ in some way from daily consumption practices; but at the same time, the ritual symbolism of feasts is constituted through a complex semiotic relationship to daily consumption patterns, and both form part of a common semiotic field (see Douglas 1984; Elias 1978). To adapt a concept from linguistic analysis, feasts may be viewed as the "marked" form to the "unmarked" meal. To illustrate this idea through a simple example, the "communion" event of the Catholic mass may be seen as essentially a feast involving the ritual distribution and consumption of bread and wine. The meaning of this consumption event both derives from and plays upon its original meaning in the context of daily meals, but is, at the same time, dramatically transformed by the symbolic framing devices that distinguish the mass as a theater of ritual action. Of course, quotidian meals are also, to a certain extent, "ritualized" events in that they are highly structured sequences of action that serve to shape the "habitus" (Bourdieu 1990) of individuals (inculcating dispositions guiding practice and naturalizing the social order) and their constituent elements can be manipulated subtly to make political statements (Appadurai 1981). But they differ from more formal ritual "feast" events in being generally less consciously public performances. The ways in which feasts are symbolically marked as distinct from daily practice are variable, and extremely important for archaeologists to understand. More will be said about this later. For the moment, it is important to recognize that this relationship between feasts and daily meals is crucial both to understanding the symbolic significance of feasts and to our very ability to identify feasting archaeologically.

At this point, it is necessary to expand the discussion slightly and set feasts in a broader theoretical context by saying a few words about the emerging anthropological understanding of the nature of ritual in general and its relationship to politics and power. One consistently common feature of recent views in cultural anthropology is a rejection of assumptions that continue to underlie many archaeological interpretations: that ritual is a straightforward reflection of social and political structure and/or an inconsequentially epiphenomenal aspect of the "superstructure" of society. The older Durkheimian functionalist view of ritual as an adaptive mechanism (a kind of all-purpose adhesive substance) for the maintenance of social solidarity (or "system equilibrium," in the terminology of one of the more archaeologically popular versions of functionalism) is also now generally recognized to be a partial and flawed understanding. This is not to deny or ignore that rituals frequently serve to create and reproduce a sense of *communitas* (Turner 1969; van Gennep 1960). But anthropological understanding of the symbolic work of ritual has moved well beyond this feature, and attention has now turned to the historically instrumental role of ritual in creating, defining, and transforming structures of power.

The relationship between ritual and politics is seen to be an intimate one: to paraphrase one recent review of the subject, there is no ritual without politics and no politics without ritual (Kelly and Kaplan 1990:141). However, this relationship is also a complex one that has generated an extensive, and often contentious, literature in anthropology (cf. Apter 1992; Bell 1996; Bloch 1989; Cohen 1979; Comaroff and Comaroff 1991, 1993; Kelly and Kaplan 1990; Kertzer 1988; Tambiah 1985; Turner 1969). In this latter vein, many scholars (e.g., Bloch 1989) see ritual as essentially a conservative authoritarian force that acts to mystify asymmetrical relations of power, while others (e.g., Apter 1992; Comaroff and Comaroff 1991, 1993; Kertzer 1988) view it as an important historical force for both the reproduction and the transformation of relations of power. This latter, more fluid, practice-oriented perspective approaches ritual as an instrument of both domination and resistance, as an arena for the symbolic naturalization, mystification, and contestation of authority. It should go without saying, but let me reiterate an earlier caveat by noting that, in treating the political dimension of ritual, one is not attempting to reduce rituals, such as feasts, to an activity that is *only* about politics. There is clearly a lot more of considerable significance going on. But rituals and politics are inseparably linked in ways that are important to understand.

The effectiveness of ritual in this domain stems from several features. As Cohen (1979) has noted, the most emotionally compelling and effective political symbols are those that are not overtly political but rather tend to have an ambiguous "bivocality" melding intense personal experience of existential identity issues with broader structures of power. By "condensing meaning" in this way, ritual symbolism infuses social norms and categories with emotion (Turner 1967:29). This is one reason that traumatic life-crisis events, such as death, so commonly serve as a major ritual arena for the manipulation of political symbolism (Morris 1992). The emotional power of rituals also stems from certain theatrical media and sensory mechanisms commonly employed (in various combinations) in performance that tend to frame ritual as symbolically pregnant action marked off from other kinds of daily practice, thus focusing people's attention and rendering them receptive to episodes of heightened emotional experience. These devices include such things as music, dancing, rhythmic verse, role acting, evocative staging and costumes, and intoxication. Dramaturgical techniques such as the creation of images through contrast and the dialectical resolution of contradictions merge emotional catharsis with important pedagogical functions. Symbolic references to the past are commonly invoked to create an impression of seamless continuity, and highly formalized, repetitive sequences of action serve to limit the perception of alternatives and to naturalize the projected order by linking it to the "natural" experience of the passage of time (cf. Bloch 1989; Dietler and Herbich 1993; Moore and Myerhoff 1985; Tambiah 1985; Turner 1967).

Like all ritual, feasts provide a site and a medium for the highly condensed symbolic representation of social relations. However, again as with other ritual, they express idealized concepts: the way people *believe* relations exist, or should exist, rather than how they are necessarily manifested in daily activity. Such representations may either camouflage, naturalize, or contest asymmetries of power, and struggles over the control of representations and their interpretation by differentially situated actors are an important site of historical change. However, in addition to this idealized representation of the social order, rituals also offer the potential for manipulation by individuals or groups attempting to alter or make statements about their relative position within that social order as it is perceived, presented, and contested. As such, feasts are subject to simultaneous manipulation for both ideological and more immediately personal goals. In other words, individuals can use feasts to compete against each other without questioning a shared vision of the social order that the feast reproduces and naturalizes, or they can use feasts to simultaneously struggle for personal position *and* promote contrasting visions of the proper structure of the social world.

Feasts are a particularly powerful form of ritual activity that also have the pragmatic virtue of being potentially visible in the archaeological record. Because of their inherent emotive and symbolic power, feasts are very often intimately embedded in *rites de passage* or life-crisis ceremonies, such as funerals; and it is this feature that often renders them archaeologically detectable as distinct events. Moreover, the culinary nature of feasts generally necessitates the use of containers for both preparation and consumption. Very frequently, over the past 10,000 years of human history at least, a substantial portion of these containers has tended to be made of ceramic or metal, which preserve extremely well in the archaeological record even when broken. Detecting feasts in the Paleolithic is, of course, considerably more difficult (see Dietler 1996; Marshall 1993; Perlès 1996); and the political dimensions of feasting are somewhat different among forager societies (see Hayden, Chapter 2; Wiessner 1996) than among the agrarian societies discussed here.

The previously asserted potency of feasts as a particular form of ritual activity derives from the fact that food and drink serve as the media of expression and commensal hospitality constitutes the syntax in the context of a ritual of consumption. Food and drink are highly charged symbolic media because they are "embodied material culture": that is, a special form of material culture produced specifically for ingestion into the body. They are a basic and continual human physiological need, which are also a form of "highly condensed social fact" (see Appadurai 1981:494) embodying relations of production and exchange and linking the domestic and political economies in a highly personalized way. Moreover, although eating and drinking are among the few biologically essential acts, they are never simply biological acts. Rather, they are learned "techniques du corps" (Mauss 1935)—culturally patterned techniques of bodily comportment that are expressive in a fundamental way of identity and difference. Alcoholic beverages frequently have a privileged role in the feasting context because they are essentially food with certain psychoactive properties resulting from an alternative means of preparation that tend to amplify their significance in the important dramaturgical aspects of ritual (Dietler 1990). Moreover, this property of fermentation as a quasi-magical transformation of food into a substance that, in turn, transforms human consciousness augments the symbolic value of alcohol in the common liminal aspects of rituals.

Both food and drink are also a highly perishable form of good, the full politico-symbolic potential of which is realized in the drama of public-consumption events that constitute a prime arena for the reciprocal conversion of what Bourdieu (1990) metaphorically calls "symbolic capital" and economic capital. Public distribution and consumption of a basic need derives added symbolic salience from its demonstration of confidence and managerial skill in the realm of production. More importantly, however, consumption is played out in the extremely powerful idiom of commensal hospitality. I believe this feature is crucial to understanding the political dimensions of feasts, and it is for this reason that I have chosen to emphasize what I have called "commensal politics."

Anigbo has asserted that "Commensality is not essentially about expressing love or intimacy" (1996:101–102), because it is clear that even individuals aggressively opposed to each other may use commensality to define their relationship. However, commensality is a powerfully expressive trope of intimacy that creates and reproduces relationships capable of encompassing sustained aggressive competition by effectively euphemizing it in a symbolic practice that encourages collective misrecognition of the self-interested nature of the process. And as Bourdieu has pointed out

> In the work of reproducing established relations—feasts, ceremonies, exchange of gifts, visits or courtesies, and, above all, marriages—which is no less vital to the existence of the group than the reproduction of the economic bases of its existence, the labour required to conceal the function of the exchanges is as important as the labour needed to perform this function. (1990:112)

Hence, one begins to glimpse the symbolic force at the heart of commensal rituals. Feasts act as a form of symbolic "metaproduction," constituting and euphemizing broader social relations in terms of the basic commensal unit.[4]

Furthermore, commensal hospitality may be viewed as a specialized form of gift exchange that establishes the same relations of reciprocal obligation between host and guest as between donor and receiver in the exchange of other more durable types of objects (Mauss 1966). The major difference is that food is destroyed in the act of commensal consumption at a feast; and, moreover, destroyed by ingesting it into the body. This is a literal "embodiment" or "incorporation" of the gift and the social debt that it engenders. Aside from the powerful symbolic dimension of this practice, it also results in the pragmatic fact that, unlike durable valuables, the food consumed cannot be recirculated (or "reinvested") in other gift-exchange relationships: food must be produced anew through agricultural and culinary labor in order to fulfill reciprocal obligations.

A clarification should be raised here, however, because food can also be used for nondestructive exchange in the same fashion as durable valuables. In contrast to the prepared food consumed at feasts, this food may be either raw (e.g., yams, sacks of flour), processed (e.g., cooked or smoked meat), or even live potential food (e.g., chickens, goats, cattle). In the case of live animals, in particular, the potential for long-term reinvestment is obvious; but even the more perishable forms may be quickly redeployed to a certain extent in other local exchange networks or in subsequent commensal hospitality. The exchange of food in this manner may take place completely outside of a commensal-consumption context that one would properly call a feast; or a feast may serve as the arena for such exchanges. In the latter case, different kinds of foods may sometimes be used for the feast and the exchange transaction. Although both of the two political uses of food described above (commensal consumption and nondestructive gift exchange) may take place at feasts, it is important for the analytical purposes of this discussion that the distinction between them not be obscured by subsuming them both under the general term *feasting*. They are not the same thing (Dietler 1996).

Commensal consumption (which, to reiterate, is here taken to be a definitive attribute of feasts) places obvious limitations on the possibilities of the guest/receiver to redeploy the food (s)he has received in the fulfillment of reciprocal obligations of other exchange relationships: it removes goods permanently and immediately from circulation. It is thus a more temporally restrictive use of food in manipulating social relations than is the nondestructive exchange pattern that may or may not accompany a feast. Because of the commensal aspect, it is also a potentially even more subtle manipulation.

The critical point to retain is that commensal hospitality centering on food and drink distribution and consumption is a practice, which, like the exchange of gifts, serves to establish and reproduce social relations. This is why feasts are often viewed as mechanisms of social solidarity that serve to establish a sense of community. However, as Mauss (1966) long ago pointed out, these are relations of reciprocal obligation that simultaneously serve to create and define differences in status. The relationship of giver to receiver, or host to guest, translates into a relationship of social superiority and inferiority unless and until the equivalent can be returned. "As the Bemba [of Zambia] say, 'You have eaten *namba* (the sticky gum from the *munamba* tree) and it sticks to your stomach'. . . i.e., you have filled your stomach with food from some one and it puts you under a permanent obligation to him" (Richards 1939:135). In this feature, the potential of hospitality to be manipulated as a tool in defining social relations, lies the crux of commensal politics. The hospitality of feasting is, of course, only one of many potential fields of political action that may be variably articulated. As will be shown in more detail in the later discussion of the Luo case, feasting may be strategically used by individuals either to complement or to compete against forms of prestige and power derived from other domains of competition for symbolic capital, such as warfare, magic, gift giving, public oratory, etc. (cf. Bourdieu 1990; Lemonnier 1990; Modjeska 1982). However, the special attribute of feasting is that, because of the intimate nature of the practice of sharing food and the symbolic power of the trope of commensality, of all forms of gift prestation it is perhaps the most effective at subtly euphemizing the self-interested nature of the process and creating a shared "sincere fiction" (in Bourdieu's apt phrase) of disinterested generosity.

MODES OF COMMENSAL POLITICS

I will now turn to some selected African empirical contexts in order to further explicate several previously defined theoretical constructs: specifically, three different modes of commensal politics, or general patterns in the ways that feasts operate symbolically in serving as sites and instruments of politics (Dietler 1996). One can, of course, propose a variety of more or less useful classifications of feasts based upon a range of criteria, such as scale of inclusion (household, neighborhood, community, etc.), specific cultural context (funerary feasts, marriage feasts, initiation feasts, etc.), or manifest and latent social and economic functions (religious feasts, labor feasts, community celebrations, etc.; see Hayden 1996 and various chapters in this volume for some alternative classifications). However, the value of a classification is entirely relative to the problem it is intended to solve.

The distinctions outlined here are analytical constructs designed to further understanding of the specific problem of the political dimensions of feasting ritual. As will become clear in the discussion to follow, a concept such as the "empowering feast" crosscuts many of the other potential categories noted above because it highlights the ways that certain political processes are operative in all these apparently different feasting contexts. Hence, I am not really proposing here a typology of "kinds of feasts" that can be linked directly to, for example, certain patterned deposits of archaeological material (insofar as that might be possible). Rather, I am attempting a heuristic dissection of the politico-symbolic dimension of feasting as an institution. The application of insights derived from this analysis to the archaeological record must always rely upon complex contextual arguments that accommodate the specific cultural conditions of a given case (see Dietler 1990, 1996, 1999a).

The first of these three modes of commensal politics to be analyzed is directed toward the acquisition or creation of social (and economic) power and the latter two are directed toward the maintenance of existing inequalities in power relations. The first two operate primarily through an emphasis on quantity, and the last operates through an emphasis on style. The first two work through the idiom of donor/receiver, superiority/subordination relations within an inclusive binding exchange dyad, whereas the latter works through the idiom of diacritical exclusion in an insider/outsider relationship.

EMPOWERING FEASTS

The first of these feast patterns, which I call the "empowering feast," involves the manipulation of commensal hospitality toward the acquisition and maintenance of certain forms of symbolic capital, and sometimes economic capital as well. The term covers a range of symbolic consumption practices that are instrumental in negotiating social positioning. In previous publications (Dietler 1996, 1999a), I have referred to this category as the "entrepreneurial feast," but subsequent discussions have led me to believe that this term has the potential to create some misunderstanding. It was intended simply as a convenient trope, but runs the risk of being interpreted literally as a sort of crude neoclassical economic concept. The change in terminology also, I believe, helps to underline the fact that I am not attempting to distinguish a type of specialized feast involving openly aggressive competitive contests (as distinct from, for example, a "harmonious egalitarian" community celebration). Rather, I use the more passive term "empowering" as a way to indicate an effective political role of feasting events of various kinds rather than necessarily an overt intention of the hosts. Although this role is sometimes fully, or at least partially, recognized by the participants, much of the effectiveness of this political mechanism derives from the fact that it often entails a kind of collective misrecognition or euphemization of the self-interested nature of the practice. It involves what Bourdieu characterizes as a "sincere fiction of disinterested exchange" (1990:112). Indeed, a major part of Bourdieu's argument about habitus is that the skill and grace of the genuinely competent social actor relies upon that actor being unaware of the principles that inform his or her actions. Awareness arises in the context of mistakes, of alternative actions that raise uncertainties about precisely how one should act. Although the limited role of consciousness in social action is an aspect of Bourdieu's work that is perhaps overstated and subject to some question and criticism, nevertheless, I believe that he is correct in identifying the euphemization of self-interest as an important aspect of ritualized forms of exchange, such as feasts.

Another preliminary preemptive disclaimer is necessary to clarify the fact that I have previously referred to empowering feasts as a domain of inherent social "competition" (Dietler 1990, 1996). This word also has the potential to give rise to misunderstandings, particularly in traversing linguistic frontiers in which the cultural coding of the term differs.[5] Hence, let me reiterate that in using the term *competitive* I am manifestly not referring only to activities that involve an overt agonistic challenge to monopolize power, with resulting explicit "winners" and "losers." I have something more subtle in mind than the ideology of free-market capitalism or football! Nor am I referring only to feasts that involve an escalating scale of ostentatious reciprocal hospitality (of the well known New Guinea "big-man" type: see Lemonnier 1990, 1996).

Rather, I mean that feasts are inherently *political*, but with an understanding of power in the sense it has acquired in the wake of work by Bourdieu (1990), Foucault (e.g., 1980), and others: as a *relational* phenomenon rather than as a limited good. Hence, the symbolic capital realized through empowering feasting is an inherently "competitive" phenomenon in that it describes conditions of *relative* asymmetries in relationships between people, and, moreover, asymmetries that must be renegotiated continually through symbolic practices. This "competition" is not necessarily one that strives toward aggressive domination and relentless accumulation of power: it is often simply one of maintaining status among peers or of defining one's peers. Nor is it necessarily one that directs an explicit challenge to particular individuals or groups: it often involves simply a positive affirmation of the prestige of the host and his/her group that implicates others only in a relative, indirect, general sense. There is clearly a significant difference between, for example, maintaining friendly reciprocal obligations with one's neighbors in hosting small beer parties and the agonistic attempts by New Guinea big-men to crush their rivals with hospitality. There are generally culturally specific behavioral sanctions and moral philosophies of legitimate power that restrict the escalation of such commensal practices and assure that cases of the latter extreme form are fairly unusual. But some degree of competition is involved in all these empowering feast contexts. Those who do not keep up fall behind. Such practices always affect the *relative* status and influence of participants and the quality of relationships. In this sense, commensal politics is always competitive in its effects, even though the political implications may be subtle, limited, and thoroughly euphemized.

Consequently, it must also be recognized that, for example, feasts conceived sincerely by the participants as harmonious celebrations of community identity and unity are *simultaneously* arenas for manipulation and the acquisition of prestige, social credit, and the various forms of influence, or informal power, that symbolic capital entails. These are not mutually exclusive functions that require, or even enable, one to assign a given feast event to one of two alternative categories (e.g., solidarity vs. competitive). Rather, one must recognize the complex political polysemy of feasts. They both unite and divide *at the same time*. They simultaneously define relationships and boundaries. This feature may well entail certain structural contradictions of interest, but it does not necessarily result in conflict, or even the perception of incongruity, in the course of practice.

Finally, let me also emphasize that, in treating the political dimension of things such as religious feasts, I am manifestly not attempting to make a vulgar reductionist argument of the bottom-line "practical reason" variety. I do not wish to reduce the participants to unidimensional cynical manipulators and deny their religious sincerity and the affective motivational force of religious belief. Quite the contrary. Rather, I believe this is an issue of audience: it must be remembered that all rituals, including feasts, have simultaneous multiple audiences. Religious feasts, for example, are clearly directed at communicating with gods, ancestors, or spiritual forces: they are a sincere attempt to "bring them to the table," so to speak. But they are simultaneously directed toward an audience of living humans, and perhaps several groups or categories of living humans. Feasts are polysemous, in terms of audience, motivation, and forms of empowerment. Concentrating on an analysis of the political should not be interpreted as a denial of the importance of other dimensions.

Symbolic capital translates into an ability to influence group decisions or actions. This influence derives from the relations created and reproduced in the process of personal interaction. In the case of feasting, those are multiple relations of reciprocal obligation and temporary sentiments of social asymmetry between host and guests created through displays of hospitality. The "power" derived from this sort of commensal politics may range from a subtle and temporary affirmation of elevated status (such as attitudes of gratitude or deference) to demands for special rights and leading managerial roles in group decisions. In societies without formal specialized political roles, hosting feasts is very often a major means of acquiring and maintaining the respect and prestige necessary to exercise leadership. It does not create the power to command, but it does imbue individuals with the moral authority that is a necessary condition to exert persuasive influence.

In societies where institutionalized political roles or formal status distinctions exist, but without fixed hereditary rules for determining who may fill them, hosting feasts is often the means by which individuals assume and hold these roles and statuses. In all such cases, this kind of power is continually being renegotiated, sustained, and contested through commensality. This form of commensal politics has been described by various anthropologists in many contexts across Africa (not to mention the Pacific, Latin America, Asia, and the rest of the world). Among the Yoruba of Nigeria, for example, men move up the social hierarchy by taking titles. This is accomplished by displays of prestige in feasts furnished with large quantities of beer or palm-wine (Obayemi 1976). Among the

Dorze of Ethiopia, assumption of the title of *balak'a* and its elevated political status requires the hosting of feasts so lavish that there is even some reluctance to undertake the initiation procedure (Halperin and Olmstead 1976). Similarly, among the Koma of Cameroon, there is a formalized age-grade system that leads to the possibilities for individuals to become high-ranking initiates and respected makers of policy within the village as they progressively gain access to more secret religious knowledge with each step. Moving up through this system requires the sponsorship of special feasts known as "cattle dances" that are held by a man to honor his wife and are fueled with a great deal of millet and sorghum beer and beef. These can be held by a man only six or seven times in a lifetime, and the ability to hold such a feast is decided by fellow villagers who judge whether an individual has acquired the necessary symbolic and economic capital for the rank to which he aspires. There are, of course, many other feasting contexts for acquiring personal prestige that are not tied directly to the age-grade structure. These include beer parties hosted for gatherings on market days, for work feasts, and for various ritual activities (Garine 1996).

In societies with an egalitarian political ethos, the self-interested manipulative nature of the process may be concealed or euphemized by the fact that it is carried out through the socially valued and integrated institution of generous hospitality, and it may even be perceived by the participants as a leveling device. However, this apparent leveling is, in a sense, merely the conversion of economic capital into symbolic capital. In fact, feasts may be used as a form of what Firth (1983) has called "indebtedness engineering" every bit as much as the prestation of valuables. This is quite clear in the cases where feasting is recognized by the participants to be openly aggressive, as with the escalating beer feasts between exchange partners among the Mambila of Nigeria where the failure to return a yet more copious feast results in jeering and ridicule (Rehfisch 1987). But it can be equally operative in cases where competitive manipulation is more subtly euphemized and where there is no escalation of prestation.

Commensal hospitality may be manipulated in the empowering feast pattern for economic advantage as well as for political power, especially through the institution of the "work feast"; and this was particularly true of societies in the past. As this institutionalized practice is more thoroughly analyzed elsewhere in this volume (see Chapter 9), I will simply note here that the "work feast" is a form of labor mobilization practice found throughout Africa (and indeed, around the world). It constitutes one pole in a continuum of labor mobilization practices, here called "collective work events" (CWE), for which the other pole is the "work exchange." The work feast is an event in which a group of people is called together to work on a specific project for a day and the participants are then treated to food and/or drink, after which the host owns the proceeds of the day's labor. Before the development and spread of the capitalist monetary economy, such CWEs were virtually the only means (excluding slavery) by which a group larger than the domestic unit could be mobilized for a project requiring a larger communal effort. This is particularly true of societies without centralized political authority, but even obligatory forms of labor (*corvée*) organized by chiefs or kings operate within this idiom.

Work feasts are extremely important in the political economy because of the context they provide for the acquisition and conversion of symbolic and economic capital. In the first place, as with all other types of feast, they provide an opportunity to make public statements about prestige and acquire symbolic capital. A lavish work feast augments the reputation of the host in the same way that sponsoring a communal ritual does. However, it also provides a means of harnessing the labor of others in order to acquire economic capital that can subsequently be converted to symbolic capital by several means. In effect, work feasts act as a mechanism of indirect conversion in multi-centric economies that can provide a potential catalyst for increasing inequality in social relations (see Chapter 9).

SOCIOECONOMIC PARAMETERS OF EMPOWERING FEASTS

The empowering feast pattern operates on a variety of scales and in numerous contexts within a given society. It may extend from the private hosting of a pot of beer among a small group of friends, to the hosting of trade partners from another community, to the sponsorship of major community life-crisis ceremonies and religious festivals. Guests may include members of the local community or people from other communities. The extent of the symbolic capital derived from these activities varies according to the context, the lavishness of the hospitality provided, and the range of guests convened. The host may be either an individual household, a kinship unit, or an entire community. In the latter cases there are usually certain individuals who act as managers and derive prestige from their role in successfully organizing and executing feasts that represent the group to outsiders; hence prestige accrues to both the hosting group as a whole and to certain influential individuals who can mobilize group activities.

Although most households will engage in some form of this kind of feasting behavior, hosting large-scale feasts requires considerable planning, time, and labor (for both agricultural production and culinary preparation), as well as large surplus stocks of food and/or drink. The kinds of food and drink traditionally available in most African agrarian societies (and most prehistoric societies) would generally have had very limited storability, especially once prepared for consumption. This would necessitate, in most cases, a large labor force for final preparation and serving just prior to the feast as well as command of a large ready supply of agricultural produce. The institutional arrangements for mobilizing these large supplies of labor and food vary a great deal from society to society, but in all cases the organization and execution of a large feast requires the host to be a good manager. It is usually advantageous for a household sponsoring a feast to be able to provide a large portion, if not the bulk, of the labor and raw materials from its own reserves, and a high incidence of polygyny among big-men and other types of informal leaders is often cited in this connection (cf. Boserup 1970:37; Geschire 1982; Friedman 1984; Lemonnier 1990).

In some cases work feasts may also be employed to harness the labor of others in differentially increasing the productive base of certain households (see Chapter 9). In most cases of very large feasts, however, the host must mobilize additional food and labor contributions through personal networks of social obligation. These networks of support are established by adept building up of symbolic capital over the years through various arenas of prestige competition and various deployments of economic capital. Hence a large, lavish feast is not just an isolated event. It is a moment of public ritual drama in a continuous process of political manipulation that serves as an advertisement of the scale of the support base that a social manager has been able to construct through various transactions, at the same time that it produces further symbolic capital.

It is important to underline the significant scale of the resources that are devoted to this kind of communal political activity in most societies, and especially to note the resources devoted to the production of alcoholic beverages for such purposes (see Dietler 1990:361–362). One frequently sees archaeological estimates of "subsistence" food production requirements that both ignore the importance of alcoholic beverages and do not take such crucial festive requirements for social reproduction and politics into account. Yet, where attempts have been made to measure such things in ethnographic contexts, the figures are consistently impressive. Haggblade (1992), for example, noted that households in Botswana consume 15–20 percent of all the grain produced in the form of sorghum beer, much of it consumed in work feasts during the harvest time when many men remain intoxicated most of the time. Similarly, Richards (1939:80) estimated that an average household among the Bemba of Zambia used about 400 pounds of millet per year in brewing beer, out of a total production of about 2,400 pounds of grain (i.e., about 17 percent); and for chiefs, who commonly drink beer every day as part of their duties of hospitality (and may virtually subsist on it), the quantity is much higher. Netting (1964) estimated that the Kofyar of Nigeria consume about 40 gallons (151 liters) of millet beer per person each year, while annual consumption estimates for the city of Ouagadougou in Burkina Faso ran to 236 liters of traditional beer per person, with half the annual grain consumption for a family being in the form of beer (Pallier 1972; Saul 1981). Likewise, Garine (1996) noted that among the Koma of Cameroon sorghum beer provides about a third of the total calories consumed during the year. He further calculated the large investments involved in hosting different kinds of feasts. For one age-grade ceremony, one needs 70 pots of beer (490 liters made from about 100 kg of cereal), plus another 50 kg of sorghum flour for 24 porridge balls, plus a number of cattle (that are worth up to $400 each); for a cattle dance, one needs 75 pots of beer, 20 porridge balls, and the most prestigious cattle; and for the funeral of a woman, one needs 37 pots of beer (Garine 1996). Similarly, Rehfisch (1987) noted that, among the Mambila of Nigeria, one beer feast in the competitive series he studied mobilized over 480 pots of beer (plus 47 chickens, 1 sheep, a dog, kola nuts, and tobacco) to counter a previous feast in which 430 pots of beer (and 30 chickens) had been offered. In Manga (a Mossi town of about 7,000 inhabitants in Burkina Faso), memorial ceremonies called *kuure* are the occasions for the most lavish beer feasts. In one week, five *kuure* were held in one ward, consuming 1,900 kg of red sorghum made into beer (with seven cartloads of wood—1,400 kg—required for brewing and cooking for one of these feasts alone); and, during a single dry season, within the town as a whole, 10 tons of sorghum were converted into beer for these memorial feasts alone, with a total annual festive consumption estimated at 14 tons of grain brewed for beer (Saul 1981). Finally, among the Luo of Kenya, funerals are the occasions for the most lavish feasts mounted in this society. These events frequently result in the serious impoverishment of the hosting family, and the Kenyan government has even attempted to intervene legally to limit the scale of Luo funerals.

All of this represents a substantial investment of agricultural and culinary labor in the essentially political activity of acquiring and maintaining symbolic capital and creating and sustaining social relationships. Moreover, contrary to some persisting archaeological conceptions of economically autonomous domestic units, it represents a substantial portion of domestic agricultural production that is regularly dedicated from the beginning to flowing outside the household and being consumed by people in other domestic units. Hence, it is clear that recognizing the importance of feasting for both social reproduction and political action in agrarian societies should provoke a corollary recognition of the scale of productive labor and resources necessarily devoted to these crucial features of social life. Feasts are an instrumental force in the organization of production as well as in the structuring of social relations and power.

PATRON-ROLE FEASTS

The second major mode of commensal politics that may be distinguished I will call the "patron-role feast." This involves the formalized use of commensal hospitality to symbolically reiterate and legitimize institutionalized relations of asymmetrical social power. This corresponds to a specific form of what has traditionally been called "redistribution" in the literature of economic anthropology (cf. Polanyi 1957; Sahlins 1972). The operative symbolic trope behind this form of commensal politics is the same as for the previous mode: the relationship of reciprocal obligation engendered through hospitality. In this case, however, the expectation of equal reciprocation is no longer maintained. Rather, the acceptance of a continually unequal pattern of hospitality symbolically expresses the formalization of unequal relations of status and power and ideologically naturalizes it through repetition of an event that induces sentiments of social debt. On the one hand, those who are continually in the role of guests are symbolically acknowledging their acceptance of subordinate status vis--vis the continual host. On the other hand, the role of continual and generous host for the community at large comes to be seen as a duty incumbent upon the person who occupies a particular elevated status position or formal political role. Institutionalization of authority relies on this binding asymmetrical commensal link between unequal partners in a patron/client relationship.

This is the principle that lies behind the regular lavish hospitality expected of chiefs and kings in almost all societies where they exist, and certainly those in Africa. This sense of obligation for generosity in a commensal context is nicely encapsulated in the Baganda definition of the essential qualities of a good chief: "beer, meat and politeness" (Mair 1934:103). Among the Nyoro, also of Uganda, the king was expected to regularly hold great feasts and give gifts, and many of his special names emphasize this expected generosity. A decline in the lavishness of the feasts provided by the king was cause for complaints. Chiefs under the king were also expected to follow this pattern on a more local level (Beattie 1960). Similarly, among the Pondo of South Africa, Hunter noted that "Generosity is a primary virtue and the mark of a chief." It was particularly important for the chief to dispense generous hospitality, and "there was always much beer at the great places." Indeed, the Pondo word for "chief," Inkosi, is also the word in everyday usage for "thank you" (1961:387–388). Dillon provides a more detailed idea of the scale of such obligations among the Metá of Cameroon:

> The foremost duty of a fon [village chief] in the mind of any Metá person was to feed his people. This was done most lavishly when he provided several grand feasts at the time of his installation. Yet the fon also entertained more modestly on a regular basis. Each time that the villagers worked for him he was obligated to feed them when they had finished their task, and he hosted the entire village whenever he held an annual celebration involving dancing. Likewise, if the village went to war, . . . the fon . . . had to provide the returning warriors with an appropriate reception. But even if no such activities had taken place within a year, the people sometimes still expected the fon to give them a feast simply because he was their leader.

Besides hosting the entire village on special occasions, the *fon* frequently entertained individuals and small groups. He was expected to have wine ready for such
visitors at any time, as well as for the *mikum si* [senior village notables] when they
met on the village rest day. Moreover, if there was a market in his village, he held
court in a house just outside of it, providing palm wine for both the local notables
and important visitors. . . .

Since the *fon* was continually receiving visitors—on week days, on village rest
days, on special occasions, and on market days—he was in an excellent position to
use the norms of hospitality as a political tool. He could honor and reward allies as
well as cultivating the nonaligned. At the same time, he gained prestige with the entire community by feeding it well. (Dillon 1990:129–130)

Similarly, among the Bemba of Zambia, Richards noted that the chief was responsible for feeding all those who provided tribute work on his *corvée* projects,
courtiers, executive officials, visiting councilors, and others. She estimated that
during one nine-month period the main chief provided food and beer for at least
one day for 561 men and 324 women who provided labor and, among others,
about 40 tribal councilors with their wives and retinue at least twice (1939:147). As
she noted, the culinary labor for this is provided by the multiple wives of the
chief, under the direction of the senior wife who was necessarily a woman with
"a good deal of organizing ability, capable of supervising younger wives, arranging for the endless grinding and brewing required in the capital, and the stirring
of huge pots of porridge to be served in enormous eating-baskets about eight
times the size of an ordinary *icipe*" (1939:148). As she further stated, "The whole
of this system of distributing food is of course necessary to the chief if he is to
make gardens and conduct tribal business through his councilors. But it is more
than this. The giving of food, as in most African tribes, is an absolutely essential
attribute of chieftainship, just as it is of authority in the village or household"
(1939:148). Correspondingly, the failure of a chief to provide food for his subjects
considerably weakens his prestige. "The tradition of the generous king survives
as a standard against which the modern ruler is constantly measured, and measured to his disadvantage" (Richards 1939:264).

It is important to emphasize that this kind of practice is not, as has sometimes
been posited in functionalist accounts, necessarily a systemically adaptive means
of providing balanced food security for a population. Rather, it is first and foremost a politico-symbolic device for legitimizing status differences, and any nutri-
tional benefits to the population at large are highly variable (see Friedman 1984;
Hayden and Gargett 1990; Pryor 1977). This political function is underlined by the
fact that challenges to chiefly authority can also be launched through feasting.
Anigbo (1996) provides an excellent example of such a challenge among the Igbo
of Nigeria in the form of a case in which two contestants for the chiefship fought

over who had the right (by virtue of lineage seniority) to convene an important "feast of yams," which sets the date for eating new yams. This conflict culminated in a dispute over who would host the centrally important *omabe* (mask feast): each candidate ended up holding this feast on a different day, with the supporters of each boycotting the feast of his rival.

Chiefs raise food supplies for this lavish public hospitality in a variety of ways (e.g., see Hunter 1961:384–389; Richards 1939; Schapera 1938). Often tribute in food and drink furnishes an important part, with individuals obligated to provide the chief with a portion of their own production. For example, Gutmann (1926:346) noted that Chagga chiefs collected part of their tribute in the form of a portion of the banana beer brewed by households. He states that the people were happy to render this tribute because it enabled the chief to maintain a continuing open feast at his residence, which they liked to attend, but also that the chief's henchmen were constantly checking to make sure that no household brewed without paying the beer tribute.

The work feast (especially in the more obligatory *corve* form), directed toward the extensive fields of the chief, is another common mechanism for mobilizing food stocks for such purposes (see Chapter 9). Among the Bemba of Zambia, for example, Richards (1939) noted that chiefs organize the largest labor groups found in the country to work their own fields: she estimated, for example, that 275 men-days and 210 women days per year were required for the gardens of one smaller chief for cutting and clearing branches, respectively (1939:388). Moreover, chiefs are very often ostentatiously polygynous in comparison to their people, providing a large pool of household labor; and they sometimes have attached forms of dependent labor (such as, in the past, slaves).

DIACRITICAL FEASTS

The third major mode of commensal politics, which I will call the "diacritical feast," involves the use of differentiated cuisine and styles of consumption as a diacritical symbolic device to naturalize and reify concepts of ranked differences in the status of social orders or classes (cf. Elias 1978; Goody 1982; Bourdieu 1984). Although it serves a somewhat similar general function to the previous pattern (i.e., the naturalization and objectification of inequality in social relations), it differs from it in several important respects. In the first place, the basis of symbolic force shifts from quantity to matters of style and taste. Moreover, the emphasis shifts from an asymmetrical commensal bond between unequal partners to a statement of exclusive and unequal commensal circles: obligations of reciprocal hospitality are no longer the basis of status claims and power.

This is the distinction made by Goody (1982) when he differentiated between "hieratic" and "hierarchical" systems of stratification in his discussion of the origins and significance of cuisine. According to Goody, the development of such diacritical culinary practices is often linked to the development of specialized food preparers for the elite class (replacing wives in this role, who become commensal partners), and commensal exclusivity is often accompanied by class endogamy. The feasting patterns of the Hawaiian kingdoms described by Kirch (Chapter 6) are a classic example of this, and of what I mean by the diacritical feast mode. Although Goody's dichotomy may be an overly broad generalization, it is clear that the practice of diacritical feasting transforms elite feasts into what Appadurai (1986:21) has called "tournaments of value," which serve both to define elite status membership and to channel social competition within clearly defined boundaries. Diacritical stylistic distinctions may be based upon the use of rare, expensive, or exotic foods or food ingredients. Or they may be orchestrated through the use of elaborate food-service vessels and implements or architectonically distinguished settings that serve to "frame" elite consumption as a distinctive practice even when the food itself is not distinctive. Or they may be based upon differences in the complexity of the pattern of preparation and consumption of food and the specialized knowledge and taste (i.e., "cultural capital": Bourdieu 1984) that proper consumption entails.

Because this type of feasting relies upon style and taste for its symbolic force, it is subject to emulation by those aspiring to higher status. Such emulation constitutes an attempted elevation of status through representational means, which may focus on either (or both) the mimetic development of styles of action (manners, tastes, etc.) or the use and consumption of objects (foods, service vessels, etc) that are materialized signs of a particular social identity. This can result in the gradual spread through a society of foods and food practices by what Appadurai (1986) has described as a "turnstile effect." This happened in ancient Greece with the expansion of the *symposion* (wine-drinking party) from its aristocratic origins throughout urban society (Dentzer 1982; Murray 1990), and it was a common feature in the development of European bourgeois manners and food culture (Bourdieu 1984; Elias 1978). Junker (Chapter 10) offers another example among Philippine chiefdoms.

Such emulation, and the resulting devaluation of diacritical significance, can be thwarted only by the imposition of sumptuary laws that restrict consumption within clear social boundaries or by the use of exotic foods and consumption paraphernalia, access to which can be controlled through elevated expense or limited networks of acquisition. In the absence of effective means of monopolization, the weakening of diacritical symbolic force caused by emulation may provoke continual shifts in elite tastes as they react to the process of imitation. These shifts need not be solely in the direction of increasing elaboration. In many cases, this reaction may be toward ostentatiously simpler, rather than more elaborate, cuisine and/or consumption paraphernalia, depending upon the nature of the emulation being reacted against. The fluctuating trajectories of such changes depend upon both the nature of historical precedents and opportunities for strategic shifts presented by invention and the incorporation of exotic elements.

Africa is an interesting case in the analysis of the diacritical feast pattern precisely because, according to Goody (1982), one should not find it there. The Pondo of South Africa provide a good example of the kind of situation that Goody took to be typical of African societies: "In spite of the fact that chiefs were the wealthiest men in the country, chiefs always lived very much as their people, and most still do. At the great place there is more beer and meat than elsewhere, but otherwise there is no difference between the diet of a chief and that of commoners" (Hunter 1961:388).

However, although it is true that African societies do not appear to have developed highly elaborated diacritical cuisines to the same extent as the states of Europe and Asia, they are not without diacritical food practices that serve to symbolically demarcate kings, chiefs, and nobles. Often African royal or noble culinary diacritica are expressed in the form of special food avoidances or privileged consumption of certain animals of ritual significance rather than through consumption of specially elaborated cuisine. For example, among the Nyoro of Uganda, the king was not allowed to eat certain kinds of common foods thought to be of low status (e g sweet potatoes, cassava, and certain vegetables), and the men he appointed as "crown wearers" (i.e., great chiefs of high status and political authority) had to observe the same restrictions. Moreover, the king's cooks were not allowed to have sexual intercourse just before or during their alternating periods of service in the palace (Beattie 1960). Among the Metá of Cameroon, the *fon* [village chief] has exclusive rights to receive, butcher, and dispose of certain prestigious and dangerous animals known as "noble game" (e.g., leopards and pythons) from which he was believed to acquire power. He would also share specifically prescribed parts of these animals with the senior village notables (Dillon 1990:133–135, 153–157). Among the Mamprusi of Ghana, the king observes all the common food prohibitions of his subjects, but in addition he does not eat goat, black fish, or the flesh of a variety of other animals associated with earth-shrines. Moreover, his diet is restricted to highly esteemed items (e.g., guinea fowl and millet porridge) prepared separately for him by a junior wife under the supervision of the senior wife (Brown 1975:158–159). Among the Bemba of Zambia, even when traveling, a chief cannot eat cooked food offered by his subjects because "porridge cooked on 'impure' fire would endanger his life" (Richards 1939:138). Rather, raw food materials are offered by subjects and these are cooked by one of the chief's wives on a fire that she creates herself. Moreover, "chiefs visiting each other will exchange uncooked food to be prepared by their respective staffs, but only a chief's head wife could send a royal visitor dishes of porridge and relish" (Richards 1939:138). Finally, among the Igala of Nigeria the king is considered to be divine and is believed to not eat at all. In fact, the king always eats in seclusion and his food and meals are referred to only in euphemisms (Boston 1968:204–205).

Hence, diacritical culinary practices differentiating certain elevated kinds or categories of people clearly do exist even in Africa. However, they are by no means universal among African kingdoms and chiefdoms. Moreover, these rituals are sometimes so exclusively focused as to be effectively noncommensal to the extent that they perhaps defy the definition of a feast, and they tend to mark certain institutionalized political roles rather than social classes. Nevertheless, such practices do perform the ritual work noted above of reifying asymmetrical relations of power through the symbolic manipulation of food consumption in a pattern that emphasizes difference and separation of at least a small elite segment of the society.

FEASTS AND SOCIAL BOUNDARIES

To be analytically useful, the concept of diacritical feasts requires some further cautious clarification. This is because nearly all feasts actually serve in some ways to define social boundaries while simultaneously creating a sense of community. That is, nearly all feasts serve to mark, reify, and inculcate diacritical distinctions between social groups, categories, and statuses while at the same time establishing relationships across the boundaries that they define. Gender categories and age distinctions, for example, are very commonly signaled in what I have distinguished as "empowering" feasting practices even among peoples with a strongly egalitarian political ethos. For example, among the Luo of Kenya (who do not have "diacritical feasts" in the sense defined above), categorical distinctions between men and women, between elders and younger men, and between kinship groups are signaled at feasts by spatial criteria (i.e., who sits where and with whom), temporal distinctions (i.e., the order of serving), by different types of drinking vessels and practices, and by different types of beer and food (see the later discussion of the Luo case). Similar kinds of practices, in culturally specific manifestations, are ubiquitous in the African ethnographic record (e.g., see Carlson 1990; Hunter 1961; Karp 1980; Peristiany 1939; Richards 1939; Sangree 1962). Such practices can also be a subtle but powerful means of marking the social ranking of individuals in hierarchies of prestige and influence. As Dillon noted for the Metá of Cameroon, for example, they "were very sensitive to subtle discriminations reflected in hospitality, and one man's attitude toward another might be significantly altered, depending on whether he had made a special effort to serve him or offered only lame excuses. People attending important gatherings also noted how various guests were treated, depending on their statuses and relations with the host" (1990:130).

Similarly, social groups or networks of various kinds (affines, age grades, etc.) are frequently marked by the same kinds of practices that are used to make other insider versus stranger distinctions. Concepts of ethnicity, for example, very frequently involve beliefs (of variable accuracy) about distinctive food tastes and culinary practices. The Luo love fish and know that this distinguishes them from their Kisii neighbors to the east who eschew fish. They also believe that their own revulsion at the idea of eating caterpillars sets them apart from other neighbors to the north. Feasts can be a theater for the symbolic manipulation of such culinary distinctions in the expression of sentiments of inclusion and exclusion at various levels.

Alas, the situation is yet more complicated for archaeologists looking for evidence of what are here defined as diacritical feasts because similar symbolic devices can be used to mark categories of events as well as categories of people. Particular care must be taken not to mistake the kinds of practices that may be used to differentiate feasts in general (as ritual events) from everyday informal consumption in societies without diacritical feasts for those used to differentiate social classes in societies having diacritical feasts. In many cases, this former distinction (i.e., marking feasts as ritual events) is accomplished simply by differences in the sheer quantity of food and drink proffered and consumed, or by a change in the location and timing of consumption. However, the same types of devices used as symbolic diacritica in marking social distinctions may be employed to distinguish ritual from quotidian practice by serving as "framing devices" that act as cues establishing the ritual significance of events (see Miller 1985:181–183). For example, feasts may be marked by special foods (e.g., ones that are expensive, rare, exotic, especially rich, particularly sweet, intoxicating, etc.). Among the Luo, for example, beer is not something consumed with everyday meals and beef is a food that is normally reserved exclusively for larger feasts (although accompanied by the standard range of other daily foods). Alternatively, special service vessels or other paraphernalia (including special forms of clothing or other bodily adornment), or special architectural staging, may be employed for this marking purpose. To use the Luo as an example again, they have a distinctive paired set of very large beer pots (called *thago* and *dakong'o*) that are used only at important feasts (Herbich and Dietler 1989, 1992). Hence, among the Luo, beer, beef, and certain kinds of ceramic vessels are all indexical markers of feasts as ritual events. Finally, atypical complexity in recipes or in the structured order of service and consumption may also be used to invoke such distinctions (see Douglas 1984).

Unfortunately, there is no handy, universal rule of thumb that will enable the archaeologist to distinguish readily between "diacritical feasts" and these other boundary-marking practices (i.e., those marking both boundaries between social groups and categories and boundaries between ritual and quotidian contexts). But I believe this disentangling of symbolic logic is both possible and useful in many instances. Each case will require a careful and critical evaluation of the contextual and associational patterns of the evidence and a multistranded, thickly textured interpretive argument in order to differentiate between "diacritical feasts" marking social classes and the diacritical use of cuisine to mark other social categories or to mark feasts as special ritual events. To take a highly simplified hypothetical example: special types of ceramic tableware that are found only in funerary contexts, but in *all* funerary contexts, are more likely representative of the latter (that is, marking the ritual nature of an event); whereas those found exclusively in male graves, but in *all* male graves probably imply both a ritual and categorical distinction; and large bronze drinking vessels found only in a limited number of very wealthy burials most likely indicate the operation of "diacritical feasts." But the plausibility of such an interpretation will depend upon other evidence from settlement data as well (see Dietler 1996 for archaeological examples).

It is important to point out that a general increase in, for example, the complexity or elaborateness of the decoration of tablewares in comparison to cooking wares (or of ceramics in general in comparison to a previous habitation level or archaeological period) is not necessarily an indication of the use of style in the development of diacritical feasts. This may simply be related to an increasing "complexification" of food-consumption patterns (in the sense of Douglas 1984) through more marked symbolic emphasis on distinctions such as that between ritual and quotidian dining practice. The diacritical feast pattern rests on an exclusive sumptuary use of style in food-consumption rituals by certain social classes whatever the relative complexity of food patterns within the society as a whole. More will be said about these issues later, but for the moment it is useful to open a brief parenthetical consideration of one of the most common categorical distinctions defined through feasting.

FEASTS AND GENDER

As noted earlier, gender is one cultural category of social identity that is nearly everywhere marked, reified, and naturalized to some extent through feasting practices. In fact, gender is one of the most common categorical distinctions made through food/drink-related practices in general, albeit in a wide variety of culturally specific ways (Bacon 1976; Child, Barry, and Bacon 1965; Counihan and Kaplan 1998; Dietler 1990; Gefou-Madianou 1992; Herbich 1991; McDonald 1994). As the Luo example discussed below illustrates (cf. Karp 1980; Ngokwey 1987 for other African examples), such categorical boundary marking at feasts may be based upon various permutations of symbolic diacritica, including: (1) *spatial distinctions* (that is, segregation or other structured differential positioning of men and women while eating), (2) *temporal distinctions* (such as order of serving or consumption), (3) *qualitative distinctions* (for example, in the kinds of food, drink, or service vessels men and women are given or are allowed to consume), (4) *quantitative distinctions* (in the relative amounts of food or drink served to men and women), or (5) *behavioral distinctions* (that is, differences in expected bodily comportment between women and men during and after feasting, including such things as permissible signs of intoxication, talking while eating, reaching for food, serving or being served, withdrawing from the meal first, and so on).

An important feature to signal here is that, where diacritical feasting (in the sense defined above) is in operation, these patterns of gender differentiation may vary greatly between social classes. In other words, gender may be marked in quite different ways within the feasting practices of each class. For example, Goody (1982) noted a frequent pattern in which, with the development of endogamous social classes marked by restricted commensal circles and diacritical culinary practices, one often notes a shift in the position of women *of the elite class* from food servers and prepares to commensal partners (with a corresponding development of specialist food preparers and servers, who are sometimes male). This does not imply any corresponding change in gendered practices in feasting among the non-elite classes; and one can anticipate in such cases a marked difference between the classes in, for example, the spatial and behavioral distinctions by which gender is marked.

It is also important to reiterate that feasting practices, although marking boundaries of gender identities in the ways noted above, simultaneously express relationships of mutual dependence across those boundaries that, in turn, represent and naturalize ideologies structuring larger societal relations of production and authority. This leads to a more general point I wish to emphasize: that understanding the gender relations that underlie, and are reproduced through, feasts is a crucial part of the project of theoretical analysis that is necessary to make feasting a productive focus of archaeological inquiry. That is because, in addition to the various aspects of symbolic representation noted above, feasting frequently is sustained by a gendered asymmetry in terms of labor and benefits. Specifically, female labor (producing and processing the agricultural supplies that are essential for feasts) often largely supports a system of feasting in which men are the primary beneficiaries in the political arena. This is one of the main reasons why there is such a strong linkage between polygyny and male political power in Africa and elsewhere (cf. Boserup 1970:37; Clark 1980; Friedman 1984; Geschire 1982; Lemonnier 1990; Vincent 1971; also see Dietler and Herbich, Chapter 9).

Female labor is often of major, or even primary, importance in agricultural production, although the relative gendered contribution in this domain is by no means uniform (Boserup 1970; Guyer 1988). However, even more common is a dominant female contribution to the crucial culinary and serving labor that transforms raw food ingredients into feasts (Friedl 1975; Goody 1982). Moreover, although cases such as the Luo (described below), in which women provide the agricultural, culinary, and serving labor for male political activities are quite common (e.g., see Bohannan and Bohannan 1968; Clark 1980), examples of the inverse pattern (where men consistently provide the agricultural, culinary, and serving labor that underwrites feasts formally hosted by women) are extremely rare, if they exist at all.

At first glance, it may be tempting to interpret this fact as a systematic form of labor exploitation, in line with Marx's observation that women probably constituted the first exploited class (Meillassoux 1975:78). However, the question of exploitation frequently hinges upon a subtle contextual consideration of the question posed by Clark for the Kikuyu: are women "controllers of resources or themselves resources controlled by men?" (Clark 1980:367). Although exploitation is frequently a justifiable analytical conclusion, this is by no means a pattern that is universal or even generalizable in a simple way. For example, in some societies there is typically a more balanced, or even male-dominated, pattern of labor in the production of feasts (although this generally does not extend to the preparation of daily meals). Moreover, women may share in the status and political benefits from their labor by being members of an influential household or lineage (in matrilineal contexts). Their labor (and male dependence upon it) may also be overtly recognized and valued, and women may even derive considerable categorical and individual status from their central role in the furnishing of hospitality or in maintaining commensal relations with the gods (e.g., see Gero 1992; March 1998). And, in many societies, women do host their own work feasts and other feast events, although usually on a smaller scale than men. For example, among the Tiv of Nigeria, women host smaller work feasts than men, but these "underscore the prestige of important women. If a woman calls a big hoeing party and supplies generous amounts of food and beer, she will be called 'important woman' (*shagba kwase*) for months afterwards" (Bohannan and Bohannan 1968:73). Finally, the common traditional female monopolization of cooking and brewing responsibilities has, with the penetration of the monetized market economy, frequently presented women with opportunities for gaining a source of income (e.g., through beer sales), and this has sometimes enabled them to acquire considerable economic independence and intrafamilial power under changing socioeconomic conditions (e.g., see Colson and Scudder 1988; Netting 1964).

The relationship between feasts and gender is clearly a complex but analytically rich and important one. Feasts are intimately implicated in the representation, reproduction, and transformation of gender identity, as well as in the gendered structuring of relations of production and power in society. This means both that feasting is an important and potentially productive avenue for understanding gender relations and roles in archaeological contexts, and that gender must be an essential consideration in any analysis of feasting.

RELATING THE MODES OF COMMENSAL POLITICS
Let us now return to the consideration of the different modes of commensal politics outlined earlier, because it is also necessary to say a few words about the relationships of these modes to each other. The first thing to emphasize is that they should decidedly not be interpreted as evolutionary stages that can be correlated with, for example, outmoded evolutionary typologies of political organization (band, tribe, chiefdom, state, etc.). There is, to be sure, an obvious correlation to some extent with increasing social stratification and complexity of structures of political power (for example, diacritical feasts, as defined here, are generally a feature encountered exclusively among state societies—but not all states will have diacritical feasts). However, rather than describing a series of successive evolutionary stages, these feasting modes should be viewed as constituting a progressively expansive repertoire of forms of political action through feasting. One form does not replace another; some forms simply expand the range of commensal politics in operation. It is true that there have been, and are, societies in which only empowering feasts are operative: this is the most basic and fundamentally ubiquitous mode of commensal politics. However, societies in which diacritical feasts are found are also certain to have each of the two other forms as well. In other words, where cuisine is used as a diacritical symbolic device separating classes, the politics of commensality will still be used by individuals or groups jockeying for relative status within those classes. Furthermore, kings, chiefs, and others in patron positions will often simultaneously employ unequal commensal hospitality in the patron-role pattern to legitimize institutionalized political authority roles. Likewise, both empowering and patron-role feasts are likely to be operative where the latter type is found: the use of redistributive hospitality by institutionalized patrons (e.g., "chiefs") to maintain the authority vested in their roles does not preclude the use of hospitality by others to define their relative statuses below that of such patrons, or its use by chiefs of different areas to negotiate and define their relative statuses vis-à-vis each other, or indeed its use to contest chiefly authority. Whatever kings, chiefs, or elite classes are doing with their food, common households will continue to hold feasts in their own way to establish community and personal relationships, mobilize labor, and build symbolic capital. Hence, the "festive landscape" in any given society will most likely be a palimpsest of several different modes of commensal politics operating in different contexts.

A second point to bear in mind is that the distinctions between the three modes of commensal politics are not precisely of the same order—and this fact has important implications for the role of feats in social change. The difference between empowering feasts and patron-role feasts is really one of establishing a transitional division along a continuum of expectations. The symbolic logic of both is quite similar: both operate by defining a single "consumption-community" within which asymmetries are expressed and naturalized to different degrees by the sharing of food. It is really the extent of institutionalized acceptance, or expectation, of a continuing pattern of unreciprocated or unbalanced hospitality that defines the difference. As the example in the following section will show, there is often a subtle distinction between the two, and it is not difficult to imagine how the patron-role feast may crystallize out of certain forms of empowering feasts. It is also important to recognize that tensions and conflict may actually be created when groups approach such feasts with different understandings of their political logic: for example, when the hosts view the feast in the patron-role mode and the guests view it in the empowering mode. This is particularly a risk with feasting across cultural boundaries, where, for example, hosts and guests are members of different ethnic groups that do not share the same cultural codes and behavioral expectations. But it can also be manipulated consciously by individuals or groups who are quite aware of the conventions but who, for example, choose to challenge chiefly authority by refusing to acknowledge a patron-role feast as such and treating it instead in the competitive empowering mode. This form of "festive revolution" is, of course, one of the many ways in which feasting can become a site of contestation and a dynamic agent in political change.

In contrast to the other two modes, the diacritical feast manifests a symbolic logic that differs in kind. It serves to reify asymmetries along lines of class or social order by defining the boundaries of separate "consumption-communities." It also, of course, serves to solidify identity within those consumption-communities through food sharing and the cultivation of shared tastes. Again, it is important to emphasize that all feasting rituals involve boundary-defining practices. Social categories such as age and gender, for example, are very commonly marked in the ways noted in previous sections; and it is important for archaeologists to be aware of the operation of such diacritical devices. But these other distinctions are established *within* commensal networks through variations in food-sharing practices. What are here called "diacritical feasts" represent a special kind of boundary-defining practice based upon commensal exclusion that I believe is sufficiently different and heuristically valuable to merit distinguishing categorically. As prior studies of prehistoric European contexts have shown (see Dietler 1996, 1999a), it can be a productive category for archaeological analysis.

LUO FEASTS

In order to further clarify some of the more abstract points made earlier, I will briefly treat several aspects of feasting among the Luo of western Kenya in somewhat more detail than the other examples raised in the discussion. The Luo are a Nilotic-speaking people who inhabit a region of about 10,000 km^2 surrounding the Winam Gulf, in the northeast corner of Lake Victoria. They have a patrilineal kinship system and live in homesteads scattered across the countryside, which are occupied by polygynous extended families with a patrilocal postmarital residence pattern (see Dietler and Herbich 1989, 1993; Evans Pritchard 1949; Herbich 1987; Herbich and Dietler 1992, 1993; Shipton 1989; Southall 1952).

Agriculture provides the base of their diet, and this is carried out by women in scattered sets of small plots in the vicinity of the homestead. Grain crops include several varieties of sorghum, millet, and maize. Root crops, especially sweet potatoes and cassava, are also important, as are various kinds of beans, greens, lentils, and wild leaves. In some areas, bananas are also grown. Protein sources include milk, fish (caught in the Gulf and traded widely throughout the region), chickens, sheep, and goats. Beef is also highly prized, but cattle are an important symbol of wealth and are usually slaughtered only for feasts. Aside from purchased fish and sporadic "target" buying and selling of grain at the local markets, most households grow most of the food they eat. There is little reliance on food stuffs imported from outside the region (aside from salt and a few luxuries, such as tea, sugar, and tobacco).

With these basic ingredients, the Luo manage to maintain a relatively varied repertoire of dishes, and there are regional and family preferences for recipes. The main meals are constituted around a thick, bread-like porridge (called *kuon*) made from boiled sorghum or maize flour. This is the symbolically central ingredient of the diet, and a Luo who has not eaten *kuon* will say that (s)he has not eaten. Various stew-like dishes made from vegetables, fish, or meat serve essentially as a condiment to *kuon*. Snacks and lesser meals consist of a maize and bean mixture (*nyoyo*), a thin millet or maize porridge (*nyuka*), sweet potatoes and sour milk, and other such dishes. The main alcoholic beverage is beer (*kong'o*) made from millet and/or maize, although a distilled alcohol known as *chang'aa* has also become popular in recent decades. These alcoholic beverages are not items consumed with daily meals; rather, they are essential components of feasts.

As with many African societies, there is usually a seasonal period of hunger just before the main harvest of the year, when grain supplies tend to run low and must be stretched. Luo history is also marked by periodic episodes of major famine caused by crop failures and cattle epidemics. These episodes are known by name and they were important enough to constitute many of the main hinges of collective memory (see Dietler and Herbich 1993), or what Shipton (1990:375) has aptly called "the hitching-posts of history."

Feasts are an important element of Luo life, and they play most of the various roles attributed to the "empowering" mode in the earlier discussion. The largest feasts, and indeed the largest gatherings in the society outside of markets, take place at funerals. These events are held at the homestead of the deceased and are marked by the provision of large quantities of beer and beef, along with the standard *kuon* and other foods. They are accompanied by ritual dramaturgical practices such as parading of cattle, dancing, singing, speeches, and the recitation of praise songs that recount the accomplishments of both the deceased and the speakers. They often last for several days, during which a large group of lineage members, affines, and neighbors must be kept satisfied with copious amounts of food and drink. The prestige of the deceased and his/her family are thought to be reflected in the size of the gathering capable of being assembled and sustained at the funeral feast and the lavishness of the hospitality provided. Influential men have the most ostentatiously lavish funerals, but every Luo is concerned about having an impressive funeral mounted for him/her. This concern is often voiced by older widows as a major reason for joining religious groups, as these assure their followers of a proper funeral. As noted earlier, the scale of hospitality at funerals is often so great that at least temporary impoverishment of the family may result, and the lavishness of such feasts among the Luo and other west Kenyan peoples is the subject of frequent harangues by government ministers and members of other ethnic groups (e.g., Mburu 1978).

Less spectacular feasts are also held for marriages, harvest celebrations, collective labor mobilization, the founding of a new homestead, and a host of other things (such as ceremonies concerning the birth of twins). Small-scale gatherings of elders or meetings between friends are also often marked by sharing a pot of beer. In general, feasts are distinguished from daily meals by several features. Most commonly, these include the consumption of beer (and/or *chang'aa*) and beef, which are not everyday foods. They are also sometimes marked by the location of consumption and the use of special containers.

In the territory of Alego, for example, homesteads have a special shaded area known as *siwanda* that serves as the place where senior men at feasts gather together to drink beer and eat.[6] At feasts of some importance, these elders will consume unfiltered beer out of a special large pot called a *thago* (Fig. 3.1). A *thago* may be larger than a meter in diameter and a meter tall, and it is supported by being partly buried in the ground at the *siwanda*. The men sit around the pot in a circle drinking from long straws (*oseke*) made of hollow vine stems with a woven filter on the end (Fig. 3.2). The possession of a personal straw, which one carries to

Figure 3.1. Photograph of Luo communal beer drinking pot *(thago)*, on left, and beer fermentation pot *(dakong'o)*, on right. Scale in cm. (Photo by M. Dietler and I. Herbich)

beer drinks in a special bamboo core, is a clear sign of senior male status. Another large pot, called a *dakong'o* (Fig. 3.1), in which the beer has been brewed, always stands near the *thago*, and beer is removed from it and mixed with hot water for consumption from the *thago*. Younger men will generally drink and eat in the clear area in front of the house (known as *laru*). They will also usually drink filtered beer that is served in a pot called *mbiru*, which is much smaller than a *thago*. They will consume their beer by dipping large cups made from half of a hollowed gourd *(agwata;* sometimes now tin cans or enamel mugs) into the *mbiru*. Women may also consume some beer in this fashion (Herbich 1991). Every household will have at least one *mbiru*, but the same is not true of *thago*. These latter are large, expensive pots that may be owned by only a few of the wealthier homesteads in neighborhood. Other homesteads will have to borrow a *thago* when they wish to organize an important feast. These are highly prized pots that usually are known within a neighborhood by a specific name, and many examples we found in homes were over 50 years old, some much older. Figure 3.3 offers a splendid iconic representation of such a feast, and the marking of social categories by these practices. It is a mural from an abandoned beer hall in a Luo market center (such beer halls were outlawed by the Kenyan government during the 1970s as part of a longstanding, and unsuccessful, struggle by the colonial and

Figure 3.2. Photograph showing how beer is consumed from *thago* through a long vine-stem straw *(oseke)*. (Photo by M. Dietler and I. Herbich)

postcolonial Kenyan governments to exert state control over alcohol: see Ambler 1991).

The consumption of food is also done on a communal basis. A "loaf" of *kuon* will be served on a basket plate and shared by several diners who will break off morsels and dip them into a common ceramic bowl *(tawo)* of the stew/sauce (sometimes these serving containers are now replaced by imported enamel dishes). These serving containers are generally not different from those used in everyday meals.

Figure 3.4 is a photograph that rather ironically encapsulates the gendered relations of production that underlie Luo feasting. It portrays a woman working at

Figure 3.3. Photograph of a mural on the exterior of an abandoned beer hall showing an iconic representation of a Luo feast. Note the elder men drinking from a large communal pot *(thago)* through long straws *(oseke)* while younger men and women drink from cups, and a woman acts in a serving capacity. (Photo by M. Dietler and I. Herbich)

drying *sinoho* (a processed grain flour product resulting from an initial stage in the *chaîne opératoire* of the beer fermentation process: see Herbich 1991) on the floor of another abandoned beer hall with a feasting mural in the background. This is one of the many laborious steps necessary to produce, store, and process a sufficient quantity of grain to mount a feast. Women are the agricultural and culinary labor force that lies behind the production of all Luo feasts, although they share in the ensuing prestige and other benefits only indirectly, as wives of the generous host. Women grow the crops, process them, and do the cooking, brewing, and serving. This is one of the reasons that, in this polygynous society, having many wives is not only a sign of wealth, but is essential for being able to mount large feasts. Acquiring wives requires wealth and is a gradual process because one must give a large amount of bridewealth to the woman's family in the form of cattle and, now, often money (formerly, iron hoes were also given). However, multiple wives considerably expand the possibilities for a homestead to offer lavish hospitality, which, as further discussion will show, has important political implications (see also Dietler and Herbich, Chapter 9).

The Luo do not have anything resembling the agonistic competitive feasting of New Guinea big-men or the escalating Mambila (Nigeria) bear feasts (Reh-

Figure 3.4. Photograph of a Luo woman engaged in drying *sinoho* (one step in the laborious *chaîne opératoire* of beer production) on the floor of an abandoned beer hall with a mural showing an idealized representation of a Luo feast in the background. (Photo by M. Dietler and I. Herbich)

fisch 1987). Yet generosity in commensal hospitality is an essential practice in maintaining a man's prestige and influence, and the funeral feast is a final dramatic affirmation of status. Luo feasts also provide a prime context for demonstrations of oratory, which is a highly valued skill that also brings prestige. This oratory includes forms of ritualized boasting in which men extol their own achievements and denigrate those of their rivals. Specialized praise singers, who accompany their songs on a form of lyre (*nyatiti*), may also be employed for this purpose.

Obviously, the Luo do not have diacritical feasts in the sense defined earlier (at least those in the countryside—the situation of the Luo who have moved to the capital city of Nairobi is somewhat different). The question of patron-role feasts is a little more complicated, and the issue is worth discussing in some detail because the Luo case highlights the fluid boundary between empowering and patron-role feasts noted earlier. Although they now live with a system of "chiefs" constructed by the British colonial government and continued by the postcolonial Kenyan state, the Luo have traditionally had a strongly egalitarian political ethos and lacked centralized authority. They do, however, have an indigenous term, *ruoth*, that is used to refer to modern chiefs. In the precolonial era this term more likely meant something closer to "leader" or "man of influence" than to the institutionalized political role it has come to signify. However, oral histories indicate that the degree to which individuals in the past were able to transform their informal influence into naturalized positions of authority and power varied somewhat from region to region.

Whisson (1961) offers an interesting case study of this process in the territory of Asembo that both illustrates the means available of concentrating power in the precolonial era (including feasting) and the ramifications this had during the imposition of the colonial administration and its structure of institutionalized chiefs.[7] Traditional Luo political organization has been described as a classic case of the segmentary lineage system (Evans-Pritchard 1949; Southall 1952). The modern administrative boundaries within Luo territory, which were defined during the colonial era, effectively froze into static form what had previously been a series of highly dynamic factional and territorial struggles between competing subgroups organized according to lineage affiliation and military expediency. Based on oral histories, Whisson describes competition for leadership in the context of such factional struggles during the immediately precolonial and early colonial eras in Asembo, the territory of the Luo subgroup known as JoAsembo along the north coast of the Winam Gulf.

One of the main functions of precolonial leaders was the arbitration of disputes within the smallest local territorial unit, the *gweng'*. Becoming an influential leader required the building of prestige and moral authority, and these qualities were acquired from several possible sources. The most immediate criteria were genealogical position and the strength of the lineage: the most genealogically senior member of the dominant lineage of the *gweng'* had responsibilities to settle disputes within the *gweng'*, and he met with other similar leaders to attempt to resolve disputes between *gwenge*.[8] Disputes that could not be settled peacefully were resolved by fission and migration, or by armed conflict. The segmentary lineage ideology structuring patterns of alliance and opposition in conflict created opportunities for leadership by members of strong lineage segments at all the points of segmentation. However, this was also augmented by the creation of pragmatic alliances in which strong lineages would secure the support of weaker *"jodak"* (tenant) lineage groups that had settled in their territory after being forced out or fissioning elsewhere.

Hence, as Whisson (1961:7) pointed out, the main sources of power that an individual could manipulate came from: (1) being a senior member of a powerful lineage, (2) personal ability in warfare, and (3) the capacity to marshal a significant amount of support in the face of conflict. Skill in the use of magical power (*bilo*) was particularly important in winning prestige in the sphere of warfare. *Jobilo* (magicians) were feared and respected for their powers of divination and their ability to use killing magic on enemies. The ability to rally support depended upon the accumulation of wealth and prestige, and it is in this domain that feasting played an important role. Wealth in this context would be reckoned in terms of cattle and wives, both of which were essential for the production of feasts. Acquiring large numbers of cattle was greatly aided by skill in raiding (which was itself a source of prestige). These cattle were used for prized meat at feasts, but also for the payment of bridewealth that was necessary to acquire wives. A large number of wives greatly increased the capacity of the homestead for agricultural and culinary labor, so that wealthy men were able create and use food surpluses to host feasts for the lineage leaders who assembled to discuss political and judicial matters. As Whisson noted, this wealth (in cattle, wives, and crops) was used to entertain "the leaders of the clans and subclans forming the nucleus of a council or court and meeting in the home of the richest or most respected man. This man became *ruoth*, the leader" (1961:7).

The strongest leaders would be able to draw upon all three of the mutually enhancing sources of power noted above. But a skilled *jabilo* from a weaker lineage who had accumulated the cattle and wives to host lavish feasts could even overcome a genealogical handicap by rallying the support of other lineages and creating political alliances. The British colonial government attempted to squeeze this fairly loose and fluid set of political relations into their preconceived model of "chiefdoms" operating as a hierarchical administrative system. They imposed a model of institutionalized central authority with formalized political roles and rules of succession upon a much more dynamic and competitive set of political practices sustained by cultural perceptions of authority that were far more contingent.

The process by which the British "identified" Luo chiefs and the manipulations that went on among competing Luo men of influence seeking to be named chiefs is a complex tale. What is important to retain for the purposes of this discussion of feasts is that the colonial situation under which these new chiefs operated created contradictions that sometimes undermined their authority. These new chiefs were agents of the state, but their ability to perform the functions that the state demanded of them depended upon maintaining the traditional forms of symbolic capital. However, the suppression of warfare and raiding eliminated both a major former arena for the acquisition of prestige and an important source of the cattle that produced the wives and feasts necessary to operate successfully in the other major arena of political action. Government pay was not sufficient to compensate for this loss and the state took a dim view of augmenting income through bribery. As in the case of an early Asembo chief named Odindo, those who were unable to keep up the lavish hospitality that people expected of a traditional *ruoth* sometimes fell from power in the face of continual scheming by rivals from other lineages (Whisson 1961:11). Others were able to survive by better adapting to their role as agents of the state by having their sons sent to mission schools and gaining the skills of literacy that the government particularly prized. It is noticeable, however, that successful chiefs today are still conspicuously more polygynous than the rest of their people. For example, one chief in our research area had 45 wives when we arrived and over 50 when we left three years later.

CONCLUSION

The Luo examples should serve to give a better sense of the experience of commensal politics that lies behind the more abstract theoretical discussion offered earlier. In particular, one can begin to understand the way in which the hospitality used in empowering feasts to acquire and maintain symbolic capital can become transformed into the institutionalized expectation of the patron-role feast; and one can see how a failure to meet those expectations can seriously weaken credibility and undercut authority. One can also get a better sense of the way that feasting either combines or competes with other sources of symbolic capital (prowess in warfare, oratorical skill, powers in magic, genealogical pedigree, gift giving, etc.) to establish prestige and influence. Feasting is by no means the only arena of political action, but it is very frequently an extremely important, if not crucial, one. The Luo case also illustrates the subtle ways in which social categories and boundaries are symbolically marked by the ritual practices of feasts, and why those operative among the empowering feasts of the Luo are quite different in their symbolic logic from those described for the diacritical feast. Finally, this case also highlights the often unremarked gendered relations of production that support commensal politics. The division of labor and symbolic capital along gender lines is certainly not always identical to, nor so starkly realized as, that among the Luo; but this is always an important consideration in the theorization of feasting.

For archaeologists, the implications of the discussion presented in this chapter are several and important. In the first place, it is clear that feasts commonly serve a variety of crucial structural roles in articulating the political economy of a wide array of societies. It is also clear that feasts are a prime arena and instrument of political action by individuals and social groups pursuing economic and political goals and competing for influence within their social worlds. However, the ways in which feasts serve the acquisition and transformation of symbolic and economic capital are extremely complex, and archaeologists need a well-developed theoretical understanding of the nature of feasting ritual if we are to understand political life in ancient societies in something more that mechanistic typological terms. In my view, it is critical that we begin to tackle issues of situated agency and the role of practice in transforming structure if we wish to say anything of insightful significance about the historical development of different forms of social inequality. In this paper I have tried to present several theoretical constructs based upon comparative analysis of ethnographic data that I believe hold some promise in analyzing feasting ritual, and I have elsewhere tried to demonstrate how they may be applied to archaeological cases in ways that yield fruitful new insights (e.g., Dietler 1990, 1996, 1999a, 1999b). However, this is by no means a definitive formulation, and I look forward to the emerging dialogue on these issues that is promised by the convergence of perspectives in this volume.

ACKNOWLEDGMENTS

My thinking on this issue has been evolving for over a decade, and it has greatly benefited from the opportunity to receive challenging comments on different papers exploring this theme from audiences in a variety of contexts, most particularly the "Food and the Status Quest" symposium at the Ringberg Castle of the Max Planck Institute in Germany (1991), the "Les Princes de la Protohistoire et l'Emergence de l'État" symposium at the Centre Jean Bérard in Naples, Italy (1994), a seminar while a visiting professor at the École des Hautes Études en Sciences Sociales (1996), the SAA symposium that generated this book (1998), and a symposium on "Consuming Power: Feasting as Commensal Politics" convened at Cornell University (1999) in which my work served as a keynote for lively critical discussion. I am grateful to all the participants of these various sessions for their comments (including those with whom I disagree), and most particularly to Michel Bats, Maurice Godelier, Brian Hayden, Pierre Lemonnier, Jean-Paul Morel, Michel Py, Nerissa Russel, André Tchernia, Terry Turner, and Polly Wiessner. Special thanks are due to Ingrid Herbich for generous sharing of data and invaluable intellectual collaboration.

NOTES

1. To avoid possible confusion, let me emphasize that I use the word *commensal* in its original sense, rather than its peculiar biological adaptation. The word derives from the Latin *com mensalis*, indicating the sharing of a table—hence, eating together. Needless to say, many people around the world manage to eat together quite well without using a table. Moreover, in a number of cases the sharing of food is

accomplished without the host and guests actually eating in the same space—in some contexts it is actually considered impolite for the host to be present when his/her guests consume their food (e.g., see Richards 1939:135–136). However, despite the minor drawback of being grounded in a Eurocentric cultural trope, the term *commensal* does provide a convenient way of indicating a range of forms of communal food consumption. Other possible alternative terms in common usage, such as adjectival versions of *companion* (indicating the sharing of bread; from Latin) and *symposium* (the sharing of drink; from Greek), have even more problematic semantic histories and associational problems. And the game of inventing neologisms, such as *co-alimentary, co-gustatory,* or the innumerable other possibilities, seems a needlessly pedantic exercise.

2. The comparative ethnographic focus of this chapter is limited to agrarian societies in Africa, as this presents a more than sufficiently complex array of issues. Those interested in the issue of feasting among "foragers" and "complex hunter-gatherers," including African examples, are directed to the works of Wiessner (1996) and Hayden (1990, 1996).

3. All unreferenced descriptions of practices among the Luo people in this paper are derived from research conducted by Ingrid Herbich and me in western Kenya from 1980 to 1983 (see, e.g., Dietler and Herbich 1993; Herbich 1987, 1991; Herbich and Dietler 1991, 1993). Thanks are due to the National Science Foundation, the Wenner-Gren Foundation, the Boise Fund of Oxford University, the Office of the President of Kenya, the National Museums of Kenya, and especially our Luo and Samia hosts and our research assistants, Rhoda Onyango, Monica Oyi**ng**, and the late Elijah Ugutu.

4. I owe the "metaproduction" formulation to an insightful comment by Terry Turner.

5. Several French colleagues, in particular, have noted that the word "competition" evokes a strongly agonistic struggle for dominance with markedly negative connotations. Unfortunately, English lacks a convenient means to mark the subtle distinction between *compétition* and the more positively viewed *concurrence*. Hence, my use of the English term "competition" should be understood to cover the entire range of such possible relationships. My thanks to Pierre Lemonnier, Michel Py, and André Tchernia, in particular, for challenging me to clarify this usage.

6. For the sake of simplicity, I use terms in this paper that are, in fact, specific to the territories of several Luo subgroups in Siaya district (such as the JoAlego). These terms vary in other areas. Similarly, the *siwanda* is not a formally defined space in the homesteads of all Luo groups.

7. To avoid cluttering the text with multiple citations of the same work, I will simply point out here that the historical information in the following discussion is largely a selective summary of parts of Michael Whisson's (1961) excellent paper "The Rise of Asembo and the Curse of Kakia."

8. I use the words "he" and "man" here purposely to indicate the gender-specific nature of these leadership roles. For one thing, Luo women are not members of the lineage into which they marry. Hence they do not have the genealogical standing to acquire authority in matters relating to the lineage of the area where they live after marriage.

REFERENCES

Ambler, C. H.

1991   Drunks, Brewers, and Chiefs: Alcohol Regulation in Colonial Kenya 1900–1939. In *Drinking Behavior and Belief in Modern History*, edited by S. Barrows and R. Room, pp. 165–183. Berkeley: University of California Press.

Amselle, J.-L.

1998

[1990]   *Mestizo Logics: Anthropology of Identity in Africa and Elsewhere*. Translated by C. Royal. Stanford: Stanford University Press.

Anigbo, O. A. C.

1996   Commensality as Cultural Performance: The Struggle for Leadership in an Igbo Village. In *The Politics of Cultural Performance*, edited by D. Parkin, L. Caplan and H. Fisher, pp. 101–114. Oxford: Berghahn Books.

Appadurai, A.

1981   Gastropolitics in Hindu South Asia. *American Ethnologist* 8:494–511.

1986   Introduction: Commodities and the Politics of Value. In *The Social Life of Things: Commodities in Cultural Perspective*, edited by A. Appadurai, pp. 3–63. Cambridge: Cambridge University Press.

Apter, A.

1992   *Black Critics and Kings: The Hermeneutics of Power in Yoruba Society*. Chicago: University of Chicago Press.

Bacon, M. K.

1976   Cross-Cultural Studies of Drinking: Integrated Drinking and Sex Differences in the Uses of Alcoholic Beverages. In *Cross-cultural Approaches to the Study of Alcohol: An Interdisciplinary Perspective*, edited by M. Everett, J. Waddell and D. Heath, pp. 23–33. The Hague: Mouton.

Barth, F.

1967   On the Study of Social Change. *American Anthropologist* 69:661–670.

Bayart, J. F.

1993   *The State in Africa: Politics of the Belly*. London: Longman.

Beattie, J.

1960   *Bunyoro: An African Kingdom*. New York: Holt, Rinehart and Winston.

Bloch, M.

1987   The Ritual of the Royal Bath in Madagascar: The Dissolution of Death, Birth, and Fertility into Authority. In *Rituals of Royalty: Power and Ceremonial in Traditional Societies*, edited by D. Cannadine and S. Price, pp. 271–297. Cambridge: Cambridge University Press.

1989   *Ritual, History, and Power: Selected Papers in Anthropology*. London: Athlone.

Bohannan, P., and L. Bohannan

1968   *Tiv Economy*. Evanston: Northwestern University Press.

Boserup, E.

1970   *Women's Role in Economic Development*. London: Allen and Unwin.

Boston, J. S.
1968   *The Igala Kingdom*. Ibadan: Oxford University Press.

Bourdieu, P.
1984   *Distinction: A Social Critique of the Judgment of Taste*. Cambridge: Harvard University Press.
1990   *The Logic of Practice*. Stanford: Stanford University Press.

Bradbury, R. E.
1973   *Benin Studies*. London: Oxford University Press.

Brown, S. D.
1975   *Ritual Aspects of the Maprusi Kingship*. Cambridge: African Studies Center.

Cannadine, D.
1987   Introduction: Divine Rites of Kings. In *Rituals of Royalty: Power and Ceremonial in Traditional Societies*, edited by D. Cannadine and S. Price, pp. 1–19. Cambridge: Cambridge University Press.

Cannadine, D., and S. Price, eds.
1987   *Rituals of Royalty: Power and Ceremonial in Traditional Societies*. Cambridge: Cambridge University Press.

Carlson, R. G.
1990   Banana Beer, Reciprocity, and Ancestor Propitiation among the Haya of Bukoba, Tanzania. *Ethnology* 29:297–311.

Child, I. L., H. Barry, and M. K. Bacon
1965   A Cross-Cultural Study of Drinking. 3. Sex Differences. *Quarterly Journal of Studies in Alcohol* (Supplement) 3:49–61.

Clark, C. M.
1980   Land and Food, Women and Power, in Nineteenth Century Kikuyu. *Africa* 50: 357–370.

Cohen, A.
1974   *Two Dimensional Man: An Essay on the Anthropology of Power and Symbolism in Complex Societies*. Berkeley: University of California Press.
1979   Political Symbolism. *Annual Review of Anthropology* 8:87–113.

Colson, E., and T. Scudder
1988   *For Prayer and Profit: The Ritual, Economic, and Social Importance of Beer in Gwembe District, Zambia, 1950–1982*. Stanford: Stanford University Press.

Comaroff, J., and J. Comaroff
1991   *Of Revelation and Revolution: Christianity, Colonialism, and Consciousness in South Africa*. Vol. 1. Chicago: University of Chicago Press.
1993   Introduction. In *Modernity and Its Malcontents: Ritual and Power in Postcolonial Africa*, edited by J. Comaroff and J. Comaroff, pp. xi–xxxvii. Chicago: University of Chicago Press.

Counihan, C. M., and S. L. Kaplan, eds.
1998   *Food and Gender: Identity and Power*. Amsterdam: Harwood.

Crumley, C.

1987   A Dialectical Critique of Hierarchy. In *Power Relations and State Formation*, edited by T. C. Patterson and C. W. Gailey, pp. 155–159. Washington, D.C.: American Anthropological Association.

Dentzer, J.-M.

1982   *Le motif du banquet couché dans le Proche-Orient et dans le monde grec du VIIe au IVe siècle avant J.-C.* Bibliothèque des Écoles Françaises d'Athènes et de Rome, 246. Paris: Boccard.

Dietler, M.

1989   The Work-Party Feast as a Mechanism of Labor Mobilization and Exploitation: The Case of Samia Iron Production. Paper presented at 88th Annual Meeting of the American Anthropological Association, Washington, D.C., November.

1990   Driven by Drink: The Role of Drinking in the Political Economy and the Case of Early Iron Age France. *Journal of Anthropological Archaeology* 9:352–406.

1996   Feasts and Commensal Politics in the Political Economy: Food, Power, and Status in Prehistoric Europe. In *Food and the Status Quest*, edited by P. Wiessner and W. Schiefenhövel, pp. 87–125. Oxford: Berghahn Books.

1998   Consumption, Agency, and Cultural Entanglement: Theoretical Implications of a Mediterranean Colonial Encounter. In *Studies in Culture Contact: Interaction, Culture Change, and Archaeology*, edited by J. Cusick, pp. 288–315. Carbondale: University of Southern Illinois Press.

1999a   Rituals of Commensality and the Politics of State Formation in the "Princely" Societies of Early Iron Age Europe. In *Les princes de la protohistoire et l'émergence de l'état*, edited by P. Ruby, pp. 135–152. Cahiers du Centre Jean Bérard, Institut Français de Naples 17—Collection de l'École Française de Rome 252, Naples.

1999b   Reflections on Lattois Society during the 4th Century B.C. In *Lattara 12: Recherches sur le quatrième siècle avant notre ère à Lattes*, edited by M. Py, pp. 663–680. Lattes: Association pour la Recherche Archéologique en Languedoc Oriental.

Dietler, M., and I. Herbich

1993   Living on Luo Time: Reckoning Sequence, Duration, History, and Biography in a Rural African Society. *World Archaeology* 25:248–260.

Dillon, R. G.

1990   *Ranking and Resistance: A Precolonial Cameroonian Polity in Regional Perspective.* Stanford: Stanford University Press.

Donham, D.

1994   *Work and Power in Maale, Ethiopia.* New York: Columbia University Press.
[1979]

Douglas, M.

1984   Standard Social Uses of Food: Introduction. In *Food in the Social Order*, edited by M. Douglas, pp. 1–39. New York: Russell Sage Foundation.

Douglas, M., and C. Isherwood
 1979 *The World of Goods: Towards an Anthropology of Consumption*. New York: Norton.
Elias, N.
 1978 *The History of Manners*. New York: Pantheon.
 [1939]
Erasmus, C. J.
 1956 Culture Structure and Culture Process: The Occurrence and Disappearance of Reciprocal Farm Labor. *Southwestern Journal of Anthropology* 12:444–469.
Evans-Pritchard, E. E.
 1949 Luo Tribes and Clans. *Rhodes-Livingstone Journal* 7:24–40.
 1971 *The Azande*. London: Oxford University Press.
Firth, R.
 1983 Magnitudes and Values in Kula Exchange. In *The Kula: New Perspectives on Massim Exchange*, edited by J. W. Leach and E. Leach, pp. 89–102. Cambridge: Cambridge University Press.
Fortes, M., and E. E. Evans-Pritchard, eds.
 1940 *African Political Systems*. London: Oxford University Press.
Foucault, M.
 1980 *Power/Knowledge: Selected Interviews and Other Writings*, edited by C. Gordon. New York: Pantheon Books.
Friedl, E.
 1975 *Women and Men: An Anthropologist's View*. New York: Holt, Rinehart and Winston.
Friedman, J.
 1984 Tribes, States, and Transformations. In *Marxist Analyses and Social Anthropology*, edited by M. Bloch, pp. 161–202. London: Tavistock.
Garine, I. de
 1996 Food and the Status Quest in Five African Cultures. In *Food and the Status Quest: An Interdisciplinary Perspective*, edited by P. Wiessner and W. Schiefenhövel, pp. 193–218. Oxford: Berghahn Books.
Gefou-Madianou, D., ed.
 1992 *Alcohol, Gender, and Culture*. London: Routledge.
Gero, J. M.
 1992 Feasts and Females: Gender Ideology and Political Meals in the Andes. *Norwegian Archaeological Review* 25:15–30.
Geschire, P.
 1982 *Village Communities and the State: Changing Relations among the Maka of Southeastern Cameroon since the Colonial Conquest*. Translated by J. Ravell. London: Kegan Paul.
Godelier, M.
 1980 L'État: les processus de sa formation, la diversité de ses formes et de ses bases. *Revue International des Sciences Sociales* 32:657–671.

Goldschmidt, W.

1976   *Culture and Behavior of the Sebei: A Study in Continuity and Adaptation.* Berkeley: University of California Press.

Goody, J.

1982   *Cooking, Cuisine, and Class: A Study in Comparative Sociology.* Cambridge: Cambridge University Press.

Gutmann, B.

1926   *Das Recht der Dschagga.* Munich: Beck.

Haggblade, S.

1992   The Shebeen Queen and the Evolution of Botswana's Sorghum Beer Industry. In *Liquor and Labor in Southern Africa,* edited by J. Crush and C. Ambler, pp. 395–412. Athens, Ohio: Ohio University Press.

Halperin, R., and J. Olmstead

1976   To Catch a Feastgiver: Redistribution among the Dorze of Ethiopia. *Africa* 46:146–165.

Hayden, B.

1990   Nimrods, Piscators, Pluckers, and Planters: The Emergence of Food Production. *Journal of Anthropological Archaeology* 9:31–69.

1996   Feasting in Prehistoric and Traditional Societies. In *Food and the Status Quest: An Interdisciplinary Perspective,* edited by P. Wiessner and W. Schiefenhövel, pp. 127–148. Oxford: Berghahn Books.

Hayden, B., and R. Gargett

1990   Big Man, Big Heart? A Mesoamerican View of the Emergence of Complex Society. *Ancient Mesoamerica* 1:3–20.

Herbich, I.

1987   Learning Patterns, Potter Interaction, and Ceramic Style among the Luo of Kenya. *The African Archaeological Review* 5:193–204.

1991   The Flow of Drink in an African Society: An Ethnoarchaeological Perspective. Paper presented at the 56th Annual Meeting of the Society for American Archaeology, New Orleans, April.

Herbich, I., and M. Dietler

1991   Aspects of the Ceramic System of the Luo of Kenya. In *Töpferei- und Keramikforschung,* 2, edited by H. Lüdtke and R. Vossen, pp. 105–135. Bonn: Habelt.

1993   Space, Time, and Symbolic Structure in the Luo Homestead: An Ethnoarchaeological Study of "Settlement Biography" in Africa. In *Actes du XIIe Congrès International des Sciences Préhistoriques et Protohistoriques, Bratislava, Czechoslovakia, September 1–7, 1991, Vol. 1,* edited by J. Pavúk, pp. 26–32. Nitra: Archaeological Institute of the Slovak Academy of Sciences.

Hunter, M.

1961   *Reaction to Conquest: Effects of Contact with Europeans on the Pondo of Southern Africa.* London: Oxford University Press.

Karp, I.
1980   Beer Drinking and Social Experience in an African Society. In *Explorations in African Systems of Thought*, edited by I. Karp and C. Bird, pp.83–119. Bloomington: Indiana University Press.

Kelly, J. D., and M. Kaplan
1990   History, Structure, and Ritual. *Annual Review of Anthropology* 19:119–150.

Kertzer, D. I.
1988   *Ritual, Politics, and Power*. New Haven: Yale University Press.

Laburthe-Tolba, P.
1981   *Les seigneurs de la forêt*. Paris: Publications de la Sorbonne.

Lemonnier, P.
1990   *Guerres et festins: Paix, échanges, et compétition dans les Highlands de Nouvelle-Guinée*. Paris: CID—Editions de la Maison des Sciences de l'Homme.
1996   Food, Competition, and the Status of Food in New Guinea. In *Food and the Status Quest: An Interdisciplinary Perspective*, edited by P. Wiessner and W. Scheifenhövel, pp. 219–234. Oxford: Berghahn Books.

Lentz, C.
1998   The Chief, the Mine Captain, and the Politician: Legitimating Power in Northern Ghana. *Africa* 68:46–66.

Mair, L.
1934   *An African People in the Twentieth Century*. New York: Russell and Russell.
1977   *African Kingdoms*. London: Clarendon.

Mandala, E. O.
1998   Hospitality, Women, and the Efficacy of Beer. In *Food and Gender: Identity and Power*, edited by C. M. Counihan and S. L. Kaplan, pp. 45–80. Amsterdam: Harwood Academic Publishers.

Marshall, F.
1993   Food Sharing and the Faunal Record. In *From Bones to Behavior: Ethnoarchaeological and Experimental Contributions to the Interpretation of Faunal Remains*, edited by J. Hudson, pp. 228–246. Carbondale: Southern Illinois University.

Mauss, M.
1935   Les techniques du corps. *Journal de Psychologie* 32:271–293.
1966   *The Gift: Forms and Functions of Exchange in Archaic Societies*. Translated by
[1925]   I. Cunnison. London: Routledge and Kegan Paul.

Mburu, J. G.
1978   West Kenya Funerals: Expensive and Immoral. *Umma* 8:9–14, 18–19, 22–23.

McDonald, M., ed.
1994   *Gender, Drink, and Drugs*. Oxford: Berg.

Meillassoux, C.
1975   *Maidens, Meal, and Money: Capitalism and the Domestic Community*. Cambridge: Cambridge University Press.

Middleton, J., and D. Tait, eds.

1958   *Tribes without Rulers*. London: Routledge and Kegan Paul.

Modjeska, N.

1982   Production and Inequality: Perspectives from Central New Guinea. In *Inequality in New Guinea Societies*, edited by A. Strathern, pp. 50–108. Cambridge: Cambridge University Press.

Moore, M. P.

1975   Cooperative Labour in Peasant Agriculture. *The Journal of Peasant Studies* 2:270–291.

Moore, S. F.

1994   *Anthropology and Africa: Changing Perspectives on a Changing Scene*. Charlottesville: University of Virginia Press.

Moore, S. F., and B. G. Myerhoff

1985   Introduction—Secular Ritual: Forms and Meanings. In *Secular Ritual*, edited by S. F. Moore and B. G. Myerhoff, pp. 3–24. Assen/Amsterdam: Van Gorcum.

Morris, I.

1992   *Death-Ritual and Social Structure in Classical Antiquity*. Cambridge: Cambridge University Press.

Murray, O.

1990   Sympotic History. In *Sympotica: A Symposium on the Symposion*, edited by O. Murray, pp. 3–13. Oxford: Clarendon.

Netting, R.

1964   Beer as a Locus of Value among the West African Kofyar. *American Anthropologist* 66:375–384.

Ngokwey, N.

1987   Varieties of Palm Wine among the Lele of the Kasai. In *Constructive Drinking: Perspectives on Drink from Anthropology*, edited by M. Douglas, pp. 113–121. Cambridge: Cambridge University Press.

Obayemi, A. M. U.

1976   Alcohol Usage in an African Society. In *Cross-cultural Approaches to the Study of Alcohol: An Interdisciplinary Perspective*, edited by E. Everett, J. Wadell and D. Heath, pp. 199–208. The Hague: Mouton.

Pallier, G.

1972   Les dolotières de Ouagadougou (Haute-Volta). *Travaux et documents de géographie tropicale* 7:120–139.

Peristiany, J. G.

1939   *The Social Institutions of the Kipsigis*. London: Routledge.

Perlès, C.

1996   Les stratégies alimentaires dans les temps préhistoriques. In *Histoire de l'alimentation*, edited by J.-L. Flandrin and M. Montanari, pp. 29–46. Paris: Fayard.

Polanyi, K.
    1957   The Economy as Instituted Process. In *Trade and Markets in the Early Empires*, edited by K. Polanyi, C. Arensberg, and H. Pearson, pp. 243–269. New York: The Free Press.

Pryor, F. L.
    1977   *The Origins of the Economy: A Comparative Study of Distribution in Primitive and Peasant Economies*. New York: Academic Press.

Rehfisch, F.
    1987   Competitive Beer Drinking among the Mambila. In *Constructive Drinking: Perspectives on Drink from Anthropology*, edited by M. Douglas, pp. 135–145. Cambridge: Cambridge University Press.

Richards, A. I.
    1939   *Land, Labour, and Diet in Northern Rhodesia*. London: Oxford University Press.

Sahlins, M.
    1972   *Stone Age Economics*. London: Tavistock.

Sangree, W. H.
    1962   The Social Functions of Beer Drinking in Bantu Tiriki. In *Society, Culture, and Drinking Patterns*, edited by D. J. Pittman and C. R. Snyder, pp. 6–21. New York: Wiley.

Saul, M.
    1981   Beer, Sorghum, and Women: Production for the Market in Rural Upper Volta. *Africa* 51:746–764.
    1983   Work Parties, Wages, and Accumulation in a Voltaic Village. *American Ethnologist* 10:77–96.

Schapera, I.
    1938   *A Handbook of Tswana Law and Custom*. London: Oxford University Press.

Schatzberg, M.
    1993   Power: Legitimacy and "Democratisation" in Africa. *Africa* 63:445–461.

Scott, J. C.
    1990   *Domination and the Arts of Resistance*. New Haven: Yale University Press.

Shipton, P.
    1989   *Bitter Money: Cultural Economy and Some African Meanings of Forbidden Commodities*. American Ethnological Society Monograph Series, 1, Washington, D.C.
    1990   African Famines and Food Security: Anthropological Perspectives. *Annual Review of Anthropology* 19:353–394.

Southall, A. W.
    1952   Lineage Formation among the Luo. *International African Institute Memorandum 26*. London: Oxford University Press.
    1956   *Alur Society: A Study in Processes and Types of Domination*. Cambridge: Heffer and Sons.

Tambiah, S. J.

1985   *Culture, Thought, and Social Action: An Anthropological Perspective.* Cambridge: Harvard University Press.

Turner, V.

1967   *The Forest of Symbols: Aspects of Ndembu Ritual.* Ithaca: Cornell University Press.

1969   *The Ritual Process: Structure and Anti-Structure.* Ithaca: Cornell University Press.

van Gennep, A.

1960   *The Rites of Passage.* Translated by M. B. Vizedom and G. L. Caffee. Chicago: University of Chicago Press.

Vincent, J.

1971   *African Elite: The Big Men of a Small Town.* New York: Columbia University Press.

Whisson, M.

1961   The Rise of Asembo and the Curse of Kakia. In *East African Institute of Social Research Conference Proceedings*, no pagination. Kampala: Makarere College.

Wiessner, P.

1996   Leveling the Hunter: Constraints on the Status Quest in Foraging Societies. In *Food and the Status Quest: An Interdisciplinary Perspective*, edited by P. Wiessner and W. Schiefenhövel, pp. 171–192. Oxford: Berghahn Books.

4

OF FEASTING AND VALUE

ENGA FEASTS IN A HISTORICAL PERSPECTIVE
(PAPUA NEW GUINEA)

Polly Wiessner

Papua New Guinea is at once the land of feasting and the land of political in-trigue,[1] and the two are intertwined. Virtually every event of importance is ac-companied by feasting, and during feasts an array of strategies are played out. The strong political orientation of Papua New Guinea societies no doubt con-tributes to the fact that over 800 different languages are spoken in this small island nation of some three and a half million inhabitants. A meaningful classification of feasts by the social, economic, or political designs they entertain is difficult to frame, particularly for the western highlands of Papua New Guinea where many personal or group projects unfold under the umbrella of feasting, no matter what the proclaimed purpose of the event.

Nonetheless, since feasting is a composite event in which certain conditions, social behaviors, and provisioning activities coalesce to form the final occasion, a breakdown of feasts by their components is useful for understanding when and why certain strategies are deployed. Here I will briefly outline the essential components of feasting, suggest some possible archaeological correlates of each, and mention some of the social and political strategies they facilitate. Then, drawing on an ethnohistorical study of feasting and exchange among the Enga of highland Papua New Guinea, I will outline the complementary role of secular and sacred feasting in the development of the great ceremonial exchange networks of Enga and go on to focus on the role of feasting in the construction of the value and meaning of things.

The Enga case illustrates: (1) how material goods are differentially valued in the context of feasting; (2) how the natural properties of things valued affects the course of production and competition; and (3) how cultural constructions of value are constantly tested against the realities of the surrounding world. When contradictions occur, as they did in Enga, feasting can be called on to revalue goods and redirect the course of change.

COMPONENTS OF FEASTING

Of what is feasting composed? First, feasting requires the aggregation of people. Aggregation in and of itself does not require feasting, though it is greatly facilitated by it; if no food is available, crowds must disperse before long. Aggregation should be detectable in the archaeological record, for example through the presence of unusually large sites or a diversity of styles in artifacts found at a given site.

Second, feasting involves food sharing and food distribution. Food sharing appears to have its roots in the parent-child relationship and thus can be a way of expressing affection and extending familial behavior to distant or non-kin in order to bond larger groups (Eibl-Eibesfeldt 1989). By contrast, food distribution, which often requires returns at a later date, creates temporary imbalance between donors and recipients and permits the construction of inequality. Food sharing and food distribution during feasting may be inferred in the archaeological record from faunal distribution or the collection of food remains from a broad catchment area at one place. Sharing is more likely to leave remains at the site than food distribution, where a good portion of the food may be carried away from the distribution site.

Third, most feasts are held for a specific occasion: to appease ancestors, initiate youth, marry, bury the dead, pay compensation, or assemble a labor force. The goal of feasts may be inferred from the presence of certain archaeological features or artifacts.

Fourth, feasting usually involves some form of display, whether this is display of food, objects, individuals, or groups. Artifacts or structures constructed for display include special vessels, platforms, graves, or houses.

Fifth, and very importantly, feasting requires abundance. A party where the food does not go round or runs out is not a good party. Abundance is perhaps the single most important factor in determining which strategies can be played out during a feast. Mere sufficiency permits a limited array of strategies; abundance furnishes many more. In foraging societies and simple horticultural societies, conditions of abundance may be difficult to achieve or to time, so that feasts take place when food is available, constraining political strategies. Depending on what is consumed in a feast or how food is presented, abundance may be more or less archaeologically visible.

Finally, since feasts are about the consumption of abundance, they place demands on production. If these demands are accelerating, they may be reflected in changing patterns of land use.

If all of these conditions for feasting are met, they coalesce to evoke excitement, warmth, and festivity, lending spirit to the occasion. What is experienced in such an atmosphere usually makes deep impressions. The festive spirit may be reinforced by emotionally laden aesthetic experiences during communal song or dance.

The social components of feasting behavior, when combined, make possible a number of political strategies. Table 4.1 breaks down the above elements of feasting and relates them to specific social or political strategies.

FEASTING AND VALUE

All of the political strategies listed in Table 4.1 were played out during Enga feasts. Here I will concentrate on the construction of value. It is well-established in anthropology that the value of things is based on several criteria: capital input, labor input, utility, abundance or scarcity, exchange rate, and "social" value, including religious and political significance (Appadurai 1986; Parry and Bloch 1989; Thomas 1991). Although the first three criteria may be predictable on the basis of economic models, exchange value and social value are culturally constructed.[2] The cultural construction of value in material culture applies to both gifts and commodities, for these categories often describe different stages or uses in an object's life history. For instance, a pig can be purchased in barter and then given as a gift. Feasting provides the ideal conditions for the valuation of objects for a number of reasons. First, feasts gather people so that certain permutations of value and meaning can be broadly introduced. Second, during feasting selected items are put in the focus of attention. For example, they may figure prominently in cult procedures, be worn by central figures, exchanged publicly, or placed in a culinary display. Studies in ethology in humans and other primates have established that being the focus of attention is the primary means of gaining status (Chance 1967; Hold 1976); the same principle appears to be ap-

TABLE 4.1

The Social Components of Feasting and Corresponding Political Strategies

Social Components	Aggregation	Food Sharing	Food Distribution	Special Purpose	Display	Abundance
Bonding groups	xxx	xxx	x	xxx	x	x
Creating external ties						
a. Between individuals	x	xx	xx	x	x	x
b. Between groups	xxx	xxx	x	xx	xx	xx
Establishing social position						
Equality						
a. Between individuals	x	xxx		x	x	x
b. Between groups	xxx	xxx		x	xx	xxx
Inequality						
a. Between individuals	x	xxx	xxx	xx	xxx	xxx
b. Between groups	xxx	xxx	xxx	xxx	xxx	xxx
Production (work parties)	xxx	xxx		xxx		x
Manipulating social norms and values	xxx	xx	xx	xxx	xxx	xx
Constructing value of goods and valuables	xxx	x	xx	xxx	xxx	xx

xxx = very important   xx = important   x = less important

plicable to material goods. Third, the special purpose of a feast is instrumental in giving the objects utilized or displayed specific meanings. Fourth, the spirit generated during the communal feasting, song, and dance turn fleeting impressions into lasting ones.

THE ENGA: A CASE STUDY

The subjects of this case study, the Enga, are highland horticulturalists numbering about 200,000 and well known in the anthropological literature through the works of Meggitt (1965, 1972, 1974, 1977), Feil (1984), Wohlt (1978), Lacey (1975), and Waddell (1972), among many others. Their staple crop, sweet potato, is cultivated in an intensive system of mulch mounding to feed large human and pig populations. The Enga population is divided into a segmentary lineage system of phratries or tribes composed of some 1,000 to 6,000 members, and their constituent exogamous clans, subclans, and lineages.[3] The politics of land, social networks, and exchange occupy much of men's time and effort, while women devote themselves primarily to family, gardening, and pig husbandry. Frequent and destructive warfare creates sharp divisions between clans (Meggitt 1977) that are periodically repaired through ceremonial exchanges to reestablish peace. All men are defined as potentially equal, though those who excel in public mediation, organization of events, oratory, and the manipulation of wealth make names for themselves as big men. Women exert considerable influence over both production and exchange in the private realm.

The Enga hold a rich body of oral traditions that include myth, song, poetry, spells, incantations, and historical traditions (*atome pii*), which are distinguished from myth or stories (*tindi pii*), in that they are said to be founded in eyewitnessed events of the past. Historical traditions contain information on such matters as tribal locations and subsistence practices some eight to ten generations ago, wars and migrations, agriculture, the development of cults and ceremonial exchange networks, leadership, trade, environmental disasters, and innovations in song and dress. Genealogies of eight to twelve generations permit a rough scheme of sequencing or dating (Table 4.2). The material on which I will draw comes from a study of these historical traditions conducted with an Enga colleague, Akii Tumu, in 108 Enga tribes (Wiessner and Tumu 1998). Working on such a broad scale made it possible to identify regional trends that occurred within the span of Enga oral history and to check for consistency by using converging lines of evidence.

The period covered by Enga historical traditions begins just prior to the introduction of the sweet potato, continues through first contact with Europeans in the 1930s, and onward into the present (Table 4.2). As the introduction of the sweet potato is placed early within the span of historical traditions, it is beyond

119

TABLE 4.2
Chronological Scheme of Events Discussed in Text

Prehistory

50,000 B.P.	First immigrants arrive in Papua New Guinea by sea from Asia
12,000 B.P.	Earliest archaeological evidence for Enga: Yuku cave in eastern Enga, hunting and gathering site at ca. 1,300 m
10,000 B.P.	Kutepa rockshelter in western Enga, hunting and gathering at 2,300 m
4000–2000 B.P.	Pollen evidence indicates forest clearance for horticulture in eastern Enga
400–250 B.P.	Introduction of sweet potato to Enga and beginning of Enga historical traditions

Historical Traditions

Generation before present

8	Population shift from high altitudes to lower valleys
	Beginning of early Tee cycle
7	Kepele cult first practiced by horticulturalists of western Enga
6	Beginning of Great Ceremonial Wars
5 (ca.1855–1885?)	Kepele cult imported into central Enga, called Aeatee
4 (ca.1885–1915)	Tee cycle expanded to finance Great Ceremonial Wars
	Aeatee cult expanded to coordinate Tee cycle and Great Ceremonial Wars
	Female Spirit Cult imported into eastern Enga
3 (ca.1915–1945)	Tee cycle begins to subsume Great Ceremonial Wars
	Aeatee/Kepele cult used to organize the Tee cycle
	First contact with Europeans in 1934
	Last Great Ceremonial War fought 1938–1941
	Tee cycle subsumes Great War exchange routes
	Ain's cult 1941–1942
2 (ca.1945–1975)	Colonial period begins—late 1940s in east, 1950–60s in west
	Female Spirit cult spreads
1 (ca. 1975–2005)	1975 Papua New Guinea's independence

the scope of reliable genealogical dating. Our best estimate is that it arrived between 250 and 400 years ago, releasing many constraints on production owing to its high yield per acre, ability grow well in poor soils and at high altitudes, resistance to blight, and superiority as pig fodder (Watson 1965a, 1965b, 1977). The sparse population of Enga that had previously subsisted by taro gardening or hunting and gathering was able to expand into higher niches, produce a substantial surplus, and store it "on the hoof" in pig populations. Another 200–350 years passed before European gold prospectors and patrols entered the Papua New Guinea highlands.

DEVELOPMENTS WITHIN THE SPAN OF ENGA HISTORICAL TRADITIONS

Descriptions from the earliest generations of Enga history portray a lifestyle very different from that of more recent times. In the fertile valleys of eastern Enga, where most of the land lies under approximately 1,900 m, sedentary agriculturists cultivated taro, yams, bananas, sugarcane, and other crops, supplementing their diet with hunting. In central Enga at altitudes between 1,900 m and 2,200 m, where taro and yams are not as productive, historical traditions describe shifting horticulturalists who cultivated mixed gardens and hunted. In the less fertile and more rugged valleys of western Enga, the population was divided by niche. Mobile groups who depended heavily on hunting and gathering inhabited regions above approximately 2,100–2,200 m. To these "hunters"[4] were attributed great physical strength and possession of powerful ritual and magic. Shifting horticulturalists, who subsisted on taro and other garden products, supplemented by hunting, inhabited the steep, narrow valleys below. There is mention of regular intermarriage and exchange between people of the high country and those of the valleys, as well as a good deal of tension and misunderstanding. Throughout Enga the population is described as sparse with long distances between settlements. Wars were fought and problems ultimately solved by dispersal in space; compensation to allies was paid with land and gifts of food for feasting. At this time, prized gifts and commodities included stone axes, salt, and items for self-decoration, the latter of which were displayed prominently at traditional feasts and dances. The plots of historical traditions from this period often revolve around hunting, trade, traditional dances, or warfare. Pigs were apparently kept in small numbers, but enter only peripherally into the oral record.

Acceptance and utilization of the sweet potato varied by region, though historical traditions from all areas report shifts in population distribution, eventual population growth, and the expansion of ceremonial exchange, religious ritual, and feasting in response to increased social and political complexity (Wiessner and Tumu 1998). The purposes, structure, and content of such responses in eastern, central, and western Enga differed greatly. In eastern Enga the sweet potato slipped into the garden regime with little note in historical traditions. Its initial impact was only an indirect one—to stimulate the immigration of people from higher regions to the south and east in pursuit of good garden land. These immigrants, who came from clans closer to the sources of ax stone and other valuables, threatened the positions of big-men in the trade of eastern Enga. In response, big-men of the Saka Valley took action and constructed a new system of finance through which to raise the wealth necessary to maintain regional prominence. As the legend goes, they sent messages and initiatory gifts to their partners along established trade routes asking them to provide wealth in the form of pigs and valuables on credit, rather than by barter, and for them to en-courage their respective partners down the line to do the same. When wealth ar-riving along these chains of finance reached the Saka Valley, they invested it in marriages and other relationships that would increase their spheres of influence. Returns from these investments, together with wealth from home production, were used to pay creditors in a public Tee festival. Thus through the concatenation of trade partnerships based on kinship ties, chains of finance were constructed to compose the skeleton of what was to become the Tee ceremonial exchange cycle.

The early Tee was conducted on a small scale, but nonetheless it introduced a powerful innovation into Enga exchange—chains of finance that gave access to the wealth of people who were usually beyond the bounds of kinship reckoning. Some two to three generations after its conception, neighboring groups realized the advantage of the Tee for obtaining wealth to finance bridewealth payments, attract allies in warfare, pay war reparations, and secure partners along trade routes. And so it spread throughout eastern Enga (Fig. 4.1).

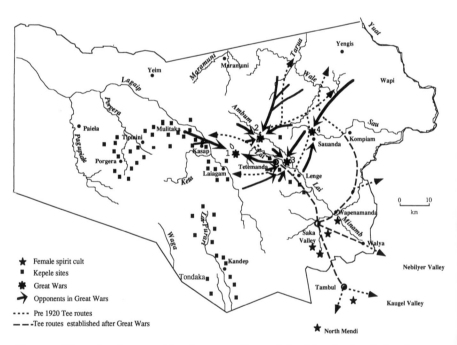

Figure 4.1. Networks of ceremonial exchange, warfare, and ritual that developed after the introduction of the sweet potato.

As it grew, the Tee developed into a three-phase cycle (Feil 1984; Meggitt 1974). During the first phase, the *saandi pingi*, initiatory gifts of small pigs, goods, and valuables were given on a private basis by individual families to Tee partners in clans to their west, more often than not adjacent clans. Initiatory gifts flowed in one direction and were intended to "pull" the *tee pingi*, the phase of main gifts. When a sufficient number of *saandi* initiatory gifts had moved westward, big-men made efforts to launch the phase of the main gifts in which full-grown pigs, cassowary, pearl shells, and other valuables were distributed by individual families during public clan festivals to partners who had given initiatory gifts. Some days or weeks after the westernmost clan in the Tee had held its distribution, the neighboring clan to the east followed suit and so the *tee pingi* worked its way westward, clan by clan, with the main gifts flowing in the opposite direction to the initiatory gifts. *Tee pingi* festivals were events of unsurpassed excitement, pomp, and ceremony. Suspense and anticipation were high throughout, for to give and receive large numbers of pigs, goods, and valuables was an indicator of political victory in controlling the flow of wealth. Part of the wealth distributed in the phase of the main gifts traveled the entire Tee network; part was pulled out to finance local events.

When the phase of the main gifts reached the easternmost clan in the network, efforts were made to launch the final reciprocal phase of the Tee cycle, the *mena yae pingi* or simply *yae*. The *yae* involved the distribution of butchered pork that traveled in the opposite direction of the main gifts, retracing its steps. Donors from the phase of the main gifts received approximately one side of butchered pork for each pig they had given. It was during the *yae* phase that extensive feasting took place, wealth in the form of pork was consumed, and demands for production renewed. However, pork received in the *yae* was not for consumption only, but also used to pay a variety of debts and establish credit with which to initiate a new cycle that would send the main gifts in the opposite direction.

In central Enga, developments that took place after the introduction of the sweet potato were quite different. Wars raged as tribes of higher altitudes sought to take land in the fertile valleys after the introduction of the sweet potato (Fig. 4.1) and large segments of the population were displaced. Here a very different system of exchange emerged: the Great Ceremonial Wars. These wars consisted of a series carefully planned, large, semiritualized tournaments lasting for weeks or months fought recurrently two to three times a generation by entire tribes or pairs of tribes. "Owners of the fight" were hosted by other tribes who supplied them with a battlefield, food, water, and allied warriors for the duration of the war. Their purpose was twofold. First, they displayed force and solidified alliances to reestablish balance of power vis-à-vis enemy groups in the face of the population shifts mentioned above. Antagonism was limited to display on the battlefield—no land could be gained or lost. Second, they were fought to brew the massive exchanges and feasts that followed the Great Wars between "owners of the fight," their hosts, and allies. These turned bonds of brotherhood established during the fighting into economic relations of exchange, putting displaced groups back on the map of trade and exchange and creating networks between four major valley systems (Wiessner and Tumu 1998). Great War exchanges, such as the Tee cycle, involved alternating distributions of live pigs and valuables and those of butchered pork, with large feasts occurring during the latter.

In western Enga, groups who were formerly dependent on hunting and gathering moved into the Lagaip Valley and settled on land acquired from relatives related through marriage. Such moves incited tension, which is evidenced in a history replete with many small wars and migrations. The people of western Enga turned to ritual life for integration. A large cult called the Kepele was crafted to assemble the tribe, reaffirm unity, and draw attention away from local disputes. Kepele cults of different tribes of western Enga were integrated into a network bound together by the exchange of ritual experts, cult procedures, innovations, and attendance by relatives from other tribes (Fig. 4.1). During the five days of Kepele celebrations, special feasts were held for those taking part in sacred events—the initiates, ancestors, ritual experts—as well as for celebrants who remained outside the sacred area—women, children, and invited guests.

Furthermore, as the population grew and conflicts accelerated throughout Enga, war reparations, which were traditionally paid to allies for men lost in battle, were extended to enemies. While formerly opponents had dispersed after warfare, one ousting the other, as the population grew and the land filled, conflicting parties had to stay put and establish peace, a condition that was achieved through wealth exchange. War reparations involved an initial payment of cooked pork and subsequent feasting, followed by a series of exchanges of live pigs, goods, and valuables. When successful, peace and balance of power were restored, former exchange ties with enemies were reactivated, and new ones created.

Initially, all of the above exchange systems depended heavily on wealth other than pigs. The early Tee cycle involved the exchange of a small numbers of pigs, but emphasis was on trade goods: salt, axes, cosmetic oil, plumes, woven netwear, shells, and other items for self-decoration. Early Kepele feasts were heavily provisioned with marsupials, cassowary, and forest products, as were the Great War exchanges. War reparations and compensation were paid with land and food for feasting. But as the population grew, the land filled, and competition accelerated, trade goods, game animals, and land no longer sufficed to fill the needs for exchange. Pigs were the only form of wealth whose production could be readily intensified to meet new demands, but their value was not high enough to encourage intensification. A number of historical traditions directly state that many people were simply not interested in the drudgery of raising more pigs. And so big-men, who realized that their ambitions as well as the needs of their own clans could only be met by increased pig production, sought to enhance the value of the pigs. Some took promising young men into their households to teach them more about pig husbandry or encouraged their daughters to demand larger number of pigs as a part of their bridewealth. They also turned to more efficient means—cults and feasting.

ENGA FEASTING: SECULAR AND SACRED

Feasting, which was so integral to the development of the Tee cycle, the Great Ceremonial Wars, the Kepele cult, and other events, was held in two contexts: the secular and the sacred. Sacred and secular feasts were distinctly separated, though the two complemented one another. Most secular feasts were embedded in exchange events composed of two- or three-phase wealth distributions separated by weeks, months, or years, similar to those discussed earlier for the Tee cycle. Usually, two of these phases involved the exchange of live pigs, game, goods, and valuables, and at least one involved the exchange of butchered pork, vegetable foods, and wild game meat. Secular feasting adhered to the principles of the economic exchange, that is to say, individual contributions of pork were coordinated into a clanwide public distribution of wealth on the local ceremonial ground. However, the actual donations were not pooled and redistributed by a big-man, but given by individuals to their partners in the recipient group(s) with obligations for future reciprocation. Individuals stood to gain status from giving generously and from indebting others.

At the domestic level, secular feasts included: work party feasts to recruit assistance in household production, planning feasts for upcoming events, marriage feasts, payments to maternal kin to mark the growth of children or compensate for their injury, and funeral feasts in which maternal kin were compensated for the loss of an individual who was born and raised by them. In all of these feasts, except work feasts and planning feasts, contributions from the clan, subclan, or lineage were given to affinal or maternal kin outside the clan to initiate or maintain long-term exchange relationships. In addition to domestic feasts, larger secular feasts were held to secure interclan relations as well as interfamily ties—for example, payments to compensate the clans of allies killed in warfare, payments to enemies to compensate losses and terminate hostilities, or the distribution of cooked pork in the final phase of the Tee cycle repaying wealth received in earlier phases and to demonstrate the prosperity and generosity of the donor clan. Accordingly, large secular feasts usually involved display in a competitive context. Smaller secular exchanges and feasts were often timed to plan and finance larger ones.

Interestingly, most secular feasts were not events that united the two parties in communal consumption. Vegetable foods prepared to welcome guests were eaten on the spot, sometimes with scraps of pork, but the substantial contributions of pork or marsupials were handled as exchange items. In most secular distributions, even weddings, recipients collected their shares and soon after set off for home before darkness fell to distribute them within their extended families or to those who had helped finance the exchanges. Public distribution permitted individuals and groups to gain prestige, but the bonding of the two groups was truncated by separate consumption in the absence of song, dance, and other festivities. Though not eaten communally with donors, consumption of meat received in exchange was nonetheless seen as a form of indirect commensality, for Enga did not consume meat stemming from groups who were considered to be enemies. Moreover, consumption of pork among the Enga, whose daily diet is one of vegetable foods, is an event of excitement and great pleasure that draws praise, warmth, and gratitude for the food donors. And so, despite the absence of communal consumption in Enga secular feasts, the addition of a round of exchanges involving highly divisible foods that pleased many consumers added a significant social element to secular exchange cycles.

Benefits obtained by ambitious men for arranging exchanges and accompanying secular feasts were substantial. They gained "name" for their organizational efforts, and they gained wealth from successful exchange. Some of this was applied to clan needs, but enough was left to pursue personal interests and social position—to procure the wealth necessary to pay bridewealth for one or more wives, to attract allies in warfare, to recruit disabled individuals or war refugees to assist in production, and to secure trade partnerships.

Two features of secular feasting affected its potential for serving social and political ends. The one was the lack of communal consumption, and the other, the fact that the food distributed carried exchange obligations. The absence of communal consumption involving donor and recipient limited the potential of secular feasts to generate feelings of unity. And maintenance of a certain distance may have been intentional, for even though strong supportive ties were formed outside the clan through exchange, these had to be suspended in times of warfare. The fact that economic goals were embedded in secular feasting meant that all moves of big-men to bring about changes were regarded as economically driven and subject to scrutiny. Such an atmosphere was not conducive to manipulation of norms and values. Nonetheless, the incorporation of a phase of feasting into secular exchange allowed big-men to put increasing numbers of pigs in the center of distributions and actively demonstrate their potential as a social and economic currency.

Sacred feasts followed different principles than secular ones and offered different opportunities for the enterprising. At their core was commensality with humans and the spirit world united through celebration, rites, incantations, song, and food sharing. Sacred cult feasts were held at many levels from the consumption of a single pig at small healing ceremonies to cults for the ancestors that drew together hundreds of people in festivities lasting up to five days or longer. Sacred feasts were "nested"—smaller ceremonies were held first, and if unfavorable conditions persisted, ever larger ones were held. Some tribes had a repertoire of up to ten different cults and accompanying feasts that could be held for the ancestors, "sky people," and other spirits. A tribe or clan's repertoire of cults was periodically revised through the importation of new cults from other groups who appeared to be thriving or through the invitation of ritual specialists from other groups who introduced additional rites.

The largest sacred feasts, organized by big-men, gathered clan or tribal members for five days of communal consumption at the cult site and entertained invited guests from other tribes. Unlike secular feasts that involved competitive provisioning and distribution, in sacred feasts every household contributed equally and everybody received freely to reaffirm equality of group members—it is said that even the dogs did not go hungry. Food produced for cult feasts was grown specifically for that purpose and never used to incur or discharge obligations related to secular exchange and feasting. The commensality of sacred feasts allowed for strong bonding at the group level that did not occur in secular feasts. As a result, entire tribes could be united.

Ritual experts who presided over cult rites were paid lavishly and stood to gain economically, although they did not have the social networks to invest their earnings in such a way as to wield power. In contrast, the benefits for big-men who organized these impressive events were other than financial ones. One benefit was the prestige that accrued from their ability to coordinate the production, cooperation, and participation necessary to stage successful cult performances and feasts. Prestige brought more than personal satisfaction—it was license to excel. In this society where all men were potential equals and equality was staunchly defended, name was only accorded to those who offered strong benefits to the group as a whole. Prestige signaled a man's ability to do just that. Accordingly, a man of renown won praise rather than protest for the number of wives he could marry, servants he could recruit, and wealth he could produce or obtain through exchange. Moreover, big-men who could organize intergroup events were considered too important to be killed senselessly in warfare. The protective umbrella of "good name" was not insignificant in a society where approximately 25 percent of men die in warfare (Meggitt 1977).

A second benefit open to big-men through participating in the organization of cult performances was the opportunity to alter norms and values. Big-men participated in importing new cults from groups who appeared more successful, summoning chosen ritual experts from other groups, and rearranging cult procedures to better communicate with the ancestors. In doing so, they were able to align norms and values with their personal projects. Because all cult-related decisions were made in the name of group betterment and detached from economically oriented exchange, the motives of big-men were not subject to the same scrutiny as were their maneuvers in secular feasting and exchange. To give some examples: through importing the praise poetry of bachelors' cults from other groups and making additions in the process, big-men could update the ideal for males; cults expressing equality of all men in the eyes of the ancestors could be timed appropriately to appease grudges emanating from emergent economic inequalities; and very importantly, goods and values were revalued through their prominent presentation in association with the sacred.

Different though they were, the relation between sacred and secular feasts was a complementary one. In a sense, sacred feasts laid the groundwork of rules from which competitive exchange could proceed. They defined all males and their family units as potential equal competitors for exchange, they displayed what was valued before the eyes of the ancestors, and when exchange depended heavily on group participation, they established a spirit of cooperation among corporate groups. When these conditions were met, individuals could go out and pursue their careers in secular exchange to benefit themselves and their clans. In turn, success in secular exchange and feasting established the practical value of items valued during sacred feasts and reaffirmed the importance of regular cult feasts to secure the goodwill of the ancestors for economic enterprises. Alternately, failures in exchange called for new cults, new rites, or in some cases, new values.

In an archaeological context, secular and sacred feasting left different signatures. The absence of communal consumption in secular feasts had a profound effect on the remains. When food was distributed and carried home, only traces of structures for food display and distribution remained at the aggregation site— postholes from display platforms, small amounts of bone from meat consumed during food preparation, and in some cases large earth ovens near the ceremonial ground to steam pork, though much meat was prepared at individual houses. The fact that meat was not consumed at the distribution site caused the majority of faunal remains to end up around household steaming pits in other clans. For sacred feasts,[5] by contrast, prolonged aggregation required the construction of a feasting site with shelters for the participants; communal consumption of all food left extensive faunal remains on the feasting site;[6] the gathering of celebrants and guests called for divided sacred and secular areas to separate insiders from outsiders; and on larger Enga cult sites, special structures were constructed for sacred rites, each of which had its own area for food preparation or consumption.

Significant also is the differential impact of competitive secular feasting and noncompetitive sacred feasting on food production and associated utilization of the landscape. Figure 4.2 compares the number of pigs given by big-men and their wives in the main phase of the Tee cycle with the number contributed by big-men to provision the Kepele cult by generation. It starts in the seventh generation before present just as the Tee cycle was beginning and pigs were being introduced into the Kepele. It ends in the third to second generation (the beginning of the colonial period) with a Tee held in the early 1950s and the last Kepele performances held before Christianity took hold in western Enga. Approximately a third of the pigs given in Tee are produced by the household (see also Feil 1984) and two thirds received as gifts; approximately half of the pigs distributed in Tee were slaughtered in the final phase of feasting and the others invested into bridewealth, compensation, and other payments. All of the pigs contributed to the Kepele cult performances were produced at home and consumed during the cult. As is clear in Figure 4.2, the overtly competitive distribution of wealth in secular events and accompanying opportunities for individual investment and economic gain fostered rapid growth in comparison to the more gradual growth in the noncompetitive Kepele. Although such growth might not be apparent from the sparse remains left on secular feasting sites, its impact is apparent in patterns and extent of land clearance and use.

Returning to the role of feasts in the valuation of material goods, below I will give one example of an elaborate cult centered on feasting, the Kepele of western Enga, through which pigs were made prominent in an area where pig production was arduous. Then I will go on to discuss the consequences of using complementary strategies in secular and sacred feasting to value the pig and construct ever-larger exchange networks, the complexities that were generated, and subsequent efforts to devalue the pig or shift value to other items.

THE KEPELE CULT

The Kepele had its roots in a pre–sweet potato cult to assemble dispersed hunting and gathering tribes of the high country in western Enga and initiate young men into the secrets of the spirit world.[7] After the introduction of the new crop, when these tribes acquired land from relatives and settled in the lower valleys, they brought the Kepele with them. There it was restructured to fit needs of a horti-

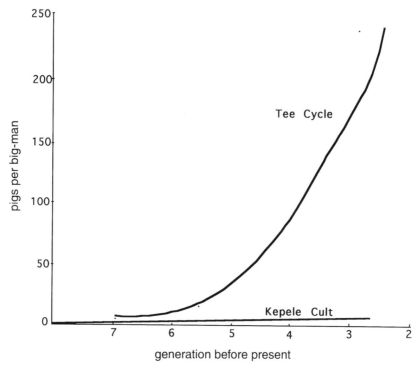

Figure 4.2. Comparison of the growth of secular competitive exchange and feasting with noncompetitive sacred feasting as measured in number of pigs contributed by big-men.

These figures are approximate. For the Tee cycle, number of pigs distributed is taken from the historical traditions detailing the lives of major big-men from the Yakani and Apulini tribes of central Enga. It is not possible to verify the accuracy of figures for earlier generations. However, since trees were planted at the end of lines of pigs distributed to mark the accomplishments of each generation of big-men, the order of magnitude should be correct. Prior to about the fourth generation, only wealthier clan members participated in the Tee cycle; after the fourth generation, most families distributed at least a few pigs as a matter of pride and sign of economic independence. Figures presented here are the maximum for major big-men who were Tee cycle organizers; in the second and third generations, big-men of less powerful clans might present 40–150 pigs, minor big-men, 30–50 pigs, and ordinary men fewer than 10.

Figures for Kepele cult performances were calculated on the basis of claims that early cult performances were provisioned with marsupials and later ones increasingly with pigs. From approximately the fourth generation on, it was stipulated that every male tribal member should contribute one pig and one pig only. Big-men with more male children would thus contribute more pigs as well as provide some pork for organizational activities, but their contributions did not greatly outstrip those of other clan members.

cultural lifestyle, including pig production, and to integrate the new settlers and their hosts (Wiessner and Tumu 1998).

The cult was called when poor environmental conditions, particularly the poor growth of gardens, children, pandanus, and pigs, indicated that the ancestors were discontented. Word was sent out to each clan to bring specific materials and foods from their own area for the construction of the tribal cult house where rites for the ancestors would be held. On the appointed day, the clans converged on the cult site in full ceremonial dress, singing and dancing. Each clan or subclan bore designated material for building the cult house, a perimeter post representing their group, and special foods from their area for the feast. Men from all clans of the tribe jointly constructed the cult house. Upon its completion, a large feast was held for all contributors and their families.

While rites for building the cult house appear to have long been a feature of the Kepele, formerly the feast had been provisioned with marsupials and other forest products. After the introduction of the sweet potato, pigs or pork were added to existing conventions and made integral to all new rites instituted. For example, during the communal feast in the house construction stage, each tribal segment was expected to bring pigs of a specific color, stake them out, club them, butcher them, and then divide the meat between all celebrants from the tribe. In this way pigs were used to underwrite the central political metaphor of the cult—the division of the tribe into independent segments, on the one hand, together with their mutual obligations to help one another, on the other. Celebrants then feasted and went home, leaving the house to deteriorate for several months to a couple of years until preparations for the major phase of the Kepele had been made.

As time for the major phase of the Kepele drew near, word was sent out to celebrants and guests to plant gardens and fatten pigs, gather materials, and to assemble young men for initiation. Requirements stipulated that every male tribesman provide one pig, whether he be adult or child. The sacred area for the cult was fenced off, the Kepele ancestral cult house repaired and decorated, and additional houses built for the initiation of boys, the steaming of pork, and the housing of ritual experts, men, and boys who would participate. When the celebrants had arrived, all of the pigs that had been brought for the ceremony were staked out and clubbed before the throngs of spectators. For the larger ceremonies of this century, 300–500 pigs were provided. Three pools were constructed at the site, one to collect the blood, another for the entrails, and a third to wash the intestines. Pigs to be used in the most sacred rites were slaughtered within the enclosed sacred area. In some cult performances, the skulls of the pigs were taken to the major cult house where they were placed on shelves for all male celebrants to see (Gibbs 1978). The pork to be used in ritual procedures was carefully separated from that given to women, children, uninitiated men, and relatives from other tribes, and pork was prepared very differently for each category of celebrant: the initiates, initiated adult males, ritual experts, and old men who would soon join the ancestors. Preparation of pork thus endorsed social divisions within Enga society. The large pig kill marked the onset of five days of sacred rites. Meanwhile women, children, and visitors remained outside the sacred area singing, dancing, feasting, trading, arranging marriages, or engaging in other social activities.

Men took designated pigs inside the sacred area and steamed them in pits for the various rites. One pig was specially slaughtered for a ritual expert who retired to a small hut and filled a gourd with the sacred water of life to be given to the initiates. The fluid was composed of the condensed breath of the ritual expert who blew on a cool stone ax blade and let the droplets roll into a gourd container where it was supplemented by pork fat and sugarcane juice. All of these substances were considered critical for the growth and long life of young men. When night fell, the initiates were taken to the cult house where they witnessed secrets of the spirit world and then were given the "water of life" from the gourd. Boys who had been through these rites were considered to be weaned from their mothers, on their way to becoming true men, and ready to witness the mating and feeding of the sacred ancestral objects. Thereafter they could consume pork that had been ritually prepared for the cult and no longer remain outside the sacred area eating ordinary pork like women and children.

The rites for the sacred objects, as far as we could determine, were added to the Kepele in the post–sweet potato era, when western Enga settled in lower valleys. The sacred objects consisted of stones in shapes reminiscent of male or female genitalia and a basketwork figure (*yupini*) fashioned to look like a man who represented the male ancestors.[8] The *yupini* was paraded to the Kepele site and placed in the Kepele house, while the sacred stones were unearthed from their resting place in the ground. In the cult house the *yupini* (or male ancestral stone) was made to simulate copulation with the female stones, while spells to promote fertility were recited. After copulation, the *yupini* was fed with pork fat, and the sacred stones were greased in it. Meanwhile, the celebrants and initiates feasted on pork that was prepared separately for each age group and category of participant. On the last day of the ceremony, the stones were wrapped in pork fat and buried. The ancestors were believed to have feasted with their human descendants during these rites and to be content to sleep thereafter, leaving human affairs to proceed unhampered and prosperous. At some cult sites, skulls of deceased tribal members were deposited over the years in a tribal skull house within the Kepele site where a pig was killed and small rites performed for each to appease the ghost. During the Kepele ceremony, the skulls that had accumulated were placed in a pyre between layers of all edible plant foods, pig fat, and firewood and ceremonially cremated. When cult rites were concluded, some of the cult houses were destroyed; it was believed that the goodwill of the ancestors had been evoked and fertility would prevail.

And so in the generations following the introduction of the sweet potato, pigs were introduced into all feasts and rites of the Kepele cult that had formerly been furnished by game and forest products. In this context, pigs and pork were given a multiplicity of meanings. During the cult house construction pigs represented tribal divisions; in subsequent feasts, these divisions were dismantled through the sharing of pork. The consumption of pork fat, among other things, was put forth as means of transforming boys to men. Pork was used to appease the ghosts of the dead and symbolically shared with the ancestors to bring about good fortune. The preparation of pork in different ways for different age groups and social positions reaffirmed the structure of Enga society. The demand that each male produce one pig for the Kepele reinforced equality of male tribesmen and gave incentive for pig production. The great feasts for the public that took place outside the sacred area gave a tangible reward for production to women, children, and invited guests who were not involved in the sacred rites.

Location of Kepele sites conformed to no specific pattern predictable for archaeologists. Sites were placed centrally in tribal territory so that they were accessible to families whose houses were widely scattered over clan land. Some Kepele sites offered magnificent views, while others were nestled on lower terraces. All Kepele sites were planted with a wide array of trees and ceremonial shrubs—some of the largest and older trees in the Enga landscape are on ceremonial grounds or cult sites. Remains left on Kepele sites would attest to the gradual valuation of pigs and the multiple meanings conferred on them. Most striking for archaeologists would be the number of structures and the presence of pig bones in association with every one as well as the association of particular pig bones, such as skulls, with specific structures (Fig. 4.3). The grand enclosure of the site and highly differentiated areas within it might suggest a ritual of unification for a given social unit and the legitimization of internal divisions within.

PROMOTING PIGS AND COMPETITION: THE OUTCOME

The upshot of enhancing porcine value though ritual, feasting, and exchange was that by the fourth to fifth generation before present, eastern, central, and western Enga offered diverse economic and ritual institutions that can all be counted as networks of ceremonial exchange and that were all grounded in a common currency—the pig. Big-men took full advantage of this similarity and diversity, weaving competitive and cooperative elements of the exchange systems of east-

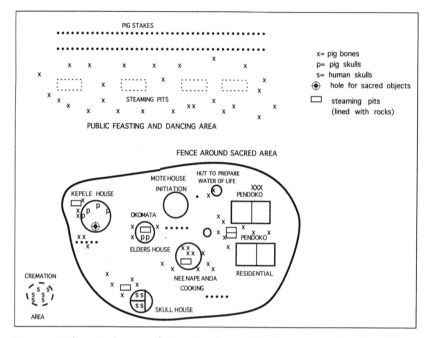

Figure 4.3. Schematic drawing of a Kepele cult site. This diagram is based on descriptions of informants while visiting Kepele sites, not the measuring and mapping of a single site. Though Kepele sites vary, many have the features presented here. Large sites may cover an area of 200 m by 200 m or more.

ern, central, and western Enga to craft the final Tee cycle. Specifically, the thin web of the early Tee cycle with its cooperative chains of finance was called on to fuel the Great Ceremonial Wars, removing the limitation of finance by home production. This began in the fourth generation before present around 1890 (Table 4.2). As the Great Wars expanded under the forces of dramatic intergroup competition, big-men involved in the Great Ceremonial Wars constructed longer Tee chains to tap into the wealth of the east and to reinvest the great mass of wealth that flowed out of the Great War exchanges. The Tee was thereby transformed from a relatively discreet stream of finance to a network flooded with wealth. The spheres of exchange carved out by alliance in the Great Ceremonial Wars later provided the pathways for the Tee cycle to expand (Fig. 4.1).

The cost, conflicts, and complexity of organization of the Great Ceremonial Wars and Tee cycle then became formidable. Big-men in tribes straddling the Tee cycle and Great Wars, aware of the different strategies that could be employed in secular and sacred feasting and the benefits of their juxtaposition, imported the Kepele cult from the west into central Enga. There it was called Aeatee, a term used for the Kepele in song.[9] The reasons for its import in the fifth generation are not stated, but initial performances were said to be held on a small scale. In the fourth generation, Aeatee rites to unite the tribe and express equality of members were elaborated into a six-stage performance spread out over five to ten years with each stage involving extensive feasting. Aeatee feasts were interdigitated with phases of the Tee cycle to facilitate its organization and timing (Table 4.3). The first stage of the Aeatee assembled the tribe for a marsupial feast and established unity within. For the second and third stages, when the ground was prepared and the cult house constructed, big-men from clans to the east who organized the Tee cycle were invited as spectators and guests for the accompanying feasts.

TABLE 4.3
The Six Stages of the Aeatee Cult of Central Enga
and Its Relation to the Tee Cycle

Stage	Feast	Purpose	Relation to Tee Cycle
Collection of building materials for the cult house	Communal hunt; marsupial feast	Unites tribe	None
Trampling of the grass on the building site	Marsupial feast	Unites tribe; expresses tribal structure	Big-men come from the east to plan the Tee
Construction of the Aeatee house	Major pork feast; one pig per male tribesman	Unites tribe; expresses tribal structure and complementarity of clans; reasserts equality of tribal members appeases ancestors	After feasts, initiatory gifts sent to launch Tee cycle
Cleaning of the house site, redecoration of the walls	Communal hunt; marsupial feast	Tribe united	None
Rites for the sacred ancestral stones	Large pork feast	Ancestral stones fed and buried; tribal prosperity assured	Big-men set off for the east to request major phase of Tee cycle
Burning of the Aeatee house	Largest pork feast	Marks end to successful performance of the Aeatee cult for the ancestors; rival tribes in the Great Wars compete to burn the cult house	Main phase of Tee arrives at western end of Tee cycle; return *yae* phase of butchered pork initiated

Upon witnessing the performance, they realized that tribes of western Enga were unified, prosperous, and that it was time to "talk Tee." This was done on the side in the quiet of men's houses. Following the great feast of the third phase, big-men from the east were sent home with gifts to launch the *saandi pingi* (phase of initiatory gifts) of the Tee cycle. In the fourth stage of the Aeatee, a large pork feast was held for the occasion of the feeding and mating of ancestral stones. Afterwards, big-men from the west set off with their Tee associates from the east to try to launch the phase of the main gifts in the east. The fifth stage of the Aeatee was held when the phase of the main gifts in the Tee had worked its way to the westernmost point. At this time the largest pork feast for the ancestors was held to mark the end of a successful cult performance that expressed equality, cooperation, wealth, and assured prosperity through communication with the ancestors; in the sixth stage the cult house was burned. Once these goals were achieved, individuals were allowed to go out to pursue their own interests. The *yae* phase of the Tee cycle, that involving the distribution and consumption of butchered pork, was initiated thereafter.

Throughout, Aeatee and Tee performances and feasts were separated in time and space, no pork was passed from one event to the other, and knowledge of their relationship was kept from the public—big-men concealed the role of the Aeatee in facilitating their goals for the Tee cycle. In short, the feasts of the Aeatee were used by big-men to mediate tensions, reaffirm old values, introduce new ones, realign feelings of tribal members, and demonstrate to participants and spectators that the tribe was strong, wealthy, and able to act as a corporate unit. Once these goals were achieved and all men proclaimed as potential equals, individuals were allowed to pursue their own interests to make a name in exchange.

During the decades before first contact with Europeans, the Great Ceremonial Wars collapsed under their own weight and their spheres of exchange were supplanted by the expanding Tee cycle (Wiessner and Tumu 1998). By first contact with Europeans in the 1930s the Tee cycle involved some 40,000 people and the exchanges of tens of thousands of pigs. The Tee cycle recorded by ethnographers and missionaries in the 1950s–1970s (Bus 1951; Elkin 1953; Meggitt 1972, 1974; Feil 1984) was thus formed by forging three vast systems of feasting and exchange in the decades before first contact with Europeans.

The results of some five generations of increased agricultural potential, the valuation of the pig, and the merging of exchange systems was that competition in Enga accelerated at a runaway pace, with the sons of each generation outdoing their fathers in number of pigs distributed. Mounting pressure was put on production, for example, while in the seventh generation pigs are said to have depended primarily on foraging for their sustenance, by the late 1960s Waddell

(1972) found that over 60 percent of the sweet-potato harvest was fed to pigs in the Aruni tribe of eastern Enga. And now for the most interesting part: competition and accelerated production cannot escalate indefinitely. Something must give. On the eve of first contact with Europeans, a number of responses to curb competition were initiated that involved, among other things, resituating the pig in the Enga scheme of value and meaning.

RESPONSES IN THE WEST: AIN'S CULT

The less fertile, rugged valleys of western Enga were the first to come up against environmental constraints, for the shift from game animals and trade goods to the pig as the primary currency of ritual and exchange imposed a heavy workload on residents in western areas. By the early twentieth century, warfare had become endemic, and nutritionally related diseases prevalent. Elders interviewed voiced the dismay they felt at the time over demands on small household labor forces to produce large numbers of pigs for ritual, social, and political occasions, particularly for Kepele cult performances, war reparations, and to help finance relatives within the sphere of the Tee cycle. Pressures for pig production in turn incited conflict over pigs and good garden land, setting off a spiral of rampant and destructive warfare that took the lives of many. So dire were the circumstances that it was said that the lives of men seemed to have little more value than the life of pigs. These perceptions corresponded to predictions from a powerful cult, the Dindi Gamu, that environment and society were on a downward spiral and that the end of the world was imminent (Wiessner and Tumu 2000, in press). Diseases introduced by Europeans and rumors of European intrusion contributed to the misery and created a feeling that change was in the air.

In the early 1940s a new cult was launched by a family of big-men and ritual experts from the northwestern corner of Enga—Ain's cult or the Mata Katenge. Its goal was to stave off disaster through ritual intervention (Meggitt 1973; Gibbs 1977; Feil 1983). Among other things, the pig, perceived as being at the root of the problems, was devalued by cult prescriptions. First, demands for pig production were decreased by abolishing events that required or celebrated pigs—warfare and thus war reparations and major cults such as the Kepele. Second, the greater part of the pig population was removed from circulation by the slaughter of pig herds and their sacrifice to the sun. Though feasting after sacrifice was a part of the cult, disrespect for pork was shown through great wastage (Meggitt 1973:26), a practice very atypical in Enga where pork is precious. As the cult swept through western Enga it took on millenarian aspects—promises that new wealth would come in the form of giant celestial pigs and pearl shells. Competition would cease, for wealth would come freely and equally to all, requiring no productive effort. When the promised wealth did not appear, the cult collapsed, but not before the greater part of the pig population of western Enga was slaughtered. Shortly afterwards, patrols and missionaries entered the area.

RESPONSES IN THE EAST: THE FEMALE SPIRIT CULT

The impact of accelerating competition and intensification of pig production was not so heavy in eastern Enga, where the soil was richer and environment more forgiving. However, an unintended consequence of valuing pigs, rather than items with more limited availability, was that all able-bodied Enga could produce pigs, distribute them, and thereby become competitors in exchange. With a growing population and expanding networks of exchange, the number of competitors became unmanageable—the plans of even the most powerful big-men were foiled by competitors on the rise. In this context, big-men of the fourth generation introduced gold-lip pearl shells cut into crescent shapes as valuables into the Tee cycle and other exchanges as part of an effort to consolidate power. Pearl shells, unlike pigs, could not easily be obtained by ordinary men who did not have a long-standing control of trade networks to the south and southeast (see Clark 1991). Furthermore, they did not have to be fed or slaughtered, but could be retained indefinitely, accumulated, and passed on to descendants (Lemonnier 1990, 1996). Pearl shells were gradually accepted as valuable by tribes of easternmost Enga because they were prized by their eastern and southern neighbors. Daughters of wealthy men began to demand these valuables in their requests for bridewealth.[10] However, the central Enga, key participants in the Tee cycle, rejected the eastern valuation of pearl shells, preferring pigs, stone axes, and cowry shells.

Big-men then attempted to influence the valuation of pearl shells by another means—through importing the Female Spirit cult, which placed pearl shells at its center and in association with prosperity and fertility. Initial motivations for importing the cult from non-Enga groups to the south (Strathern 1970, 1979a), as stated in historical traditions, were to enhance clan or tribal fortune as well as to host an event similar to the Aeatee cult of central Enga, which would draw people from near and far to plan the Tee cycle. Historical traditions tell of voyages taken by big-men from eastern Enga, laden with goods and valuables contributed by themselves and fellow clanspeople, to purchase the sacred objects, spells, and rites of the cult as well as the services of a ritual expert to institute the cult in their clans.

The Female Spirit cult was directed at a spirit woman who came to men as a bride but remained a virgin with a closed vagina, giving men protection against the contaminating menstrual fluids of women but bringing fertility to them and their families. Two houses were constructed, one male and one female, and segregated from public areas by three elaborately decorated fences. Male celebrants were divided into two moieties, one representing males and one females to express the cult's central theme: that male and female must be separated but indissolubly linked (Strathern 1979a). This theme was timely for the expanding ceremonial exchange networks that depended on women's work and cultivating ties with affinal and maternal kin. After a suspenseful day of secretive rites in the cult house for which thirty to sixty pigs were slaughtered, male participants emerged from the cult house in a dramatic parade, holding pearl shells before them, level with their eyes. They danced with stamping movements around the ceremonial grounds to the awe of the crowds and then paraded back to the cult house, reemerging with the net bags of pork for the communal feast. When the feast was over, invited guests from central Enga talked Tee just as they had done after Aeatee performances. No doubt the prominence of the shells in the cult and their association with fertility and prosperity did not escape evaluation by these shrewd men.

As the Female Spirit cult spread through clans of eastern Enga, many details of performance and meaning were lost or altered as it was adapted to new situations (Wiessner and Tumu 1998). The parade, which presented pearl shells as a coveted valuable with a sacred dimension, was perpetuated. The acceptance of pearl shells as items of great economic and symbolic value spread. However, before their impact on the social and political order could be determined, Europeans intervened, airlifting literally millions of pearl shells into the highlands to be used as a currency in dealings with indigenous populations. Inflation of pearl shells occurred and their value subsequently declined. Whether the pearl shells would have been accepted as the ultimate valuables, whether their circulation would have narrowed the field of competition, relieved pressure for pig production, or led to institutionalized social inequalities through the inheritance of wealth remain open questions (see Feil 1984 and Strathern 1979b).

By contrast to the case of pigs in Kepele feasts, no direct archaeological evidence would be likely to be found for the valuation of pearl shells via the Female Spirit cult. However, indirect inferences could be made from the appearance of cult sites with a new structure at the same time that pearl shell fragments, or the plaques of hardened resin on which shells were mounted, showed up in the archaeological record in greater numbers.

SUMMARY

Within the span of Enga historical traditions, the oral record illustrates how new value and meaning were conferred on pigs during sacred feasts, and reaffirmed during secular ones. Pigs had some noteworthy attributes. That they could be produced by all permitted unbridled competition on the one hand; on the other, the fact that they must be slaughtered and consumed to profit from labor invested made them an inappropriate form of wealth for the consolidation and transmission of power. So once pigs were endowed with sufficient value to become an all-purpose currency for social, political, and religious matters, competition accelerated at a runaway pace. When such competition reached the point where it introduced tensions and contradictions into Enga society and ran up against constraints of the external world, cults and their accompanying feasts were then sought by big-men to either devalue the pig or shift value to items with limited availability and greater durability, for example, pearl shells.

To conclude, I would like to make the following points. First, the event of feasting is a composite one and emphasis on its different components will have an effect on strategies that can be played out during feasting, as well as the structure of remains in the archaeological record. By juxtaposing feasts that permitted different strategies, such as secular and sacred ones, complex institutions such as the Enga Tee cycle can be formed. Second, a good portion of the value and meaning of material goods is culturally constructed. Feasting, by combining a number of social activities and behaviors, provides an optimal setting for brewing such connotations. Third, strategies couched in feasting, including the valuation of things, should be identifiable in certain archaeological contexts. And fourth, the attributes of items for which value is promoted, such as requirements for production, availability, durability, divisibility, lifespan, and disposal, have a strong impact on the course of social, economic, and political competition. Many social strategies ride piggyback on the natural properties of goods and valuables as demonstrated in the Enga case. Accordingly, altering the values and meanings of things through feasting can direct or redirect the course of change.

NOTES

1. There are some excellent publications on feasting in the New Guinea literature, to mention a few: Rappaport 1968; Young 1971; Strathern 1971; Lemonnier 1990, 1996; Kahn 1986; Knauft 1993.

2. Exchange value is an interesting issue for it involves mediating between values placed on items by those in different segments of a society or different societies.

3. The term *phratry*, as used by Meggitt (1965) is perhaps the most accurate anthropological term for *tata andake* in Enga—political units composed of aggregates of clans united by an origin tradition and genealogy that link members to a common ancestor. As discussed elsewhere (Wiessner and Tumu 1998), we have chosen to use *tribe*, a less precise notion, in order to use a term comprehensible to the Enga themselves.

4. History portrays groups in the high country as hunter-gatherers; apparently they maintained a sense of identity as such. However, it is possible that they cultivated small gardens as well.

5. Sites for smaller feasts, both sacred and secular, would not be visible archaeologically.

6. Enga use banana and breadfruit leaves for serving food, not wooden or ceramic vessels.

7. Procedures and rites for the Kepele varied from tribe to tribe and performance to performance. The one given here is a general description of major activities performed at the majority of cult houses.

8. The sacred stones used in Enga ritual were frequently mortars and pestles made by former inhabitants of Enga, perhaps their distant forebears. Pestles represent male ancestors and mortars female ones. The *yupini* figure appears to have been imported from the Sepik region. Sacred stones had been used by surrounding groups in lower fertile valleys prior to the introduction of the sweet potato, however they were new to the Kepele cult of western Enga.

9. Many Enga names, such as clan or cult names, have a special term used to refer to them in song. Aeatee was the song term for Kepele.

10. Enga brides reside in their future husbands' residences for some weeks before marriages are finalized. At this time they sing songs to their husbands' clansmen asking for specific items to be paid as part of the bridewealth (Kyakas and Wiessner 1992). Demands of brides can thus have an impact on the value of items. While stone axes were requested by brides of central Enga within living memory, pearl shells were requested in the east.

REFERENCES

Appadurai, A.
    1986   *The Social Life of Things: Commodities in Cultural Perspective*. Cambridge: Cambridge University Press.

Bus, G.
    1951   The Te Festival or Gift Exchange in Enga (Central Highlands of New Guinea). *Anthropos* 46:813–824.

Chance, M. R. A.
    1967   Attention Structure as the Basis of Primate Rank Orders. *Man* 2:503–518.

Clarke, J.
    1991   Pearlshell Symbolism in Highland Papua New Guinea, with Particular Reference to the Wiru People of Southern Highlands Province. *Oceania* 61:309–339.

Dietler, M.
    1996   Feasts and Commensal Politics in the Political Economy: Food, Power, and Status in Prehistoric Europe. In *Food and the Status Quest: An Interdisciplinary Perspective*, edited by P. Wiessner and W. Schiefenhövel, pp. 87–126. Oxford: Berghahn Books.

Eibl-Eibesfeldt, I.
    1989   *Human Ethology*. New York: Aldine.

Elkin, A.
    1953   Delayed Exchange in Wabag Sub-District, Central Highlands of New Guinea with Notes on Social Organization. *Oceania* 3:161–201.

Feil, D.

1983　A World without Exchange. *Anthropos* 78:89–106.

1984　*Ways of Exchange: The Enga Tee of Papua New Guinea.* St. Lucia: University of Queensland Press.

Gibbs, P.

1977　The Cult from Lyeimi and the Ipili. *Oceania* 48:1–25.

1978　The *Kepele* Ritual of the Western Highlands, Papua New Guinea. *Anthropos* 73:434–447.

Hayden, B.

1996　Feasting in Prehistoric and Traditional Societies. In *Food and the Status Quest: Interdisciplinary Perspectives,* edited by P. Wiessner and W. Schiefenhövel, pp. 127–148. Oxford: Berghahn Books.

Hold, B.

1976　Attention-Structure and Rank Specific Behavior in Preschool Children. In *The Social Structure of Attention,* edited by M. Chance and R. Larsen. London: Wiley.

Khan, M.

1986　*Always Hungry, Never Greedy: Food and Expression of Gender in a Melanesian Society.* Cambridge: Cambridge University Press.

Knauft, B.

1993　*South Coast New Guinea Cultures.* Cambridge: Cambridge University Press.

Kyakas, A., and P. Wiessner

1992　*From inside the Women's House: Enga Women's Lives and Traditions.* Brisbane: Robert Brown.

Lacey, R.

1975　Oral Traditions as History: An Exploration of Oral Sources among the Enga of the New Guinea Highlands. Unpublished Ph.D. thesis, University of Wisconsin.

Lemonnier, P.

1990　*Guerres et Festins: Paix, échanges, et compétition dans les Highlands de Nouvelle-Guinée.* Paris: Maison des Sciences de l'Homme.

1996　Food, Competition and Status in New Guinea. In *Food and the Status Quest: An Interdisciplinary Perspective,* edited by P. Wiessner and W. Schiefenhövel. Oxford: Berghahn Books.

Meggitt, M.

1965　*The Lineage System of the Mae-Enga of New Guinea.* New York: Barnes and Noble.

1972　System and Sub-System: The "Te" Exchange Cycle among the Mae Enga. *Human Ecology* 1:111–123.

1973　The Sun and the Shakers: A Millenarian Cult and Its Transformation in the New Guinea Highlands. *Oceania* 44:1–37 and 109–126.

1974　"Pigs Are Our Hearts!" The Te Exchange Cycle among the Mae Enga of New Guinea. *Oceania* 44:165–203.

1977   *Blood Is Their Argument*. Palo Alto: Mayfield.

Parry, J., and M. Bloch

1989   *Money and the Morality of Exchange*. Cambridge: Cambridge University Press.

Rappaport, R.

1968   *Pigs for the Ancestors: Ritual in the Ecology of a New Guinea People*. New Haven: Yale University Press.

Strathern, A.

1970   The Female and Male Spirit Cults in Mount Hagen. *Man* 5:572–585.

1971   *The Rope of Moka. Big-men and Ceremonial Exchange in Mount Hagen, New Guinea*. Cambridge: Cambridge University Press.

1979a   Men's House, Women's House: The Efficacy of Opposition, Reversal, and Pairing in the Melpa *Amb Kor* Cult. *Journal of the Polynesian Society* 8:37–51.

1979b   Gender, Ideology, and Money in Mt. Hagen. *Man* 4:530–548.

1994   Lines of Power. In *Migration and Transformations: Regional Perspectives in New Guinea*, edited by A. Strathern and G. Stürzenhofecker. pp. 231–256. Pittsburgh: University of Pittsburgh Press.

Thomas, N.

1991   *Entangled Objects: Exchange, Material Culture, and Colonialism in the Pacific*. Cambridge: Harvard University Press.

Waddell, E.

1972   *The Mound Builders: Agricultural Practices, Environment, and Society in the Central Highlands of New Guinea*. Seattle: University of Washington Press

Watson, J.

1965a   The Significance of Recent Ecological Change in the Central Highlands of New Guinea. *Journal of the Polynesian Society* 74:438–450.

1965b   From Hunting to Horticulture in the New Guinea Highlands. *Ethnology* 4:295–309.

1977   Pigs, Fodder, and the Jones Effect in Post-Ipomoean New Guinea. *Ethnology* 6:57–70.

Wiessner, P., and A. Tumu

1998   *Historical Vines: Enga Networks of Exchange, Ritual, and Warfare in Papua New Guinea*. Washington, D.C.: Smithsonian Institution Press.

1999   A Collage of Cults. *Canberra Anthropology* 22 (1): 34–65.

2000   Averting the Bushfire Day: Ain's Cult Revisited. In *Ecology and the Sacred:*
(in press) *Engaging the Anthropology of Roy A. Rappaport*, edited by M. Lambek and E. Messer. Ann Arbor: University of Michigan Press.

Wohlt, P.

1978   *Ecology, Agriculture, and Social Organization: The Dynamics of Group Composition in the Highlands of New Guinea*. University Microfilms: Ann Arbor.

Young, M.

1971   *Fighting with Food: Leadership, Values, and Social Control in a Massim Society*. Cambridge: Cambridge University Press.

5

AKHA FEASTING

AN ETHNOARCHAEOLOGICAL PERSPECTIVE

Michael J. Clarke

This chapter presents the results of two field seasons (1996, 1997) of ethnoarchaeological research on the feasting practices of the Akha of Northern Thailand. The main argument that I will present is that the Akha place great
importance on feasting in their society because (1) feasts function as social
mechanisms that facilitate the creation and maintenance of a life-crisis support
network, and (2) feasts provide arenas for competition between extended family
groups for control over basic socioeconomic resources such as land, labor, and
political influence. I will discuss the nature of the Akha resource base and the
difficulties associated with it, some of the various forms of feast types that function to cope with these difficulties, and lastly, archaeological indicators of feasting activity.

The goals of my research have been to document the ways in which feasting interacts with social structure, to construct a typological system for feasting, and to search for material correlates of feasting activity that might serve as archaeological indicators of feasting activity in the past. For the purpose of this study, I define a feast as any ritualized meal that is consumed by two or more people. By 'ritualized,' I mean that the meal is not eaten solely for sustenance, but rather, is considered as only one facet of a greater social event.

ETHNOGRAPHIC BACKGROUND

The Akha (also known as the Kaw or E-Kaw) are an ethnic minority living in the northern mountainous regions of mainland Southeast Asia. Although their exact population is not known, it is generally believed that they number somewhere around 500,000 individuals (Tribal Research Institute 1995). The vast majority of Akha live in Yunnan Province, China though significant numbers have been migrating southward for the past century or longer, and many now live in Kentung State, Myanmar, as well as Northern Thailand, Laos, and Vietnam. They are members of the Lolo branch of the Tibeto-Burman linguistic group, and it is believed that they (along with most other Hill Tribes) originated from the Tibetan plateau and slowly migrated east and south toward their present homeland. The exact date of the Akha's first entry into Thailand is not known, but it is probably as recent as the late 1800s. Most Akha in Thailand live in Chiang Rai province, and their total population is in excess of 48,500 people living in 258 villages (Tribal Research Institute 1995).

The majority of Akha in Thailand still prefer to live along the mountain ridges at approximately 1,000 m elevation where they can practice a traditional method of shifting cultivation. They grow dry rice, millet, corn, ginger, peppers, peanuts, and a variety of other vegetables for consumption and sale. Recently, due to Thai governmental efforts to halt migration and to eradicate opium production, many Akha now tend sustainable fruit orchards, tea plantations, and cabbage farms. Crop production is often inadequate for consumption needs, and people supplement their diet by gathering wild plants and hunting, and also by occasionally working for wages as farm laborers. Hunting and gathering is not as common as it was in the past. They raise a variety of domestic animals for use in their many sacrifices and ceremonies, as well as for sale. These include many varieties of fowl (chicken, duck, turkey), in addition to cattle, water buffalo, pigs, goats, and dogs. The Akha are pantheists who place great emphasis upon ancestor worship, spirit placation, and rice fertility rituals.

Each Akha village is an independent political unit composed, ideally, of members of at least three patriclans (Lewis 1992:208). The most basic social unit is the extended family, with the oldest male in each family acting as the head of that family. He functions as family priest in regular offerings made to the ancestors. The patrilineages (groups of related extended families within a village) mediate all relationships involving kinship ties, marriage, residential patterns, and rights of succession.

Although the Akha are nominally egalitarian, there are institutionalized administrative positions in each village. A description of these positions is germane to this discussion because the people who hold these offices are key players in the feasting complex. It is their favor which is often courted in feasts held by less influential persons, and they themselves are very active feast givers because their positions are very often based on proof of spiritual potency which is demonstrated through economic success. Oftentimes, their major role in office is to be the focal point of lineage-wide or village-wide feasting.

Foremost among these administrators is the *Dzuma*, or Village Founder-Leader (Kammerer's [1986] term). Each Akha village must have a Village Founder-Leader, and his role is primarily a religious one. He is responsible for all village-wide religious events, of which there are a great many. However, in Akha culture, the realm of the sacred is not clearly distinguished from that of the profane, and consequently, it is often the Village Founder-Leader's duty to arbitrate in disputes, to fine people for social infractions, and to validate decisions made by the council of elders regarding secular issues. He is considered the 'Father of the Village,' which has both familial and authoritarian connotations. Ideally, the Village Founder-Leader is a ritually pure man who was the first settler in a new location. Once his position is established, it is considered hereditary. However, it is not unknown for men to be removed from this office by the assembled village elders. If the Village Founder-Leader is a strong-willed man with many relatives in his village, he can be extremely powerful and influential. He is always invited to feasts as it is in everyone's best interest to court his favor.

There are two more quasi-political positions that are recognized by the Akha, both of which are religious in nature. The first is a ritual specialist called a *Bu Moe*. These men are Ritual Reciters (Kammerer's [1986] term), and they are responsible for performing rites for individuals in times of sickness, death, and other such matters relating to the spirit world. This position carries a great amount of respect, and in any village where a Reciter resides, he will be an influential man. Furthermore, almost all religious services that he provides involve the sacrifice of animals and a subsequent feast. He is a key player in the Akha feasting complex, and it is often through using his sacred services that an Akha family can host a feast that will have significant social consequences in the secular realm of village politics.

The third official village position is that of the *Baji*, the village Blacksmith. In traditional times, the Blacksmith would have been an important person to have in a village, and thus, he was treated with great respect and ritualized deference. Today, however, the Akha import their tools from Thai market towns, and the role of the Blacksmith has been reduced to its ceremonial minimum. Nevertheless, he is still an influential man, and in terms of Akha cosmology, he is next only to the Village Founder-Leader in importance.

All villages also have a less important political headman who tends to deal with more secular village-wide issues such as relations with the Thai government. The headman is usually appointed by a council of elders in whose hands the real power lies. The elders are all of the men in the village over the age of about fifty. They, as grandfathers, are the paternal heads of multiple households, and they each look out for the interests of their respective families in terms of the village decision-making process. For example, when the village must decide whose land to appropriate in order to build a new school, the elders will hold council and make the final decision. In the villages in which I have conducted research, I have noted that certain elders will form coalitions and essentially dominate village politics via their joint control of the majority of the population. These coalitions are formed and maintained through vigorous and ongoing feasting between the parties involved. The elders are also the figureheads of any individual's main support group, the lineage. As such, their households are often the location of lineage solidarity feasts, and it is through the elders and their indulgence that junior members may move up the ranks of influence and security within the lineage. Elders play a pivotal role in the feasting complex, and, by tradition, all elders are welcome to attend any feast that is given within the village (although they usually only attend those feasts given by friends and relatives). This tradition serves to illustrate the dynamic relationship between sociopolitical power and feasting in Akha society.

THEORETICAL BACKGROUND AND DISCUSSION

The Akha are a transegalitarian society, as discussed by Hayden (Chapter 2). This means that, for the most part, their society maintains an egalitarian ethos, but that there are sizable differences in wealth and power between individuals and family groups. These material-resource and social-power inequities result in the emergence of subtle class-like distinctions. However, the nature of the resource base of many traditional transegalitarian societies (which will be discussed presently) generally does not allow social-class distinctions to develop fully, and there are many instances, of which Leach's (1956) study of the Kachin is the seminal example, where there is actually a regression toward greater social equality and individual self-autonomy. Table 5.1 gives some examples of the material inequities that exist between three of the richest men and three of the poorest men in my main study village of Mae Salep.

TABLE 5.1

Comparison of Rich and Poor Families

Family Heads	No. in Family	Producers	House (m²)	Land (m²)	Buffalos	Sales ($US)
Rich Men						
Latche (a)	8	5	121.1	60,800	12	340
Latche (b)	27	15	236.25	84,800	0	3,600
Latche (c)	7	4	175	43,200	19	4,504
Poor Men						
Latche (x)	5	4	34.8	20,800	0	0
Labu (y)	5	3	70	12,800	0	0
Latche (z)	3	2	77	11,200	0	0

Note: "Producers" is the number of workers in the home. Buffalos are included because they are the pinnacle of wealth accumulation. "Sales" only regards animal sales for the years 1995 and 1996. Latche (b) has no buffalos only because he sold a large herd the year previously, and he owns many cattle.

In Akha society, socioeconomic inequity, competition, and aggrandizing behavior emerges primarily between the lineages and clans as a whole, rather than between individuals, and this, more than anything, serves to define transegalitarianism in the Akha case. Individual households in Akha society, even if they are rich, do not become socially dominant in the way that individual households become dominant in more complex transegalitarian or stratified societies where power is more easily centralized. Particular lineages, on the other hand, can and do become socially dominant. For the purpose of this study, I follow Hayden and Maneeprasert (1996) and define clans as patrilineally related families living in separate communities, and lineages as patrilineally related families (smaller segments of clans) living in the same community.

Clan/lineage relations among the Akha are structured in a systematic way through long tradition and cultural norms. They are both the explicit village sociopolitical structure, and the implicit supraregional sociopolitical structure (Kammerer 1986). Feasting is integral to the dynamics of clan/lineage relations, and as such, is an "institution" (in the same sense as parliament, or the democratic system) that can be used and manipulated by individuals and groups to effect changes in the sociopolitical sphere.

The nature of the Akha economy affects both social structure and feasting practices. Hill Tribe swidden horticulture allows for a relatively high population density, compared to hunting and gathering, and consequently, presents unique organizational challenges. Hill Tribe villages, which may have up to several hundred people in residence, are, of necessity, segmented into various allied factions. In Akha society, the prime dividing line seems to be lineage/clan membership.

However, because the ownership of swidden fields (in traditional times) was only temporary, and families eventually had to change residence once the land was no longer fertile, the long-term (multigenerational) monopolization of the resource base by one allied group was not possible. Furthermore, because of the availability of new land, socially weaker and subdominant groups always had the option of moving out of a village and farming in a new locale. Consequently, the formation of a wealthy land-owning gentry class was not possible. No one could depend on long-term economic security, and even mere economic survival was a precarious and transitory thing for every family. Hence, there was, and still is, a need for a structured and dependable life-crisis support network.

All individuals in Akha society are aware of the precariousness of their economic situation, and most people realize that they may have to depend on the help of friends and family when they are faced with hard times (i.e., crop failures, sickness, disputes, or other misfortunes). Furthermore, at certain points in the agricultural year it is necessary to organize cooperative work groups (for field clearing, for example), which are essentially based on friends and family reciprocating labor. It is important to maintain these relationships.

There are many ways in which a drastic change of fortune can occur. The literature makes ample reference to bandits and armies robbing entire villages (i.e., Lewis 1969, 1970; Kammerer 1986); rich individuals are sometimes held for ransom; crops can receive inadequate or excessive rain, and disease or insects can destroy entire fields. In the past, famine was not unknown among the Hill Tribes. For instance, some of the richest families in Sam Soong village lost almost all of their pigs to disease in the past two years; one family lost nearly 80 pigs (see Fig. 5.1).

The Akha resource base is in some ways similar to that of a generalized hunting and gathering people's resource base: it is fluctuating, to some degree unpredictable, and not strictly nucleated. In other ways, however, it is similar to the resource base of more complex societies: it is labor intensive; increased extraction labor does not make resources vulnerable to overexploitation but increases total output; the economy allows for the production of occasional surpluses; not all land is of the same quality; and land that is cultivated is effectively private property.

On the basis of the field data collected, it is clear that to cope with these unique resource qualities, the Akha employ a mixture of hunter-gatherer and complex-society social strategies, especially feasting techniques. The typical hunter-gather problems (the precariousness and fluctuations of the food supply) are dealt with by alliance formation and mutual assistance created in part by feasting *within* the clan and lineage, and to some extent, within the village. There is little or no aggrandizing or competitive behavior at these feasts. Some examples of intralineage solidarity feasts are the thirteen annual family ancestor offerings, the sickness-curing feasts, and newborn naming feasts.

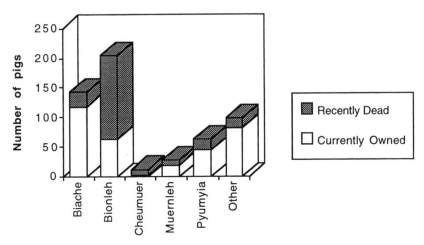

Figure 5.1. Compound bar graph illustrating the number of pigs that each clan in Sam Soong village owns, and how many of those pigs recently died of disease.

The typical complex-society problems that the Akha encounter (the competition for labor, spouses, land, and political control in general) are dealt with to a great extent by feasting *between* the clans and lineages (e.g., feasts that foster alliances between groups such as weddings, or which are grandiose enough to validate a claim to power such as funerals). These larger feasts serve to advertise the wealth and productivity of the host lineages. These kinds of feasts exhibit some mildly aggrandizing attributes (such as food delicacies and an abundance of alcohol and narcotics) and have the emic purpose of being impressive. The more ostentatious Akha funeral feasts fall into this category.

Advertising household and/or lineage success is adaptive and advantageous for at least two reasons. First, because it attracts and maintains a large and reliable work force in the form of healthy, hard-working wives from influential families marrying into the family and relatives moving into the village. Since village political matters (especially litigations) are often decided by the votes of the elder men who represent the various lineages in the community, it stands to any person's advantage to have as many relatives as possible in their village. Furthermore, hard-working wives increase a farm's production level. Second, success advertisement is advantageous because it encourages deference. Wealthy men are seen as both blessed and intelligent. Their opinions hold more weight than an average person's.

It is more appropriate to conceptualize the above division of feasting activity

—hunter-gather-type solidarity feasting and complex-society competitive feasting—as two degrees, rather than as two categories of feasting activity. They are not mutually exclusive divisions. A wedding feast, for example, will tend to be promotional, and therefore competitive in nature, but will also always foster a certain degree of intraclan solidarity and alliance enhancement. A poor family's wedding will emphasize intralineage solidarity (most guests being from within the lineage) whereas a rich family's wedding will emphasize the promotional aspects (many guests being from other lineages). This is why it is so difficult to create feasting classification categories based on function alone; although each feast category may share a structural homogeneity (i.e., all weddings have a certain prescribed ordering of ritual and food consumption), most feasts have a variety of functions, which are all manifested to varying degrees. The degree to which any function is made manifest, whether it be social bonding, wealth advertisement, or outright debt fostering, is contingent upon many factors. The primary factors seem to be the host's wealth, relative sociopolitical position, and ambitions.

AKHA FEAST TYPES

Akha life is rife with feasting. Some feasts are small, involving only a few people and the ritualized consumption of a very small amount of food, whereas other feasts are enormous, involving many hundreds of people and the consumption of several water buffalos, pigs, and chickens over a period of weeks. There is no significant secular or religious event that is not accompanied by a feast of some kind, except for possibly a few political meetings. For instance, the Akha hold feasts for purifications, divorces, menopause, field ceremonies, and all initiations of office.

Feast quality (i.e., expensive, overtly public, or modest and subdued) is in most cases a function of the distance of the guests (genetically, geographically, and physically) from the host. Greater, more intense, and more symbolic measures are required to communicate social messages to people who are farther apart. In most cases, it is only the larger types of feasts, such as weddings and funerals, that have guests participating in them who are not in some way already intimate with the host.

A large variety of occasions merit a feast in Akha society. What all feasts have in common, however, is that there is always some sort of meat consumed. Because the daily Akha diet consists mostly of rice and vegetables, meat of any kind is considered a treat. In this sense, all feasts contain a desirable delicacy and entitle the host to a certain degree of gratitude and respect.

Feasts are generally held inside a home. The young men do most of the cooking, except for the rice, and the middle-aged men act as servers. Women and men sit in opposite halves of the house, and both male and female elders are given seats of honor upon a raised sleeping platform. There is very little ostentation displayed at Akha feasts by the host. It is never considered appropriate to brag or to boast. However, some of the larger Akha feast "types" can be characterized as promotional in nature because they contain a great variety of food delicacies, alcohol, and other desirable goods. It is often at these larger feasts where the women will don their full silver ornamental headdresses and accompanying bangles, which are a family's main repository of surplus wealth (Fig. 5.2). They literally display their family's wealth upon the top of their heads (although they see it simply as formal wear).

Table 5.2 is a summary of most of the important and more common Akha feasts. It is in no way exhaustive (for a more detailed account see Clarke 1998). Many of the feasts listed, such as purification and penalty feasts, have a wide variety of possible forms and functions. Some purifications are simply small ceremonies meant to cleanse a holy place, others are larger events that relate to specific problems involving an individual, whereas still others operate more in the social realm and are concerned with social events such as divorce and adultery. Furthermore, some of the larger feast types, especially the funeral, are actually a series of small and large feasts spread over a period of time.

Figure 5.2. Elder lineage women and peer guests feasting at the women's table of honor during an Akha marriage feast. Note the elaborate and valuable headdresses and beadwork worn for this occasion. (Photo by B. Hayden)

TABLE 5.2

Akha Feast Types

Feast Type	Attendance	Cost (US$)	Function
Ancestor offering	3–10	$5	Family solidarity
Newborn naming	3–7	$5	Family solidarity
Sickness curing	10–25	$20–$50	Solidarity / allies
Butchers'	5–15	$10–$15	Solidarity / allies
Workmen's	5–30	$10–$50	Acquire labor
Penalty	5–10	$2–$150	Social control
Purification	5–50	$5–$300	Solidarity / control
Gate rebuilding	5–10	$10–$30	Village solidarity
Lords of Earth	5–10	$10–$30	Village solidarity
Harvest	Each household	$5–$20	Village solidarity
New Year's	Each household	$5–$75	Village solidarity
Dzuma's annual	(?)10–50	?	?
Wedding	20–200	$25–$500	Promotion
New house	20–300	$25–$600	Promotion
Menopause	(?) 20–100	$100–$250	Promotion
Funeral	15–1,000	$25–$1,000+	Extreme promotion

The feasts shown in Table 5.2 have been arranged in loose order of size, start-ing from the smallest and most intimate at the top, and finishing with the largest and most public at the bottom. The first two feasts, ancestor offerings and new-born naming, are small household events that are held fairly frequently, the an-cestor offerings being made thirteen times a year. A chicken, along with some rice, whiskey, and tea is consumed at these events.

Butchers', curing, and workmen's feasts are medium-sized events that operate mostly at the lineage level. Curing feasts can be given to people, usually children, whether they are ill or not. Curing feasts are an opportunity for lineage elders to meet, reassert their spiritual potency (as part of the ritual), and offer the younger clan members an opportunity to ingratiate themselves (Fig. 5.3). Butchers' feasts are given to the elders when an animal (almost always a pig) is slaughtered for sale. Theoretically, all village elders are welcome, but in my field observations, I have noted that only those elders related to, or closely allied to, the hosting butcher attend. Workmen's feasts are purely secular. They are a form of recogni-tion for men who have helped with a building project (usually a house). These co-operative work feasts generally include lineage members, and they are characterized by the serving of dog meat (a delicacy not appropriate for ritual consumption) and copious amounts of whiskey.

Figure 5.3. Lineage elders (the three men at the left), a Ritual Reciter (center rear), and the younger lineage host (right, holding child) at a curing feast. One of the lineage elders is tying a string around the child's wrist for spiritual protection as the Reciter looks on. (Photo by B. Hayden)

Purifications and penalty feasts have a wide range of forms. Most are small in size, and they are held infrequently. These feasts are a means of enforcing conformity to social norms and of asserting the power of the ruling elder males. It is the council of elders who decide the size, and hence the cost, of penalty and purification feasts.

There are five annual village-wide feasting events: the ceremonial gate rebuilding, the offering to the Lords (i.e., Spirits) of the Earth, the harvest festival (also known as the swinging festival), the New Year's festival, and the annual feast given by the Village Founder-Leader (*Yo la la*). The first two annual feasts, the gate rebuilding and the offering to the Lords of the Earth, are small feasts that the elders celebrate at the location of the ceremonial gate and the village water source, respectively. The expense for these feasts comes out of a village fund. The harvest and New Year festivals are typified by each family feasting in their own home, with possibly the elders invited to a special meal at the Village Founder-Leader's house. For the harvest festival, the villagers will purchase shares of a water buffalo, which they will take away and consume at home. For the New Year festival they generally eat pork and drink copious amounts of whiskey. Some households will have many guests visiting them during the New Year festival and may be inclined to spend a fairly large sum of money. The annual Village Founder-Leader's feast is considered a payback to the villagers for the support they have given him, and it is also a time to thank the special protective spirit of the Village Founder-Leader.

The last four feasts outlined in Table 5.2, wedding, new house, menopause, and funeral feasts, tend to be the largest and most costly for individuals. It is at these feasts where obvious delicacies, such as candy, betel nut (a narcotic), and beer start to appear on a regular basis. It is not uncommon (in recent years) for printed invitation cards to be delivered to guests. All of these characteristics point to the fact that these feasts are intended to be grandiose and, hence, promotional.

Wedding feasts can vary greatly in size, depending upon the wealth of the host, but in general they are quite expensive (relative to income) and last for three days. One or two large pigs and several chickens are usually consumed. New House feasts are very similar to wedding feasts. They tend to have more guests but are shorter in duration, lasting for only one full day and night. Menopause feasts are events that initiate women into a new ceremonial role, that of the White-Skirted Woman, and they are not given to every woman, only to a select few who qualify and can afford the necessary ceremonial sacrifices.

Menopause feasts can be very costly: several large pigs, numerous chickens, and in some areas, goats are required in order to perform the ceremony. If the ceremony is widely publicized, then the family may also have to kill a buffalo in order to feed the many guests who will arrive. There is no compulsion to perform this ceremony once menopause is reached, and, in fact, Kammerer (1986) has noted that it is usually the husband who insists that the ceremony be completed. It is very honorable to have a White-Skirted Woman as a member of one's household; it is also thought to bring great blessing and fortune, but more importantly, from an ethnoarchaeological perspective, it is an opportunity for a family to display its success, wealth, and desirability of affiliation to the people of the general region.

Akha funerals are by far the most emically important of all ceremonial events. The Akha people attach great religious importance to them, but funerals also fulfill very practical social functions. They are a venue at which successful and powerful households can reassert their claim to distinction and deference, and they are an avenue along which lineages and clans can compete for status and recognition. A wealthy family's funeral for an elder will consist of the sacrifice of 1–7 water buffalo, 5–20 pigs, and numerous other animals. The family will pay the presiding ritual specialist and his assistants in silver. Funerals are incredibly expensive relative to the income of the people. The cost of a funeral can easily be the equivalent of several years' income. However, donations for the funeral very often are collected from a wide range of clan and lineage members.

A FEASTING EXAMPLE

I would now like to relate the events surrounding a specific Akha wedding feast, which will illustrate some of the points that I have made thus far. The wedding took place in an Akha village called Mae Salep, situated near the Myanmar border. There are nine different clans represented in Mae Salep, and the total village population is 267. One clan, the Latches, forms the majority of the population, and it is this clan that essentially governs village life. The Latche families have formed a close alliance with the second most populous clan, the Labus, and together the elders of these two clans dominate village politics. This alliance was created by, and is maintained by, reciprocal feasting between the various families within these two clans.

This particular wedding feast was held for the son of the most prominent Labu man in the village, Mae Salep's Ritual Reciter. This is a very traditional household, and this wedding was in many ways a very typical example of a large Akha feast.

The feast took place in the home of the father of the groom and lasted for three days. On the day preceding the actual celebrations, the groom and the bride performed a brief ritual involving the passing of an egg back and forth between them. Although this ritual is considered the actual initiation of the marriage, it is given relatively little importance. No one is expected to pay attention to this ceremony; instead, the members of the household were busy making the preparations for the feast. The feast itself is considered the public announcement and recognition of the union. This illustrates the role that ritualized public consumption of food plays in the formation of the Akha community structure.

In order to feed the guests, the father had to provide a large, fat, corn-fed, castrated boar, as well as several chickens. This in itself is a considerable economic investment, but there were also large expenditures made on other delicacies such as whiskey, candy, cigarettes, and on staples such as rice, cabbage, and tea. The various meals at the three-day event were truly excessive in terms of the amount and variety of food when compared to daily fare. Meat itself is a delicacy in Akha society. The wedding also provided people with an opportunity to gamble and to smoke opium.

Over the three days, more than 75 people attended, although many did not participate for the full duration. It is significant to note that elders from other villages came to participate. These men were representatives of related lineages living in nearby villages, and it was important to maintain contact with them because the Akha generally relocate several times during their lifetime, frequently to relatives' villages (Kammerer 1986). The host also made a point of inviting the generally disliked Thai school administrators. These men look down on the Akha because of their poverty, but the Akha can do little about this because they often depend on the head administrator's cooperation in regards to matters of citizenship and land rights. If the wedding had been considered a purely festive event, then the host would probably not have invited these Thai administrators, but because these men are very powerful, the host used the wedding as an opportunity to court their favor.

In order to cook such copious amounts of food, the family had to have (or borrow) a large assortment of cooking and serving vessels. These included one very large wok 50 cm in diameter, and four pots, one 55 cm in diameter, one 45 cm, and two 30 cm in diameter (Fig. 5.4). They also had about 50 serving bowls, 25 drinking glasses, and 27 blue ceramic whiskey cups. What should be noted is that these figures are far in excess of the average Akha family's daily cooking/serving vessel assemblage. Normally, a family of this size will need only one or two woks of about 30 cm in diameter, and two or three pots ranging from 15 cm to 30 cm in diameter. On average, they will own ten to fifteen serving vessels and around five drinking glasses. This difference is significant because the relative size and number of cooking and serving vessels is a strong archaeological indicator of feasting

Figure 5.4. Large cooking pots and woks used for preparing large quantities of food for large feasts. (Photo by M. Clarke)

activity. My research has determined that families who are actively engaged in ongoing feasting will own a disproportionate amount of these vessels, and that the remains of these vessels will be deposited in the middens surrounding their house.

The wedding feast served as a solidarity-reinforcing event on many levels. Firstly, in terms of the greater community support group, all of the elder males representing the various lineages in the village were in attendance, with the exception of those who had converted to Christianity and thus had opted out of the traditional village cooperative unit. Their absence was very evident, and made a very clear statement of disassociation. At the lineage level, it is worth noting that Latche clan members assumed prominent roles as organizers, workers, and servers in this Labu family wedding, and this was a very symbolic act of friendship and cooperation, which is a reflection of the sociopolitical alliance that the two clans have formed in Mae Salep.

On an individual level, this particular feast served to integrate the young groom and his new household into the greater lineage support group, and it also served as a platform on which his father, the host, could advertise his family's success and revalidate his position as the village Ritual Reciter. For instance, at one point in the wedding, the young groom walked among the assembled guests and shared a small drink of whiskey with the men present. These men then made a small cash donation to the household. This is considered "begging for blessing," and the money is to help defray the cost of the feast and to help the young couple set up a household. However, it is also a symbolic act of inclusion within the greater lineage and, as such, the people are expressing their cooperative ethos while the young groom is acknowledging his indebtedness to his lineage.

ARCHAEOLOGICAL INDICATORS OF FEASTING ACTIVITY

I have alluded to a number of archaeological correlates of feasting activity in the preceding sections, but I would now like to discuss them in a more systematic fashion. Although the following observations were made in a culturally specific context, and no ethnoarchaeological generalization can be considered a cross-cultural archaeological truism, the relationships that I present have been structured in a manner that is largely based on the material requisites for feeding large groups of people simultaneously using traditional technology. These relationships are not intended to be a checklist of evidence for archaeologists to consult when they find similar data at their sites, but rather, it is hoped they will provide insights that will help archaeologists explain hitherto unexplained phenomena, as well as being complementary to other data that is used in archaeological analyses of feasting. The systematic occurrence of large-scale feasting is evident in the multimodal size distribution of cooking vessels in large assemblages such as those of entire villages (Fig. 5.5).

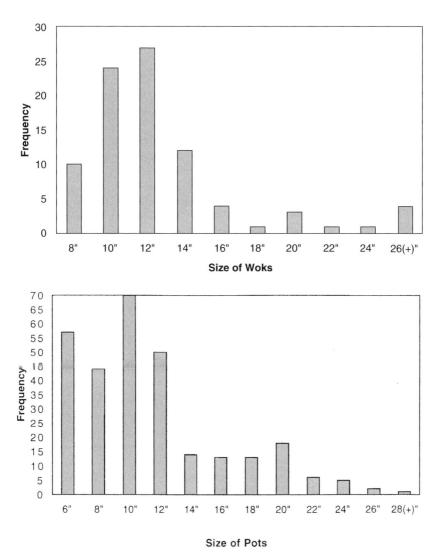

Figure 5.5. Histograms showing the multimodal size distribution of woks and pots in an Akha village. Sizes of both woks and pots in the 6- to 14-inch diameter range represent normal food-preparation vessels. Modal peaks in the 20- to 26-inch range represent food-preparation vessels for feasts of increasing sizes.

COOKING VESSELS

As already noted for wedding feasts, the size and number of cooking vessels can be used as a measure of feasting activity. Vessels greater than a certain size are really only practical to use when one is cooking for large numbers of people and large volumes of food must be produced. Furthermore, daily meals generally consist of a maximum of two to three dishes (excluding rice) though it is not uncommon for feasts to consist of five to ten different dishes. In order to be able to prepare such a wide variety of dishes at the same time, several cooking vessels are necessary for each dish. The average Akha household consists of approximately ten people, and a family will usually provide for its daily cooking needs with one or two small woks, three or four small pots and one large pot approximately 50 cm in diameter to cook pig food in. In all cases, households that exceeded this norm in the cooking vessel assemblage did so because they owned, or borrowed, vessels for feasting purposes.

SERVING VESSELS

The relative number of serving vessels per household (or other corporate group) may be indicative of feasting. It would seem obvious that everyone would have a functional minimum of these items, but families with excessive numbers must use them for other purposes. In traditional Akha villages, no families acted as merchants for such vessels. In some societies, special elaborate serving vessels have a specific feasting function; however, this is not the case for the Akha. The only thing that is indicative of feasting for the Akha, in terms of serving vessels, is their number.

An average Akha family may own 10–15 serving bowls and plates, 1–10 drinking glasses, and 4–6 rice baskets. For some of the larger feasts, hundreds of these vessels are required. Not only are more vessels required because of the greater number of guests, but also because of the larger variety of food and drink available.

No one ever owns the hundreds of vessels needed for the very large feasts. Instead, they borrow what is needed from their relatives. However, those households that engage in regular small- to medium-scale feasting always own an adequate number of serving vessels for these events, and this is always greater than the village average.

TROPHY BONES

Very often after a feast, the host will save the jaw or horns of a large sacrificed animal for display. It must be remembered that meat is not a daily component of the diet, and the offering of an expensive animal for sacrifice is reason enough to gain prestige. The display of water buffalo horns is particularly prestigious, as the sacrifice of one or more water buffalo at a funeral is a very auspicious event.

Much more common however, is the display of pig mandibles; some homes can have as many as twenty displayed on the wall (see Fig. 2.8).

COOKING FIRES

The relative size and number of hearths is also a good indicator of feasting activity. This may prove difficult to recognize archaeologically. Families that actively participate in traditional feasting often have large kitchens with extra hearthrings and braziers. It is frequently necessary to expand the area of the hearth for a feast. In the case of the Akha, very traditional homes, with the division between male and female halves, have discrete ash dumps for each hearth in the home. This is because women and men maintain their own hearth, and both men and woman have a separate entrance to the house. Each sex dumps the ash outside of their respective entrances, indicating the two major cooking areas.

TEMPORARY KITCHENS

The construction of temporary kitchens may also be archaeologically recognizable. These would only be needed for very large feasts. Their construction is sometimes necessary if the existing kitchen is not large enough to accommodate the feasting preparation. In the Akha case, and I suspect in most other cases, temporary or extra kitchens are added on to original permanent kitchens. This was because most of the implements needed for cooking could be shared between the two, and also because the preparations are easier to coordinate that way.

GARBAGE FIRES

Garbage fires with many feasting remains in them are very indicative of feasting in the Akha case. Normally, small bits of refuse are tossed away indiscriminately, or swept through the space in the floorboards. Large amounts of trash are tossed away, downslope, from the house into a toft area. There are only two occasions that seem to merit the effort of a garbage fire. One is the generation of a large amount of waste produced from some kind of plant-processing activity, husking corn for example. These types of garbage fires, because of the singularity of their contents, produce a very homogeneous type of ash. The second occasion where a garbage fire is necessary is following a large feast, and the ash from these fires always contains a very large variety of contents, from bone and food remains, to whiskey bottles and broken ceramics. Garbage fires were always lit outside, in front of the house.

FAUNAL REMAINS

The Akha predilection for dicing up their meat completely, bones and all, created some problems in terms of the analysis of faunal remains. Pigs and chickens are almost completely consumed. The people chew and swallow the well-cooked bones, and most of those that they cannot manage to ingest are generally eaten by the numerous dogs and pigs that are always at hand. This consumption pattern, of course, must change when people are eating large animals such as cows or water buffalos. Although I have never had the opportunity to witness a water buffalo being butchered, I am sure that they would not have attempted to completely dice up and eat such large, thick bones.

The remains of a small cow that was eaten at a new house feast provided some minor insight into large-mammal taphonomic processes. It was only at these large feasts that an entire animal was ever eaten all at once and in one location. Consequently, these are the only times when large portions of the skeleton of an animal are ever deposited all in one dumpsite. In all other Akha cases, and I suspect in many tribal societies everywhere, portions of butchered animals are distributed among friends and family members throughout the village. Consequently, the bones are deposited in different middens throughout the village.

It is possible that the Akha might choose to butcher and preserve (i.e., smoke or salt) a large animal, and then deposit its bones all in one dumpsite, but I have never seen this done (although Lewis [1969] claims that in Burma they salt and dry large game animals). The practical necessity of immediate consumption aside, it also serves a greater social function to divide up the meat. In one instance, a family caught a gopher and rather than just eating the small animal themselves, they divided it up into quarters and spread them around to their relatives in the village.

Finally, faunal remains in human graves have sometimes been cited as evidence of feasting. In the Akha case, this seems to hold true. According to Lewis (1969), at different points in the funeral, feasting food is offered to the deceased, and some sacrificed animals are hung over the coffin. They are subsequently buried with the body.

SUMMARY

I believe that feasting is a social phenomenon of great significance that often leaves recognizable traces in the archaeological record. There is a growing body of evidence that suggests that promotional or competitive feasting may have been of central importance in the initial transition of early humans from simple hunter-gatherers to complex horticulturalists (see Bender 1978; Hayden 1990, 1992a, 1992b; Keswani 1994; Liden 1995). The ethnographic record is able to lend insight into the various ways in which feasting can play a dynamic role in the creation and maintenance of social structure.

Studying the Akha, as one specific example of complex horticultural-society feasting practices, has provided us with some rudimentary insights into the role that feasting can play in traditional nonmoney economies. It is evident that in Akha society, feasting functions primarily as a social mechanism that creates and maintains a life-crisis support group, bringing people together in solidarity-enhancing events. Similarly, feasting can be used as an articulation point between allied corporate groups (in this case clans and lineages). The feast provides potential allies with a venue to express their desire to ally and to prove the sincerity of that desire through gifts of highly desired food, drink, and narcotics. Feasting can also be an avenue for people to jockey for power positions within their greater support group.

Related to feasting as a way of maintaining a support group is the Akha's use of feasting as a form of wealth and success advertisement. Promoting the economic success of the household allows families to attract and hold high-quality labor and spouses, to create and maintain trading contacts, and to engender sociopolitical deference within their community. In fact, it is considered necessary for officeholders (those who make special claims based on spiritual potency) to constantly revalidate their social position through the hosting of regular feasts. In Akha culture, economic success is seen to be based on spiritual purity and power (similar to the idea of 'mana' in the South Pacific). Blessings are given by the ancestors and are a sign of sacred connectiveness. Therefore, people who make claims to official political power positions must be able to demonstrate their ritual potency through economic success. Similar concepts pervade many other Southeast Asian cultures and feasting complexes, as argued by Friedman (1975).

Much work still needs to be done in order to advance our understanding of feasting among the Hill Tribes. There are several other groups that inhabit the mountainous regions of mainland Southeast Asia that also have highly developed feasting complexes. As yet, little is known about the feasting of these other groups. The practice of feasting is closely tied to the economics of production, and although a great deal of data have been gathered on the specifics of Akha feasts, much more data is still required on the economy which makes this feasting possible.

REFERENCES

Alting von Geusau, Leo
    1983   Dialectics of Akhazan: The Interiorization of a Perennial Minority Group. In *Highlanders of Thailand*, edited by Jon Mckinnon and Wanat Bhruksasre, pp. 243–277. Kuala Lumpur: Oxford University Press.
Appadurai, A.
    1986   *The Social Life of Things: Commodities in Cultural Perspective*. Cambridge: Cambridge University Press.

Arnold, J.

    1993   Labor and the Rise of Complex Hunter-Gatherers. *Journal of Anthropological Archaeology* 12:75–119.

Blitz, John

    1993   Big Pots for Big Shots: Feasting and Storage in a Mississippian Community. *American Antiquity* 58 (2): 80–96.

Bender, B.

    1978   Gatherer-Hunter to Farmer: A Social Perspective. *World Archaeology* 10:204–222

Blau, P.

    1964   *Exchange and Power in Social Life.* New York: John Wiley.

Blumberg, Rae Lesser

    1978   *Stratification: Socioeconomic and Sexual Inequality.* University of California, San Diego: Wm. C. Brown.

Cashdan, E.

    1980   Egalitarianism among Hunters and Gatherers. *American Anthropologist* 82:116–120.

Clarke, Michael J.

    1998   Feasting among the Akha: An Ethnoarchaeological Case Study. M.A. thesis, Department of Archaeology, Simon Fraser University, Burnaby, B.C.

Cooper, Robert

    1984   *Resource Scarcity and the Hmong Response.* Singapore: Singapore University Press.

Crabtree, Pam

    1990   Zooarchaeology and Complex Societies: Some Uses of Faunal Analysis for the Study of Trade, Social Status, and Ethnicity. In *Advances in Archaeological Method and Theory*, vol. 2, edited by M. Schiffer, pp. 155–160. Tucson: University of Arizona Press.

Dietler, Michael

    1990   Driven by Drink: The Role of Drinking in the Political Economy and the Case of Early Iron Age France. *Journal of Anthropological Archaeology* 9: 352–406.

Douglas, M.

    1984   Standard Uses of Food: Introduction. In *Food and the Social Order*, edited by M. Douglas, pp. 1–39. New York: Columbia University Press.

Earle, T.

    1997   *How Chiefs Come to Power: The Political Economy of Prehistory.* Stanford: Stanford University Press.

Falvey, Lindsay

    1977   Ruminants in the Highlands of Northern Thailand. Thai-Australian Highland Agronomy Project, Tribal Research Institute, Chiang Mai University, Chiang Mai.

Fiddes, Nick

    1991   *Meat: A Natural Symbol.* New York: Routledge.

Friedman, Jonathan
 1975 Tribes, States, and Transformations. In *Marxist Analyses and Social Anthropology*, edited by M. Bloch, pp. 161–202. London: Malaby Press.
Hanson, Rev. O.
 1913 *The Kachins: Their Customs and Traditions*. New York: American Baptist Mission Press.
Hayden, Brian
 1990 Nimrods, Piscators, Pluckers, and Planters: The Emergence of Food Production. *Journal of Anthropological Archaeology* 9:31–69.
 1992a Ecology and Complex Hunter/Gatherers. In *A Complex Culture of the British Columbia Plateau*, edited by B. Hayden. Vancouver: University of British Columbia Press.
 1992b Models of Domestication. In *Transitions to Agriculture in Prehistory*, edited by Anne Birgitte Gebauer and T. D. Price, pp. 273–299. Santa Fe: Prehistory Press.
 1995a Pathways to Power: Principles for Creating Socioeconomic Inequalities. In *Foundations of Social Inequality*, edited by T. Douglas Price and Gary Feinman, pp. 15–85. New York: Plenum.
 1995b A New Overview of Domestication. In *Last Hunters—First Farmers*, edited by T. D. Price and A. Gebauer, pp. 273–299. Santa Fe: School of American Research Press.
 1996 Feasting in Prehistoric and Traditional Societies. In *Food and the Status Quest: An Interdisciplinary Perspective*, edited by P. Wiessner and W. Schiefenhövel, pp. 127–148. Oxford: Berghahn Books.
 1998 The Dynamics of Wealth and Poverty in the Transegalitarian Societies of Southeast Asia. Unpublished paper, Dept. of Archaeology, Simon Fraser University, Burnaby, Canada.
Hayden, Brian, and Ralana Maneeprasert
 1996 *Feasting among the Akha in Thailand*. Unpublished report to the National Research Council of Thailand.
Janse, Olov
 1944 *The Peoples of French Indochina*. Smithsonian Institution War Background Studies Number Nineteen, Washington, D.C.
Kammerer, Cornelia
 1986 Gateway to the Akha World: Kinship, Ritual, and Community among Highlanders of Thailand. Ph.D. dissertation, Anthropology Department, University of Chicago, Chicago.
Keswani, Priscilla Schuster
 1994 The Social Context of Animal Husbandry in Early Agricultural Societies: Ethnographic Insights and an Archaeological Example from Cyprus. *Journal of Anthropological Archaeology* 13:255–277.
Kim, Seung-Og
 1994 Burials, Pigs, and Political Prestige in Neolithic China. *Current Anthropology* 35 (2): 119–131.

Kirsch, A. T.

1973   *Feasting and Social Oscillation: A Working Paper on Religion and Society in Upland Southeast Asia.* Southeast Asian Data Paper No. 92. Ithaca: Cornell University, Dept. of Asian Studies.

Leach, Edmund

1956   *Political Systems of Highland Burma.* Boston: Beacon Press.

Lefevre, E.

1995   *Travels in Laos: The Fate of the 'Sip Song Pana' and 'Muong Sing'* (1894–1896). Bangkok: White Lotus.

Lewis, Paul

1969   *Ethnographic Notes on the Akhas of Burma*: Vols. 1–2. Human Relations Area Files, New Haven, Connecticut.

1970   *Ethnographic Notes on the Akhas of Burma*: Vols. 3–4. Human Relations Area Files, New Haven, Connecticut.

1991   *Thai Hill Tribes Phrase Book: Lonely Planet Language Survival Kit.* Victoria, Australia: Lonely Planet Publications.

1992   Basic Themes in Akha Culture. In *The Highland Heritage: Collected Essays on Upland North Thailand,* edited by Anthony Walker. Singapore: Double-Six Press.

Lewis, Paul, and Elaine Lewis

1984   *Peoples of the Golden Triangle.* London: Thames and Hudson.

Liden, Kerstin

1995   Megaliths, Agriculture, and Social Complexity: A Diet Study of Two Swedish Megalith Populations. *Journal of Anthropological Archaeology* 14:404–417.

Maneeprasert, Ralana

1988   Ban Mae Salaep Akha: Chiang Mai. Report on file at the Tribal Research Institute, Chiang Mai.

Marshall, F.

1993   Food Sharing and the Faunal Record. In *From Bones to Behaviour: Ethnoarchaeological and Experimental Contributions to the Interpretation of Faunal Remains,* edited by J. Hudson, pp. 228–246. Carbondale: Southern Illinois University.

McGuwere, R., and R. Paynter

1991   *The Archaeology of Inequality.* Oxford: Blackwell.

Schrock, John

1970   *Ethnographic Study Series: Minority Groups in Thailand.* Washington, D.C.: Cultural Information Analysis Center, Center for Research in Social Systems.

Schubert, Bernd

1986   *Proposals for Farming Systems–Oriented Crop Research of Wawi Highland Agricultural Research Station in Northern Thailand.* Center for Advanced Training in Agricultural Development: Technical University of Berlin, Berlin.

Smith, M. E.

1987   Household Possessions and Wealth in Agrarian States: Implications for Archaeology. *Journal of Anthropological Archaeology* 6 (4): 297–335.

Tai Landa, Janet

1994   *Trust, Ethnicity, and Identity: Beyond the New Institutional Economics of Ethnic Trading Networks, Contract Law, and Gift-Exchange.* Ann Arbor: University of Michigan Press.

Tribal Research Institute

1995   *The Hill Tribes of Thailand:* Fourth Edition. Chiang Mai, Thailand: Technical Services Club, Tribal Research Institute, Chiang Mai University.

Visitpanich, Theera, and Lindsay Falvey

1980   A Survey of the Highland Pig Industry. *Thai Journal of Agricultural Science* 13:259–267.

6

POLYNESIAN FEASTING IN ETHNOHISTORIC, ETHNOGRAPHIC, AND ARCHAEOLOGICAL CONTEXTS

A COMPARISON OF THREE SOCIETIES

Patrick V. Kirch

What could be more visually evocative of a "classic" Polynesian scene than a feast? In the public mind, the Hawaiian *lu'au* has indeed become a potent symbol of Polynesian-ness. Yet the critical role of the feast in Polynesian societies is ethnographically and ethnohistorically verifiable (Bell 1931), not merely a late capitalist invention of the multinational tourist industry. Just as the last Hawaiian king, Kalakaua, used the *lu'au* as a political stage to entertain such international figures as Robert Louis Stevenson, so his chiefly (and priestly) predecessors ritually incorporated the first European explorer to the archipelago, Captain James Cook, in a symbolic act of feeding upon the temple platform of Hikiau (see Sahlins 1995). For generations before Cook burst through the boundaries of Kahiki, Hawaiian chiefs had elaborated the feast as a social nexus wherein the surplus fruits of production—extracted from the populace by cooperation or by coercion (both martial and ideological)—were put to work furthering chiefly political aspirations. To invoke the Marxist conception of a social formation, the feast occupies strategic terrain at the interface between infrastructure and superstructure. Through the complex act of feast giving, the structures of heterarchy and hierarchy were continually renegotiated.

Douglas Oliver (1989:291–292), in his definitive comparative ethnography of Oceanic societies, advances several criteria differentiating feasts from ordinary domestic eating. First, feasts are *quantitatively* distinguished by larger numbers of participants, incorporating consumers from more than a single household unit. Second, feasts involve "larger amounts of food per intended eater." Third, there are important *qualitative* differences, such as the inclusion of delicacies or ritually marked foods in feasts. In Polynesian societies, these special foods include, for example, pork, dog, or fowl, prized species of fish (such as pelagic game fish), sea turtle, "fancy puddings" (usually incorporating an emollient such as coconut oil), or "well-aged fermented breadfruit." In some Polynesian societies, human flesh was also a component of feasts.[1] Fourth, there are spatial differences in the ways and places in which feast foods were consumed, further differentiating them from domestic eating. In many Polynesian societies there were spatially defined feasting places, although these vary in the extent to which they were architectonically marked by permanent structures. Finally, the disposal of the remnants of feasts sometimes differed from the ways in which ordinary household food remains were disposed of. The detritus of religious feasts might be given special treatment, for such ritually charged garbage could be dangerous to those who came into contact with it.

One of the great strengths of the Polynesian ethnographic record lies in the opportunities for controlled comparison among a range of societies all characterized as *chiefdoms*, yet displaying a remarkable range of variability in degree of hierarchy or stratification, in size of populations and scale of political units, in the levels of production intensification, and similar variables. The classic comparative studies of Marshall Sahlins (1958) and Irving Goldman (1970) exploited these opportunities to derive from the Polynesian record some general models of cultural evolution in pre-state, ranked societies.

The ethnographic and ethnohistoric literature on Polynesian feasting is vast,[2] grist for a monograph of its own. Here I limit myself to the role of feasts in three Polynesian societies, each representative of one of the categories in Goldman's sociopolitical classification (Table 6.1). These societies are: (1) Tikopia, a small-scale "Traditional" Polynesian chiefdom; (2) the Marquesas, an exemplar of mid-range "Open" societies given to fluidity in their social structures; and, (3) Hawai'i, a chiefdom so complex and stratified that it is sometimes characterized as an "ar-

TABLE 6.1

Key Contrasts between Tikopia, Marquesas, and Hawaiian Case Studies

Attribute	Tikopia	Marquesas	Hawai'i
Goldman's class	Traditional	Open	Stratified
Island size (km²)	4.6	1,057	16,692
Total population	1,250	50,000	300,000+
Population of maximal political unit	1,250	1,500–3,000	30,000–50,000
Degree of stratification	Minimal (2 levels, little status marking)	Intermediate	High (class endogamy between chiefs and commoners)

chaic state." I explore the extent to which variation in traditional feasting within these three Polynesian societies displays regularities—or signal distinctions—with respect to differences in scale, stratification, or other indices of sociopolitical complexity. I do this by examining three aspects of feasting: (1) the *functions* of feasts, whether emically or etically construed; (2) the *foods* prepared for and consumed in feasts, especially as these are differentiated from everyday cuisine; and (3) the *architectonic space* within which feasting was practiced. These latter two features of feasts may be of particular salience in developing an "archaeology of feasting" within Polynesia.

TIKOPIA: FEASTING AND KINSHIP

Although Tikopia qualifies as a "chiefdom" society, it is governed more by culturally ingrained concepts of *kinship* than by the political pronouncements of its four *ariki*, or hereditary chiefs (Firth 1936). "We, the Tikopia," *Matou Nga Tikopia*, is an indigenous slogan encapsulating this notion of a closely knit community in which everyone is bound to everyone else through consanguineal or affinal ties. The role of food in Tikopia was summed up Sir Raymond Firth in these words: "Food serves as a most important material manifestation of social relationship, and through it kinship ties, political loyalty, indemnity for wrong, and the canons of hospitality are expressed" (1939:38).

The cover term for "feast" in Tikopia is *anga*, meaning either the feast itself, or the "specific assemblage of food for [a] stage in ceremony" (Firth 1985:11); however, there are many specific indigenous lexical categories of feast, not all of which are called *anga* (Table 6.2).[3] Functionally, we may subdivide Tikopia feasts into three main groups: (1) domestic or secular feasts; (2) chiefly feasts; and (3) ritual feasts. The latter are associated with particular religious ceremonies that make up the annual cycle known as the "Work of the Gods" (Firth 1967).

TABLE 6.2
Principal Kinds of Feasts in Tikopia

Functional Category	Indigenous (Lexical) Category and Subtypes
Secular/domestic feasts	1. Initiation of young men: *te umu lasi* ("the great oven") 2. Marriage: *te umu tanakianga* ("the oven of joining"); *te anga*
Political/chiefly feasts	**General term: *anga*** 1. *Moringa*, feast of newly elected chief 2. *Pungaumu (anga fi)*, midcareer feast of chief 3. *Aroarorima (anga soro)*, feast as chief ages 4. *Fakatangata (anga soro)*, feast late in chief's career 5. *Fakamatua*, final feast of chief
Ritual/religious feasts	**Associated with all key components of the "Work of the Gods" cycle, e.g.:** 1. Recarpeting ancestral temples 2. Dance to Quell the Wind *(Taomatangi)* 3. Proclamation at Rarokoka

Domestic feasts typically celebrate key stages—rites de passage—in the life cycle of members of households. Important feasts of this kind are those of new male initiates at the time of circumcision, and marriage feasts. In both cases more than a single household unit is involved, and the exchange of food between households is a key social function of these events.

Major *anga* feasts are also given by chiefs at particular points in their careers. Of these chiefly feasts, Firth writes that:

> From the point of view of the chief the *anga* marks a stage in the progression of his reign. It gives an opportunity to display his food resources and to assert his rank; it secures for him ceremonial expressions of thanks from his chiefly guests and of loyalty from his clanspeople; and in the later stages demonstrates his own fidelity to his gods and thereby ensures their continued interest in him. (1939:222)

There are, in theory, a progression of such *anga* throughout the life of a chief, beginning with the *te moringa* feast held soon after his election, through midcareer feasts of a type known as *anga soro* because of the immense quantities of grated taro (*soro*) involved, to the *fakamatua*, or "making elderly" feast, held when the chief determines that the end of his life is approaching.

Feasts marked virtually all of the many rites and ceremonies held throughout the course of the ritual year (Firth 1967), such as the major island-wide rituals called the "Dance to Quell the Wind" (*Taomatangi*), and the "Dance of the Flaming Fire" (*Urangafi*), or the week-long ritual extraction of the sacred turmeric dye (*Nuanga*).[4]

In the foods accumulated, prepared, and consumed in these various kinds of *anga* among the Tikopia, we can distinguish differences from ordinary domestic consumption, although the main distinction is quantitative rather than qualitative. Because the Tikopia do not keep dogs or pigs for food, there is no particular emphasis on special flesh foods for their feasts.[5] Rather, feasts are characterized by the preparation of special kinds of "fancy puddings," concoctions of starch staple mixed with an emollient, usually coconut cream or coconut oil.[6] One such feasting food is the *roi*, a pudding made from "taro, breadfruit or ripe banana mixed with sago flour and coconut cream, then cooked overnight" in the earth oven (Firth 1985:403). This *roi* is a key component in many Tikopia rites, such as the Proclamation of Rarokoka (Firth 1967:280).[7] In the annual Work of Somo-somo, for example, all of the men who have married women from a particular clan during the previous year made a gift of *roi* to the clan chief. In quantity, such gifts could be prodigious, as much as 40 baskets from a single man, requiring "preparations . . . begun months in advance" (Firth 1967:393). Archaeologically, however, none of these special foods are likely to be preserved, with little probability of a qualitatively distinctive signature for feasting in the Tikopia archaeological record.

The architectonic context of Tikopia feasting varies depending upon the type of feast. Secular feasts such as those for initiation and marriages take place within the normal domestic quarters. Indeed, all food preparation for both domestic feasts and chiefly feasts utilized the same cookhouse facilities as for ordinary household food preparation. Ritual feasting, however, was spatially associated with the lineage and clan temples, located in the sacred district of Uta, along the inner shore of the lake. In most respects, these temples (which also had associated sacred cookhouses) were like ordinary domestic dwellings, and indeed, historically they were the former dwellings of ancestors, which had become sacred, "holy houses" through generations of use and through the burial of ancestors within them (see Kirch 1996, 2000). Whether such ritual spaces could be separately distinguished from domestic spaces in the archaeological record—without the aid of the ethnographic evidence—is a serious question, again raising the possibility that a prehistoric record of feasting in Tikopia may well be refractory to archaeological analysis.

THE MARQUESAS: FEASTING AND COMPETITIVE INVOLUTION

In marked contrast to Tikopia, the Marquesas Islands and their population never comprised a single, integrated community linked by bonds of kinship, or even by politically induced integration. Although the Marquesan islanders shared a common language and many aspects of culture (all of which marked them as distinct from other, related Polynesian groups), politically they were divided into a larger number of independent tribal units, each typically focused on a single valley, or at most uniting several adjacent valleys (Handy 1923; Thomas 1990). These political units were frequently at war with each other, with acts of warfare ranging from limited raiding to obtain sacrificial victims, to more extensive raids aimed at the destruction of an enemy's productive resources, to outright wars of territorial conquest (Thomas 1990:87 passim).

Proto-historic Marquesan society falls into a group (along with such other Polynesian societies as those of Mangaia and Rapa Nui) characterized by Irving Goldman (1970) as "open." In contrast to "traditional" societies such as Tikopia, the open societies were marked by more fluidity and negotiation among competing status positions of chief (*haka'iki*), warriors (*toa*), and priests (*tau'a*). In Goldman's words, these systems were "more strongly military and political than religious," and stability was "maintained more directly by the exercise of secular powers" (1970:20). Elsewhere (Kirch 1991:144), I have characterized proto-historic Marquesan society as marked by "an involuted cycle of prestige rivalry and competition." As ethnohistorian Nicholas Thomas (1990) observes, the two main arenas in which such competition took place were those of *warfare* and *feasting*. In such a highly competitive society, it is not surprising that Greg Dening describes the Marquesan *ko'ina*—the feast—as a kind of "market":

> *Enata* had no wealth that could be accumulated. What they accumulated were the obligations they were owed by the distribution of their wealth. *Koina*, the feast, was their marketplace. All the foods, all the ornamentation, all the energy used in dance and song were expended in a short time. What remained was a lien on tomorrow. (1980:63)

The Marquesan cover term for "feast" is *ko'ina*, with many specific kinds of feast designated by an adjectivally modified form of *ko'ina*, as in *ko'ina tupapa'u*, "feast for the dead" (Table 6.3). In addition, the specific terms *mau*, for "memorial feast," and *heana*, for "cannibalistic feast," were primary lexical designations for two significant kinds of feast/festivals (Thomas 1990; Dening 1980). As in Tikopia, there was in traditional (pre-mission) Marquesan life a considerable diversity of feasts, as outlined in Table 6.3. Because of the severe collapse of Marquesan society after European contact, the nature of many of these feasts is incompletely known, since they were abandoned well before systematic ethnographic observation commenced in the early twentieth century, and can be reconstructed only through early visitors' accounts and oral testimony of older Marquesans. Here I follow the account of Handy (1923:203–223) who carried out "salvage ethnography" in the archipelago in 1920.

Among the main domestic or secular feasts were *ko'ina* for betrothal and marriage, and to celebrate the tattooing of a young man. Marquesan society was con-

TABLE 6.3

Principal Kinds of Feasts in the Marquesas

Functional Category	Indigenous (Lexical) Category and Subtypes
Secular/domestic feasts	1. Betrothal feasts *(ko'ina tuia)*
	2. Marriage feasts *(ko'ina hunona)*
	3. Tattooing feasts *(ko'ina tuhi tiki)*
Chiefly/political feasts	1. Competitive entertainment feast *(ko'ina hakahiti)*
	2. Memorial feasts for deceased chiefs *(mau)*
	3. Memorial feasts for deified priests *(ko'ika oke, ko'ika vaihopu, and ko'ika u'upua)*
	4. Harvest festivals *(ko'ina tapavau)*
War/cannibalistic feasts	*Ko'ina heana*

siderably more hierarchically differentiated than that of Tikopia, and only "wealthy" families would ordinarily command the resources to carry out such feasts. These included the households of chiefs *(haka'iki)* and other elites, such as priests *(tau'a)*, warriors *(toa)*, and various kinds of experts *(tuhuna)*.

Of greater significance were the memorial festivals "held in honor of the departed spirit of a man" (rarely were these celebrated for women), called *mau*, or in the case of festivals to deify a deceased priest, *ko'ika* (Handy 1923:212 passim). *Mau* and *ko'ika* feasts were impressive displays, both of prestige foodstuffs such as numerous baked hogs, and of special starch and fermented breadfruit preparations, as well as of bodily ornamentation for elite participants and dancers. Handy writes that "the greatest of all feasts were the memorial festivals celebrated long after the actual death of chiefs and chiefesses, inspirational priests, or ceremonial priests for the purpose of deifying their spirits" (1923:216). Another category of feast associated with chiefs and held under their aegis was the harvest festival *(ko'ina tapavau)*, held after the completion of the breadfruit harvest and the successful filling of the silos of fermented breadfruit.[8]

Finally, there were feasts held at the successful conclusion of a war against an enemy tribe, "celebrating the capture of human victims" (Handy 1923:218), called *ko'ina heana*, or simply *heana*. According to Handy's all-too-brief account, these *heana* were rather solemn affairs, lacking the elaborate dancing and singing that typically accompanied other feasts. Rather, "the *ko'ina heana* consisted merely of a feast at the dance area [*tohua*], where human flesh, pig, and *popoi* [fermented breadfruit paste] were consumed" (1923:219). The bodies of sacrificial victims intended as offerings to the gods were apparently not consumed, but those of other victims were eaten by the chiefs, warriors, and priests.

Marquesan feasting was thus distinguished *qualitatively* as well as quantitatively from ordinary eating, not only in the preparation of special starchy puddings (as in Tikopia), but in the emphasis on prestige flesh foods, particularly pigs but also in the *heana* feasts, human flesh. As elsewhere in Polynesia, the pig had a particular association with rank and status, and may have been reserved primarily, if not exclusively, for consumption by males.

Turning to the architectonic or spatial context of feasting, the contrast with Tikopia is striking. Beginning—on archaeological evidence—during the Expansion Period (ca. A.D. 1100–1400), the Marquesans began to construct unique feast places, called *tohua*. Essentially, these consisted of large, rectangular dance plazas, usually a leveled terrace, surrounded by platforms (*paepae*). These platforms included foundations for temples (*me'ae*), chiefs' houses, and viewing platforms for spectators who witnessed the elaborate dances that accompanied feasting. There were also associated cookhouse structures where the baking of pigs and other food preparations were carried out.[9] *Tohua* were often of considerable size, with individual platforms of "megalithic" dimensions; the terrace of Tohua Vahangeku'a in Taipi Valley (Nukuhiva) measures 174 m long by 26 m wide, and is surrounded by a complexity of ancillary structures and platforms (Fig. 6.1; see also Suggs 1961:102–103). *Tohua* were often architecturally ornamented with relief or freestanding sculpture of anthropomorphic character, in some cases commemorating individuals who had been deified in *mau* or *ko'ika* feasts (Linton 1925:85).

An exemplar of Goldman's "open" class of Polynesian societies, the Marquesan pattern of feasting displays important differences from that of "traditional" Tikopia. Despite similarities in categories of feasts (as in the domestic marriage feasts), there are critical differences, with Marquesan feasts playing an important role in the overall emphasis on competition and status/prestige rivalry (the commemorative, deification, and cannibalistic feasts). Whereas in Tikopia there was little if any qualitative distinction between ordinary and feast foods, the Marquesan feasts emphasized the provision of prestige flesh foods, especially pig, and in the case of *heana* feasts to celebrate success in war, of human flesh itself.[10] In the architectonic sphere, the great emphasis accorded feasting as an aspect of sociopolitical competition is matched by the Marquesan development of a special feast place, the *tohua*, construction of which required substantial labor investments. Archaeologically, both the emphasis on qualitatively different (and taphonomically preservable) animal foods, and the construction of permanent and architecturally elaborate feast spaces, greatly enhance the likelihood that a pre-

Figure 6.1. The main ceremonial plaza of Ta'a'oa *tohua* on the island of Hivaoa, Marquesas Islands. Informants state that the platform in the foreground was for the cooking and display of human sacrificial victims. (Photo by P. V. Kirch)

historic record of the long-term development of feasting behavior might be possible for the Marquesas.

The key differences in Tikopian and Marquesan practices of feasting reflect fundamental differences in the two societies. In the small-scale community of Tikopia where all members of society are linked by bonds of kinship, the feast serves as a mechanism for assuring social solidarity, binding the community together in commonly perceived purpose. In the larger-scale, multitribal society of the Marquesas, the feast had become an instrument of prestige rivalry and competition, a means of 'fighting with food.' As Thomas writes, "the medium of food, its movements, and the differing qualities and quantities of particular presentations must have, as a totality, provided an index to virtually everybody's situation of power or dependence" (1990:97).

HAWAI'I: FEASTING AND KINGSHIP

In turning to the Hawaiian Islands, we move from the realm of Goldman's "open" level of chiefdom society into the "stratified." Indeed, on a variety of criteria, the proto-historic polities of Hawai'i[11] are among the most complex chiefdoms ethnohistorically or ethnographically documented, arguably described as "archaic states." In these Hawaiian polities, the chiefly class had elaborated itself into as many as nine grades of chiefs, practiced virtual class endogamy (as well as sibling marriage to maintain the purity of the blood line), had alienated direct control of land and other means of production from the commoner class (instituting a system of usufruct rights subject to regular tribute payments), supported a body of craft specialists as well as warriors and household retainers, and were ideologically legitimated by a religious system based on the cults of Ku (god of war) and Lono (god of dryland agriculture), the former requiring human sacrifice. With genealogies that proclaimed them to be direct descendants of the gods—indeed, god-like "raging blazes" who walked on earth—it is a matter of semantics whether we choose to designate the highest ranked, paramount leaders of Hawai'i as "chiefs" or "kings."[12] I shall here adopt the latter terminology, and refer to the political system of proto-historic Hawai'i as one of *kingship*. The question of immediate moment, then, is how the Polynesian patterns of feasting that we have examined for Tikopia and the Marquesas were further transformed as Hawaiian society moved from a structure based on kinship to one based on kingship.

One of the most salient features emerging from a perusal of the Hawaiian ethnographic and ethnohistoric literature, with regard to feasting, is the relative dearth of references to feasting among commoners (the *maka'ainana*), and the concomitant richness of description for feasts among the chiefly class (the *ali'i*). The consumption of vast quantities of food—even on a daily basis—had become virtually a defining attribute of the *ali'i*, marked reciprocally by their corpulence.[13] As the Russian explorer von Kotzebue observed of the Waialua chiefess Pi'ia in 1824, "I can . . . bear testimony to another qualification, *of equal importance in her estimation*—she has certainly the greatest appetite that ever came under my observation" (1830:vol. 2, 223; emphasis added). In their endomorphism, the Hawaiian chiefs had carried to an extreme the widespread Polynesian cultural logic that chiefs should naturally be bigger than their subjects.[14] But it appears they had also co-opted the feast as *a distinctly chiefly form of consumption*, yet one more means of distinguishing and differentiating themselves from the common folk.

In Tikopia and the Marquesas, domestic feasts such as those accompanying initiation, marriage, or tattooing, comprise a major category in the functional classifications of feasts. For Hawai'i, however, such domestic feasts are but little remarked, even by such indigenous ethnographers as Kamakau (1964:25–26). Far more important for the *maka'ainana*, were small feasts (usually focused on the sacrifice of a pig) to celebrate the cutting of a new canoe, or the successful harvest of a set of irrigated taro terraces (Kamakau 1976:119, 36–37), both critical aspects of production and both largely male-focused arenas.

The chiefs, in contrast, could virtually be found feasting every day of their lives. From many early-nineteenth-century documents pertaining to the chiefly estate at Waialua, O'ahu, Kirch and Sahlins (1992) chronicle the ceaseless demands put upon the common people of that district for taro, *poi*, pigs, fish, and other foodstuffs to support the bloated chiefly establishment in Honolulu. Qualitatively distinctive foods, which in other Polynesian societies might be reserved for special feast occasions, had become the daily fare of *ali'i* households. While only the male chiefs ate pork (on a daily basis), the female chiefesses developed a great fondness for puppies, and hundreds of small *poi*-dogs (fattened upon the starchy taro paste) were raised in pens for the latter's regular enjoyment.

When the chiefs and their retainers were not resident in one of their principal locales (such as Waipi'o or in Kona on Hawai'i, or after European contact in Lahaina or Honolulu), they traveled about their domains literally feasting off the produce demanded up of their subjects. Thus in September of 1833, the king Kauikeaouli (Kamehameha III) traveled with his substantial household to Waialua, descending as the resident missionary Emerson put it, "like a company of locusts" upon the common folk. Emerson's wife penned in her journal: "I shall be glad when it's over. Pigs, dogs, fish and fowl have been slaughtered in large numbers, and ever so many calabashes of *poi* have been prepared" (both Emerson quotes in Kirch and Sahlins 1992:145–146).

In the proto-historic Hawaiian polities, and continuing up until the abandonment of traditional religious practice during the later reign of Kamehameha I (and ceasing completely after his death in 1819), the other great arena for feasting was at the great cult temples dedicated to Ku and Lono (see Valeri 1985). Here the feasts were formal components of highly elaborated temple rituals, presided over by a cadre of priests (*kahuna*) and the chiefs, and in which (some) male commoners were allowed to participate as observers and at times as consumers of certain feast foods, but from which women were wholly excluded. I cannot here go into the complex matter of gender differentiation in Hawaiian food consumption, except to note that this was highly systematized, and included prohibitions (*kapu*) on the eating of such ritually marked items as pork, certain kinds of bananas, certain species of fish, and so forth.

The quantitative scale of such feasts could be grand indeed, as the nineteenth-century Hawaiian scholar David Malo described for a feast to conclude the dedication of a new *luakini heiau*, a temple dedicated to the war-god Ku:

> That night a large number of hogs, as many as 800 (*elua lau*), were baked; and the priests were separated into two divisions, one on this side and one on that side of the *mana* [house], each division taking part in the service alternately.
>
> The pork was also divided into two portions, 400 of the hogs being assigned to the priests seated at one end of the building and 400 to the priests seated at the other end (*kala*). The priests and their men ate the flesh of the swine and continued their prayers, without sleep, until morning.
>
> The next morning, which was Kupau, the *kuili* service was kept up, and continued without intermission all day. That day 400 pigs were served out to the worshippers, 200 (*elima kanaha*) to those at one end of the temple and 200 to those at the other end.
>
> The service was still kept up during the ensuing night, 240 pigs being baked and served out—120 to priests at this end of the temple and 120 to those of the other end of the temple. The service continued all night.
>
> During the next day, Olekukahi, the *kuili* service still went on, and 400 pigs were baked and divided out equally between the priests at the two ends of the temple. (Malo 1951:172)

All this (1,440 pigs, to be exact), moreover, was *merely preliminary* to what Malo calls the "great feast" following the girding of the Ku image with a sacred loincloth, at which the number of slaughtered hogs is unfortunately not specified.[15]

Clearly, for two of the three attributes of Polynesian feasting upon which I have focused—function and the nature of feast foods—the Hawaiian pattern had been considerably transformed in the context of a hierarchically differentiated society. No longer a significant aspect of commoner life, feasting was a virtually mundane, ubiquitous aspect of the chiefly *habitus*. Prestige foods, especially pigs, were essential to chiefly feasts, whether for daily consumption or for ostentatious display during temple rituals. Hawaiian feasting was likewise differentiated architectonically, since it was spatially concentrated in two kinds of venue: the chiefly residence, and the principal temples.

As with the Marquesas, the possibilities for recovering an archaeological record of feasting in Hawai'i seem good. Although Hawai'i lacked formal feasting centers such as the *tohua*, the main Hawaiian temples (*heiau*) were principal loci of feasting, and refuse pits associated with these structures should contain the remains of temple feasts. Likewise, chiefly residences ought to be differentially marked from commoner habitations by the presence of prestige food items, especially the bones of pigs, dogs, and certain kinds of fish (such as pelagic game fish). There is indeed support for such differential faunal assemblages in the Hawaiian archaeological record (Weisler and Kirch 1985).

CONCLUSIONS

I conclude this all-too-brief comparison of feasting in three Polynesian societies with two general observations. The first concerns variation in feasting behavior in relation to key structural characteristics of these societies. At risk of sounding like an old-time Malinowskian structural-functionalist, the case can be argued that differences in feasting between Tikopia, the Marquesas, and Hawai'i do correlate closely with such attributes as sociodemographic scale, degree of stratification and hierarchy, and extent of aggressive competition (war). In a small-scale society such as Tikopia, where kinship underwrites the Durkheimian sense of community, feasts are largely organized at the immediate suprahousehold level, and are partaken of by commoners and chiefs alike. Indeed, in Tikopia chiefs are expected to give feasts *for* the common people at key stages in their careers. In the Marquesas, some differences emerge, correlating with the larger scale of Marquesan polities, but more particularly with the increased hierarchy of Marquesan society and with the involutionary emphasis on overt competition. In the Marquesas, the feast became less of a medium for regular social communion than an instrument of political competition. The Hawaiian case takes us the farthest from the Durkheimian mode, in which the feast was co-opted as a virtual prerogative of the ruling class, less an instrument of power than a pervasive, daily reminder of the immense gulf of social distinctions that separated *ali'i* from *maka'ainana*.

It is only an illusion that Tikopia, the Marquesas, and Hawai'i appear to represent ideal stages along some kind of evolutionary continuum for chiefdom societies. None of these is actually ancestral to the other, and all are ethnohistoric endpoints preceded by millennia of history. To trace the real history of feasting in Polynesia requires that we pull back the ethnohistoric tapestry, and enter the messy realm of the "archaeological record." In this chapter, I have alluded briefly to the potentials for an archaeology of feasting, and I have been mixed with regard to my assessments of these possibilities. For Tikopia, I frankly think that the likelihood of developing a robust archaeological record of feasting behavior over time is not very good. Tikopian feasting has little to distinguish it qualitatively from ordinary eating, nor is there any elaboration of the architectonic contexts within which feasting occurs. Indeed, although I spent two long field seasons excavating in Tikopian sites (Kirch and Yen 1982), I cannot say that I dug up the remains of anything specifically identifiable as a feast.

For the Marquesas and Hawai'i, and other Polynesian societies of their "types," the possibilities for an archaeology of feasting seem more feasible. This reflects both the emphasis on qualitatively different kinds of feast foods (especially pig), and the architectural elaboration of feasting places (whether *tohua* in the Marquesas, or chiefly residences and temple sites in Hawai'i). Indeed, for Hawai'i there are tentative archaeological identifications of chiefly residential sites based on distinctive faunal assemblages (Weisler and Kirch 1985), as well as great potential for the reconstruction of feasting behavior associated with temples. In short, an archaeology of feasting in Polynesia is likely to be—to adopt a metaphor from contemporary "local" Hawaiian eating—a "mixed plate." But then, such has always been the nature of our historical science.

NOTES

1. The revisionist stance of Arens (1979), which argues that cannibalism is entirely a Western construction of the indigenous Other, does not stand up to the ethnographic or archaeological records for various Pacific Islands. Sound documentation—either ethnographic or archaeological, or both—for the consumption of human flesh exists for Fiji, the Marquesas, Mangaia, Easter Island, and probably New Zealand.

2. Oliver observes that for Oceania generally, "feasting occupies a larger part of many Islands' ethnographies than any other kind of activity . . . and perhaps deservedly so—not because of the drama usually associated with it but because of the political relations it represented and revealed" (1989:291).

3. Elsewhere, Firth writes that the term *anga* applies both to feasts given by chiefs, and also "to the accumulations of food for initiation and marriage rites" (1939:222).

4. In 1978 I participated in the *Nuanga* of the Ariki Tafua, the second-ranked chief of Tikopia. This is one part of the Work of the Gods that had not been abandoned as a result of the conversion to Christianity. Although the extraction and purification of the turmeric dye was the focus of this ritual activity, and not feasting per se, the *Nuanga* met all of the key criteria for feasting, such as the participation of large numbers of people, the accumulation of significant quantities of food, the preparation of special foods (such as taro puddings), and the consumption of food in a special precinct, that of the chief's house and adjacent compound.

5. One exception to this is the marine turtle (*Chelonia mydas*), a food associated with chiefly status. When turtles are taken, they are usually brought to the chief, and may be kept for days or even weeks before being slaughtered and consumed on a feast occasion. Their flesh, however, is not exclusively reserved for the chief, and will be shared out with other participants.

6. For another ethnographic case of the importance of such puddings (*faikai*, literally "made food") in another traditional Polynesian society, see Kirch (1994:95–100, 189–213) on Futuna.

7. Firth writes that "the sacredness of the *roi* depends upon its being used to provide offerings in the most important religious ceremonies. It is said then to be made by the chiefs' elders for their respective deities. 'Each makes it for his god'" (1967:280).

8. Marquesan subsistence depended more than virtually any other Polynesian society (except perhaps that of the Society Islands) on arboriculture or orchard gardening, with specific emphasis on the breadfruit (*Artocarpus altilis*). Since the breadfruit harvest occurs in a short period, the vast yield of starch is preserved through a method of semi-anaerobic pit fermentation and ensilage (see Kirch 1984:132–135).

9. Suggs (1961:72–73, fig. 25b) reports excavating such an "oven complex" at the Hikoku'a *tohua* site in Hatiheu Valley, Nukuhiva.

10. Of course, quantity was also important in Marquesan feasting, as Thomas points out: "Prestige depended not simply upon returning the equivalent of what had previously been received, but upon giving more, and particularly more than the receivers could eat" (1990:101).

11. There were four main, competing chiefdom polities in the archipelago at the time of European contact, centered on the principal islands of Kaua'i, O'ahu, Maui, and Hawai'i.

12. Historical ethnographers Sahlins (1995) and Valeri (1985) have used the term *king*, I believe justifiably.

13. On the corpulence of Hawaiian chiefs in the early nineteenth century, see Kirch and Sahlins (1992:vol. 1, 78–79).

14. As one Tongan informant put it to the ethnographer E. W. Gifford, "Can't you see he is a chief? See how big he is" (1929:124).

15. Human sacrifice was also an essential aspect of such *luakini* ritual, but unlike the Marquesan situation, human flesh was not generally consumed, other than the symbolic eating of the victim's eye (see Valeri 1985).

REFERENCES

Arens, W.
    1979   *The Man-Eating Myth*. New York: Oxford University Press.
Bell, F. L.
    1931   The Place of Food in the Social Life of Central Polynesia. *Oceania* 2:117–35.
Dening, G.
    1980   *Islands and Beaches: Discourse on a Silent Land, Marquesas 1774–1880*. Honolulu: University of Hawaii Press.
Firth, R.
    1936   *We, the Tikopia*. New York: American Book Company.
    1939   *Primitive Polynesian Economy*. George Routledge and Sons.
    1967   *The Work of the Gods in Tikopia*. New York: Humanities Press.
    1985   *Tikopia-English Dictionary*. Auckland: Auckland University Press.
Gifford, E. W.
    1929   *Tongan Society*. Bernice P. Bishop Museum Special Publication 61. Honolulu.
Goldman, I.
    1970   *Ancient Polynesian Society*. Chicago: University of Chicago Press.

Handy, E. S. C.
  1923   *The Native Culture in the Marquesas.* Bernice P. Bishop Museum Bulletin 9. Honolulu.
Kamakau, S. M.
  1964   *Ka Po'e Kahiko: The People of Old.* Bernice P. Bishop Museum Special Publication No. 51. Honolulu.
  1976   *The Works of the People of Old.* Bernice P. Bishop Museum Special Publication 61. Honolulu.
Kirch, P. V.
  1984   *The Evolution of the Polynesian Chiefdoms.* Cambridge: Cambridge University Press.
  1991   Chiefship and Competitive Involution: The Marquesas Islands of Eastern Polynesia. In *Chiefdoms: Power, Economy, and Ideology,* edited by T. Earle, pp. 119–45. Cambridge: Cambridge University Press.
  1994   *The Wet and the Dry: Irrigation and Agricultural Intensification in Polynesia.* Chicago: University of Chicago Press.
  1996   Tikopia Social Space Revisited. In *Oceanic Culture History: Essays in Honour of Roger Green,* edited by J. Davidson, G. Irwin, F. Leach, A. Pawley, and D. Brown, pp. 257–274. Dunedin: New Zealand Journal of Archaeology Special Publication.
  2000   Temples as "Holy Houses": The Transformation of Ritual Architecture in Traditional Polynesian Societies. In *Beyond Kinship: Social and Material Reproduction in House Societies,* edited by R. Joyce and S. D. Gillespie, pp. 103–114. Philadelphia: University of Pennsylvania Press.
Kirch, P. V., and M. Sahlins
  1992   *Anahulu: The Anthropology of History in the Kingdom of Hawai'i.* Chicago: University of Chicago Press.
Kirch, P. V., and D. E. Yen
  1982   *Tikopia: Prehistory and Ecology of a Polynesian Outlier.* Bernice P. Bishop Museum Bulletin 238. Honolulu.
Kotzebue, O. von
  1830   *A New Voyage Round the World in the Years 1823, 24, 25, and 26.* 2 vols. London: Colburn and Bentley.
Linton, R.
  1925   *Archaeology of the Marquesas Islands.* Bernice P. Bishop Museum Bulletin 23. Honolulu.
Malo, D.
  1951   *Hawaiian Antiquities.* Bernice P. Bishop Museum Special Publication 2. Second Edition. Honolulu.
Oliver, D. L.
  1989   *Oceania: The Native Cultures of Australia and the Pacific Islands.* Honolulu: University of Hawai'i Press.
Sahlins, M.
  1958   *Social Stratification in Polynesia.* Seattle: American Ethnological Society.

1995   *How "Natives" Think: About Captain Cook, for Example*. Chicago: University of Chicago Press.

Suggs, R. C.

1961   *The Archaeology of Nuku Hiva, Marquesas Islands, French Polynesia*. Anthropological Papers of the American Museum of Natural History, No. 49. New York.

Thomas, N.

1990   *Marquesan Societies: Inequality and Political Transformation in Eastern Polynesia*. Oxford: Clarendon Press.

Valeri, V.

1985   *Kingship and Sacrifice: Ritual and Society in Ancient Hawaii*. Chicago: University of Chicago Press.

Weisler, M., and P. V. Kirch

1985   The Structure of Settlement Space in a Polynesian Chiefdom: Kawela, Moloka'i, Hawaiian Islands. *New Zealand Journal of Archaeology* 7:129–158.

7

FEASTING FOR PROSPERITY

A STUDY OF SOUTHERN NORTHWEST COAST FEASTING

James R. Perodie

Feasts, potlatches, and related activities may have been significant factors in the transition from egalitarian to ranked societies (see Chapters 2, 3 and 9; also Clark and Blake 1994:17, 25, 28, 29; Hayden 1990:32, 37, 1993:225, 1995:24, 25, 74). Thus, any inquiry into the emergence of socioeconomic inequality should include a study of feasting, potlatching, and related activities. Indeed, questions naturally arise as to why individuals of indigenous cultures expended significant time, energy, and resources on feasting and potlatching. The Northwest Coast region is a good area for studying these phenomena because feasts and potlatches were central elements of the indigenous cultures, and because abundant ethnographic information provides valuable emic data for analyzing Northwest Coast feasts and potlatches. The Kwakiutl, Nootka, Coast Salish, and Twana were chosen for this analysis because they are sufficiently similar culturally to treat as one group for the purpose of analyzing feasting behavior. Due to the incomplete nature of observations in individual ethnographies it is necessary to examine feasting as a regional phenomenon. No single ethnography or ethnographic collection has relevant information on all cultural aspects pertinent to this investigation. Other researchers have assumed or argued that some or all of these groups can be considered culturally similar for general analytical purposes (Barnett 1968:10, 21; Boas 1897:317; Codere 1990:370; Drucker 1951:456; Elmendorf 1971:356; Ferguson 1984b:267; Rosman and Rubel 1971:6).

Feasts and potlatches can be differentiated by the nature of the distribution that occurred on each occasion. According to Drucker (1951:370, 372), feasts were occasions when an individual (the sponsor) would distribute food to four or more invited guests, whereas at potlatches nonfood property was also distributed to invited guests (Fig. 7.1). By stipulating that "four or more" invited guests must be present, Drucker is probably more concerned with distinguishing potlatches and feasts from simple nuclear family meals or informal visits than he is with defining rigid attendance requirements.

Figure 7.1. A potlatch at Alert Bay prior to 1914. Of particular note are the sacks of flour and pots of food that are to be given away as well as the full ceremonial regalia of the major participants standing at the far end of the display area. (Photo by J. Welsh RBCM 2307-b, courtesy Vancouver Public Library)

Because there is a wide variety of feasts and because the definition of potlatch varies widely from ethnographer to ethnographer, indeed, because almost any type of feast has been called a "potlatch" by various authors, it is important to distinguish carefully between different types of feasts as discussed below. *Feast* will be used as a comprehensive term for feasts and potlatches. In some cases, the term *potlatch* will be retained for convenience if it is used by original ethnographers. The distinctions between potlatches and other feasts, in any event, are not critical to the new analytical approaches that follow. Of much greater importance is whether the distributed materials were returned to the sponsor, and how and when this occurred.

Many anthropologists have studied Northwest Coast feasts and come up with widely different opinions on the role or function of feasts in Northwest Coast societies. For example, Boas states: "The underlying principle [of the potlatch] is that of the interest-bearing investment of property" (1966:77). According to Boas, "the principal motivation in the behavior of the [Kwakiutl] Indians is the desire to obtain social prestige" (1966:51). Acquiring and maintaining high prestige required correct marriages, and wealth accumulated via industry and potlatch investments (Boas 1966:51).

Codere (1966:127–129) concludes the Kwakiutl potlatch was a form of nonviolent "warfare" utilized to increase social prestige. Codere states that the Kwakiutl were characterized by "their limitless pursuit of social prestige (1966:118) and that at one time warfare and potlatching were probably "interchangeable means of gaining prestige" (Codere 1966:122). However, at least partly as a result of European influences, warfare subsided and potlatching became the only significant method of establishing or maintaining high social prestige (Codere 1966:118, 127–129).

Drucker (1951:377, 386; Drucker and Heizer 1967:134) and Barnett (1938b:351, 1955:253, 256, 1968:123) argue that the potlatch announced and reasserted the hereditary claims (i.e., seats, dances, properties) of the sponsor and his heirs, and therefore their claims for social status. Barnett (1938b:353, 357, 1955:250, 1968:123) adds that Northwest Coast cultures emphasized liberality and generosity, or their simulation, and that the potlatch was "characterized by . . . an implied equation of social worth with institutionalized liberality" (Barnett 1938b:357). Drucker notes that "the Nootkan data are in very close harmony with Barnett's . . . appraisal" (1951:386).

Suttles (1960:302–304) argues that the potlatch was a redistribution mechanism that enabled a network of interacting communities, each of which had varying economic opportunities and capabilities, to maintain high levels of food production and equal food consumption among all members of the network. Suttles states that "the drive to attain high status is clearly not the explanation of the potlatch" (1960:304). Piddocke (1965:244, 245, 258) also argues that the potlatch was a redistribution mechanism. However, he (1965:258) states that the potlatch had multiple functions, and that in addition to redistributing food and wealth, potlatch distributions were the potlatch sponsor's opportunity to secure and validate his social prestige by demonstrating his generosity (Piddocke 1965:245, 257, 258).

And Rosman and Rubel (1971:205, 206) argue that potlatches were individual and group rites of passage that occurred at critical social junctures when position holders would turn over prerogatives to successors. They assume that prestige and status were prime motivators.

The explanatory framework used in the present analysis differs because (1) it assumes that time-consuming and costly behavior that persists over time ought to be associated with some practical benefit, as Hayden argues in Chapter 2; (2) it assumes that sponsors of the most elaborate and expensive feasts were ambitious individuals and that their supporters utilized feasts for advancing their own ambitions, and (3) it identifies the specific practical benefits ambitious individuals were seeking with various types of feasting activities. This perspective is similar to Boas's in that Boas acknowledges one practical benefit of some feasts as increasing wealth. Codere may have viewed increased wealth and control as practical beneficial outcomes of warfare, and hence potlatching. However, she (1966:118) maintained that the potlatch was an agent for increasing social prestige and did not detail any specific practical benefits of this prestige in the manner that I discuss in the following pages.

I suggest that ambitious individuals who want to maintain and increase their economic and political control, control over labor, and wealth, need to achieve several specific goals. In order to control labor, labor must somehow be attracted and held. Increasing economic and political control requires a multitude of alliances with other groups in order to increase access to resources, security, and other support. Ambitious individuals need a consistently available mechanism for increasing their wealth and political power. All of these goals can be accomplished with feasting to create alliances, to indebt others, to escalate the production of surpluses, and to disproportionately concentrate control of debts, alliances, and surpluses in the hands of the organizers of feasts—in the hands of aggrandizers. Most of the remaining paper is dedicated to detailing why these goals are important to ambitious individuals, and how they are achieved with feasting. Brian Hayden has developed the theoretical feasting model that is used in this chapter in several unpublished manuscripts (e.g., Hayden and Maneeprasert n.d.).

ASSUMPTIONS

There are five assumptions underlying the model used in analyzing Northwest Coast feasting. The assumptions and their justifications are:

1. Ambitious individuals, or "aggrandizers" (after Clark and Blake 1994), on the southern Northwest Coast participate in feasting activities for their

own benefit. Numerous ethnographers note that a feast distribution "was no free and wanton gift" (Codere 1966:69), rather it was given to further the donor's own interests (Barnett 1938b:350, 1968:77–78, 126; Boas 1966:51; Kamenski 1917:48; Mauss 1967:3; Sproat 1987:80). One of the main goals of this chapter is to identify the specific advantages that aggrandizers derive from various types of feast giving. In recent years, George Buchanan was awarded a Nobel Prize for developing economic models in which individuals participating in a system of exchange are assumed to act for their own self-interest (Lewin 1986:941).

2. When individuals systematically invest significant amounts of time, energy, and resources in an activity, they expect to gain specific, practical benefits. This assumption extends the first assumption by stipulating that terms such as *status* and *prestige* are too vague to account for an individual's ambitious program of feast giving (see Chapter 2). Specific, practical benefits being sought must be identified (Hayden 1995:21; Young 1971:211).

3. The majority of support group members (usually lineages, corporate groups,[1] or communities) must at least tacitly approve of the aggrandizer's activities (Hayden 1995:21). Intragroup conflict would erupt otherwise (and undoubtedly did on occasion), inhibiting the efforts of aggrandizers. There is abundant ethnographic evidence that sponsoring a feast required a high degree of group cooperation among members of support groups (e.g., Barnett 1968:123; Boas 1921:1341; Codere 1966:78; Drucker 1951:268). It seems unlikely that any individual could successfully sponsor a large feast if faced with a concerted opposition.

4. The elaboration of feasting on the Northwest Coast was a function of the region's environmental richness. This richness originally enabled the amassing of food and property for distribution (Barnett 1938:118, 1968:76; Drucker 1951:37, 59).

5. An aggrandizer's main objective is to increase control by indebting others. In discussing the Kwakiutl, Walens (1981:13) states that a "nobleman" attained success only by indebting others. Hayden (1995:24, 69) argues that ambitious individuals increased their power by indebting others and creating return obligations. Gosden (1989), Mauss (1967:73), Wohlt (1978:100), and Strathern (1971:215–216, 219) all make similar points: power and prosperity resulted from indebting others.

FEASTING TYPES

Hayden (Chapter 2—see also 1995:27; also Hayden and Maneeprasert n.d.:5–9) proposes that all practical benefits or goals of feasting can be categorized into (at least) eight general types that can be conceptualized as ideal feast types. Ambitious southern Northwest Coast individuals maintained and increased their economic and political control, control over labor, and wealth, by sponsoring feasts of these eight general types, although purposes often overlapped or were combined in a single event.

1. *Solidarity*. Feasts promoting cooperation within a group (e.g., household, lineage, corporate group, village) are considered solidarity feasts. Solidarity within a group will enhance economic productivity and security, promote mutual support between group members in conflicts with other groups, and ensure support for group leaders. In solidarity feasts, hierarchical differences should be downplayed, food should be the main product distributed, contributions from all participants frequently occur, no debts or return obligations should result, and participation and attendance should be widespread.

2. *Reciprocal*. Reciprocal feasts *initiate* and *maintain* alliances between groups for the purposes of security, marriage, and economic benefits (e.g., increased access to resources or exchange partners). Two or more groups or their representatives must be involved, and each group generally tries to impress the other(s) without being overtly competitive so as to maintain an amiable atmosphere.

3. *Solicitation*. Solicitation feasts are feasts given to solicit favors or support from more powerful individual(s). Solicitation feasts are probably unidirectional exchanges where the solicited powerful individual receives food and/or gifts without incurring the expense of a specific return feast.

4. *Promotional*. Promotional feasts advertise group success and prosperity in order to *attract* desirable potential labor, allies, exchange partners, and other supporters. Group success and prosperity is promoted by making public distributions to important and specifically invited individuals with whom a relationship is desired (e.g., families with potential marriage partners, or potential security allies). Distributions are also made to other miscellaneous guests and supporters in order to promote the host group to as wide a circle as possible.

5. *Competition*. Competitive feasts create material profit for the feast sponsor because invested feast distributions are returned at a future feast with interest. Competitive feasts are large, lavish events where the sponsor endeavors to maximize his contractual obligations and profit by distributing enormous amounts of food and property.

6. *Political Support*. Political support feasts are sponsored in order to obtain or increase political support.

7. *Acquisition of Political Positions*. Feasts that function as a formal criterion for political advancement are categorized as feasts for acquiring political positions.

8. *Work-Party Feasts.* Work-party feasts obtain labor for specific labor-intensive projects such as house building. Individuals provide their labor in exchange for participation in feasting activities.

9. *Child-Growth Feasts.* A ninth type of feast might be added to Hayden's proposed ideal feast types. Child-growth feasts are feasts that invest surpluses in children in order to increase their worth so that wealth exchanges at marriages will be maximized, and alliances between families for other purposes will be strengthened.

Separating feasts in this manner is artificial because the feast types obviously overlap, and a single feast will probably involve a combination of these proposed types. However, identifying these specific practical benefits of feasts facilitates this analysis by clarifying the components.

FRAMEWORK

In order to simplify the analysis of feasting in the study area, the Kwakiutl, Nootka, Coast Salish, and Twana feasts will be separated into three more basic categories: (1) feasts where the sponsor does not expect the recipients of food or gifts to invite him to a future feast, which I will call no-return feasts; (2) feasts where the sponsor expects the main recipients of his food or gifts to invite him to a future feast and return equivalent amounts to him, which I will call equal-return feasts; (3) feasts where the sponsor expects to receive an increased return at a future feast, which I will call greater-return feasts. It is important to emphasize that Drucker (1951:290–291, 381), Drucker and Heizer (1967:79–80), Elmendorf (1960:332, 343), Boas (1966:51), Barnett (1938a:132, 1955:190, 255, 257, 1968:30, 84, 100), Sproat (1987:80), and Birket-Smith (1967:12, 13, 15, 35) all state that on at least certain occasions potlatch and feast distributions obligated the recipients to return the feast and gifts.

The return expected by a feast sponsor helps indicate which of the nine general purposes for holding feasts is involved, which in turn identifies the practical benefit sought by the feast sponsor. How the different feast types fit into this framework, and how aggrandizers used them to increase their wealth and control, will be discussed in the coming sections.

In order to understand feasting goals and dynamics, it is necessary to examine the question of who the main feast sponsors are. Details will be provided throughout the chapter; however, the principal individuals who sponsor feasts, whether they are no-return, equal-return, or greater-return feasts, appear to be highly motivated hereditary elites ("chiefs") with the power and capability to amass the required resources for lavish or larger feasts. "No one but a chief of high rank could potlatch for himself" (Drucker 1951:182; also see Barnett 1955:134; Drucker 1939:64, 1951:72, 193, 141, 143, 243, 247, 286, 370, 376, 377, 439; Elmendorf

1960:322, 327, 338, 343, 353, 361–63, 388, 404–405, 410, 443, 1971:361). Barnett (1955:141) and Elmendorf (1960:333, 427, 433) state that elite individuals were verbally trained from an early age to be ambitious. Barnett states that the potlatch "expresses purely personal intentions and ambitions" (1968:126). Boas (1897:343; also in Barnett 1968:5) makes the same points. Although sponsorship is sometimes attributed to a single individual such as a household head, the principal sponsor can be regarded as representing his own interests, the interests of the corporate group's upper-class members, and to a lesser extent the interests of other free corporate group members (see Barnett 1938b:350; Drucker 1939:64).

Daughters could inherit titles and property (e.g., Barnett 1938a:131, 1955:251; Boas 1925:67–69, 91, 105; Codere 1990:367; Rosman and Rubel 1971:135), but this occurred less frequently, if at all, before contact (Barnett 1995:251; Codere 1990:367). For this reason I will refer to feast sponsors and aggrandizers in the masculine third person.

NO-RETURN FEASTS

No-return feasts have been defined as those feasts in which the sponsor does not necessarily expect a return feast. Nevertheless, as will be seen, even on these occasions the sponsor can be viewed as pursuing his own interests.

Solidarity Feasts

In order to attain their ambitions, aggrandizers needed control over a supply of labor. Resource sites were definitely privately or corporately owned (Barnett 1955:59, 241, 250, 251, 1968:78; Boas 1921:1345, 1966:35–36; Drucker 1951:42, 43, 47, 247, 248, 256–257, 454; Suttles 1960:300; Walens 1981:13, 71). Hereditary chiefs who owned such productive resource sites needed workers to collect and process the resources at their hunting, fishing, or gathering sites (Drucker 1951:279, 454; Suttles 1960:300). The output from these resource sites fed the chiefs' families and retainers (Drucker 1951:244) and enabled aggrandizers to accumulate surplus food for feasting and exchanging.

Control over labor secured several other benefits for aggrandizers: first, it increased security for both the group and its leaders. Second, it secured control over production of nonfood goods such as canoes (Boas 1913:1338; Drucker 1939:64), which could be used for exchanging or distributing. Third, controlling labor provided the opportunity for acquiring privately owned "henchmen" (Barnett 1938:130; Drucker 1951:251; Walens 1981:38) who enforced the aggrandizers' orders.

The two crucial points are: (1) that aggrandizers needed control over labor in order to prosper (Barnett 1955:247, 1968:113; Boas 1921:1333, 1334; Drucker 1951:244, 280, 323, 454; Elmendorf 1971:372); and (2) that aggrandizers required a means of controlling the individuals who fished, hunted, gathered, or otherwise supported them. Aggrandizers indebt the members of their group by providing food for subsistence, and other perks such as giving them economic rights, naming their children at feasts, giving them their own prestigious names such as war chief names, and lending them ceremonial privileges such as hair ornaments for their daughters' puberty feasts so that they are able to sponsor their own small feasts (Drucker 1951:47, 140–141, 245, 257, 270, 273, 280, 381, 383–384; Elmendorf 1960:324; Walens 1981:13). Some retainers might even receive a wife as a reward for their service, which the retainer might not be able to afford otherwise (Drucker 1951:273; Mozino 1970:32–33). In his discussion of indigenous economic systems of the Northwest Coast and elsewhere, Herskovits (1952:462–463, 470, 482) notes that the supporters of aggrandizers may be rewarded with prestigious titles or given assistance in accumulating their marriage gift. Indebting, rewarding, and controlling group members in these or other manners results in the group members becoming the retainers of the group elites (for additional descriptions of group members as tenants or retainers see Barnett 1968:45; Boas 1921:1333, 1334; Drucker 1951:43, 271–272; Elmendorf 1960:325).

Solidarity feasts were one way aggrandizers kept their group members content, productive, and supportive. The way feasts were employed to *attract* labor will be discussed under promotional feasts. According to Drucker, young chiefs "were told that they must 'take care of' their people . . . providing them with food, giving them feasts, winning the good will and affection of the commoners, for 'if your people don't like you, you're nothing'" (1951:131). Young chiefs were advised "to 'be good to their people, treat them kindly, and give them many feasts to make them happy'" (Drucker 1951:454; also see Drucker 1951:439–440). And according to Barnett, a chief "gave frequent feasts and entertainments to the members of his family group to maintain their good will" (1955:246). That is, there were no guests from other groups, or at least no essential guests. Similar considerations may have been responsible for the community feasts held in more complex chiefdoms and early states such as described by Kirch (Chapter 6), Junker (Chapter 10), and Schmandt-Besserat (Chapter 14).

Due to the private or corporate ownership of productive resource sites, people who did not own property could only survive by aligning themselves with a group in order to gain access to subsistence resources (Barnett 1938a:130, 1955:244; Boas 1921:1345–1347; Drucker 1939:59; Elmendorf 1960:268; Walens 1981:71). Examples are cited stating that individuals caught using a resource site without the proper right might be killed (Barnett 1955:244; Boas 1921:1345–1347; Boas 1966:35–36). "Service and deference were traded for economic security" (Barnett 1938a:130; also see Rosman and Rubel 1971:79).

Moreover, for free individuals, group membership was not static; members were able to choose the group with which to affiliate according to the relative benefits they would receive (Barnett 1938b:350–351, 1955:193; Drucker 1951:71, 279; Elmendorf 1971:358–359; Rosman and Rubel 1971:173; Walens 1981:39). The treatment retainers received determined whether they remained with the current house group, or aligned themselves with another (Barnett 1938a:129, 1955:246, 1968:45; Boas 1921:1333; Drucker 1951:453, 454). And as Drucker (1951:131, 280, 439–440, 454) and Barnett (1955:246) indicate, feast participation was a deciding factor in whether an individual continued to align with a particular group. Feast participation included the benefits of celebrating group membership, accessing abundant or special feasting foods, and enjoying a party atmosphere. Drucker's informants told him that individuals did not mind working for a chief because they knew they would receive a feast in return (Drucker 1951:251).

The majority of the food distributed at solidarity feasts appears to have come from the output of group members (Boas 1921:1334; Drucker 1951:251, 371). Boas cites several examples of tribute amounts. Salmon fishers and berry pickers might give 20 percent of their catches (Boas 1921:1335), bear hunters gave one for every three caught (Boas 1921:1338), and mountain goat hunters gave five out of ten goats obtained (Boas 1921:1334). However, ethnographic accounts do not seem to detail specific distributions at solidarity types of feasts. On the other hand, there are more detailed accounts for larger, more conspicuous feasts. Many of the commonly known feasts such as naming feasts or puberty feasts were probably not solely solidarity feasts. Many feasts would have had solidarity features because the sponsor's group would have participated. It seems likely that feasts that were held for strictly solidarity purposes occurred regularly, were small and informal with rank differences being downplayed (Barnett 1955:246). For example, Drucker and Heizer (1967:37) cite an occasion when a chief returned from a potlatch and provided an informal feast to "his people" who did not accompany him, relating to them the festivities that occurred. Barnett (1955:266) notes an instance when a feast sponsor thanked his household supporters by making a small distribution to them the day after all invited guests had departed. These are probably typical examples of small household solidarity feasts.

Work-Party Feasts

Work-party feasts are also given by wealthy elites without an expectation of a return feast. The feast sponsor provides the feast in exchange for labor on a specific project such as building a house: "Building a house . . . [required] control of a considerable amount of manpower, which in turn depended on economic resources to support the people while they worked, with enough surplus to give feasts and other diversions to entertain them" (Drucker 1951:72).

Barnett (1938b:352), Boas (1925:339), Elmendorf (1960:152, 312), and Rosman and Rubel (1971:163) observed that feasts were exchanged for labor on projects such as house building, post carving, and post raising. Details specifying where the invited workers were from, and the amounts of food and property that were distributed, are minimal. In the instance Boas (1925:313) cites the house was being built by one of the Fort Rupert septs (i.e., "subtribes") and the laborers were members of the other three Fort Rupert septs. Barnett (1938b:352) states that laborers were not from the house builder's own group. Elmendorf (1960:312) indicates that labor, and the distributed food and property, was provided by both the house builder's group and other households. Work-party feasts were probably intracommunity events, and most of the distributions were probably produced by the house builder's retainers. Alternatively, the distributed goods might have been accumulated with credit exchange transactions. Loans were utilized for financing many types of feasts, including work-party feasts. Loans were a critical mechanism for amassing resources and indebting others, and will be examined in the equal-return section.

It seems likely that at least some lower-class members of the house builder's group participated in the feasting activities, either as a result of providing labor for the construction project or as a result of helping orchestrate the feast (see Barnett 1938b:352). Therefore, some solidarity aspects were probably involved with large work-party feasts. It is even possible that work-party feasts reinforced alliances. For example, the relatives of the house builder's spouse might have been among those who provided labor and participated in the feasting activities, thus solidifying relations between the two families or groups.

Solicitation Feasts

It seems likely that on occasion individuals made solicitation feasts and distributions in order to elicit favors or support from wealthy or powerful individuals. These feasts were probably on a very small or medium scale with no return feast expected. However, the only evidence I encountered came from Elmendorf who notes that a feast distribution might have been made to an individual "whose 'heart one wants to grease' preparatory to a request" (1948:626 note). Solicitation feasts were evidently not major occasions, and were probably subsumed with other feast types (e.g., reciprocal feasts) or were too small to be of much importance for most ethnographers.

EQUAL-RETURN FEASTS

Some preliminary observations on equal-return feasts should be made before discussing specific types of feasts in this category. Ambitious hereditary elites were also the principal organizers and sponsors of equal-return and greater-return feasts. However, because these feast types have different goals than no-return feasts do, it is more likely that the principal recipients of equal-return and greater-return feasts were themselves hereditary elites rather than retainers—in contrast to many no-return feasts where the main recipients of food and gifts were retainers. Thus, the principal recipients of equal-return or greater-return feast distributions were hereditary elites from outside the sponsor's group (Barnett 1955:255, 266; Boas 1925:353–357; Drucker 1951:377; Elmendorf 1960:337, 338, 443–444). Depending on the occasion, guests might have included powerful corporate heads who were prospective defensive allies (Ferguson 1984:315), families or corporate leaders of groups with prospective marriage partners for the sponsor's children (Elmendorf 1960:443), or potential wealth exchange partners who were judged by the sponsors to be good credit risks (Barnett 1968:81–82). With feast invitations it was implicit that an invited guest could also bring other members of his household or village to the feast (Elmendorf 1960:339). Hence, intergroup feasts often included numerous miscellaneous guests in addition to the specifically invited guests. The choice of which household members accompanied chiefs to these feasts was undoubtedly another coveted reward that chiefs used to control labor and supporters within their groups.

Furthermore, the distribution of food and gifts to the principal guests at inter-village feasts was given in ranked order and amounts (Barnett 1955:255, 1968:27; Codere 1966:65; Drucker 1951:379, 1948:232; Elmendorf 1960:324, 341–342). Intravillage feasts, such as solidarity feasts, apparently did not have ranked distributions (e.g., Barnett 1955:255; Boas 1925:119–125). However, it seems probable that ranked distributions occasionally occurred (depending on the situation) if more than one family or household group was involved.

In addition, as Hayden (1995:52) acknowledges, the return furnished at subsequent return feasts might not always meet the original sponsor's expectations. Drucker and Heizer (1967:79–80) write that a difficulty (at least in aboriginal times) in assessing returns was caused by the exchange mediums: no two canoes, slaves, native blankets, pelts, or olachon containers were identical (also see Barnett 1968:84). Consequently, an exact comparison between what was given, and what was returned, was impossible. Therefore, an individual expected to provide an equal return must have been obligated to return an "approximately equal" amount.

Promotional Feasts

Promotional feasts on the southern Northwest Coast can be considered either as no-return or equal-return feasts. No-return promotional distributions included the incidental food and gifts given to miscellaneous guests and participants who were not principal guests, such as retainers accompanying the principal guests. These distributions were part of the overall expense of sponsoring a feast, and ensured the feast was a "good show," dissipated envy, guaranteed that everyone felt involved, rewarded supporters, and so on (Hayden 1995:46, 68). For example,

Elmendorf (1960:324, 342) noted that commoners received token gifts of low value after the ranked distributions to the main guests (also see Boas 1925:231–233; Drucker 1948:232, 1951:299, 438).

However, many equal-return feasts (including maturation and "life-crisis" feasts) were equally, if not more, important as promotional opportunities because they also involved distributions to specific *prospective* allies, marriage partners, or other important contacts. For example, potential suitors from a girl's own village, and from other villages, were invited to her puberty feast and informed of her availability for marriage (Elmendorf 1960:443–444; also see Barnett 1955:151). The privileges to be inherited by her future children, and to be given at the time of her marriage, might also be displayed at a girl's puberty feast (Drucker 1951:141).

Aggrandizers also publicized their heirs, and simultaneously advertised group success to prospective partners and supporters by sponsoring lavish naming feasts for their children (Drucker 1951:124–125, 247; Elmendorf 1960:385–386). Naming feasts were expensive (Barnett 1955:132), and the sometimes extravagant distributions (e.g., 300 silver dollars [Elmendorf 1960:387]; $100 at one individual's naming feast and $160 at another [Barnett 1955:139]) were intended to advertise group success and the benefits of affiliation (see Barnett 1955:142, 143). In many, if not most cases, the sponsors of these maturation, or other promotional feasts would themselves be invited to similar feasts hosted by the guests who were within the group of potential future in-laws or allies. Much of the distribution costs of promotional feasts would be recouped at such subsequent feasts (Barnett 1955:134, 255, 257). Barnett does not specify a time span for such return invitations, but return invitations were probably received within a few years. As a result of the above considerations, I have decided to examine Northwest Coast promotional feasts in the equal-return section.

Promotional feasts were opportunities for aggrandizers to advertise group prosperity, and the benefits of group affiliation, in order to attract productive or skilled labor, allies, marriage and exchange partners, and other supporters with critical abilities (Hayden 1995:52). This goal is recognized by Schulting (1995:15, 183) who observed that some feasts were used to attract supporters. Barnett (1938b:353–354), too, reported that feasts gained the sponsors publicity and recognition ("prestige" or "status") outside of their group and that this recognition was required to achieve their aims. Barnett does not specify what these aims were, or how publicity helped the aggrandizers achieve them, but the publicity probably helped aggrandizers to attract labor, marriage, and exchange partners, and other supporters, in the manner outlined below.

Skilled and powerful supporters were especially important for success in conflict situations. The lack of powerful allies or supporters resulted in a weak pub-

lic image, and "perceived weakness invited attack" (Ferguson 1984b:308). Therefore, promoting the group as being prosperous and well connected increased security. In fact, Ferguson states that warfare might even be motivated by the desire
to obtain resources that could be redistributed to "attract individual followers
and ally groups" (1984a:49).

As Drucker puts it, an aggrandizer's goal was "to attract lower rank people to
his house . . . [which] he did by good treatment, generosity (giving many feasts
and potlatches)" (1951:280). Promotional feasts demonstrating the benefits of
group membership attracted the labor that aggrandizers required to harvest resources at sites they owned or controlled, to produce exchange goods, and to
support their feasting activities. Some aggrandizers also sought to attract followers for military campaigns (Ferguson 1984b:272), and promotional feasts would
have helped here as well. Aggrandizers were sometimes even willing to accept
slothful retainers because rejecting these individuals might provoke their more
industrious relatives to also leave (Drucker 1951:280).

Families of desirable workers, hunters, or craftsmen "would be courted [by a
chief] to the extent of giving them economic and ceremonial rights, to entice
them to associate" with him (Drucker 1951:280). And prospective tenants took advantage of their position to promote their own self-interest. Residence "choices
are made on the basis of a type of strategy involving rank of seat obtainable,
rank of group involved, and its size and power" (Rosman and Rubel 1971:173; see
also Hayden 1995:66). Aggrandizers' promotional displays of wealth and prosperity influenced tenants' and lower elites' perceptions of which groups were most
successful, most powerful, and most likely to support tenants' aspirations.

Child-Growth Feasts

Wealthy hereditary elites sponsored the most lavish maturation and life-crisis
feasts (Barnett 1955:134; Drucker 1951:139, 141, 143; Elmendorf 1960:388, 410, 443).
Maturation and life-crisis feasts were probably primarily promotional opportunities for aggrandizers to advertise themselves and their groups. The leading guests
who were invited from other villages and the amounts of property distributed
varied with the family's wealth and ambitions (Barnett 1955:255, 257, 261; Drucker
1951:141, 148; Elmendorf 1960:385, 386, 443, 460). Poor families either kept these occasions private and did not have feasts larger than the nuclear family, or held very
small gatherings where they invited the chiefs of their household and delivered a
small gift (Barnett 1955:132, 143; Drucker 1951:124–125, 141, 149; Elmendorf
1960:409, 410).

However, the puberty and naming feasts mentioned above also exemplify another aspect of maturation feasts: "child-growth" investments (Hayden 1995:44,
45, 54, 55, 59; Mauss 1967:6, 26; Oberg 1973:33, 35, 81, 121; Rosman and Rubel

1971:174, 187, 195, 198). Maturation feasts for children such as naming (Barnett 1955:134, 138, 139; Boas 1925:119–130; Drucker 1948:208, 1951:124–125; Elmendorf 1960:385–386), ear piercing (Drucker 1951:124–125; Elmendorf 1960:410, 418), and puberty (Barnett 1955:151; Boas 1966:370; Drucker 1948:212, 213, 1951:139–145; Elmendorf 1960:410, 418) were essentially investments made by the parents with the expectation of increased compensation or levels of wealth exchange at future marriage and perhaps funeral exchanges (Hayden 1995:44, 45). With every expensive maturation feast given for a child, the level of wealth exchange at their marriage undoubtedly increased, providing a means of recouping the initial feast expenses. Barnett (1955:180) reports that wealthy families enhanced the value and desirability of girls by secluding them to the extent that they could hardly walk properly. Drucker (1951:143) makes similar observations.

In terms of investing wealth in children through maturation feasts, increasing the cost of marriages serves the needs of aggrandizers by stimulating surplus production and creating increasingly large debt relationships throughout the community (Hayden 1995:44, 45, 54, 55)—a topic to be taken up again shortly. To prosper at utilizing wealth to control others (Mauss 1967:73) aggrandizers need competitors. Rivals also engage in production of surpluses, increasing the total wealth available for manipulation and escalating the scale of contractual obligations. Rosman and Rubel say it succinctly: "one needs one's rivals" (1971:159, 172). That is one reason "lazy men" are despised (Barnett 1938a:131, 1955:248; Drucker 1951:328; Hayden 1995:46, 48). Lazy people thwart the aggrandizer's ambitions by not producing surpluses, by not exchanging wealth, and by "mooching" off elite surpluses when in need. Child-growth investments probably at least occasionally, and eventually, yielded a surplus return; however, due to the lack of immediate returns or compulsory returns from the full range of elites invited (only some of whom might actually enter into more formal reciprocal exchanges), as well as the more uncertain nature of the returns, child-growth investments are examined here under equal-return feasts.

Previously it was mentioned that production by retainers was one manner in which food and property were amassed for feast distribution. A second important method involved credit exchanges or loans. Individuals from all four of the Northwest Coast cultures examined here amassed property by borrowing it (Barnett 1938a:135, 1955:135, 258–259, 1968:81; Boas 1897:341, 1966:78–79; Codere 1966:69–71; Drucker 1948:233; Elmendorf 1960:330, 338, 358). The borrowed property was then distributed to supporters of aggrandizers with a contractual agreement that an equal or greater value to the goods loaned out would be given back to the aggrandizer within a given amount of time or when needed. The initial loan was then repaid when the ambitious borrower received his return goods from supporters at a future feast (e.g., Boas 1966:79; Elmendorf 1960:358). Some groups required that interest be paid on loans. The northern Coast Salish groups asked for 100 percent interest on a loan (Barnett 1938:135, 1955:258–259), the southern Coast Salish (Barnett 1955:258–259) and the Twana (Elmendorf 1960:330) did not require interest, and the Kwakiutl had variable interest rates that depended on the term: 20 percent for less than six months, 40 percent for six months, and 100 percent for 12 or more months (Boas 1897:341, 1966:78–79; Codere 1966:69–71). Furthermore, an individual's "credit rating" (i.e., reputation, "status," past performance) affected his borrowing capabilities and the interest he paid where applicable (Barnett 1968:81; Boas 1897:341, 1966:78; Elmendorf 1960:330; Rosman and Rubel 1971:30). Individuals burdened with poor credit had to pawn their name for a year, and paid exorbitant interest rates, even over 200 percent, to get reestablished (Boas 1897:341, 1966:78; Codere 1966:70). As Hayden (1995:52) states, it seems likely that loans were not always returned according to these specified rates.

Even without interest on loans, there were obvious advantages in this system for borrowers and lenders. Borrowers were able to amass property and indebt others with their secondary distributions. Lenders increased their claims over others, forcing borrowers to actively engage in ongoing production and wealth exchanges. Lenders who were faced with defaulting borrowers might have been able to "foreclose" on resource sites or other property that belonged to the borrower either in lieu of payment or until late payments and "late charges" were paid. In some cases defaulters may even have been enslaved, or served with some other potential penalty such as being forced to direct members from their household to labor for their creditors. Furthermore, lending property and distributing wealth at feasts enabled aggrandizers to maintain full production of food and goods without worrying about storage, security, or spoilage (Hayden 1995:45). Importantly, an individual's ability to lend or borrow, his credit rating, the interest rates he paid, and the network of borrowing and lending contacts he had, were all undoubtedly affected by the promotional feasts he sponsored, his past record of transactions, and the degree of support from successful, hereditary corporate groups.

The contractual claims created over an individual by indebting them via loans or feast distributions were exacting. An individual who failed to repay his debts almost certainly lost allies, supporters, the chance for a good marriage, and his credit rating or "prestige." More seriously, warfare or the threat of warfare was often the result of defaulting on obligations (Hayden 1995:35, 40, 60; Mauss 1967:3, 11). If ordinary tenants had to pawn their "name" (i.e., reputation) for a year to assure repayment (Boas 1897:341, 1966:78; Codere 1966:70), elites must have had similar liens on each other to give force to these contractual debts. In extreme cases, violence could be used. Ferguson states that "war is an exchange gone bad" (Ferguson 1984a:17–18, 41), and that unfulfilled "social" obligations motivated warfare. McIlwraith (1948:I:320, II:376; Ferguson 1984b:307) reports an instance when a Bella Bella group destroyed a Rivers Inlet Kwakiutl village for failing to repay their potlatching debts. Boas (1897:366, 1966:54) gives an example of an unveiled threat to a father-in-law who was trying to evade repaying the marriage gift: the son-in-law drowned a wooden effigy of his wife by putting a stone around the image's neck and dropping it in the sea. And Drucker states that an individual's name might be "seized if a debt was not paid" (1939:63). This is an extreme penalty, considering that an individual's name represented all his economic and ceremonial rights (Barnett 1955:134; Drucker 1939:62). Presumably an individual was not enslaved when it was his name, not his person, that was seized although this might have varied according to the amount involved in defaulting. Presumably, he minimally lost the valuable ceremonial songs, dances, and other privileges connected with his name, as well as ownership of productive resource sites the name bestowed. Thus, potentially, a person's power and influence may have been destroyed by not fulfilling his contractual feasting obligations.

Reciprocal Feasts

Reciprocal feasts were ongoing reciprocal wealth exchanges between groups that initiated and maintained alliances between groups for the purposes of security, marriage, and economic benefits (e.g., access to resources or exchange partners). The ongoing nature of reciprocal feasts fulfilled several important needs for the self-interest of aggrandizers (Hayden 1995:42–44, 47): first, it reinforced the concentration of wealth and power in the hands of those who already had it. Wealthy and powerful groups tended to reciprocate and marry with each other, further distancing themselves from lesser groups. Second, surplus production was maintained, increasing the wealth aggrandizers could manipulate. Third, continuous exchanges provided a perpetual opportunity for the creation of contractual obligations between elite groups, and also enabled aggrandizers to indebt less wealthy individuals who borrowed wealth in order to marry, or to establish other types of alliances that would advance elite sponsors and their interests.

Intergroup marriage feasts, and the ongoing feast exchanges they initiated are good examples of reciprocal feasts (Barnett 1955:182, 183, 184, 190, 194; Drucker 1951:275, 286, 291–292; Elmendorf 1960:349, 358, 362). The Twana, Nootka, and southern Coast Salish had equal-return marriage feasts; the Kwakiutl, Pentlatch, and Comox (northern Coast Salish) expected a surplus return and therefore these feasts will be examined under greater-return feasts (Barnett 1938:132, 1955:188, 190, 207; Boas 1966:51, 53; Codere 1966:63, 68–69; Drucker 1951:377, 381).

In addition to wealth-exchange benefits, marriage feasts provided other benefits. First, they initiated and maintained security alliances between groups, protecting one or both groups from attack and slave raids (Barnett 1955:182, 183, 270; Drucker 1951:302; Elmendorf 1960:349, 561; Ferguson 1984b:285). Second, marriages with significant wealth exchanges established resource alliances that enabled access to another group's resource sites (Drucker 1939:59, 1951:267, 268; Elmendorf 1960:267–268; Ferguson 1984b:288; Suttles 1960:299). Drucker (1951:248) cites an example of a rich salmon stream obtained by a chief through marriage. Third, marriage feasts with wealth exchanges increased credit-exchange opportunities because the spouse's relatives became additional contacts for lending, borrowing, or other support (Barnett 1968:50, 51; Drucker 1951:430; Elmendorf 1960:361–362). Barnett notes that if a groom's father did not have enough property for the marriage gift to the bride's family "he called upon . . . his wife's brothers . . . for their contributions to swell the total of the marriage gift" (1955:185). Fourth, marriage feasts with wealth exchanges forged alliances that expanded an individual's political connections and helped increase political control within and between groups (Barnett 1938:133, 1955:182; Jewitt 1987:19). And fifth, marriage alliances secured the transfer of titles and privileges from the bride's family to the groom and his family. Among the Twana, Nootka, and most Coast Salish groups, these titles and privileges were intended for the couple's future children (Barnett 1955:189, 1968:31; Drucker 1951:291; Elmendorf 1960:381, 384). If no children resulted, the titles and privileges reverted to the bride's family (Drucker 1951:291). However, despite the claim that the titles and privileges were solely for the couple's future children, it seems likely that the groom or his family controlled the titles and privileges at least until the couple's children reached independent maturity (Drucker 1951:266, 269; Barnett 1955:251).

Kwakiutl, Pentlatch, and Comox marriages contrasted with those of the Twana, Nootka, and other Coast Salish groups, because the groom himself overtly received and controlled the titles and privileges given by the bride's family (Barnett 1955:189, 290, 294, 1968:31; Boas 1966:62–63, 71; Codere 1990:367; Rosman and Rubel 1971:173). As a result, the creation of a family was often a secondary consideration compared to acquiring wealth, allies, resource rights, privileges, and titles (Boas 1966:51, 56). Multiple (sequential monogamous and polygamous) marriages were sought in order to accumulate titles and privileges (Barnett 1955:194; Codere 1990:368; Drucker 1948:277). Sham marriages between two men, a man and a household dog, or one man and part of another's body, were practiced solely for acquiring titles and privileges and presumably as a pretext for exchanging wealth as well (Barnett 1938a:133, 1955:203; Boas 1897:359, 1966:55; Codere 1990:368; Drucker 1948:215). The amounts of property exchanged at large, elite marriages between corporate groups or villages clearly indicate that it was the well-connected wealthy elites who were reaping the benefits listed above (Drucker 1948:279, 1951:286; Elmendorf 1960:353, 361–363, 1971:361). Elmendorf (1960:550) states that group exogamy, not necessarily village exogamy, was the principal concern behind elite marriages. Thus, in addition to establishing a variety of alliances with other villages, elite marriages potentially brought increased access to allies, labor, and other supporters within a village. At one southern Coast Salish marriage exchange the groom's party delivered a marriage-feast gift of $200 cash, 20 Indian blankets, 70 trade blankets, and 400 loaves of bread. Three years later the bride's family returned 1,000 loaves of bread and $100 cash (Barnett 1955:200). The return was seemingly less than the original gift, thus this exchange also illustrates that in reality an "equal return" might have been less than the original gift, or equal to it, or a little more. Usually only food was exchanged in the subsequent reciprocating feasts (Barnett 1955:192, 199; Drucker 1951:296–297).

The subsequent reciprocal feasts could go on indefinitely for as long as the bride and groom wished to remain married, or for as long as their respective groups wish to remain allied. It seems likely that an exchange occurred every few years in order to affirm ties between the two groups involved (Barnett 1955:190, 194; Elmendorf 1960:358). After each complete gift and return cycle either party was free to "divorce" the other without further payment, except of course for the privileges that reverted to the bride's family if the couple was childless (Barnett 1955:195; Drucker 1951:291, 302). To perpetuate the marriage and the alliance, a new cycle of exchanges had to be initiated by the groom or his representatives (Barnett 1955:195; Boas 1966:54–55).

A groom's marriage gift might be returned immediately (Barnett 1955:190, 200; Drucker 1951:291), in one year (Barnett 1955:188, 191, 199) or in several years, for example after the birth of children (Barnett 1955:189, 200; Drucker 1951:291, 297; Elmendorf 1960:355). An immediate return could only be made by the wealthiest individuals, and would publicize their wealth and power. Alternatively, by delaying the return, the bride's father (or family head) was able to amass resources for returning the marriage gift by distributing and investing the bridewealth receipts among his own network of influential partners (Barnett 1955:198, 200, 1968:59; Drucker 1951:291).

The groom or his family did not always make the initial distribution in a reciprocal wealth exchange. If a suitor was poor "but skilled professionally and gave every assurance that he would be an asset to the [bride's] family" (Barnett 1955:193), the bride's father might accept the suitor without a marriage gift. Alternatively, a prospective father-in-law might discreetly loan a poor but desirable suitor a modest sum for a marriage gift. In both of these cases the groom paid his debt to the father-in-law by laboring for him, often staying in the father-in-law's house as a member of his household (Barnett 1955:193, 203). Drucker and Heizer (1967:72) even report an instance when a groom desired a larger marriage gift return than his father-in-law could or would provide. Ultimately, the groom him-self provided his father-in-law with the resources to make an enormous marriage gift return. These situations do not seem to fit the typical pattern of ongoing re-ciprocal wealth exchanges between two groups, however, it is clear that mutually beneficial alliances were created. These illustrations are good examples of norms being bent to accommodate practical benefit considerations.

Distributing the receipts from the marriage gift accomplished at least three ob-jectives: first, the bride's father paid off any existing debts. Doing so perpetuated his reputation as a good credit risk, ensuring he could borrow again. Second, the bride's father created additional claims over individuals by indebting them with his distributions. And third, production of surplus goods for the marriage gift re-turn could proceed without the burden of storing the marriage gift items. The opportunity for both the bride's and groom's families to create contractual obli-gations was probably a primary reason for the lavish nature of elite marriages. The feast given by a groom when he distributed the marriage gift payback was "often the greatest of his career" (Drucker 1948:279).

Considering the numerous benefits that resulted from reciprocal feasts, it is easy to agree with Rosman and Rubel (1971:173–174) that marriage involved a strategy in which the resources, military strength, credit rating, positions, and in-fluence of a prospective spouse's family were scrutinized in order to maximize the practical benefits that would accrue to the participating families (Drucker 1951:287–288; Elmendorf 1960:335). The fact that marriages were arranged for elite children, frequently of a very young age, substantiates the inference that this strategy was being followed by families (Boas 1897:362; Drucker 1951:143, 287; El-mendorf 1960:353). Moreover, polygamous marriages enabled the wealthiest, most ambitious individuals to multiply the advantages of this strategy (Barnett 1955:193; Drucker 1951:301; Elmendorf 1960:367–368; Hayden 1995:43).

The marriages of commoners contrasted markedly with elite marriages, al-though of course, there was a continuum of intermediate marriages (Drucker 1951:286, 288–289, 292, 293; Elmendorf 1960:370). Lower-class individuals typically did not marry outside of their own community (Elmendorf 1960:353, 404, 550). Some commoners "just woke up in bed together" (Elmendorf 1960:370) indicat-ing little or no formal marriage ceremony, feasting, or ongoing wealth exchanges. In other cases the parents made an informal agreement, invited a few guests to a meal and distributed token gifts (Barnett 1955:192; Drucker 1948:279, 1951:292, 299; Elmendorf 1960:370, 1971:361).

Marriage feasts were not the only type of reciprocal feasts. This discussion has focused on them because of the abundant and detailed ethnographic records of marriage feasting and wealth exchanges. However, other feasts such as the Twana Intervillage Eating Festivals (Elmendorf 1960:139–141) achieved similar results. It seems likely that less formal and less well-documented feasting between elites from different houses or corporate groups occurred and also achieved similar results.

Feasts for Political Positions and Support

Political support feasts and feasts to acquire political positions will be grouped together because they were similar (although not identical), and because increasing political support was so tightly connected with many feasting types (e.g., solidarity, promotion, reciprocal) that it is difficult to distinguish feasts solely for this purpose.

The main feast that functioned as a formal condition for political advancement is the funeral feast. Funeral feasts occurred when an elite heir announced he was taking over the positions and property of the deceased (Barnett 1955:220; Birket-Smith 1967:20; Drucker 1951:148; Drucker and Heizer 1967:132), as well as the deceased's credit and debt obligations (Drucker and Heizer 1967:132; Codere 1966:69; Hayden 1995:65). Thus, the funeral feast was the heir's statement assuring other elites that he would keep the debt and exchange cycle operating (Hayden 1995:65). Importantly, the heir did not necessarily continue the deceased's specific contractual relationships by distributing property to the deceased's former exchange partners (Drucker and Heizer 1967:131). However, the heir *could* legitimately affirm his intention to maintain the debt and exchange cycle by destroying property and by distributing property to commoners who were present at the funeral feast (Drucker and Heizer 1967:131). (Drucker and Heizer do not specify whether or not the commoners who received property distributions were related to the deceased, but the heir's goals could probably be attained whether the commoners were related or not.) Even in cases when a new contractual obligation was not initiated with specific elite individuals, the heir would still be more or less reimbursed for his distribution when he became a leading guest at future funeral feasts for other community members (Barnett 1955:259, 261; Hayden 1995:66). Therefore, funeral feasts functioned as equal-return feasts.

Rosman and Rubel (1971:170) state that funeral feasts were important occasions of succession among some northern tribes (e.g., Tsimshian, Haida, Tlingit), but in the south (e.g., Kwakiutl) the inheritance had already been received at feasts during the lifetime of the original holder (Rosman and Rubel 1971:170, 171, 175). But the potential for competition between several rival heirs at funeral feasts contradicts Rosman and Rubel. Drucker and Heizer (1967:131, 132) state that competition for a deceased's property and positions could occur, and Boas (1925:89) implies that competition erupted if another individual doubted a prospective heir's claims. In addition, although an heir's father or uncle might give the heir nominal ownership of important seats and privileges, the father or uncle retained control over the seats and privileges until their death (Barnett 1955:251; Drucker 1951:266, 269). It was only after the funeral feast that the "apprenticeship" ended and the heir began exercising control (Drucker 1951:145). In order to permit heirs to firmly establish their network of credit and debt, elite funeral feasts were generally held one to two years after the actual death of a chief or high-ranking elite, although interim funeral feasts might also be held to reassure rivals and creditors of the heir's intentions and capabilities (Barnett 1955:219, 220; Drucker 1951:148–149).

At the funeral feast the heir needed to prove he was worthy of succeeding the deceased. Sponsoring an impressive feast indicated that he had the necessary industry, ambition, group support, wealth, and resources to do so. Boas (1925:75–89) cited a situation in which an important Kwakiutl chief had died and his nephew was to replace him. The men from thirteen Kwakiutl tribes were invited to the funeral feast, fed, and then 2,000 blankets were distributed among the 658 seat holders of the thirteen tribes. Sponsoring this feast would have been an enormous undertaking for anyone, and the heir must have had considerable assistance from his supporters. The stakes were high. The heir's uncle's seat, a house, two valuable coppers, four feasting dishes, and various other songs and privileges could all have been forfeited if the heir had failed to display the required control over the economic and social resources of the corporate group.

Depending on the deceased's influence, guests might be from other tribes (Boas 1925:75–89) or strictly from the deceased's village (Elmendorf 1960:459). A claimant to a more powerful or contested position needed to sponsor a more extravagant feast than a claimant to a lesser position. Drucker (1951:148, 149) reports that for lesser chiefs and wealthy commoners the heir invited only the local chiefs to a feast and gave them gifts. For lesser individuals, funeral feasts probably occurred shortly after death, and they probably exhibited more traits of solidarity feasts for nuclear or extended families. It is doubtful that slaves had any funeral feasts at all.

GREATER-RETURN FEASTS: THE COMPETITIVE FEAST
Competitive feasts were the only feast type in which greater returns were required on initial feast distributions, thus creating material profits for sponsors and supporters alike. "Competitive feasting involving interest payments is clearly one of the most common strategies used for extending personal power and wealth . . . [on] the Northwest Coast" (Hayden 1995:58–59). Investments and wealth exchanges were necessary to increase wealth beyond the limited surpluses provided by retainer labor (Hayden 1995:59). Boas (1897:341, 1966:77) states that the underlying principle of the potlatch distribution "is that of the interest-bearing invest-

ment of property." In addition to increasing wealth, competitive feasts enabled aggrandizers to increase the scale of their contractual obligations with larger and larger exchanges (Hayden 1995:52).

Competitive feasts were sponsored by wealthy individuals (Elmendorf 1960:338, 343) and involved enormous property distributions with hundreds or thousands of people in attendance. Eells (Castile 1985:310, 323) documented 425 people and 1,200 people attending two specific feasts of this kind. The pretext might be any of the common feast occasions such as marriages (Boas 1897:359; Barnett 1955:257), secret society initiations (Elmendorf 1960:337, 343), maturation feasts (Barnett 1955:263), or spring intertribal meetings (Barnett 1955:255, 257). Codere (1966:68–69, 70), Boas (1897:343, 359), and Barnett (1938a:132, 1955:188, 202) all state that competitive feasting returns were expected to be twice the initial distribution, although short-term loans within a household or extended family might carry interest rates as low as 25 percent or none at all (Boas 1966:78).

As an example of a highly attended competitive wealth exchange with vast amounts of property being transferred, Boas (1925:236–357) recounts a succession of wealth exchanges initiated by a marriage involving two very high-ranking Kwakiutl families from two different Fort Rupert septs (see Table 7.1 [also summarized in Rosman and Rubel 1971:161–163]). The ratio of property given to property returned seems obscure because they are not in identical currencies. However, Boas (1966:51) assures readers that "the value of the goods paid (at a marriage gift return) is far in excess of what the bride's father has received."

Sponsoring a competitive feast required years of preparation (Barnett 1968:4; Boas 1898:682, 1925:236–357; Elmendorf 1960:338) with time periods of five to ten years or longer generally being cited (e.g., Castile 1985:310; Hayden 1995:60). The aggrandizer spent these years amassing property by financing smaller-scale loans and feasts (Barnett 1955:258–259; Codere 1966:70), as well as by demanding surplus production from retainers. Ultimately, or ideally, all outstanding credits were collected to finance one enormous feast distribution that would be invested for a few years until being returned with a profit (Barnett 1955:258, 259; Boas 1925:237, 347; Codere 1966:70).

Surplus returns enabled aggrandizers to pay off their supporters with a profit in addition to increasing their wealth in terms of material property, titles, privileges, and the scale of their contractual obligations. Providing profits to supporters motivated supporters to continue producing surpluses that aggrandizers could manipulate, and attracted the surpluses of other parties interested in profitable exchanges (Hayden 1995:52).

In addition, a profitable feast return of more property than could be amassed by small exchanges or tenant labor provided the aggrandizer with a rare oppor-

TABLE 7.1
Marriage Wealth Exchanges between Two High-Ranking Kwakiutl Families

Occasion	Property Distributed	Invited Guests	Comments
Groom's marriage gift	500 blankets	12 tribes	Groom amasses blankets by calling in outstanding loans.
Father-in-law's immediate return	300 blankets; a ceremonial title; the "great copper" named Sewa		Groom sells copper two years later for 600 tins of grease. Grease used to finance a feast for several tribes.
Groom's second distribution to father-in-law	1,000 blankets		Occurs four years after the initial exchanges.
Father-in-law's return	300 blankets; 50 shawls; 20 pairs gold earrings; 20 gold bracelets; 25 silver earrings; 25 silver bracelets; 50 pair abalone shells; 50 silk kerchiefs; 10 phonographs; 35 sewing machines; 250 wooden boxes; 40 dressers; 50 masks; 250 dancing aprons; 25 canoes; 15 boats; a box of crests	10 tribes	Occurs four years after in Groom's second distribution. Bride's father amasses property by calling his outstanding loans. Groom immediately distributes the goods to the important chiefs of the 10 invited tribes.

Source: Boas 1925:236–357. Presumably this exchange cycle continued until economic limits of increase were reached and it became impossible to exchange escalating amounts.

tunity—the massive quantities of returned property could be distributed to wealthy and powerful guests from other villages with whom the aggrandizer wanted to indebt or establish a relationship for purposes of resource access, security, or political support. In Boas's (1925:236–357) account of the marriage between two high-ranking Fort Rupert families, the groom used the proceeds from the father-in-law's first return to sponsor a feast for several tribes (Boas 1925:289), and he distributed the father-in-law's second return to the ranking chiefs of the ten guest tribes attending the event (Boas 1925:353–357; also see Barnett 1955:255, 266, 1968:59; Elmendorf 1960:337, 338).

Finally, the Kwakiutl took competitive feasting to extreme forms with rivalry feasts "in which sums to be given back and forth were pyramided until one rival was broken" (Drucker 1951:381) and significant property destruction occurred. In some of these feasts, blankets were destroyed, grease and canoes were burned, and slaves were killed (Boas 1897:353–354, 1966:93, 98; Codere 1966:77–78, 1990:369). No other groups destroyed significant amounts of property in competitive feasts (as opposed to funeral feasts), and only the northern Coast Salish Comox approached the intensity of the Kwakiutl rivalry feasts (Barnett 1938b:357, 1955:265, 265–266, 1968:81; Drucker 1948:232, 1951:377, 381, 383). Rivalry feasts were probably the ultimate competitive arena for attracting and maintaining labor, political support, exchange partners, and other supporters (Mauss 1967:72). As Boas (1897:353–354) reports, the broken rival lost his influence and undoubtedly his supporters and many economic rights. He was, in essence, bankrupt. Although often characterized as the "typical potlatch," these feasts with increased surplus returns were clearly extreme forms on the Northwest Coast, and reciprocal and no-return feasts were much more common.

CHANGES WITH CONTACT

At this point there is no evidence to indicate that the feasting activities described by ethnographers are fundamentally different in principle from precontact feasting activities, except perhaps for the more extreme forms of competitive and destructive feasting (Barnett 1968:104, 105; Drucker 1951:457). This is supported by Codere (1966:v, 61) who argues that postcontact changes reflected *existing* tendencies in Kwakiutl culture. Thus, this analysis should provide a useful model for the indigenous development of social inequality, rather than just documenting European-induced adaptations in Northwest Coast culture.

Many differences between precontact and postcontact feasting have been cited. Before European arrival (1) the goods distributed were native-manufactured (Barnett 1955:256–257; Codere 1966:94, 1990:369); (2) property was distributed less often and in smaller amounts due to difficulties amassing large quantities of native goods (Barnett 1968:105; Codere 1966:124, 1990:369; Drucker 1951:376–377); (3) fewer guests from other villages were invited, due to more hostile relations (Barnett 1955:256–257; Codere 1990:369); and (4) only the wealthiest hereditary elites could afford to sponsor a feast (Barnett 1968:105; Codere 1990:368; Drucker 1939). Depopulation, wage labor, and merchandise brought by Europeans increased the scale of feasting and enabled more people, including more commoners and women, to be involved in sponsoring feasts (Barnett 1968:105, Codere 1966:125, 1990:363, 369, 371; Drucker 1951:13, 181). However, the underlying motivations and fundamental principles of feasting activities do not seem to have changed from precontact to postcontact.

CONCLUSION

Feasts were sponsored on the southern Northwest Coast to serve the sponsors' interests and ambitions. They constituted important strategies and techniques for promoting self-interest via the acquisition of wealth and power. Ambitious individuals striving to increase their own power and prosperity needed to accomplish several goals.

First, they needed to attract and bind labor to themselves or their group. High-quality labor supported the aggrandizers and their activities such as house building and harvesting resources at privately or corporately owned resource sites. Good supporters also increased group security and provided surplus food and other products that aggrandizers could manipulate.

Second, ambitious individuals needed to form alliances with other powerful groups in order to increase political support, increase security, and gain access to greater exchange networks and marriage partners.

And third, aggrandizers needed a means to invest initial surpluses so that their wealth and prosperity could cycle and multiply.

Various forms of feasting accomplished all of these goals. Throughout this paper references and examples of distributions were provided to demonstrate that (1) the principal feast sponsors were wealthy hereditary elites, and (2) the principal recipients of equal- and greater-return feast distributions were powerful individuals capable of mutually assisting the sponsors in pursuing their goals for potential exchange partners, political supporters, and security allies. One of the key foundations underlying feasting distributions was contractual debt. Aggrandizers' feasting distributions indebted retainers, allies, exchange partners, and other recipients with harsh consequences for unfulfilled obligations.

Many proposals for the "function" of the potlatch exist, but as we have seen, there is no single potlatch phenomenon. Rather, there is a wide range of feasts with different purposes. Therefore, it is illusory to search for a general meaning beyond that of promoting the practical self-interest of organizers and supporters under conditions of extractable resource abundance. Social Structural explanations such as Rosman and Rubel's approach neglect the practical benefits that provided the impetus for the Northwest Coast feasts. Suttles's argument that the potlatch was a redistribution mechanism is inconsistent with Northwest Coast ethnographic data documenting that individual motivations, competition, group solidarity, and the control of surpluses were important aspects of potlatching. Explanations that focus solely on the investment aspect of feasting provide an incomplete analysis of feasting because they do not address the numerous other practical benefits or goals of feasting. Similarly, equating feasting with warfare is misleading. Equating feasting with warfare may imply that at least some feasting participants were motivated by their own self-interest, but such explanations fail to identify and differentiate the solidarity, promotional, investment, and other aspects involved in many feasts and potlatches. Explanations based on "status" or "prestige" are deficient because they emphasize vague psychological yearnings for approval without acknowledging practical consequences. Thus, explanations citing warfare, prestige, hereditary claims, or investments, offer incomplete or unspecific answers, which by themselves create misleading impressions concerning the psychological motivations, strategies, and practical goals associated with feasting. I suggest that the present surplus-based model of self-interested aggrandizers integrates a much greater variety of theoretically and ethnographically important factors and observations in a more satisfactory fashion than previous models. It is only regrettable that even more detailed ethnographic observations are not available on the critical variables that have been discussed. Perhaps the ultimate utility of this approach will only be demonstrable by other cross-cultural studies that support the same kinds of interpretations that I have offered here.

NOTE

1. Corporate groups can be defined as cooperative groups that are enduring and hold joint rights and responsibilities in resources or property ownership and also maintain sociopolitical relationships with other groups or individuals (see Hayden and Cannon 1982).

REFERENCES

Barnett, H. G.

1938a   The Coast Salish of Canada. *American Anthropologist* 40:118–141.

1938b   The Nature of the Potlatch. *American Anthropologist* 40:349–358.

1955   *The Coast Salish of British Columbia*. Eugene: University of Oregon Press.

1968   *The Nature and Function of the Potlatch*. Eugene: University of Oregon Press.

Birket-Smith, K.

1967   *Studies in Circumpacific Culture Relations, Vol. I*. Kobenhavn: Munksgaard.

Boas, F.

1897   The Social Organization and Secret Societies of the Kwakiutl Indians. *U.S. National Museum Annual Report* 1895, pp. 311–738.

1898   Final Report on the Northwestern Tribes of Canada. *British Association for the Advancement of Science Report for* 1898, pp. 628–688.

1921   Ethnology of the Kwakiutl. *Thirty-fifth Annual Report of the Bureau of American Ethnology*, 1913–1914: I and II. Washington.

1925   *Contributions to the Ethnology of the Kwakiutl*. New York: Columbia University Press.

1966   *Kwakiutl Ethnography*. Chicago: University of Chicago Press.

Castile, G. P., ed.

    1985   *The Indians of Puget Sound: The Notebooks of Myron Eells*. Seattle: University of Washington Press.

Clark, J., and M. Blake

    1994   The Power of Prestige: Competitive Generosity and the Emergence of Rank Societies in Lowland Mesoamerica. In *Factional Competition and Political Development in the New World*, edited by E. Brumfiel and J. Fox, pp. 17–30. Cambridge: Cambridge University Press.

Codere, H.

    1966   *Fighting with Property: A Study of Kwakiutl Potlatching and Warfare 1792–1930*. Seattle: University of Washington Press.

    1990   Kwakiutl: Traditional Culture. In *Handbook of North American Indians, Vol. 7, Northwest Coast*, edited by W. Suttles, pp. 359–377. Washington, D.C.: Smithsonian Institution.

Drucker, P.

    1939   Rank, Wealth, and Kinship in Northwest Coast Society. *American Anthropologist* 41:55–65.

    1948   *Culture Element Distributions XXVI: Northwest Coast*. Anthropological Records Vol. 9, No. 3. Berkeley: University of California Press.

    1951   *The Northern and Central Nootkan Tribes*. Smithsonian Institution Bureau of American Ethnology Bulletin 144. United States Government Printing Office, Washington, D.C.

Drucker, P., and R. F. Heizer

    1967   *To Make My Name Good*. Berkeley: University of California Press.

Elmendorf, W. W.

    1948   The Cultural Setting of the Twana Secret Society. *American Anthropologist* 50:625–633.

    1960   *The Structure of Twana Culture*. Pullman: Washington State University Press.

    1971   Coast Salish Status Ranking and Intergroup Ties. *Southwestern Journal of Anthropology* 27:353–380.

Ferguson, R. B.

    1984a   Introduction. In *Warfare, Culture, and Environment*, edited by R. B. Ferguson. New York: Academic Press.

    1984b   A Reexamination of the Causes of Northwest Coast Warfare. In *Warfare, Culture, and Environment*, edited by R. B. Ferguson, pp.267–328. New York: Academic Press.

Gosden, C.

    1989   Debt, Production, and Prehistory. *Journal of Anthropological Archaeology* 8:355–387.

Hayden, B.

    1990   Nimrods, Piscators, Pluckers, and Planters: The Emergence of Food Production. *Journal of Anthropological Archaeology* 9:31–69.

    1993   *Archaeology: The Science of Once and Future Things*. New York: Freeman.

1995   Pathways to Power: Principles for Creating Socioeconomic Inequalities. In *Foundations of Social Inequality*, edited by T. Douglas Price and Gary M. Feinman, pp. 15–86. New York: Plenum.

Hayden, B., and A. Cannon

1982   The Corporate Group as an Archaeological Unit. *Journal of Anthropological Archaeology* 1:132–158.

Hayden, B., and R. Maneeprasert

n.d.   Feasting among the Akha in Thailand. Ms. in possession of B. Hayden, Simon Fraser University, Burnaby, British Columbia.

Herskovits, M. J.

1952   *Economic Anthropology*. New York: Alfred A. Knopf.

Jewitt, J. R.

1987   *The Adventures and Sufferings of John R. Jewitt*. Vancouver: Douglas and McIntyre.

Kamenski, A.

1917   *Tlingit Indians of Alaska*. Fairbanks: University of Alaska Press.

Lewin, R.

1986   Self-Interest in Politics Earns a Nobel Prize. *Science* 234:941–942.

Mauss, M.

1967   *The Gift: Forms and Functions of Exchange in Archaic Societies*. New York: Norton.

McIlwraith, T. F.

1948   *The Bella Coola Indians*. 2 vols. Toronto: University of Toronto Press.

Mozino, J. M.

1970   *Noticias de Nutka: An Account of Nootka Sound in 1792*. Translated by I. H. Wilson. American Ethnological Society Monograph No. 13. Seattle: University of Washington Press.

Oberg, K.

1973   *The Social Organization of the Tlingit Indians*. Seattle: University of Washington Press.

Piddocke, Stuart

1965   The Potlatch System of the Southern Kwakiutl: A New Perspective. *Southwestern Journal of Anthropology* 21:244–264.

Rosman, A., and P. G. Rubel

1971   *Feasting with Mine Enemy*. New York: Columbia University Press.

Schulting, R. J.

1995   *Mortuary Variability and Status Differentiation on the Columbia-Fraser Plateau*. Burnaby, B.C.: Archaeology Press of Simon Fraser University.

Sproat, G.

1987   *The Nootka*. Victoria, B.C.: Sono Nis Press.

Strathern, A.

1971   *The Rope of Moka*. Cambridge: Cambridge University Press.

Suttles, W.

1960   Affinal Ties, Subsistence, and Prestige among the Coast Salish. *American Anthropologist* 62:296–305.

Walens, S.
    1981   *Feasting with Cannibals*. Princeton: Princeton University Press.
Wohlt, P.
    1978   Ecology, Agriculture and Social Organization: The Dynamics of Group Composition in the Highlands of Papua New Guinea. Unpublished Ph.D. dissertation, University of Minnesota, Minneapolis.
Young, M.
    1971   *Fighting with Food*. Cambridge: Cambridge University Press.

8

THE BIG DRINK

FEAST AND FORUM IN THE UPPER AMAZON

Warren R. DeBoer

In [the] pre-1849 period, the Kwakiutl "potlatch" does not seem to be so developed or striking an institution that there is a need for a distinctive term for it. There is nothing remarkable about the giving of gifts or even of ceremonialized giving in human society; and marriages, comings-of-age, and meetings with other villagers or outsiders are so frequently the occasion for gifts that Kwakiutl practices ... seem less particularly Kwakiutl than human.

Codere 1961:445

The feast—or its Spanish cognate *la fiesta*, which perhaps has a richer and more encompassing connotation—has long been a focus of anthropological inquiry. Yet feasts have been viewed in contrasting ways: as mechanisms for leveling or for accumulating wealth and power; as devices for aggregating dispersed populations or for reaffirming social distance in concentrated populations; as ploys for promoting solidarity or for surfacing festering divisions; as forums for accentuating or for easing rites of passage; as contests in which an often ineffable "prestige" is accrued; and as the classic arenas in which otherwise latent worldviews are exposed and dramatized. Given its protean character, the feast would appear to be a delightfully ambiguous category, one whose members are linked by faint resemblances but otherwise lack common properties. In its fuzziness, the feast could be likened to the category "game" (Lakoff 1987:16). Codere's observation, therefore, is apposite.

However ambiguous a general category, the feast may provide a useful entree into the workings of specific cultural systems. Its very unboundedness and ramifying nature resist interpretive closure and may thereby open a wide window into what is revealed and concealed in human behavior, the structures of meaning that scaffold such behavior, and, as will be argued, archaeological residues of both. Here I attempt to marshal the available evidence concerning the major traditional fiesta of the Conibo and Shipibo, denizens of the central and upper Ucayali basin in the Amazon region of eastern Peru. This fiesta, the *ani shrëati*[1] ("big drinking" in Conibo-Shipibo), was practiced as recently as the mid-1970s (d'Ans 1994; Heath 1991; Roberta Campos and Joan Abelove, personal communication, April 18, 1975) but, as far as is known, has been discontinued since that time. The evidence is of three kinds: (1) interviews with Conibo-Shipibo informants who remember the fiesta (the "memory culture" approach); (2) a fairly large but unevenly reliable corpus of references from missionaries, explorers, and a few early ethnographers;[2] and (3) material correlates of the *ani shrëati* that can be tracked in the archaeological record.

In pursuing this project, I will focus on those central themes proposed by Hayden and Maneeprasert, namely: "(1) the purpose of the feast; (2) the group involved; and (3) the amount of surplus that can be assembled for feasting purposes" (1996:18). This tripartition, however, cannot fully enfold the complexities of the *ani shrëati*, and various sorties into other aspects of Conibo-Shipibo culture will contribute context.

PURPOSE OF THE FIESTA

The manifest purpose of the *ani shrëati* was to mark and celebrate the period when a girl or cohort of girls reached, or approached, marriageable age. This straightforward statement, however, needs clarification. The fiesta, although technically a "puberty rite," did not necessarily correspond to the onset of puberty as signaled by first menstruation. In part, this is due to the custom of arranged infant betrothals, today rare but formerly more common, in which a girl as young as six years can be promised to an older, usually adolescent male (Eakin, Lauriault, and Boonstra 1980:80–83). This practice possibly accounts for the great variability noted for the timing of the *ani shrëati*, ranging from six to ten (Izaguirre 1928:234–236) through the more realistically pubescent ages of eleven to fourteen years reported by several nineteenth-century observers (Pallarés and Calvo in Larrabure i Correa 1905–1909, 9:60; Sabaté in Izaguirre 1922–1929, 10:194–195). The fiesta, therefore, celebrated marriageability more than puberty.

The word *celebrate* is perhaps somewhat infelicitous given that the focal event of the *ani shrëati* was a clitoridectomy performed by specialized female surgeons. In the Spanish literature, these specialists are variously called *ancianas* ("old women"), *madrinas* ("godmothers"), or *sacerdotas* ("priestesses").[3] Rationale for the operation is complex and leads to a consideration of Conibo-Shipibo mythology, sexual politics, precarious gender roles and, by extension, the entire fabric of culture (Odicio Román 1969; Roe 1982; Gebhart-Sayer 1987).

For archaeologists who often seem resistant to, or at least wary of, ethnographic sensibilities, let me point out that much of the following is explicated by the Conibo-Shipibo themselves. That is, it is not totally a "deep-structural" concoction on the part of foreign observers. A fundamental theme in Conibo-Shipibo thought is the opposition between "male culture" and "female nature." As procreative beings of nature, females are regarded as oversexed. This excessive concupiscence allies females with the disruptive forces of nature. In contrast, males are the guardians of culture, moderation, and order. As contextually diagnosed by Roe (1982, 1988:118–120) and more specifically targeted by Bertrand-Ricoveri (1996), this theme has both conceptual and spatial referents that can be visualized in terms of concentric circles (Fig. 8.1). An inner core constitutes the male domain of culture and consists of houses flanking a plaza kept immaculately clean (by women!). The outermost circle constitutes the exotic, a zone of libidinous females and male hunting. An intermediate circle has liminal proper-

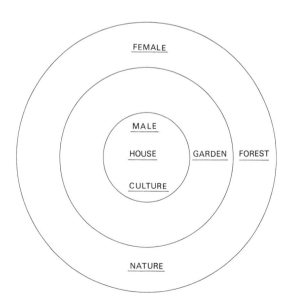

Figure 8.1. Schema contrasting male-associated core with female-associated periphery.

ties: here plants are cultivated; "garden hunting" (Linares 1976) is pursued oppor-
tunistically; and sexual intercourse, both conjugal and illicit, takes place.
Whatever else culture is about, it has to do with coming to terms with nature
and history and, in some sense, taming both. As with other Amazonian groups
(Murphy and Murphy 1974:230; cf. Bamberger 1974), Conibo-Shipibo mythic history recounts a time when women were in control, possessed phallic flutes, or,
more literally, had penises. For the Conibo-Shipibo—correctly sensing the
anatomical correlates of this history—the clitoris is a vestige of an era when male
and female roles were reversed. Periodic excision is necessary to reverse the
vengeful resurfacing of female control and the concomitant reversion to nature
and disorder that it portends. This is not a worldview without angst. Accordingly,
vagina dentata symbolism and castration anxiety are rife among the Conibo-Shipibo as well as other Panoan-speaking groups (e.g., Kensinger 1995:237–246;
Siskind 1973). That these are ancient South American, if not pan-human, beliefs is
attested clearly in Chavín iconography of the Andean Formative (Burger
1992:figs. 178–179, 207).

PREPARATION

All sources agree that hosting an *ani shrëati* was a long and arduous process.
Preparations could begin as much as two to three years before the event and entailed the clearing of gardens and the planting of manioc, *camote* (sweet potato),
and sugarcane (Samanez y Ocampo 1980:80–81, Karsten 1955:156–157, Roe
1982:97–98). From these cultigens, prodigious quantities of manioc beer and cane
liquor were brewed.[4] As the fiesta approached, many additional demands had to
be met.

Men hunted in order to provide meat. As meat storage in the humid tropics is
short-term, captive peccaries, monkeys, juvenile tapirs, and curassows were
raised and fattened as pets in anticipation of the coming feast (Odicio Román
1969:49–60, Illius 1985:586). Even manatees were caught, penned, and fed a special
diet of water plants (Heath 1991:7). New pottery vessels, especially large beer-
storage jars and beer-serving mugs, had to be manufactured (Samanez y Ocampo
1980:44; Tessmann 1928:206–207; Roe 1982:97–98, 100–101; Heath 1991:5). Women
wove new clothing and beaded new ornaments, as protocol demanded that hosts
and guests alike be dressed appropriately (Sabaté 1922–1929, 10:269–271).

In addition, a large guest house was often constructed (Díaz Castañeda
1923:407–408; Illius 1985:584). Obviously, the core sponsors of an *ani shrëati* (said
to number from one to five men, including fathers of the girls undergoing the
ceremony) had to be able to marshal and orchestrate considerable labor—labor
that, in turn, had to be fed and served beer, the basic lubricant of Conibo-Shipibo
social life.

INVITATION

Conibo-Shipibo settlements range from single households (today, usually two adjacent structures, one a domicile, the other a kitchen) to communities numbering in the hundreds. Historical and archaeological records indicate that this variability in settlement size is an old one (DeBoer 1981). Clearly, large settlements were in a better position to host large *ani shrëati*, although smaller communities hosted diminutive versions of the same. In the 1880s, Samanez y Ocampo (1980:80–81) estimated that a fiesta attracted two hundred to three hundred guests. My Conibo-Shipibo informants said that this was a typically sized gathering. At the large Shipibo community of San Francisco de Yarinacocha, guests arrived from as far as the Pisqui to the north and the Pachitea to the south, a catchment of a few hundred kilometers by river (Roe 1982:98).

Odicio Román (1969:49–60) furnishes otherwise lacking information on the mechanics of invitation. Special heralds, called *chaniti* in Shipibo, canoed upstream and downstream to announce the upcoming event. These emissaries were received with ritualized hostility. The shoreline invitees would taunt, "We want to go see our other women," to which the *chaniti* would reply, "You braggarts will get your necks cut" (as will be seen, not an idle threat).

The geography of invitation implicates another deep-seated scheme in Conibo-Shipibo culture that, although cast as concentric circles in Figure 8.2, should be

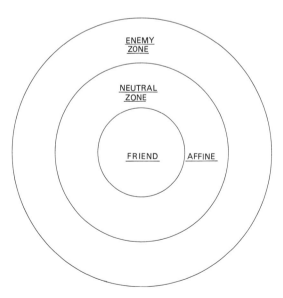

Figure 8.2. Schema contrasting friends, affines, and enemies.

viewed in terms of river distance. The ring of extralocal invitation encompasses potential affines and allies. This proximate, "neutral" zone can be contrasted with a more distant periphery inhabited by *nahua*, the generic Panoan term for "foreigners" or "enemies." That locality and the gradients of distance, both spatial and social, that surround it should be so partitioned is not unfamiliar. Siskind (1973:49–50) sketches a parallel model for the Panoan Sharanahua as does Erikson (1994:26) for the Mayoruna; much farther afield, comparable examples are legion (e.g., Cole 1945:131 for the Ifugao; Boddy 1982:694 for a Sudanese village).

FIRST ENCOUNTERS

Feasts can be viewed as drama (Goldman 1964, Gregor 1977). The arrival of canoe-borne guests to an *ani shrëati* certainly resembled an act in a well-staged play. The reception of guests was steeped in etiquette. Hosts, bedecked in finery, went to the shoreline with mugs filled with welcoming manioc beer or cane liquor. After this initial encounter, visitors, amidst a chorus of drums, flutes, and panpipes, were escorted to the newly constructed guest house where more libations were served. Confrontation was now choreographed. Host and guest males formed facing lines, each male bearing a hardwood club (called *macana* in local Spanish, *huino* in Conibo-Shipibo); light head taps were exchanged between the contestants (Sabaté 1922–1929, 10:269–271; Roe 1982:98–99). Host and guest women, in a parallel case of ritualized conflict, wrestled (Heath 1991:8). Such antagonistic "opening ceremonies" are a widespread feature in South American ethnography (e.g., Clastres 1998:225–226). In the Conibo-Shipibo case, it is interesting that such publicly acted hostilities involve females against females, males against males. Intersexual berating and bantering are evident but seem to play a less focal role than among the Sharanahua (Siskind 1973:105) or the Cashinahua (Kensinger 1995:57–58) who have elevated such ribaldry to high art.

Guest males then engaged in an archery contest in which the targets were a white-lipped peccary, a curassow, or a spider monkey tethered to a large cross of balsa wood (Odicio Román 1969:49–60; Roe 1982:99–101; cf. Eakin 1990:12–13). Some of the older accounts state that the best archers had first claim to marry the girls to be circumcised (Díaz Castañeda 1923:407–408; de Uriarte 1982:240). In contrast, Heath (1991:6–7), who actually witnessed one of the last *ani shrëati*, places the killing of these animals raised as pets later in the fiesta. In addition, she states that it is the host males who speared the captured game, the final killing being done by the very women who were to oversee the clitoridectomy. This was done by clubbing the animal with flutes, otherwise male instruments (compare Gebhart-Sayer 1987:254–259).

In terms of the schema in Figure 8.2, the animals chosen for ritual sacrifice were not a random set. Monkeys are regarded, perhaps with warrant, as shameless fornicators. Peccaries are classic Amazonian symbols of unrestrained sexuality (Roe 1982:223). Manatees and dolphins are viewed as the aquatic seducers of bathing women (Roe 1982:51–52; Kendall, Trujillo, and Beltrán 1995:27).[5] Furthermore, in the context of the *ani shrëati*, these wild animals had been raised as pets, that is, they had been domesticated and thereby had entered the "neutral" zone of affinity. It is these animal affines that were first shot by males and then clubbed to death by women wielding phallic flutes. As Heath tersely puts it: "The death of the wild animals symbolises the subduing of woman's animal-like instincts" (1991:8).

SCHEDULING AND DURATION

Sources state that the *ani shrëati* was ideally held under a full moon, although how such convenient night lighting could be guaranteed is unclear (Girard 1958:244; see Roe 1982:104–105 for the symbolic significance of the moon). With respect to duration, there are two modes that either represent a chronological shift (considered to be the more likely) or a distinction between the Conibo and their linguistic and cultural brethren, the Shipibo. For the Conibo, the *ani shrëati* is said to have lasted eight days with the clitoridectomy performed on the last night (Pallarés and Calvo, cited by Rippy and Nelson 1936:39; Díaz Castañeda in Izaguirre 1928:234–236). For the Shipibo, the fiesta is said to have lasted three days with the clitoridectomy taking place on the second night (Tessmann 1928:206–207; Karsten 1955:156–157; Roe 1982:40; Gebhart-Sayer 1987:243–259; Heath 1991). Samanez y Ocampo (1980:80–81) was certainly off the mark when he claimed that the fiesta lasted two to three months.

DANCING AND FIGHTING

The *ani shrëati* was a multimedia festival with drum, panpipe, and flute music specific to the ceremony, singing (Tschopik 1954), feasting on the game slaughtered for the event, drinking to excess, and dancing until dead drunk (Pallarés and Calvo in Larrabure i Correa 1905–1909, 9:60). Two stages in these festivities can be recognized. The first involved rather affable unisexual dancing, the men in one circle, the women in another (Díaz Castañeda 1923:407–408; de Uriarte 1982:241). At some point, the young girls to be initiated, wearing "dazzling" attire (Heath 1991:5), joined as dance-masters, orchestrating the performance of the whole. This brief appearance opened a second stage in which behavior, undoubtedly fueled by inebriation, became more frenzied and ultimately more sinister. After the public announcement of the clitoridectomy, men were said to go berserk, assaulting each other with *macanas*, and attempting to down an opponent in order to subincise the nape of his neck with a knife that was traditionally bladed with a serrated toucan beak, more recently with filed metal.[6] This knife, customarily

suspended around the neck for ready access, is called *huisháti* (Samanez y
Ocampo 1980:80–81; Díaz Castañeda 1923:407–408; Karsten 1955:157–158; Roe
1982:100–101; cf. Lauriault 1952). Accusations of adultery were said to be the primary instigation of these confrontations. Watching women at first encouraged
these scuffles but then attempted to intervene before more serious, but rarely
lethal, outcomes ensued (de Uriarte 1982:242; Karsten 1955:157–158; Odicio
Román 1969:49–60). As an aside, I should note that in the early 1970s, when conducting archaeological work on the Ucayali, several of my older Shipibo workmen bore multiple nuchal scars, proud tokens of their virility, remembered or
otherwise. While men attempted to hold center stage in drunken histrionics attendant to the *ani shrëati*, things were happening among women as well.

CLITORIDECTOMY

The actual operation, the nominal purpose of the fiesta, deserves a separate
paper, which is another way of saying that details are sparse when it comes to secretive aspects of Conibo-Shipibo culture, although both female and male anthropologists have considered the "problem." As indicated earlier, the operation was
performed by women skilled as surgeons. Called *shatöti*[7] (Illius 1985:586), it took
place in a special structure situated well away from the main plaza filled with dancing and otherwise hysterical men (the "culture" zone). This removed structure
was variously called *quischiquepiti* (Pallarés and Calvo in Larrabure i Correa
1905–1909, 9:60) or *púshuva* (Karsten 1955:155–156; Girard 1958:240). Note that this
structure (essentially a medical hut) was situated in the "neutral" zone. In this
sense, it resembles the *tanpo* (a term of possible quechua origin), or potter's shed,
where raw clay and other materials are converted into cultural form. The young
girls were anesthetized with ample draughts of cane liquor, a bit stronger than
manioc brew. Surgical implements were heated and presumably sanitized in a special clay pot, of which more later. The excision of the clitoris was done with the
sharpened nails of the *sacerdota* (Izaguirre 1928:234–236), with a sharp cane knife
(Eakin, Lauriault, and Boonstra 1980:79–80), or, as one of my *male* informants
averred, with the metal lid of a discarded tuna can. The wound was washed in a
heated solution of *piri-piri* (various plants of the Cyperaceae family—see Tournon
1984, Eakin, Laurialt, and Boonstra 1980:63–64), and then a fired clay object, the
shërvënanti (males call it *bushi*, or penis), was inserted between the vaginal labia to
prevent cicatricial complications (d'Ans 1994 relays some typically out-of-focus
photographs; also see Karsten 1955:157–158; Roe 1982 gives a different slant).

THE MORNING AFTER

"Concluido el masato y los viveres, todo el mundo se dispersa" (Samanez y
Ocampo 1980:80–81). When the beer and food are gone, everybody leaves.[8]

Samanez y Ocampo got it right by placing beer first. Food seems a lesser concern. Like the Cubeo (Goldman 1966:83–84), drink, not food, fueled the *ani shrëati*. If we look at the Panoan-speaking landscape hugging the Ucayali basin, we find that manioc beer tends not to be produced among interfluvial groups such as the Cashinahua, Yaminahua (Townsley 1994:280), or Cashibo (Frank 1994:211–212). Among the latter, for instance, *meat* sliced from the captively raised tapir is a central reward of the major feast. In contrast, among the Conibo-Shipibo, food—to play with a famous dictum—is good to think, while beer, and the altered states it can induce, is good to drink. For hosts, not to be able to offer more than guests can drink is cause for mortification and entails a consequent lowering of social and political status registered by host and guest alike (cf. Goldman 1966:83–84 for the aptly named Cubeo "drinking party").

THE ARCHAEOLOGICAL SIGNATURE

With typical aversion to understatement, the late Donald Lathrap argued:

> On surveying the average size of each of the functional classes of pottery used by the various surviving Tropical Forest groups, one is led to the conclusion that a vessel with a maximum diameter of more than 40 cm is very likely to be a fermentation vessel. The presence of such large containers in an archaeological deposit can be taken as evidence that beer was present and that the whole fiesta pattern was in full swing. (1970:55)

Lathrap was clearly basing this judgment on work among the Shipibo, a project continued by several of his students. As documented elsewhere (DeBoer and Lathrap 1979; DeBoer in press), the Conibo-Shipibo ceramic assemblage reduces to four functional classes and three size modes. As illustrated in Figure 8.3, the functional classes are cooking pots (or, more technically, pots placed over a fire and therefore unpainted), liquid-storage jars, food-serving vessels, and beer mugs. The size modes are: (1) large (*ani*, which can be glossed as "big" or "growing") vessels that are typically, but not exclusively, used in fiesta contexts; (2) "ordinary"-sized vessels (sometimes marked by the ranked subordinate terms *anicha* and *anitama*) used in quotidian activities of cooking, eating, and drinking; and (3) small vessels (*vacu*, or "kid-sized") serving as portable containers for canoe travelers. The resultant twelve-celled matrix, diagrammed in Table 8.1, not only summarizes recent Conibo-Shipibo pottery but also can be applied to the archaeological ceramics of the Cumancaya phase, dating to about A.D. 900–1000 (Raymond, DeBoer, and Roe 1975). As the Cumancaya site proper is identified as an ancestral settlement by the Conibo-Shipibo (Loriot and Hollenbach 1970), the case for historical continuity would appear to be strong. The case is made stronger still by the co-occurrence of items specific to the *ani shrëati* in both mod-

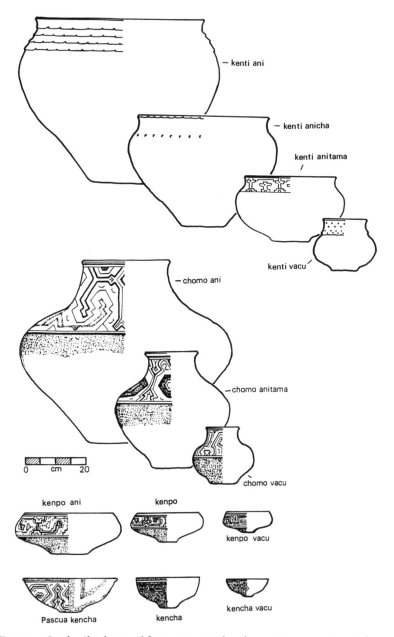

kenti ani

kenti anicha

kenti anitama

kenti vacu

chomo ani

chomo anitama

chomo vacu

0   cm   20

kenpo ani   kenpo

kenpo vacu

Pascua kencha   kencha

kencha vacu

Figure 8.3. Conibo-Shipibo vessel forms. Unpainted cooking pots are at top, painted serving vessels below.

TABLE 8.1

Classification of the Conibo-Shipibo Ceramic Assemblage, with Average Capacities in Liters

	Serving		Cooking	
	Food Bowl	Beer Mug	Jar	Olla
Small for transport	*kencha vacu*	*kenpo vacu*	*chomo vacu*	*kenti vacu*
	0.7	1.2	2.4	5.0
Medium for quotidian	*kencha*	*kenpo*	*chomo*	*kenti*
	1.7	2.8	*anitama*	*anitama*
			16.5	11.1
				kenti anicha
				29.0
Large for fiesta	*pasqua kencha*	*kenpo ani*	*chomo ani*	*kenti ani*
	3.8	7.5	103.3	80.2

Italics indicate Conibo-Shipibo terms.

ern and archaeological contexts. These include rattle-based beer mugs (Raymond, DeBoer, and Roe 1975:fig. 45k; Heath 1991:11) as well as several supplementary items that are activated specifically in a fiesta context.

Notable are the *toncoate* that were suspended on strings in order to withdraw beer from the bottom of a *chomo ani*. These vessels, alternatives to tipping beer kegs as they approach empty, took a symbolically charged form. They are modeled as dolphins (Fig. 8.4A)—notorious riverine rapists—as testicles (Fig. 8.4B), or, as shown in Tessmann (1928:Tafel 58), as testicle- and penis-crunching turtles (Kensinger 1995:237–246). Although *toncoate* have not been identified in prehistoric archaeological sites, serving vessels bearing dolphin adornos are a conspicuous feature at Cumancaya, notably in ceremonial deposits composed of smashed pottery vessels (Roe 1973).

Paraphernalia either specific to—or activated during—the *ani shrëati* include the cane knife for excising the clitoris (Fig. 8.4C), the men's knife for subincising the neck of accused adulterers (Fig. 8.4D), and the clay plug, or *shërvënanti*, inserted into the girl's vagina after the surgical removal of the clitoris (Fig. 8.4E). The latter has been found in recent Conibo-Shipibo middens as well as prehistoric ones.

Other accoutrements attendant to the *ani shrëati* include a small painted olla, the *shërvënanti kenti* (Fig. 8.5A). This form, known only ethnographically, was used to sterilize implements used in the clitoridectomy as well as the water for cleaning the wound. As a painted cooking pot, this form violates conventions in

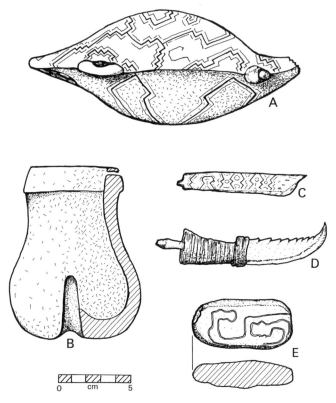

Figure 8.4. Artifacts associated with the *ani shrëati*. A. *Toncoate*, or suspended beer dipper, in the form of a river dolphin. American Museum of Natural History, Catalogue Number 40.0/4770. B. *Jobosko toncoate*, or beer dipper modeled as testicles. This specimen, unpainted and unfired, was recorded in San Francisco de Yarinacocha in 1971. C. *Paca köntsö* (Roe 1982:327), or cane knife used in clitoridectomy. Specimen formerly on display at the American Museum of Natural History, New York. D. Traditional *huisháti*, or men's knife with toucan beak blade (after Tessmann 1928:fig. 14). E. Clay plug, a probable *shërvë-nanti*, found at the Cumancaya site (after Roe 1973:fig. 63f–g).

which a pot placed over a fire should not be so decorated. It can be treated as a standard case of sacred reversal, as widely attested in world ethnography (the "contraries" of the Cheyenne—Grinnell 1923, 2:79–86—and the "opposite-talkers" of the Zuni—Tedlock 1979:503—come to mind). Another vessel form, a small, shallow bowl called *nanë ati* in Shipibo, held the black pigment used in painting the faces of girls undergoing the clitoridectomy. Roe (1973:173–174) has identified what is likely to be an archaeological example of this form at the site of Cumancaya (Fig. 8.5B).

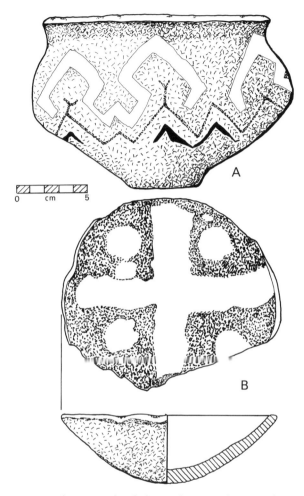

Figure 8.5. Pottery vessels associated with the *ani shrëati*. A. *Shërvënanti kenti,* or vessel used for heating water for the clitoridectomy. Recorded at the Conibo hamlet of Iparia in 1971. B. Shallow bowl with resist decoration on interior, a probable *nanë ati* or paint bowl. From the Cumancaya site (after Roe 1973:fig. 63a–b).

Given the vagaries of preservation in a humid, tropical environment, the above list of artifacts shared between contemporary fiesta-associated assemblages and imputed fiesta contexts of the past is impressive. The *shërvënanti,* rattle-based beer mug, and *nanë ati* would appear to close the case for continuity, at least as expressed in specific artifacts. The case can be strengthened further, however, by looking at patterns. As Lathrap noted in the passage opening this section, large vessels in the tropical forest are often feast vessels. Well, how large?

Samanez y Ocampo (1980:80–81) estimated that 30 to 40 "enormous" beer jars had to be manufactured for the *ani shrëati*. Farabee (1922:85–86) noted that the mother of the girl undergoing the operation made a large jar holding 20 or more gallons (80 liters or so), while Roe's (1982:97–101) informants indicated that 15 to 20 such jars were needed for a typical *ani shrëati*. Although emphasizing the symbolic rather than the volumetric, Gebhart-Sayer (1987:86–91) casts similar verdicts. As given in Table 8.1, the mean volume of large beer jars (*chomo ani*) manufactured by the Conibo-Shipibo in 1971 was about 100 liters. Thus volumetric estimates of beer produced for an *ani shrëati* might range from 1,500 to 4,000 liters, figures that correspond to Alvarez's (1970:50) comment that 3,000 liters of manioc beer could be consumed readily at a Piro festival within a few days (cf. Illius 1985:584). In size and volume, jars and serving vessels from the thousand-year-old Cumancaya and Sonochenea sites conform to their modern descendants (DeBoer in press).

No fossilized *ani shrëati*, needless to say, has been "dug up"; however, ceremonial deposits, in addition to common middens, have been sampled in excavations conducted along the Ucayali. Ceremonial deposits include linear arrays of smashed ceramic vessels, conjoinable into whole pots, and urn features containing either primary or secondary burials. Table 8.2 presents the occurrence of beer vessels (*kenpo, chomo ani*, and their prehistoric "cognates") and "other vessels" in a range of ethnographic and archaeological contexts. For contemporary Conibo-Shipibo as well as for prehistoric midden and burial contexts, beer vessels constitute about one-sixth of all ceramic containers. In "smashed vessel features," however, this ratio is essentially one. Although these smashed vessel features

TABLE 8.2

Distribution of Beer and Nonbeer Vessels in Ethnographic and Archaeological Contexts

	Beer Vessels	Other	Ratio of Beer/Other Vessels
Conibo-Shipibo vessels in use	42	220	~1:5
Sonochenea midden (vessels)	29	134	~1:4.5
Cumancaya midden (sherds)	703	2,127	~1:3
Shahuaya midden (vessels)	33	172	~1:5
Urn burials, Sonochenea and Cumancaya	7	25	~1:3.5
Smashed vessel features, Sonochenea and Cumancaya	14	16	~1:1

Data from DeBoer (1971), Roe (1973), Raymond, DeBoer, and Roe (1975), and DeBoer and Raymond (1987).

have been interpreted as mortuary deposits covering extended primary burials, there is little conclusive evidence to support this interpretation (Raymond, De-Boer, and Roe 1975:59). Their ceramic "signature" clearly indicates a feasting deposit in which beer-related vessels predominate.

The smashing of beer mugs and other vessels as ceremonial endings to fiestas such as the *ani shrëati* runs as a motif throughout Conibo-Shipibo ceremonialism (DeBoer and Lathrap 1979:135, note 8). The fact that such ritual closings, dominated by beer vessels, should be so conspicuously represented at archaeological sites such as Cumancaya and Sonochenea is further evidence for the antiquity of the Conibo-Shipibo feasting pattern. And there is more.

Decoration, specifically painted or incised designs (*quënëa*), plays a basic role in Conibo-Shipibo worldview, and it would be surprising if such designs did not figure in such salient and culturally central events as the *ani shrëati*—and they do, albeit in contradictory ways. On the one hand, decoration was made flamboyant and otherwise visually impressive in such public events (DeBoer and Moore 1982). On the other hand, design applied to the faces of girls undergoing the clitoridectomy was reduced to dots and crosses, the same designs adorning the interior of the *nanë ati*, or paint bowl, for the initiates (Roe 1982:322; Gebhart-Sayer 1985:594). Design simplification also characterized the *shërvënanti kenti* (Fig. 8.5A) and the crudely incised *shërvënanti* proper from Cumancaya (Fig. 8.4E). In terms of Conibo-Shipibo aesthetics, these designs are depauperate, they allude to an uncivilized and designless world, a peripheral netherland occupied by various brands of subhumans exemplified by the Cashibo and Amahuaca; the intermediate or interfacial zone once again serves as a middle ground, a kind of buffer in which designs are amplified to secure boundaries and are simultaneously simplified to acknowledge the permeability of all boundaries.[9]

Over the last thousand years, the Ucayali basin—a zone stretching a thousand kilometers north to south along the eastern base of the Andes—yields convincing ethnographic, ethnohistorical, and archaeological evidence for the focal role of feasts. This combined data set is somewhat privileged, in that archaeologists have routinely worked with informants whose ancestors produced the remains in question. Without such guidance, archaeologists are likely to succumb to universal and objectivist accounts that merely subsume or explain away specific facts.

DISCUSSION AND CONCLUSION

When seeking the latent functions of the *ani shrëati*, one confronts a veritable silence in ethnohistoric and ethnographic accounts (but see below). If one were to ask a Conibo-Shipibo man what the "evolutionary consequences" of this fiesta might be, a likely response would be "what's more important than women?"—an answer that would please the sociobiologically inclined but would leave unaddressed the specific form that the *ani shrëati* takes.

In pursuing a more satisfactory account, it is instructive to cite a casual comment offered by de Uriarte: "From this competitive fiesta emerged future leaders, future spouses, and future rivals. If the hosts wanted to attract skillful sons-in-law, the male guests were equally intent on obtaining wives" (Ortíz 1982:240, my translation). To appreciate this insight, additional ethnographic context is required. The Conibo-Shipibo generally follow matrilocal residence. Therefore, the *ani shrëati* not only acted as a demographic signal of the availability of nubile females but also served as a vehicle for attracting economically essential sons-in-law—men who fished and hunted, cleared gardens, constructed houses, and would come to sponsor the next generation of *ani shrëati*. Yet another factor intervened.

Until the 1930s and even 1940s, the Conibo-Shipibo were avid raiders, pillaging backwoods groups such as the Amahuaca, Isconahua, Campa, and Cashibo for slaves, booty, and wives. At least for the Conibo, such raiding was already commonplace in the late seventeenth century (DeBoer 1986). Wives captured in these raids constituted an obvious exception to the otherwise general practice of matrilocality. That is, men not only married-in, but also made up a military corps that could and did abduct wives from the outside. Even today, genealogies record the "recruitment" of such foreign women and can trace their pedigree to living descendants.

From the Conibo-Shipibo perspective—one shared by their mestizo neighbors—these foreign women, although often treated as second-class citizens and drudge labor, were nonetheless exotic, untamed, and decidedly sexy.[10] Whatever sexual fantasies were involved, both inside and "recruited" forms of female labor produced the prodigious quantities of beer needed for fiestas and gave birth to children—preferably females—who attracted another cohort of sons-in-law. During this replicative process, ideally timed to a full moon, females lost their collective clitoris for the effort. Something has got to be missing.

These ethnographic addenda force reconsideration of earlier schemata in which male culture, centered on the house plaza, was contrasted with an outer female zone of nature and wilderness. In quotidian terms, the reverse situation holds! Women ruled the home front and were part of enduring residential units of related females, while men were in-marrying strangers typically lacking supportive kin, were obliged to observe mother-in-law avoidance, and otherwise occupied precarious social positions. As Brown (1963) observed some time ago, matrilocality can be a rather formidable rite of passage for men. Warfare and the female booty it provided were, among other things, male palliatives in this predicament as it is rendered in Figure 8.6.[11]

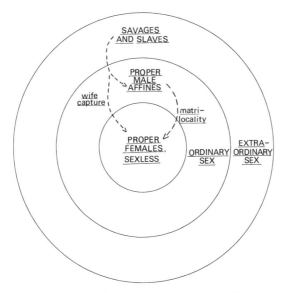

Figure 8.6. Schema for marriage and sex. Dotted lines indicate two major flows of marriage partners: (1) the customary practice of matrilocality whereby a husband moves in with his wife and her family; (2) the capture of women from enemy groups.

In Table 8.3, the schemata used to order a welter of disparate data are condensed in terms of polarities and intervening gradients. By and large, these triadic sets are less than astonishing (which accounts for their ready translation). At least one pair of seeming contradictions, however, stands out. How can female(ness) simultaneously be unbridled nature and the epitome of domesticity? Or, how can male(ness) be the custodian of culture and, at the same time, the

TABLE 8.3
Synopsis of Schematic Polarities: The Conibo-Shipibo Point of View

Inner (Civilization)		Outer (Savagery)
house	garden	forest
culture	culture-nature	nature
friend	affine	enemy
above sex	sex	dangerous sex
design	design amplified or simplified	designless
male	male/female	female
female	male	—

231

perpetrator of rapine? Such ambiguity, however—anathema to logicians and to objectivist notions of science—is the way in which humans work and the manner by which human phenomena are played out. This would seem to be particularly the case when sex—or its cultural representation, gender—is confronted. In his oft-cited yet untired verdict, Giddens put it this way: "Don't look for the functions social practices fulfill, look for the contradictions they embody" (1979:131). One only has to reread *Naven* (Bateson 1936), or this essay for that matter, to be reminded that human bodies and behavior are infected by transfiguring and otherwise queer properties.

Another matter that needs to be taken into account is the seeming longevity of the *ani shrëati*, a full millennium if our reading of the archaeological record is correct. Over this millennium, Conibo-Shipibo society and environment have undergone major changes including the wrenching dislocations effected by European colonialism in its various sequent forms (San Román 1975 provides a review). In fact, whether one can speak of the Conibo or Shipibo a thousand years ago is quizzical. As ethnic appellations that mark real-world entities, these labels are clearly inventions forged, developed, and negotiated during the period in question. Yet the *ani shrëati* survived these storms until the 1970s. The interesting issue, therefore, is not the "evolutionary potential" of this particular institution so much as its perdurance in the face of worlds being remade. The remarkable stasis of the *ani shrëati* suggests an institution that is anchored securely to the deepest values of Conibo-Shipibo culture in its becoming and maintenance. Perhaps stasis and replication are as much evolutionary processes as change itself.

The *ani shrëati* remains somewhat fuzzy with respect to the driving themes of this volume. This fiesta surely played a role in social and biological reproduction, prompted production of drink and other material goods that otherwise would not have been produced (although such "surplus" was dissipated in the gormandism of the fiesta), attracted labor essential to the planned well-being of hosting communities, but less clearly acted as a crucible leading to increased cultural complexity, however measured. Other than promised bodies, exchange of gifts or other material goods was not emphasized. Valued and increasingly essential items such as machetes, axes, chainsaws, or outboard motors simply were not written into the script of the fiesta, although the *ani shrëati* may have formed (or thwarted) social relations by which such transactions could be pursued in other contexts.

In short, the *ani shrëati* appears to have had primarily an equilibrating rather than transformative role in Conibo-Shipibo culture. The demise of this focal institution in the 1960s and 1970s was a symptom of emergent opportunities for a new brand of aggrandizers who stepped outside the traditional fold and its lingering and increasingly embarrassing vestiges of "the primitive." This new breed, as schoolteachers or political activists, increasingly turns to interfacial roles with the national economy, the international market with its rapacious desire for primitive art and extollations of the native point of view, and the entailed need to deal with an onslaught of meddling visitors, including archaeologists and ethnographers. If not all-purpose fulcra for weighing the course of culture histories, feasts like the *ani shrëati* nonetheless provide gauges for sensing the meaning congealed in the special moments that aggregate human populations, expose the agonies that accompany human existence, and underscore attempts to reset a world always in danger of going off course. As explored here, feasts—and the bodies and brains behind them—leave detectable traces along the great waterway of the Ucayali, as they do elsewhere.

NOTES

1. Also known as *pishta* (Odicio Román 1969) and *wake honéti* (Karsten 1955:155–156). As evident in citations, the present study of the *ani shrëati* leans heavily on the masterful and imaginative synthesis given by Roe (1982). Dr. Roe has also made available the important paper by Carolyn Heath (1991), who witnessed and recorded one of the last *ani shrëati* held at the settlement of Sinuya in 1976. Unfortunately, this significant document remains unpublished.

2. These accounts are often difficult to assess, as it is clear that authors were regularly using earlier sources, often without citation. I have tried to be critical in selecting what appear to be original documents, but, on another occasion, it would be useful to construct a detailed phylogeny of original and derived accounts.

3. In 1975, Roberta Campos and Joan Abelove, both of whom were then working among the Shipibo of the Pisqui, told me that the last clitoridectomy had been performed three years before when the last knowledgeable female surgeon (*"maestra"*) was still alive.

4. What portion of agricultural production was devoted to these periodic obligations is unknown. For the Cubeo, Goldman estimates that as much of one-third of a manioc crop could be destined for beer necessary for hosting ceremonies (1966:86).

5. Heath observed women wading into the enclosure in which a manatee was kept (1991:7). Before killing the captive animal by plugging up its nostrils, to facilitate drowning, and then clubbing its head, again with flutes, "they played and danced with the manatee for about half an hour, imitating the sexual act." Outside of the context of the *ani shrëati*, I have seen men similarly club to death shore-hugging dolphins because of the danger (and temptation) that these animals may have posed to bathing women.

6. The cutting of the *tësho*, or neck, can be viewed as a male counterpart to clitoridectomy. In this context, the neck is phallic, and the threatened but curtailed act of "head-taking" (*tështëa*) is a fairly convincing representation of castration (see Bettelheim 1954 for additional arguments of this kind).

7. In d'Ans's 1970 reissue of Navarro's 1903 dictionary, the entry for clitoridectomy is *maspijána chícai* or, when parsed, *maspi* ("female genitalia")-*jána* ("tongue")-*chícai* ("cut-out"). The pervasiveness of *vagina dentata* imagery is here reinforced by likening the clitoris to the tongue.

8. The legacy of any given *ani shrëati* is well encapsulated by Lathrap's general diagnosis of Tropical Forest feasting:

> The crucial mechanism by which one Tropical Forest village could achieve or maintain a position that would impress its neighbors was to give a fiesta which lasted longer, expended more beer, and unleashed more drunken brawls than any other fiesta in memory. The drunken brawls during these fiestas afforded a culturally sanctioned opportunity for discharging all the tensions and interpersonal aggression which had built up in the course of day-to-day living. In its form and functions, the Tropical Forest fiesta pattern was not unlike that of the modern cocktail party, but it lasted far longer and, on the average, more crockery and heads got broken. (1970:54)

Cocktail party may be a bit antiquated as a convincing allusion, but the diagnosis is still telling.

9. In this light, the claim made by some Conibo-Shipibo that the clitoridectomy is a custom adopted from the Cashibo—a people whom they otherwise regard to be abject savages—assumes some comprehensibility, if not historicity (Gebhart-Sayer 1985:592).

10. In 1968 at the combined Campa-Conibo mission of Shahuaya, Pancho, a mestizo patrón who had several Campa "wives," remarked that the latter were "muy ardiente" in contrast to the Conibo who were "muy frío." Whatever the case, his testimony is of notional interest.

11. It is not my intention here to explain why the Conibo-Shipibo practice matrilocality. One might cite the statistically framed hypothesis forwarded by Ember and Ember (1971) that such a residence rule disperses fraternally bound males and thereby discourages internal aggression, while favoring external aggression. One could just as well argue that male absenteeism—promoted by mercenary activities during the rubber boom era, employment in lumbering or other extractive industries, or, more recently, military service—could encourage "matrifocal" tendencies. From a Darwinian perspective, however, one can assess consequences without specifying origins. Given matrilocality, Murphy (1957) still provides one of the best accounts of the resultant "predicament" in an Amazonian society. *Mutatis mutandis*, his argument could be applied to the Conibo-Shipibo.

REFERENCES

Alvarez, Ricardo
    1970   *Los Piros: Hijos de Dios*. Lima: Santiago Valverde.
Bamberger, Joan
    1974   The Myth of Matriarchy. In *Woman, Culture, and Society*, edited by M. Z. Rosaldo and Louise Lamphere, pp. 263–280. Stanford: Stanford University Press.
Bateson, Gregory
    1936   *Naven*. Stanford: Stanford University Press.

Bertrand-Ricoveri, P.
1996   Un aspecto de la dialéctica masculino-feminino en la mitología Shipibo. *Antropológica* 14:81–104. Pontificia Universidad Católica del Perú.

Bettelheim, Bruno
1954   *Symbolic Wounds*. Glencoe: The Free Press.

Boddy, J.
1982   Womb as Oasis: The Symbolic Context of Pharaonic Circumcision in Rural Northern Sudan. *American Ethnologist* 9 (4): 682–698.

Brown, Judith K.
1963   A Cross-Cultural Study of Female Initiation Rites. *American Anthropologist* 73:571–594.

Clastres, Pierre
1998   *Chronicle of the Guayaki Indians*. New York: Zone Books.

Codere, Helen
1961   Kwakiutl. In *Perspectives in American Indian Change*, edited by Edward H. Spicer, pp. 431–516. Chicago: University of Chicago Press.

Cole, Fay-Cooper
1945   *The Peoples of Malaysia*. New York: D. Van Nostrand.

d'Ans, André-Marcel
1970   *Materiales para el estudio del grupo lingüístico Pano*. Lima: Universidad Nacional Mayor de San Marcos, Serie Lexicos 1.
1994   L'Initiation et l'excision des filles chez les Indiens Shipibos d'Amazonie. Informations Ethnographiques Provenant de Documents d'Amateurs. *L'Ethnographie* 90 (2): 9–29.

DeBoer, Warren R.
1971   Archaeological Explorations on the Upper Ucayali River, Peru. Ph.D. dissertation, Department of Anthropology, University of California, Berkeley.
1981   Buffer Zones in the Cultural Ecology of Aboriginal Amazonia: An Ethnohistorical Approach. *American Antiquity* 46 (2): 364–377.
1986   Pillage and Production in the Amazon: A View through the Conibo of the Ucayali Basin, Eastern Peru. *World Archaeology* 18 (2): 231–246.
in press   Ceramic Assemblage Variability in the Formative of Ecuador and Peru. In *Archaeology of Formative Ecuador*, edited by J. Scott Raymond and Richard Burger, Dumbarton Oaks, Washington, D.C.

DeBoer, Warren R., and Donald W. Lathrap
1979   The Making and Breaking of Shipibo-Conibo Ceramics. In *Ethnoarchaeology: Implications of Ethnography for Archaeology*, edited by Carol Kramer, pp. 102–138. New York: Columbia University Press.

DeBoer, Warren R., and James A. Moore
1982   The Measurement and Meaning of Stylistic Diversity. *Ñawpa Pacha* 20:147–162. Berkeley: Institute of Andean Studies.

DeBoer, Warren R., and J. Scott Raymond
1987   Roots Revisited: The Origins of the Shipibo Art Style. *Journal of Latin American Lore* 13 (1): 115–132.

Descola, Philippe

    1996   *The Spears of Twilight: Life and Death in the Amazon Jungle.* New York: The New Press.

de Uriarte, Buenaventura L.

    1982   *La Montaña del Peru.* Annotated by Fr. Dionisio Ortíz. Lima: Gráfica 30.
    [1942]

Díaz Castañeda, César

    1923   Kunibo. *Inca: Revista trimestral de estudios antropológicos* 1 (2): 398–409. Lima: Museo de Arqueología de la Universidad Mayor de San Marcos. (Much the same material written in 1912 appeared as "Sobre los Indios Cunibos" in Izaguirre 1922–1929, 1:301–320.)

Eakin, Lucille

    1990   *Nuevo Destino: The Life Story of a Shipibo Bilingual Educator.* Dallas: International Museum of Cultures, Summer Institute of Linguistics.

Eakin, Lucille, Erwin Lauriault, and Harry Boonstra

    1980   *Bosquejo etnográfico de los Shipibo-Conibo del Ucayali.* Lima: Ignacio Prado Paster.

Ember, Melvin, and Carol R. Ember

    1971   The Conditions Favoring Matrilocal versus Patrilocal Residence. *American Anthropologist* 73:571–594.

Erickson, Philippe

    1994   Los Mayoruna. In *Guía etnográfica de la alta Amazonía,* edited by Fernando Santos and Frederica Barclay, vol. 2, pp. 1–128. Quito: FLACSO-Sede.

Farabee, William C.

    1922   *Indian Tribes of Eastern Peru.* Papers of the Peabody Museum of American Archaeology and Ethnology X. Harvard University.

Frank, Edwin H.

    1994   Los Uni. In *Guia etnográfica de la alta Amazonía,* edited by Fernando Santos and Frederica Barclay, vol. 2, pp. 129–237. Quito: FLACSO-Sede.

Gebhart-Sayer, Angelika

    1985   Notizen zur Mädchenbeschneidung bei den Shipibo-Conibo, Ost Peru. In *Die Braut, Geliebt-verkauft-getauscht-geraubt: Zur Rolle der Frau im Kulturvergleich.* Edited by G. Völger and K. von Welck. Special issue. *Ethnologica* 11 (2): 592–597.

    1987   *Die Spitze des Bewusstseins: Untersuchungen zu Weltbild und Kunst der Shipibo-Conibo.* Hohenschäftlarn: Klaus Renner.

Giddens, Anthony

    1979   *Central Problems in Social Theory: Action, Structure, and Contradiction.* Berkeley: University of California Press.

Girard, Rafael

    1958   *Indios selvaticos de la Amazonia peruana.* Mexico City: Libro Mex Editores.

Goldman, Irving

    1964   The Structure of Ritual in the Northwest Amazon. In *Process and Pattern in Culture: Essays in Honor of Julian Steward,* edited by Robert A. Manners, pp. 111–122. Chicago: Aldine.

1966   *The Cubeo: Indians of the Northwest Amazon*. Urbana: University of Illinois Press.

Gregor, Thomas

1977   *Mehinaku: The Drama of Daily Life in a Brazilian Indian Village*. Chicago: University of Chicago Press.

Grinnell, George Bird

1923   *The Cheyenne Indians*. 2 volumes. New Haven: Yale University Press.

Hayden, Brian, and Ralana Maneeprasert

1996   Feasting among the Akha: The 1996 Report. Manuscript presented to the symposium "The Archaeological Importance of Feasting," organized by Michael Dietler and Brian Hayden, Annual Meeting of the Society for American Archaeology, Seattle.

Heath, Carolyn

1991   An *ani sheati* in the Shipibo Village of San Pablo, Rio Sinuya, Lower Ucayali River, Peru. Unpublished manuscript translated from the Spanish by Peter Roe.

Illius, Bruno

1985   Die grosse Trinken: Heirat und Stellung der Frau bei den Shipibo-Conibo, Ostperu. In *Die Braut, Geliebt-verkauft-getauscht-geraubt: Zur Rolle der Frau im Kulturvergleich*, edited by G. Völger and K. von Weick. Special issue. *Ethnologica* 11 (2): 584–591.

Izaguirre, Bernardino

1922–   *Historia de las misiones franciscanas y narración de los progresos de la geografia·*
1929   *Relator originales y producciones en lenguas indígenas de varios misioneros*, 1619–1921. 14 vols. Lima: Talleres Gráficos de la Penitenciaria.

1928   Descripción histórico-etnográfico de algunas tribus orientales del Peru. *Boletín de la Sociedad Geográfica de Lima* 45:196–236.

Karsten, Rafael

1955   Los Indos Shipibo del Rio Ucayali. *Revista del Museo Nacional* 24:154–173. Lima.

Kendall, Sarita, Fernando Trujillo, and Sandra Beltrán

1995   *Dolphins of the Amazon and Orinoco*. Bogotá: Fundación Omacha.

Kensinger, Kenneth M.

1995   *How Real People Ought to Live: The Cashinahua of Eastern Peru*. Prospect Heights, Illinois: Waveland Press.

Lakoff, George

1987   *Women, Fire, and Dangerous Things*. Chicago: University of Chicago Press.

Larrabure i Correa, Carlos

1905–   *Colleción de leyes, decretos, resoluciones i otros documentos oficiales referentes al*
1909   *Departamento de Loreto*. 18 vols. Lima: Imprenta de "La Opinión Nacional."

Lathrap, Donald W.

1970   *The Upper Amazon*. New York: Praeger.

Lauriault, E. H.

1952   El Hushati Chama. *Peru Indígena* 2:56–60.

Loriot, James, and Barbara Hollenbach

1970   Shipibo Paragraph Structure. *Foundations of Language* 6:43–66.

Murphy, Robert F.

1957   Intergroup Hostility and Social Cohesion. *American Anthropologist* 59 (6): 1018–1035.

Murphy, Yolanda, and Robert F. Murphy

1974   *Women of the Forest.* New York: Columbia University Press.

Odicio Román, Francisco

1969   *Mitos y Leyendas: Mitología Chama.* Lima, privately published.

Pallarés, Fernando, and Vicente Calvo

1975   *Historia de las misiones del Convento de Santa Rosa de Ocopa.* José Amich
[1870]   y Continuadores. Lima: Editorial Milla Batres. (Also appears in Larrabure i Correa 1905–1909, 9:1–205.)

Raymond, J. Scott, Warren R. DeBoer, and Peter G. Roe

1975   *Cumancaya: A Peruvian Ceramic Tradition.* Occasional Papers No. 2, Department of Archaeology, University of Calgary.

Rippy, J. Fred, and Jean Thomas Nelson

1936   *Crusaders of the Jungle.* Chapel Hill: University of North Carolina Press.

Roe, Peter G.

1973   Cumancaya: Archaeological Excavations and Ethnographic Analogy in the Peruvian Montaña. Ph.D. dissertation, Department of Anthropology, University of Illinois-Urbana.

1982   *The Cosmic Zygote: Cosmology in the Amazon Basin.* New Brunswick: Rutgers University Press.

Sabaté, Luis

1922–   Viaje de los padres misioneros del Convento del Cuzco a las tribus
1929   salvajes de las Campas, Piros, Cunibos, y Shipibos por el Padre Fray Luis Sabaté en el año 1874. In *Historia de las misiones franciscanas y narración de los progresos de la geografía: Relatos originales y producciones en lenguas indígenas de varios misioneros, 1619–1921,* by Bernardino Izaguirre, 10:19–304. Lima: Talleres Gráficos de la Penitenciaria.

Samanez y Ocampo, José B.

1980   *Exploración de los rios peruanos Apurimac, Eni, Tambo, Ucayali y Urubamba hecha por José B. Samanez y Ocampo en 1883 y 1884.* Lima: Sesator.

San Román, Jesus

1975   *Perfiles historicos de la Amazonia peruana.* Lima: Ital-Perú.

Siskind, Janet

1973   *To Hunt in the Morning.* London: Oxford University Press.

Tedlock, Dennis

1979   Zuni Religion and World View. In *Handbook of North American Indians,* vol. 9, pp. 499–508. Washington: Smithsonian Institution.

Tessmann, Günter

1928   *Menschen ohne Gott.* Stuttgart: Strecker und Schröder.

Tournon, Jacques

1984   Investigaciones sobre las plantas medicinales de los Shipibo-Conibo del Ucayali. *Amazonia Peruana* 5:91–118.

Townsley, Graham

1994   Los Yaminahua. In *Guía etnográfica de la alta Amazonía*, edited by Fernando
Santos and Frederica Barclay, vol. 2, pp. 241–358. Quito: FLACSO-Sede.

Tschopik, Harry

1954   Notes for *Indian Music of the Upper Amazon*. Ethnic Folkways Library Album
No. FE4458. New York: Folkways Records and Service Corp.

9

FEASTS AND LABOR MOBILIZATION

DISSECTING A FUNDAMENTAL ECONOMIC PRACTICE

Michael Dietler and Ingrid Herbich

The use of feasts to mobilize collective labor has been a widespread and fundamental economic practice of societies around the world. In fact, variants of the
practice are so strikingly omnipresent in the ethnographic and historical literature that a good case can be made for acknowledging it both as virtually a universal feature among agrarian societies (e.g., see Erasmus 1956; Moore 1975;
Uchendu 1970) and as the nearly exclusive means of mobilizing large voluntary
work projects before the spread of the monetary economy and the capitalist
commoditization of labor and creation of a wage labor market.

This fact is of enormous potential significance to archaeologists in their attempts to understand ancient societies, particularly in terms of grappling with issues such as the role of labor control and exploitation in the development of

social inequality. However, the realization of that potential has been hampered by the lack of a fully theorized understanding of the specific range of practices that enable voluntary labor to be mobilized on a scale above the household level, how the possibility for labor exploitation inheres in some of these practices, and, crucially, the ways that feasting operates as a mechanism of conversion within this realm. Despite frequent programmatic statements by archaeologists about the importance of understanding the means of controlling labor (e.g., Webster 1990) and various attempts to do such things as quantify labor inputs in public projects (e.g., Renfrew 1973; Trigger 1990), little serious consideration actually has been given to developing a theoretical explanation of collective labor-mobilization practices other than slavery. However, we would argue that a nuanced understanding of the complex and intimate relationship between feasts and labor is crucial. That is because, although feasts have a nearly universal role in this domain among agrarian societies, this does not mean that they operate everywhere in exactly the same fashion or that they have the same potential for exploitation in all cases. Hence, the devotion of a chapter in this book to an explicit theoretical dissection of this fundamental issue.

The following discussion is based upon cross-cultural analysis of ethnographic cases derived from both the anthropological literature (especially building upon the seminal works of Erasmus 1956; Moore 1975; and Uchendu 1970) and our own ethnographic and historical research in western Kenya. We begin with an attempt to define a working vocabulary and a set of analytical concepts for exposing the relationship between feasts and labor and we propose a model of "collective work events" that serves as a basis for understanding both the "conversion" functions of feasts and their potential for exploitation. We then move from this more abstract discussion to some ethnographic examples that illustrate the points we develop. Finally, we explore the implications of this analysis for archaeology, and especially for the understanding of labor exploitation and the development of social inequality in ancient societies.

COLLECTIVE WORK EVENTS (CWEs)

Work feast is the term we use to describe a particular form of the "empowering feast" mode of commensal politics (see Dietler, Chapter 3) in which commensal hospitality is used to orchestrate voluntary collective labor. That is, the work feast is an event in which a group of people are called together to work on a specific project for a day (or more) and, in return, are treated to food and/or drink, after which the host owns the proceeds of the day's labor. The *work feast,* as the term is defined here, actually constitutes one pole in a range of labor-mobilization practices that we call *collective work events* (CWEs). At the other pole of the CWE range is what we call the *work exchange* (see Fig. 9.1).[1]

241

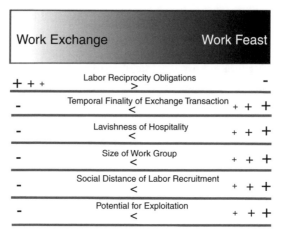

Figure 9.1. Schematic representation of Collective Work Events (CWEs) showing the correlated inverse-trend relationships among work-group size, the degree of reciprocal labor obligations, the scale of hospitality required, and the social distance of workers capable of being mobilized.

Several analytical points need to be established in order to understand the operation of CWEs. Most immediately, it must be emphasized that, from a comparative analytical perspective, work feasts and work exchanges are not binary oppositional categories, but rather terms used to describe polar tendencies along a continuum (Moore 1975). This continuum is defined by several factors (work-group size, reciprocal labor obligations, scale of hospitality, social distance of workers, etc.) that vary in a fairly predictable relationship to each other (see Fig. 9.1). Perhaps the most important defining characteristic is the inverse relationship between the degree of reciprocal labor obligation and the scale of hospitality required.

At the extreme *work-exchange* end of the scale, little if any food needs to be provided (often simply a little ordinary refreshment), but the moral obligations to reciprocate by participating in the work-exchange events of those who have participated in one's own event are very strong and explicit. This reciprocation may be either in person, or by sending a member of one's household as a substitute. At the extreme *work-feast* end of the scale, reciprocal labor obligations may be very weak (and vaguely implicit) to completely nonexistent, but the lavishness of the hospitality expected is quite significant.

In other words, crudely stated, the difference is basically one between an exchange of labor for labor versus and exchange of labor for hospitality. That is, work exchanges operate through a kind of delayed reciprocity, where the host of the event assumes a labor debt to all the participants that must be repaid at a later date. Work feasts, on the other hand, operate more as a temporally finite exchange transaction: lavish hospitality is "exchanged" directly for labor, and no further obligations exist between host and guest. In some cases the event is at least partially acknowledged by the participants as a kind of exchange, and judgments about the quality and quantity of the beer and food provided affect the amount of work done and the size of the group that participates (e.g., see Barth 1967a; Colson 1949; Donham 1994; Goldschmidt 1976; Netting 1964; Saul 1983; Hunter 1961). However, as Karp has noted for the Iteso of East Africa, the participants do not necessarily consciously envisage this as an exchange transaction; instead, the feast may be seen simply as "the vehicle through which cooperation is achieved" (1980:88). In other words, labor relations are constituted through, and euphemized as, relations of commensality.

In work exchanges, the size of the work group able to be mobilized is limited to fairly small collectives of usually less than fifteen people; and these groups are very often organized through kinship or friendship networks (Erasmus 1956). As Moore (1975) has noted, the rather precisely and explicitly reckoned reciprocal labor obligations create certain scheduling constraints that both limit the size of the groups and generally result in one of two organizational arrangements for reciprocation. In what he calls the "individual exchange" pattern, individuals will participate in several different work-exchange networks, and will thus have multiple individual obligations with several other persons who will have their own sets of obligations that only partially intersect. In the "group exchange" pattern, a consistent group of individuals will work together in a consecutive circuit on the projects of each of its members. As Moore (1975) further noted, where institutionalized differences in social rank exist, recruitment to either of these kinds of work-exchange events is normally confined to individuals of comparable status with comparable landholdings to be worked.

With work feasts, on the other hand, labor can be mobilized on a much larger scale (up to several hundred people) and projects can be undertaken that would not be possible with work exchanges. Work feasts are also more effective at recruiting workers from a wider social radius, without reference to kinship, neighborhood affiliation, or social status. It is the scale of hospitality—the copiousness and quality of the drink and food provided (and the reputation of the host for providing these things in abundance)—that draws people to participate rather than close social relationships. Furthermore, work feasts are ad hoc events that are mounted for specific projects and they do not form part of a permanent cyclical organizational structure of labor relations. This means that, as noted, work feasts (of the ideal polar form) do not entail lingering obligations on the part of the host to participate in the work feasts of his or her guests, and this feature becomes even more marked as the size of the work feast expands (Erasmus 1956; Moore 1975).

One can actually distinguish two variants of the work feast, one voluntary and one obligatory. In the voluntary work feast, people are drawn to the event simply by the prior reputation of the host for providing lavish feasts. The obligatory form, which is often referred to as *corvée* labor, exists only where there is institutionalized central authority in the form of religious leaders, chiefs, kings, or other types of state apparatus. In these cases, people are drawn to participate because a ruler or public institution has the moral authority to require their presence as a form of labor tribute. However, as will be discussed in more detail later, rulers who fail to orchestrate *corvée* projects through the same work-feast idiom, by providing a generous quantity of food and drink for the workers, will soon meet grumbling and resistance. Rulers cannot rely on coercive force to motivate participation: any stable long-term system of labor tribute must rely on the continual production of consent—which means operating through and playing upon the same practices that have symbolic resonance within the population as a whole. Hence, there is very good reason to view *corvée* labor simply as a variant of the work feast in which the composition of the labor force is predetermined by an ideology of obligation and authority. In fact, approaching this relationship from the opposite direction, Bourdieu (1990:118) sees the voluntary work feast as simply "a covert exaction of corvées"—a perspective that will be better appreciated after the discussion of exploitation below.

A second important point that needs to be made about these CWE modes is that they are not mutually exclusive and it is not possible to characterize particular societies by one or the other of them. Rather, in most societies both modes will be employed in different contexts for different purposes. For example, work exchanges may be the normal pattern for small groups performing routine agricultural tasks (e.g., weeding, harvesting, field clearing, transport of crops from field to home), while work feasts will be employed for projects requiring a larger work group (e.g., house building and repair, fence or rampart construction, road building and repair, waterworks construction and maintenance, mining, agricultural work on very large plots of land, mounting trade expeditions) or one convened for an urgent task. Moreover, within given local contexts, these different forms of CWE are often categorically marked; that is, many societies distinguish different kinds of CWE by name and conceptualize them as distinct categories (see below). In other cases, the differences are more clinal than categorical (e.g., see Chibnik and de Jong 1990; Saul 1983).

Another important related point that needs to be established is that the specific forms of CWE found in real ethnographic contexts do not necessarily closely approach the polar extreme versions used here to define the abstract analytical continuum. Nor need there be only two categories. In other words, a local version of what would be classified as a work feast on our abstract comparative scale might still involve some implicit reciprocal labor obligations (often only for participating kin); and, in the opposite direction, there might well be several categories within the work-exchange end of the continuum with decreasing hospitality obligations and decreasing size. For example, the Maale of Ethiopia have three categories of CWE: the *dabo*, the *mol?o*, and the *helma*. The *dabo* is a moderately large (up to thirty people) ad hoc work feast of variable participation at which the provision of much beer is mandatory and the quantity of beer determines the length of the workday, but at which the host also acquires some implicit reciprocal work obligations. The *mol?o* is a large (between about six and fifteen people) rotating work exchange with a formal organization and durable composition at which some beer is usually provided (but is not obligatory). The *helma* is a very small work exchange (three to four people) following a fixed cycle of rotation at which beer is not necessary; but some beer will be served if one wants the work to extend beyond the standard half day (Donham 1994; cf. Barth 1967a; Mayer 1951; Nadel 1942:248–251; Tosh 1978:41 for a range of different local classifications).

Hence, from an analytical perspective, it is important to recognize that such culturally specific forms of CWE may be located at various points along the abstract continuum according to local expectations about the relative degree of labor reciprocity obligations and scale of requisite hospitality. Moreover, in a given society, there may be no forms that closely approximate the polar extremes. As will be discussed later, this fact has important implications for understanding the potential of these practices for labor exploitation. However, for the moment, let us simply establish the semantic point that, in applying a term such as *work feast* to empirical ethnographic or archaeological cases, we are merely signifying those arrangements that tend toward the work-feast end of the abstract analytical continuum of CWEs.

It should additionally be noted that CWEs are used to congregate groups of workers performing identical tasks of a relatively unskilled nature. They are useful in contexts where the simple multiplication of the number of hands brought to bear on a task is effective in reducing the time of completion or in enabling certain feats (such as the movement of heavy objects or the construction of large structures) that could not be accomplished by members of a household alone. Tasks for which the specialized skills of an individual are more important than the multiplication of the number of workers are accomplished through other means. The example discussed later of iron working among the Samia of Kenya nicely illustrates this distinction by contrasting the mining of ore through work feasts with the compensation of smiths through payment with a part of their production (although, of course, such specialists may also be treated to some commensal hospitality). Another related feature of CWEs commented upon in many ethnographic contexts (e.g., Barth 1967a; Donham 1994; Kennedy 1978) is that the quality of work performed at work feasts is generally less good than at work exchanges, and the quality often gets worse as the size of the feast expands. This is frequently due in part to the effects of the alcohol that often accompanies the work at work feasts. However, it also stems from the different sense of reciprocal obligation that attaches to small work exchanges, as well as the increasing difficulties of supervision with increasing size.

As a final preliminary observation, it should be noted that, contrary to older conceptions of an idealized "domestic mode of production" composed of self-contained household production and consumption units, CWEs are fundamental to the operation of the agrarian economy because they mobilize the essential interhousehold communal labor flows that, in fact, sustain domestic units (see Donham 1994). Moreover, work feasts, in particular, are extremely important in the political economy because of the context they provide for the acquisition and conversion of symbolic and economic capital (to employ Bourdieu's [1990:117–119] useful terminology). In the first place, as with all other types of feast, they provide an opportunity to make public statements about prestige and acquire symbolic capital (Chapter 3). It should not be forgotten that, for the participants, a lavish work feast is, above all else, a festive social occasion (rather than simply a day of wage labor). Such an event not only mobilizes labor: it augments the reputation of the host for generous hospitality in the same way that, for example, hosting a large marriage ceremony or sponsoring a communal ritual does (e.g., see Chibnik and de Jong 1990; Colson and Scudder 1988:77; Kennedy 1978). However, its peculiar characteristic among feasts in general is that it *simultaneously* provides a means of harnessing the labor of others in order to acquire economic capital that subsequently can be converted to additional symbolic capital by several other means. As will be explained below, work feasts, in effect, act as a mechanism of indirect conversion between spheres of exchange in multi-centric economies and thereby provide a potential catalyst for increasing inequality in social relations.

WORK FEASTS IN ETHNOGRAPHIC CONTEXTS

At this stage, it is necessary to ground this schematic discussion of collective work events, especially work feasts, in some brief ethnographic examples in order both to give a sense of the everyday lived experience behind these abstract concepts and to expand upon the theoretical points made.

The importance and ubiquity of work feasts can hardly be doubted by anyone familiar with the ethnographic and historical literature.[2] In fact, work feasts have been such a common feature of agrarian societies that they have often been taken for granted as part of the expected cultural background—a self-evident feature mentioned in a various passages but not singled out for detailed analysis (with some fortunate exceptions). However, even some of the briefer analyses are quite revealing. Goldschmidt, for example, wrote of the *mayket* work feast of the Sebei of East Africa that "no institution is so central to modern Sebei life" (1976:156); and among the Kofyar of Nigeria, the concept of God is even phrased in terms of a wealthy farmer who distributes beer in return for labor (Netting 1964).

As noted earlier, work feasts were, and are, used to perform a wide variety of tasks for which the sheer multiplication of hands either allows a project to be done in a short space of time or enables a project that could not be undertaken otherwise. Most often these include agricultural tasks and construction or maintenance / repair projects, but such things as the organization of game drives, mining, and trade expeditions are also recorded. For example, the genesis of the extensive trading network of the Kamba of Kenya was due in large measure to the innovative adaptation of the traditional *mwethya* work-feast system to organize transport (Cummings 1976:92–93).

What is more, the motivational effectiveness of CWEs in inducing people to participate in working together is evident in the fact that, despite some obviously important effects on such practices stemming from the spread of wage labor and the transformation of labor into a marketable commodity under colonial regimes, work feasts and work exchanges have continued to persist alongside wage labor in many areas (Colson and Scudder 1988; Erasmus 1956; Moore 1975; Saul 1983). Indeed, during the colonial period, long after many other elements in an indigenous economy had been accepted as commodities with a monetary value, there often persisted a lingering negative feeling about exchanging labor for money (as also was the case with land). Barth (1967a), for example, noted that among the Fur of the Sudan, government workers were for some time unsuccessful in recruiting local workers by offering money wages—even when those wages were calculated to be twelve times the value of the millet beer demanded by an individual in the context of a work feast. Similarly, on Samoa and in the Cook Islands of the Pacific, Lemert (1979) noted that natives could not be recruited for agricultural work on plantations by offering money; only the promise of *mea miti* ("something to sip": i.e., several bottles of drink for a feast after the work is done) would provide a sufficient incentive.

Hunter's description of work feasts *(amalima,* singular: *ilima)* among the Pondo of South Africa nicely illustrates and highlights several of the typical features noted in the earlier discussion. These *amalima* can mobilize up to two hundred people for a particular task. Word is spread by telling the neighbors that an *ilima* will be held in a particular field on a given day, and the news quickly spreads through the district by word of mouth. There is no obligation for anyone to participate, but people are drawn by the prospect of the feast. Moreover, there is a hierarchy of preference between beer feasts and meat feasts:

an *ilima* with beer always draws more than an *ilima* with meat . . . It is known and discussed in the community beforehand how many barrels [of beer] have been prepared, and so the number of people is in some ways commensurate with the amount of beer provided, but other considerations such as the scarcity of beer at the time, the number of other festivities on, the occupation of people with their own lands, and the reputation of the owner of the *ilima* for generosity, or stinginess, affect the number attending. (Hunter 1961:89)

As Hunter describes one such event:

At one *ilima* to take mealies off the cob, five barrels of beer were provided and an average of forty people were present at one time, the number of men and women being about equal. People came and went, assisting in the work for as long as they stayed. Beer was passed round at intervals, so the amount they got depended upon the length of time they stayed. (1961:89)

As she further noted, people work hard at such events, but they come to them because they enjoy participating: "An *ilima* is a party. The crowd of people, the mixing of the sexes, and the refreshments, give even to hard work the atmosphere of play. There is conversation, and songs, and flirting" (1961:90). This means also that "Usually an *ilima* gets through a considerable amount of work, but the quality of the work, particularly in a weeding party, is apt to be poor" (1961:90).

Bohannan and Bohannan (1968) provide another illuminating description of a work feast among the Tiv of Nigeria:

The biggest [yam-] mounding party we saw was called by a man of about forty-five, Yilaun of MbaDuku/MbaYar. He called his best friend from the neighboring lineage . . . who gathered about twenty of his own agnatic kinsmen about him and came to MbaDuku late one evening. They brought drums and hoes, a hurricane lamp, and their best clothes. They danced at several compounds along the way, to songs composed for the occasion and to well-known work songs. When they got to Yilaun's compound, they danced until about 1:00 A.M. They began work the next morning at daybreak. This group was joined by Yilaun's agnatic kinsmen: all the agnatic descendants of his father's father, and a few youths with more attenuated agnatic links. Drawn by dancing and the promise of rich food, several young men of Yilaun's mother's lineage came, and two of his wives' brothers also arrived.

This group made yam mounds at a feverish pitch for about four hours. They were then given food, prepared and brought to the fields by all of the women of Yilaun's compound. They ate in groups of about half a dozen; each group was given a huge calabash of yam porridge with three different sauces. There was so much food they could not eat it all. Work was suspended during the heat of the day. They began again about four in the afternoon and worked until dark, and were fed again. That night they danced until well after midnight. The next day the procedure was repeated, and all the farms of Yilaun's compound were finished. That night they began the biggest dance of all: Yilaun furnished pot after pot of millet beer and killed two small goats. They again danced far into the night, and the next day danced for almost two hours at the local market. (Bohannan and Bohannan 1968:73–74)

By hosting this large work feast, Yilaun was actually able to use this labor to expand his farmland into disputed territory in a region where land was becoming increasingly scarce. "In addition, Yilaun reaped great prestige from his lavish treatment of the relatives of his best friend: during the dancing at the market place, his name was on the lips of all" (Bohannan and Bohannan 1968:74).

As pointed out earlier, *corvée* labor also is generally organized through the idiom of the work feast (e.g., see Dillon 1990:129; Goody 1982:67; Richards 1939; Washburne 1961:140). In making this generalizing observation, there is, of course, some potential danger in using cases from colonial contexts because in many instances "chiefs" were created by decree in societies where they did not previously exist (e.g., see Chapter 3). Hence, such neo-chiefs may simply have continued the labor-mobilization practices used by wealthy influential men who did not previously have the authority to command labor tribute. However, this danger is mitigated by the fact that even cases with long-established kingdoms seem to follow this pattern. As noted earlier, Bourdieu (1990:118) considers the voluntary work feast as simply a camouflaged version of *corvée*. While this statement obscures important distinctions within the range of events that constitute work feasts (outlined in the initial discussion of CWEs), it does quite correctly point to the potential for *some* work feasts to develop into a mechanism of labor exploitation.

SAMIA WORK FEASTS AND THE ISSUE OF LABOR EXPLOITATION

Let us now turn to a brief consideration of an ethnohistorical study on precolonial iron production conducted among the Samia people in western Kenya as a means of focusing particularly upon this issue of labor exploitation and exploring the closely related conversion function of the work feast.[3] The Samia are an agrarian society with a traditionally acephalous form of political organization. They speak a language of the Bantu family and are neighbors of the Nilotic-speaking Luo living north of the Winam Gulf in the northeast corner of Lake Victoria. Until the influx of European industrially produced iron in the 1920s, all of the iron used over a several-thousand-square-kilometer area encompassing both Samia and large parts of the neighboring Luo territory was derived from a single ore source in the Samia hills. This source, composed of hematite deposits in pockets of about 7 meters thickness, constitutes the richest iron ore source in Kenya (Brown 1995:43). The importance of the precolonial exploitation of these deposits is reflected in both the considerable quantities of iron slag found at the base of the hills and in the Luo name for the principal object produced from this ore, a large iron hoe blade called *Kwer Nyagot,* or "Hoe, Daughter of the Hills" (Fig. 9.2). The production of these hoes was based upon a system fueled by large work feasts, which was an elaborated version of the same mechanism used to mobilize labor for a variety of other projects. A wealthy man (that is, one with a large number of wives capable of raising a copious supply of millet, brewing it into beer, and preparing a generous supply of food) would call together all the willing men of the area on a given day to mine ore from the Samia hills. There was no obligation to participate, but men were drawn to do so by the prior reputation of the host for generous hospitality. After spending the day gathering ore, these men were treated to a great feast, after which they would return home and the host was left with a large supply of iron ore. No further compensation was required, and the host was considered to own the proceeds of the day's labor. A smelter and a smith were then called to convert the ore first into blooms and then into hoes, respectively. Each of these craftsmen was compensated for his labor by being given some of the hoes produced from the ore.

These hoes, some of which still survive as heirlooms in Luo and Samia homes, were extremely valuable. Although used for utilitarian agricultural purposes, they formed part of a prestige sphere of exchange in a multi-centric economy: their acquisition required the giving of livestock and they were even used along with cattle as bridewealth in marriage transactions. So important were they to the neighboring Luo that Samia travelers were exempt from attack for fear of en-

Figure 9.2. Iron hoe blade (length = 56 cm) from the precolonial era in western Kenya. These hoe blades were made in the Samia Hills and exchanged widely throughout the region. They could be used as bridewealth and to exchange for livestock. (Photo by M. Dietler and I. Herbich)

dangering exchange links, and giving a daughter to be married to a Samia man was considered highly desirable because of the exchange relationships it engendered. Furthermore, the still iron-rich slag (the smelting process was not very efficient) was often collected by those Samia who could not manage to host mining work feasts on their own, and small chunks of iron were hoarded until there was enough to make a hoe.

While this work-feast method of engaging in iron production was, in principle, open to all Samia men, in practical terms its effective manipulation was limited to those wealthy enough to provide sufficiently large feasts to mobilize large work groups. As noted elsewhere (Chapter 3), the agricultural and culinary labor required for such an event is formidable, and in Samia and Luo societies this required many wives. However, acquiring wives required the accumulation of wealth (i.e., cattle and iron hoes) for bridewealth. Moreover, there is an obvious link between subsistence production, marriage, and iron production that would insure that an initial position of advantage in access to this process would tend to have a spiraling effect in augmenting wealth and prestige (see Fig. 9.3). That is, wealth in cattle was necessary for the bridewealth to obtain the multiple wives whose labor could produce a large feast. But once achieved, the hoes gained through the institution of the work feast could be used to obtain more wives (through conversion to stock used as bridewealth or used directly in marriage transactions): and the increased productive capacity represented by these women could be used to more effectively and frequently amass the supplies for a large feast and engage again in iron production. Those men without the initial "capital" (in terms of cattle, crops, and wives) to produce a large feast were effectively excluded from the cycle and were reduced to being regular guests / workers at the work feasts of the wealthy.

This example serves to illustrate how feasts may act as a means of indirect conversion between spheres of exchange (or regimes of value) in a multi-centric economy (Fig. 9.4). Such economies, in which different classes of goods circulated in separate exchange regimes (of variable number and kind depending upon the culture) and in which there were strong moral sanctions against converting between the spheres, were a very common feature of pre-monetary economic systems that did not have a uniform and universal scale of value (Barth 1967a; Bohannan 1955; Piot 1991; Salisbury 1962); indeed, Kopytoff (1986) sees them as a universal feature, even in the Western capitalist context. In pre-monetized western Kenya, for example, one could exchange grain for pots or a range of other craft items and agricultural produce. However, grain was so low on the scale of value that no one would be willing to accept even a huge quantity of it in direct exchange for prestige-sphere goods (except, perhaps, during a famine); yet its conversion into beer and food in the context of a feast was a prime means of

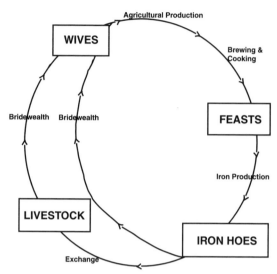

Figure 9.3. Schematic representation of the link between subsistence production, marriage, and iron production in Samia society showing how an initial position of advantage in access to this process would tend to have a spiraling effect in augmenting wealth and prestige.

both acquiring prestige and mobilizing the labor by which prestige-sphere exchange objects could ultimately be obtained. A ritual form of commensal hospitality (the work feast) was able to perform the apparently impossible function of converting lowly grain into valuables and prestige, of linking separate spheres of exchange via an indirect route involving the mobilization of labor (both culinary and productive).

The Samia example also demonstrates the way in which work feasts serve as a conduit for reciprocal conversions of what Bourdieu (1990) calls economic and symbolic capital.[4] People are drawn to participate in such events by the reputation of the host for generous hospitality. This reputation is an aspect of symbolic capital acquired through the expenditure of material capital in previous feasts. But through the institution of the work feast, this symbolic capital is used to harness the labor of others for the acquisition of further material capital, while at the same time augmenting the symbolic capital of the host by generating further prestige and embellishing his reputation for generosity.

Finally, this example also illustrates how the manipulation of this practice can sometimes lead to increasing social and economic inequality even in the context of ideologically egalitarian precapitalist societies. When one segment of a community becomes adept at managing this entrepreneurial device and begins to act consistently as hosts of large work feasts while others find themselves continually serving as guests/workers, then one has the beginnings of a pattern of labor ex-

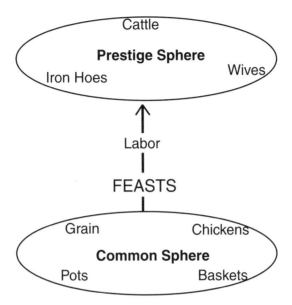

Figure 9.4. Schematic representation of the role of feasts as a privileged mechanism of indirect conversion between spheres of exchange in a multi-centric economy. This is a highly simplified rendition of one possible set of spheres of exchange; comparative ethnographic surveys show many possible permutations of numbers of spheres and valuations of objects.

ploitation by which some individuals or groups are able to dominate the system and extract wealth and prestige from the labor of others.

Barth (1967a, 1967b) noted a similar potential for "growth spirals" among the mountain Fur villages of the Sudan. There the people of the village had gradually separated into two strata: a moderately prosperous group of work-feast hosts and a less fortunate fraction who, through their frequent participation as guest/workers at the feasts of others, effectively formed a labor reserve for the more wealthy. Some of the wealthy individuals had even begun to further augment their relative advantage by expanding the use of work feasts to enter the cash-crop market.

Similarly, among the Tarahumara of Mexico, Kennedy (1978:86) noted that wealthier men were able to give more frequent and more lavish *tesgüinadas* (work feasts fueled with maize beer), and thereby to gain the labor necessary to maintain larger areas under cultivation. This allowed them not only to hold more beer feasts, but also to amass surplus maize for distribution to others in times of famine. Both of these things generated considerable symbolic capital. As he noted, the beer feast operates as a "prestige showcase" that serves "the important function of publicizing rank and power," and this feature was even more marked during the lean season before the next harvest (Kennedy 1978:118).

A similar situation was noted among the Maale of Ethiopia by Donham (1994:146–152). He calculated that in one context about two thirds of the net surplus of work-feast labor that richer villagers enjoyed came from people in the poorest categories of the village hierarchy. These were households that, on average, sponsored no work feasts at all during the entire period of his fieldwork. Moreover, what he identified as "middle villagers" (i.e., those in the middle economic stratum) on average enjoyed a small net surplus of work-feast labor, but "still showed a negative deficit in cooperation with richer villagers" (Donham 1994:148).

Hence, a potential for labor exploitation clearly inheres in some forms of the work feast. But a marked pattern of exploitation is by no means a universal result of the operation of work feasts; nor do all exploitative forms necessarily result in escalating inequalities.[5] Consequently, it is important to ask what conditions favor the development of such an asymmetrical pattern and what kinds of constraints might inhibit its spiraling expansion?

One immediate potential constraint stems from certain specific organizational arrangements of the relationship between workers and food providers. In some contexts, certain public projects may be undertaken by groups of people who share not only the work but also the provisioning of the feast. For example, among the Wamira of Papua New Guinea, Kahn (1998) notes that all men must work together to construct and periodically clear out common irrigation canals. This involves work feasts of perhaps thirty men for which food is supplied jointly by the wives of all the men. Hence, a potential for exploitation depends upon the existence of work feasts hosted by individual households, or at least by a group smaller than the collection of assembled workers/guests. Given this arrangement, Barth (1967a) located another potential brake on the system in the fact that the quality and productivity of the workforce tends to deteriorate as the group expands. As noted earlier, this feature has very frequently been remarked upon in other cases (e.g., Donham 1994; Kennedy 1978). While this may constrain the size of individual work feasts, it does not explain limitations on the expansion of the system. However, more important constraints are imposed by the cultural definition of the transaction that constitutes a work feast.

What becomes immediately clear is that those events which, by local cultural convention, conform most closely to the extreme work feast pole of the continuum of CWE possibilities are the most susceptible to exploitation. This is because the event is treated by the participants as a finite exchange transaction where lavishness of hospitality replaces any delayed obligations for reciprocal labor. Hence, the host is not limited by the time and energy constraints of taking on multiple labor-debt obligations. Moreover, this form of work feast comes closest to the concept of a labor market, while at the same time the fact that the exchange is orchestrated through a ritual of commensal hospitality subtly serves to euphemize the nature of the transaction—the exchange is represented as an act of generosity and made palatable even in societies with a strongly egalitarian ethos. Finally, the fact that recruitment of the labor pool may expand well beyond very local kin and friendship networks means that, even in those cases where some weak and implicit labor obligations might accrue, the transaction occurs between the host and a large number of individuals who are not already linked by close social relationships and who stand outside the moral community within which such obligations might be recognized (see Sahlins 1972).

As the culturally construed proper form of the work feast is located farther away from the polar type (hence as reciprocal labor obligations increase and are more explicitly and precisely calculated), such asymmetrical exploitation becomes more difficult. The accruing labor obligations restrict the future activities of the host and the size of the work group that can be assembled through a work feast. As noted earlier, the precise location on the CWE continuum of a given local version of the work feast is determined by local cultural conceptions. This can, of course, shift over time as practice responds to changing problems and historical contexts. But what is important to note is that a potential for exploitation is inherent in the upper range of the work-feast end of the continuum. This potential can be powerfully magnified through certain linkages—when work feasts are used to produce goods or materials that can be employed in external exchange circuits to increase economic and symbolic capital (for example in the case of producing iron hoes for cattle exchanges, or the use of work feasts to produce cash crops).

It is also necessary to briefly discuss another form of labor exploitation that is a more variable aspect of work feasts—that is, an intrahousehold one based upon gender. In very many cases, it is women who constitute the productive base for the agricultural and culinary labor that underwrites the operation of work feasts, yet have little or no claim to the benefits of the event (except indirectly, as members of the household). For example, in the Samia case discussed earlier, it was the multiple wives of a wealthy man who provided the crops and the culinary labor necessary to produce a feast. Yet it was largely the husband who benefited from the mining labor organized through the feast—both in terms of the prestige generated and the subsequent use of the iron hoes (for the acquisition of cattle and more wives). Hence, there was a double system of exploitation in operation. A similar pattern of the gendered division of labor is found in many agrarian societies, especially in Africa (e.g., see Clark 1980; Geschire 1982). This is, in fact, one of the attractions of polygyny and one reason that wealthy men and chiefs in patrilineal polygynous societies tend to have many more wives than other men.

It would be misleading, however, to suggest that this is a universal pattern of exploitation. In the first place, there are many cases in which men are responsible for agricultural production and, perhaps more rarely, culinary labor for their own feasts. There are also cases in which the division of agricultural labor is more balanced, and gendered patterns of crop ownership and responsibilities can, in fact, be rather complicated (e.g., see Barth 1967a:151). Moreover, in some instances women are capable of mounting work feasts on their own and have proprietary rights over the proceeds of the event. It is very common that women organize work exchanges, but somewhat less common that they are the official hosts of work feasts, especially the larger types. However, it does happen in some contexts. Moreover, CWEs of various types can be turned to novel uses that actually give women the possibility for increased economic independence and power: among the Luo of Kenya, for example, during the 1980s women began to expand the traditional work exchanges for agricultural tasks into new kinds of cooperative work-exchange associations (among some potters, for example) that enabled them to pool resources, build collective capital, and ameliorate individual risk (see Herbich and Dietler 1989). Hence, work feasts and other CWEs cannot automatically be viewed simply as a mechanism of gendered exploitation of labor. However, one can observe that gendered exploitation, where it exists, does tend to involve exploitation of female labor, whereas an inverse pattern (that is, in which men provide the bulk of the agricultural and culinary labor that supports women's work feasts) is rather rarer. It is extremely important to recognize the potential permutations of these various intersecting patterns of exploitation in understanding the labor-mobilization practices of a given society and their potential for creating and transforming structures of inequality.

CONCLUSION

As archaeologists become increasingly interested in pursuing questions concerning the transformation of social relations, the organization and institutional setting of labor is a topic that demands to be explored in much greater depth. In particular, it is extremely important to develop a theoretical understanding of the practices that enable the mobilization of voluntary collective labor.

Archaeologists have expended a good deal of energy attempting to identify, classify, and understand "craft specialists" and systems of "specialized production" (e.g., Childe 1936; Clark 1995; Clark and Parry 1990; Costin 1991; Herbich 1987; Peacock 1982). However, they have been far less engaged with exploring the forms of collective labor (voluntary and involuntary) that underlie in a more fundamental way the operation of the agrarian political economy. Within the fields of history and anthropology there exists a considerable literature analyzing forms of involuntary labor classified under the rubric of "slavery" (e.g., Finley

1985; Garlan 1988; Kopytoff 1982; Meillassoux 1991; Miers and Kopytoff 1977); although, to date, this has been of far less concern to archaeologists. The major exception to this pattern of neglect has been archaeologists working on the highly idiosyncratic form of slavery found on the plantations of North America (see Singleton 1995), although scholars working in a few other regions have also made important contributions (e.g., Arnold 1988; Daubigney 1983; Peschel 1971).

This chapter has attempted to focus an analytical lens on the even less well explored, yet extremely important, process of voluntary collective labor mobilization. A theoretical understanding of such labor-mobilization practices is crucial to archaeologists for several reasons. In the first place, a fuller awareness of the range and operation of such practices exposes the inadequacies of assumptions that have guided archaeological interpretation in the past, such as simplistic correlations between the existence of large-scale earthworks and the necessity of centralized political organization. The idea that such projects must be the result of tributary *corvée* labor is simply not warranted, as it is clear that work feasts can mobilize voluntary work groups on a similar scale for similar kinds of projects. Indeed, it should be evident at this point that *corvée* labor can only be understood when it is properly situated in the context of the full range of voluntary "collective work events" because it operates as a kind of variant of the work feast. Even large state-directed projects, at least those that depend upon the labor of free subjects rather than slaves, will usually take the organizational form of work feasts.

A theoretical dissection of work feasts also reveals how they serve the important role of operating as mechanisms of conversion between economic and symbolic capital. Like other feasts, they convert agricultural produce into immediate prestige for the host. However, they also have the advantage of simultaneously harnessing labor that can be used to generate further materials for future feast events or to produce goods that can be used to acquire other forms of symbolic capital or enlarge the household productive base (e.g., through marriage transactions). As explained earlier, this is an extremely important function of indirect conversion in premonetary multi-centric economies where there are moral sanctions against direct conversions between spheres of exchange. It is important precisely because it allows goods of little value to be used to create and acquire valuables and prestige. It provides a venue for building a career through strategic "investment."

Such an exploration of CWEs also exposes the potential that exists for some forms of work feast to enable the increasing exploitation of labor even in the context of societies with an egalitarian political ethos. Regardless of the formal ideology of a society, large work feasts that are viewed as a finite exchange transaction with no reciprocal labor obligations can result, in the course of practice, in asymmetrical labor flows, such that some individuals or households de-

rive wealth and prestige from the labor of others. This fact has profound significance for the long-term development of social relations and economic structures.
Obviously, it also has crucial implications for archaeologists attempting to understand the development and exacerbation of conditions of social inequality. Finally, it dramatically underscores yet one more reason why it is essential for
archaeologists to recognize the importance of feasts in social life.

ACKNOWLEDGMENTS

Portions of this discussion have been presented previously at various symposia and semi-
nars (e.g., Dietler 1989, 1996; Herbich 1991). We benefited particularly from discussion at
the École des Hautes Études en Sciences Sociales in Marseille and the Université de Paris I
(Sorbonne-Panthéon). Special thanks are due to Anick Coudart, Jean-Paul Demoule, and
André Tchernia.

For making possible our ethnographic research in western Kenya, thanks are due to the
National Science Foundation, the Wenner-Gren Foundation, the Boise Fund of Oxford
University, the Office of the President of Kenya, the National Museums of Kenya, and es-
pecially our Luo and Samia hosts and our research assistants, Rhoda Onyango, Monica
Oyier, and the late Elijah Ogutu.

NOTES

1. The distinction between "work feasts" and "work exchanges" corresponds
   approximately to categories with slightly different names developed in several earlier
   comparative analyses of collective labor practices. For example, Erasmus (1956)
   denoted these practices with the terms "festive labor" and "exchange labor,"
   respectively; whereas Moore (1975) called them "non-reciprocal co-operative labour"
   and "reciprocal co-operative labour." While owing an obvious major debt to these
   seminal works, we employ an alternative terminology in order to signify a particular
   analytical focus on the role of the feast *event* in orchestrating labor projects and to
   mark certain subtle differences from these earlier works.
2. Work feasts were/are found from Africa to Latin America, from the Caribbean to Asia,
   from European peasants to North American colonists and their barn-raisings. In
   addition to the works cited elsewhere in this text, see, for example, Cancian 1972;
   Eguchi 1975; Guillet 1980; Herskovits 1937:70–76; Kahn 1998; Kenyatta 1938:59–60;
   Lomnitz 1976:183; March 1998; Moerman 1968; Provinse 1937; Salisbury 1962. This is, of
   course, merely a minuscule sample cited in order to suggest the geographical extent
   of the practice.
3. All unreferenced descriptions of practices among the Luo and Samia peoples in this
   paper are derived from research conducted by us in western Kenya from 1980 to 1983
   (see, e.g., Dietler and Herbich 1993; Herbich 1987, 1991; Herbich and Dietler 1991, 1993).
4. Bourdieu's (1990) *The Logic of Practice* is a theoretical reformulation of concepts, such
   as symbolic capital, presented earlier in his (1978) *Outline of a Theory of Practice.*

Although the latter text is better known in the Anglophone anthropological community, it has been largely superseded by the later work. The adoption of Bourdieu's metaphorical use of "capital" to translate various forms of socially constructed power poses certain dangers—not least the fact that it may be easily misconstrued as advocating an extension of the simplistic and inappropriate neoclassical economic perspective to the analysis of social and cultural phenomena or as naturalizing the cultural logic of capitalism. Hence, although we have certain misgivings, the term *symbolic capital* is used here largely because it is the most useful trope we have found for illuminating the operation of the work feast. However, we issue the caution that it is used in the specific sense stemming from Bourdieu's theoretical program for the analysis of symbolic domination, and not in a neoclassical economics sense or rational actor theory sense.

5. For example, Donham (1994:146–152) provides an example of two very different patterns in the same society in Ethiopia. The Bola faction had a classic pattern of labor exploitation by the wealthy as described earlier. However, among the Dofo group, there was a very different flow of work-feast labor due to the influence of a political struggle by elders attempting to preserve their factional position. In this case, with a few exceptions, the most politically influential households had deficits of labor flows in work feasts and there was a net transfer of labor from elders' households to middle-aged men's households (the elders sent younger members of their very large households to the work feasts of junior men rather than coming themselves). In this case, "elders appeared to be transferring labor to middle-aged men in return for support and deference" (Donham 1994:151).

REFERENCES

Arnold, B.
    1988   Slavery in Late Prehistoric Europe: Recovering the Evidence for Social Structure in Iron Age Society. In *Tribe and Polity in Late Prehistoric Europe,* edited by D. B. Gibson and M. N. Geselowitz, pp. 179–192. New York: Plenum Press.

Barth, F.
    1967a   Economic Spheres in Darfur. In *Themes in Economic Anthropology,* edited by R. Firth, pp. 149–174. London: Tavistock.
    1967b   On the Study of Social Change. *American Anthropologist* 69:661–670.

Bohannan, P.
    1955   Some Principles of Exchange and Investment among the Tiv. *American Anthropologist* 57:60–70.

Bohannan, P., and L. Bohannan
    1968   *Tiv Economy.* Evanston: Northwestern University Press.

Bourdieu, P.
    1986   The Forms of Capital. In *Handbook of Theory and Research for the Sociology of Education,* edited by J. G. Richardson, pp. 241–258. New York: Greenwood Press.
    1990   *The Logic of Practice.* Stanford: Stanford University Press.

Brown, J.
    1995   *Traditional Metalworking in Kenya.* Cambridge Monographs in African Archaeology 38, Cambridge.

Cancian, F.
    1965   *Economics and Prestige in a Maya Community.* Stanford: Stanford University Press.

Chibnik, M., and W. de Jong
    1990   Agricultural Labor Organization in Ribereño Communities of the Peruvian Amazon. *Ethnology* 29:75–95.

Childe, V. G.
    1936   *Man Makes Himself.* New York: Mentor.

Clark, C. M.
    1980   Land and Food, Women and Power, in Nineteenth-Century Kikuyu. *Africa* 50:357–370.

Clark, J. E.
    1995   Craft Specialization as an Archaeological Category. *Research in Economic Anthropology* 16:267–296.

Clark, J. E., and W. J. Parry
    1990   Craft Specialization and Cultural Complexity. *Research in Economic Anthropology* 2:289–346.

Colson, E.
    1949   *Life among the Cattle-Owning Plateau Tonga.* Livingstone, Zambia: The Rhodes-Livingstone Museum Occasional Papers 6.

Colson, E., and T. Scudder
    1988   *For Prayer and Profit: The Ritual, Economic, and Social Importance of Beer in Gwembe District, Zambia, 1950–1982.* Stanford: Stanford University Press.

Costin, C. L.
    1991   Craft Specialization: Issues in Defining, Documenting, and Explaining the Organization of Production. *Archaeological Method and Theory* 3:1–56.

Cummings, R. J.
    1976   The Early Development of Akamba Local Trade History, c.1780–1820. *Kenya Historical Review* 4:85–110.

Daubigney, A.
    1983   Relations marchandes méditerranéennes et procès des rapports de dépendance (magu- et ambactes) en Gaule protohistorique. In *Modes de contacts et processus de transformation dans les sociétés anciennes,* pp. 659–683. Rome: École française de Rome.

Dietler, M.
    1989   The Work-Party Feast as a Mechanism of Labor Mobilization and Exploitation: the Case of Samia Iron Production. Paper presented at 88th Annual Meeting of the American Anthropological Association, Washington, D.C., November.

1990   Driven by Drink: The Role of Drinking in the Political Economy and the Case of Early Iron Age France. *Journal of Anthropological Archaeology* 9:352–406.

1996   Feasts and Commensal Politics in the Political Economy: Food, Power, and Status in Prehistoric Europe. In *Food and the Status Quest: An Interdisciplinary Perspective,* edited by P. Wiessner and W. Schiefenhövel, pp. 87–125. Oxford: Berghahn Books.

Dietler, M., and I. Herbich

1993   Living on Luo Time: Reckoning Sequence, Duration, History, and Biography in a Rural African Society. *World Archaeology* 25:248–260.

Dillon, R. G.

1990   *Ranking and Resistance: A Precolonial Cameroonian Polity in Regional Perspective.* Stanford: Stanford University Press.

Donham, D.

1994   *Work and Power in Maale, Ethiopia.* New York: Columbia University Press.
[1979]

Eguchi, P. K.

1975   Beer Drinking and Festivals among the Hide. *Kyoto University African Studies* 9:69–90.

Erasmus, C. J.

1956   Culture Structure and Culture Process: The Occurrence and Disappearance of Reciprocal Farm Labor. *Southwestern Journal of Anthropology* 12:444–469.

Finley, M. I.

1985   *The Ancient Economy.* London: Hogarth Press.

Garlan, Y.

1988   *Slavery in Ancient Greece.* Ithaca: Cornell University Press.

Geschire, P.

1982   *Village Communities and the State: Changing Relations among the Maka of Southeastern Cameroon since the Colonial Conquest.* Translated by J. Ravell. London: Kegan Paul.

Goldschmidt, W.

1976   *Culture and Behavior of the Sebei: A Study in Continuity and Adaptation.* Berkeley: University of California Press.

Goody, J.

1982   *Cooking, Cuisine, and Class: A Study in Comparative Sociology.* Cambridge: Cambridge University Press.

Guillet, D.

1980   Reciprocal Labor and Peripheral Capitalism in the Central Andes. *Ethnology* 19:151–167.

Herbich, I.

1987   Learning Patterns, Potter Interaction, and Ceramic Style among the Luo of Kenya. *The African Archaeological Review* 5:193–204.

1991   The Flow of Drink in an African Society: An Ethnoarchaeological Perspective. Paper presented at the 56th Annual Meeting of the Society for American Archaeology, New Orleans, April.

Herbich, I., and M. Dietler

1989   River-Lake Nilotic: Luo. In *Kenyan Pots and Potters*, edited by J. Barbour and S. Wandibba, pp. 27–40. Nairobi: Oxford University Press.

1991   Aspects of the Ceramic System of the Luo of Kenya. In *Töpferei- und Keramikforschung*, 2, edited by H. Lüdtke and R. Vossen, pp. 105–135. Bonn: Habelt.

1993   Space, Time, and Symbolic Structure in the Luo Homestead: An Ethnoarchaeological Study of "Settlement Biography" in Africa. In *Actes du XIIe Congrès International des Sciences Préhistoriques et Protohistoriques, Bratislava, Czechoslovakia, September 1–7, 1991, Vol. 1*, edited by J. Pavúk, pp. 26–32. Nitra: Archaeological Institute of the Slovak Academy of Sciences.

Herskovits, M. J.

1937   *Dahomey: An Ancient West African Kingdom*. New York: J. J. Augustin.

Hunter, M.

1961   *Reaction to Conquest: Effects of Contact with Europeans on the Pondo of Southern Africa*. London: Oxford University Press.

Kahn, M.

1998   "Men Are Taro" (They Cannot Be Rice): Political Aspects of Food Choices in Wamira, Papua New Guinea. In *Food and Gender: Identity and Power*, edited by C. M. Counihan and S. L. Kaplan, pp. 29–44. Amsterdam: Harwood Academic Publishers.

Karp, I.

1980   Beer Drinking and Social Experience in an African Society. In *Explorations in African Systems of Thought*, edited by I. Karp and C. Bird, pp. 83–119. Bloomington: Indiana University Press.

Kennedy, J. G.

1978   *The Tarahumara of the Sierra Madre: Beer, Ecology, and Social Organization*. Arlington Heights, Ill.: AHM.

Kenyatta, J.

1965   *Facing Mt. Kenya: The Tribal Life of the Gikuyu*. New York: Vintage.

Kopytoff, I.

1982   Slavery. *Annual Review of Anthropology* 11:207–30.

1986   The Cultural Biography of Things: Commoditization as Process. In *The Social Life of Things: Commodities in Cultural Perspective*, edited by A. Appadurai, pp. 64–91. Cambridge: Cambridge University Press.

Lemert, E.

1964   Forms and Pathology of Drinking in Three Polynesian Societies. *American Anthropologist* 66:361–374.

Lemonnier, P.

1990   *Guerres et festins: Paix, échanges et compétition dans les Highlands de Nouvelle-Guinée*. Paris: CID—Editions de la Maison des Sciences de l'Homme.

Lomnitz, L.
1976   Alcohol and Culture: The Historical Evolution of Drinking Patterns among the Mapuche. In *Cross-Cultural Approaches to the Study of Alcohol: An Interdisciplinary Perspective,* edited by M. Everett, J. Waddell and D. Heath, pp. 177–198. The Hague: Mouton.

March, K. S.
1998   Hospitality, Women, and the Efficacy of Beer. In *Food and Gender: Identity and Power,* edited by C. M. Counihan and S. L. Kaplan, pp. 45–80. Amsterdam: Harwood Academic Publishers.

Mayer, P.
1951   Agricultural Co-operation by Neighborhood Groups among the Gusii. In *Two Studies in Applied Anthropology in Kenya,* edited by P. Mayer. London: HMSO.

Meillassoux, C.
1991   *The Anthropology of Slavery: The Womb of Iron and Gold.* Translated by A. Dasnois. Chicago: University of Chicago Press.

Miers, S., and I. Kopytoff, eds.
1977   *Slavery in Africa: Historical and Anthropological Perspectives.* Madison: University of Wisconsin Press.

Moerman, M.
1968   *Agricultural Change and Peasant Choice in a Thai Village.* Los Angeles: University of California Press.

Moore, M. P.
1975   Cooperative Labour in Peasant Agriculture. *The Journal of Peasant Studies* 2:270–291.

Nadel, S. F.
1942   *A Black Byzantium: The Kingdom of Nupe in Nigeria.* London: Oxford University Press.

Netting, R.
1964   Beer as a Locus of Value among the West African Kofyar. *American Anthropologist* 66:375–384.

Peacock, D. P.
1982   *Pottery in the Roman World: An Ethnoarchaeological Approach.* London: Longman.

Peschel, K.
1971   Zur Frage der Sklaverei bei den Kelten während der vorrömischen Eisenzeit. *Ethnographisch-Archäologische Zeitschrift* 12:527–539.

Piot, C.
1991   Of Persons and Things: Some Reflections on African Spheres of Exchange. *Man* 26:405–424.

Provinse, J.
1937   Cooperative Ricefield Cultivation among the Siang Dyaks of Central Borneo. *American Anthropologist* 39:77–102.

Renfrew, C.

1973   Monuments, Mobilization, and Social Organization in Neolithic Wessex. In
The Explanation of Culture Change: Models in Prehistory, edited by C. Renfrew,
pp. 539–558. London: Duckworth.

Richards, A. I.

1939   *Land, Labour, and Diet in Northern Rhodesia.* London: Oxford University Press.

Sahlins, M.

1972   *Stone Age Economics.* London: Tavistock.

Salisbury, R. F.

1962   *From Stone to Steel: Economic Consequences of a Technological Change in New
Guinea.* Melbourne: Melbourne University Press.

Saul, M.

1983   Work Parties, Wages, and Accumulation in a Voltaic Village. *American Ethnologist* 10:77–96.

Singleton, T.

1995   The Archaeology of Slavery in North America. *Annual Review of Anthropology*
24:119–140.

Tosh, J.

1978   *Clan Leaders and Colonial Chiefs in Lango: The Political History of an East African
Stateless Society.* Oxford: Clarendon Press.

Trigger, B.

1990   Monumental Architecture: A Thermodynamic Explanation of Symbolic Behaviour. *World Archaeology* 22:119–132.

Uchendu, V.

1970   Traditional Work-Groups in Economic Development. In *Annual Conference
Proceedings, East African Universities, Dar es Salaam, vol. 5.* Kampala: Makerere
Institute of Social Research.

Washburne, C.

1961   *Primitive Drinking: A Study of the Uses and Functions of Alcohol in Preliterate Societies.* New York: College and University Press.

Webster, G.

1990   Labor Control and Emergent Stratification in Prehistoric Europe. *Current Anthropology* 31:337–366.

Part 2

ARCHAEOLOGICAL
PERSPECTIVES

10

THE EVOLUTION OF RITUAL FEASTING SYSTEMS IN PREHISPANIC PHILIPPINE CHIEFDOMS

Laura Lee Junker

At the time of initial Spanish colonization, the Philippine archipelago had a political landscape composed of numerous coastal and riverine chiefdoms of varying scale and complexity that interacted through maritime trade. Archaeological evidence for status-related differences in burials and regional settlement hierarchies indicate that these complex societies existed for at least a millennium prior to European contact (Hutterer 1977; Jocano 1975; Junker 1994, 1999). Historical sources suggest that these societies were ruled by hereditary chiefs. However, remarkably low population densities relative to productive agricultural land, and the consequently high value placed on control of labor, favored political units composed of shifting, alliance-structured coalitions rather than the more permanent, territorially defined constituencies characteristic of chiefdoms in many other regions of the world (Junker 1998; Kiefer 1972; also see Reid 1993:3–6; Winzeler 1976; Wolters 1982:1–15). Ethnohistoric analysis shows that these political coalitions were maintained through the strategic redistribution of resources obtained through tribute mobilization, maritime trading, raiding, and sponsored craft production to both allies and subordinates in the contexts of ritualized exchange and competitive feasting. Because of the tenuous nature of political ties, competition for wealth and followers was perpetual and fierce, with chiefs continually striving to obtain new sources of politically manipulable wealth, elite knowledge, and power.

Some time at the end of the first millennium A.D., and intensifying just prior to early sixteenth-century Spanish contact, Philippine chiefs became involved in long-distance maritime trade for prestige goods with the Chinese empire and other Southeast Asian polities (Hutterer 1977; Junker 1994). Chinese porcelain, silks, metal goods, and other exotic luxury items from outside the archipelago became key symbols of social status and political power for the Philippine chiefly elite. Archaeological and historic evidence suggest that this foreign luxury-good trade reached its height in terms of volume and interpolity trade competition in the fifteenth and sixteenth centuries, with increasing use of foreign imports as "wealth" objects in elite households and as grave accompaniments to high-status burials (Fox 1964, 1967; Junker 1993a, 1993b; Nishimura 1988). Historic sources indicate that foreign porcelains were in high demand as status-enhancing serving assemblages in ritual feasting and they were circulated as valuables in elite exchanges associated with ritual feasts. Not surprisingly, the emergence of larger and more complex chiefdoms in a number of regions of the Philippines in the two centuries prior to Spanish contact is associated with an increased involvement in the foreign porcelain trade and an expanded scale of ritual feasting (Hutterer 1973, 1977; Junker 1999).

Here, I focus on the role of ritual feasting in the evolving political economy of Philippine chiefdoms between the tenth and nineteenth centuries. Because maritime trade for porcelains, silks, metal weaponry, and other mainland Asian prestige goods became an important component of chiefly political economies in many Philippine island polities by the late first millennium A.D., their literate Chinese trade partners have provided us with nearly a millennium of historic writings on Philippine culture. These Chinese sources include a few references to ritual feasting (Junker 1998). However, the richest documentary evidence for ritual feasting and its role in chiefly political economies comes from contact-period (sixteenth-century) Spanish texts, many of which provide considerable detail on "pagan rituals" as part of Christian evangelizing efforts. Another remarkable source of information on ritual exchange and celebratory feasts are ethnographic accounts of Philippine chiefdoms in the island interiors (such as the Bagabo, Magindanao, and Bukidnon of Mindanao), complex societies that were still largely intact and independent of colonial control in the early twentieth century. In his 1913 *Wild Tribes of the Davao District*, ethnographer Fay Cooper Cole provided a particularly vivid description of human sacrifice and ritualized exchanges as part of an annual "harvest" feast among the Bagabo of southeastern Mindanao. Finally, archaeologists have recently begun to look at material evidence relevant to the long-term evolution of ritual feasting in the Philippines, studying household ceramic assemblages and subsistence remains at a number of coastal chiefly centers (Junker, Mudar, and Schwaller 1994; Mudar 1997; see Fig. 10.1).

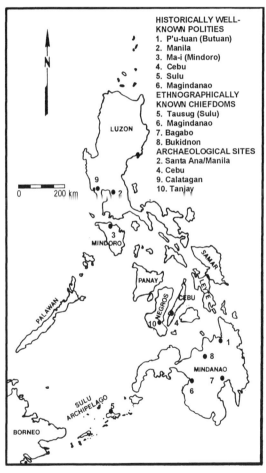

Figure 10.1. The location of tenth- to nineteenth-century Philippine chiefdoms known through Chinese accounts, Spanish records, ethnographic study, and archaeological research.

269

"Feasts of merit" in prehispanic Philippine chiefdoms, like ritual feasts in many complex societies, served to reproduce social relations. Both community cohesion and social rank differentiation were reaffirmed and continually renegotiated through exchange of valuables, chiefs' oral narratives, animal sacrifice, food prestations, and ancestor-invoking ritual. What is particularly significant about the Philippine case is that ritual feasting was highly competitive and socially transformative, with each feast realigning social and political power relations within alliance and patronage networks. Chiefs, nobles, and those with elite pretensions created the social debt fundamental to expanding power asymmetries by distributing increasingly more elaborate status foods and valuables to an ever-widening circle of participants. In many chiefdom-level societies, ritual feasting tends to focus less on overt status competition and negotiation of political relationships than on ideological reinforcement of existing power hierarchies between hereditary chiefs and their constituencies. In the Philippines, and elsewhere in island Southeast Asia, the development of strongly centralized polities with powerfully integrated political hierarchies and relatively permanent, territorially defined power bases may have been constrained by certain ecological, geographic, and demographic factors. In these weakly integrated polities, political power was transient and relied, not on control over fixed territorial bases or well-defined unilineal descent groups, but on cultivating ties of personal loyalty and expanding one's power base through frequent and elaborate gift-giving and ceremonialism. The first section of this chapter examines the complex role of ritual feasting in Philippine chiefly politics through an analysis of historic and ethnographic sources.

In the second half of the chapter, I consider evolutionary aspects of the feasting system and how it relates, in a dynamic way, to other components of an expanding chiefly political economy. Archaeological evidence for ritual feasting at prehispanic Philippine settlements documents changes in the intensity, scale, and social dynamics of these ceremonial events as more complex chiefdoms emerged in the millennia prior to European contact. The distribution of faunal and floral remains that might be associated with ritual feasting, the presence of specialized food-preparation and serving assemblages at prehispanic settlements, and the archaeological study of specific spatial contexts associated with feasting suggest some ways in which these feasting systems may have transformed over time. Increased production of high-value foods such as pig, water buffalo, and rice, and their differential distribution across elite and non-elite residential zones at some fifteenth- and sixteenth-century chiefly centers suggests widening social participation in "feasts of merit" and an inflationary scale of material inputs compared to earlier periods. Archaeological evidence from a number of chiefly centers also suggests that foreign porcelain serving assemblages become an increasingly important component of elite feasting paraphernalia in the few centuries prior to European contact. At the same time, expanded production of local status wares may be tied to the emulation of elite feasting rites by lower-ranked individuals who did not have access to elaborate foreign porcelain assemblages.

Although the archaeological data documents these material trends, we must turn once again to the ethnohistoric evidence from the Philippines and elsewhere in Southeast Asia to develop more specific ideas about how an expanding system of competitive feasting might relate to broader transformations in chiefly political economies. Integrating archaeological and ethnohistoric data, I conclude the paper with a discussion of how ritual feasting is tied to changing chiefly production strategies, escalating competition over access to foreign porcelains, and increasing interpolity warfare and slave-raiding as larger-scale chiefdoms emerged in the fifteenth and sixteenth centuries. What is clear is that material exchanges associated with ritual feasting are central to political alliance building and to the expansion of chiefly political economies. Therefore, ethnohistoric and archaeological analysis of ritual feasting is key to any study of long-term political processes in the prehispanic Philippines.

RITUAL FEASTING IN PHILIPPINE COMPLEX SOCIETIES: THE ETHNOGRAPHIC EVIDENCE

What the sixteenth-century Spaniards described as "feasts of ostentation and vanity" or "feasts of merit" (Colin 1975:175) were a central feature of the political economy of virtually all Philippine complex societies. Ritual feasts are described by Spanish observers and early ethnographic accounts as the cornerstone of social, political, economic, and religious life in these societies. These feasts were generally associated with elite life-crisis events (birth, marriage, illness, death) and events critical to the political economy (e.g., chiefly succession, trading expeditions, warfare and maritime raiding expeditions, political alliances or "peace pacts," "harvest festivals" and other ritual events associated with the agricultural cycle; Boxer manuscript 1975:190, 201, 213–214; Chirino 1904:262–271; Loarca 1903:149–151; Perez 1951:102–103, 110; Pigafetta 1975:65–66; Plasencia 1903b:190–195; Santa Ines 1990:78–79).

Ethnohistoric evidence suggests that feasting in the Philippines simultaneously transacted values of sociopolitical integration and asymmetries, wealth accumulation and generalized redistribution, socially restricted ritual potency, and supernaturally reinforced community well-being. The ability of a chief to draw on the resources of his constituency to finance a feast demonstrated a status-enhancing power to mobilize productivity. His generosity in distributing food to both nobles and commoners attending the ritual feast emphasized his role as a superior kinsman and strengthened the often tenuous bonds that held together political coalitions. Lavish gifting of valuables such as porcelain bowls or metal gongs to elite participants served to both maintain politically significant reciprocal exchange relationships (the material glue of alliance building) and to symbol overtly a particular chief's rank in a social hierarchy vis-à-vis other elites (as measured through his control of wealth).

Although contact-period Philippine chiefdoms diverged widely in terms of scale and complexity, ceremonial feasting was ubiquitous and was characterized by certain pan-archipelago features. These features include (1) sponsorship (though not always exclusively) by elite individuals (most frequently, chiefs); (2) the performance of sacrificial rites using animals (usually pigs, chickens, and/or water buffalo), other foodstuffs, people, and/or manufactured goods contributed by individuals in a tributary or subservient role to the sponsor; (3) elite exchanges of valuables (e.g., porcelain, silks, gold jewelry) as part of ongoing reciprocal exchange partnerships; (4) reallocation of meat and other feasting foods for consumption according to kinship ties and social rank relations with the sponsoring elite; and (5) the conferring of social prestige on the feast's sponsor in accordance with the feast's lavishness and the social debt created through the sponsor's prestations.

FEASTING AND THE RITUALIZED NEGOTIATION OF SOCIAL-POLITICAL RELATIONS

In an ethnohistoric analysis of the use of food in ritual contexts amongst the native American Oglala, Powers and Powers distinguish "feasts" from mundane consumption as "a food event which is somehow commemorative or celebratory of perhaps a historical or religious occasion . . . [the feasts] having some intrinsic social value which transcends the nutritive function of eating" (1984:83). Feasts are thus generally associated with ceremonial or ritual events held either periodically (or on an ad hoc basis), they generally involve commensal units larger than the usual domestic units, and they are often highly structured in terms of what is served and how it is served. Often, the most significant aspect of a feast is its ritual context, within which are generally embedded specific social goals, although Hayden (1994) points out that feasts do not invariably involve religious components or social competition (e.g., work feasts). Ritual feasts are occasions when social relations are negotiated and reaffirmed (Rosman and Rubel 1978). Because ritual feasts in the Philippines were most often sponsored by chiefs and tied closely to aspects of chiefly political economy, they were also important in reinforcing the ideology of chieftainship. To be effectively promulgated, a ruling-class ideology must be materialized in widely witnessed ceremonial events and publicly displayed symbolic objects (DeMarais, Castillo, and Earle 1996; Earle 1997:143–192). Since Philippine chiefdoms did not construct a monumental landscape as a permanent representation of political and social power relations (Junker 1999), repetitive ceremonial events were particularly important in institutionalizing power asymmetries.

Sixteenth-century Spanish sources and early ethnographic accounts of Philippine chiefdoms persisting into the modern era suggest that ceremonial feasts were held frequently throughout the year in a variety of social contexts that included both calendrical and life-crisis ritual. Life-crisis events requiring the sponsorship of a ritual feast by the kin group included the birth of a child, achievement of puberty, marriage, illness, or death of a household member (e.g., Anon. 1990a:164; Anon. 1990b:110; Boxer manuscript 1975:190–191, 193; Chirino 1904:262–271; Loarca 1903:149–151; Plasencia 1903b:190–195; San Antonio 1990:313, 316, 336–338; S;aaanchez 1617:387). The Spanish sources suggest that both elite and non-elite kin groups would hold these life-crisis ritual feasts if they possessed the necessary resources, but for chiefs and other elites these events took on significant political meaning (see below). Other noncalendrical ritual feasts are concerned with more ad hoc elite endeavors, such as the construction of a chiefly residence or war canoe, and the initiation of maritime raiding or trading expeditions. As discussed in more detail below, calendrical rituals associated with planting and harvesting agricultural crops also involved ceremonial feasting and were intimately tied to chiefly tribute-mobilization systems.

Specialist priests, known as *babaylans* in Visayan and *katulunan* in Tagalog and often elite females, performed the religious rites associated with curing or various rites of passage, as well as the ritual killing of the sacrificial animals (preferably pigs or water buffalo) to be later consumed by the guests at the ritual feast. An extended discussion of the cosmological underpinnings of these sacrificial rites are beyond the scope of the present work (see Gibson 1986; Scott 1994:77–93, 233–241; and De Raedt 1989 for more detailed analysis of this aspect of feasting). However, we note here that historical sources and ethnographic accounts suggest that animal sacrifice and consumption by the feast's participants was aimed at warding off afflicting spirits who were seen as attempting to prevent the passage of individuals through critical life stages (i.e., birth, marriage, death), who were causing illness in an individual, or who were likely to prevent the successful completion of community endeavors such as warfare, large-scale maritime trading expeditions, agricultural production, or even the construction of a chiefly residence. There is some indication that these potentially malevolent spirits were actually ancestors, who could bring misfortune on their descendants if the proper ancestral sacrifices were not made at critical points in the life-cycles of the living, and particularly if individuals had violated certain social proscriptions such as engaging in "incestuous" marriages (e.g., Cole 1913:111–120; Gibson 1986:173–176; Scott 1994:237–238).

The sacrifice had to be performed for the kin group to regain the benevolence of these ancestors or to ensure that malevolent spirits will not cross the threshold of a house to cause misfortune for the inhabitants in their various endeavors. Animals such as pigs were viewed as intermediaries between the human and spirit worlds, who exchange their lives to bring "vitality" to the individuals sponsoring the sacrifice. Anyone who participates in consuming the ritual animals' flesh is also imbued with "vitality" and to some degree shares the supernatural protection afforded by carrying out the sacrificial rites. Thus, the sacrificial rites were a reaffirmation of social connectedness, whether these social relations involved a kin-like alliance between social equals or asymmetrical patron-client ties.

RECIPROCITY AND EXCHANGE RELATIONS IN FEASTING

All of the feast participants, including chiefs and nobles as well as commoners and slaves attached to the sponsor, were obliged to make contributions to the feast (e.g., carabao or domestic water buffalo, pigs, fowl, rice, wine) and/or offerings to be used in the accompanying sacrificial ritual and in payment to religious specialists performing it. These contributions included gold, cotton, metal weapons, other prestige goods, rice, pigs, chickens, and other "high-quality" subsistence items (Bobadilla 1990:334; Chirino 1904:262–271; Cole 1913:111–120, 1956:94–117; Boxer manuscript 1975:201; San Antonio 1990:314). It is clear from both the contact-period Spanish sources and early ethnographic accounts that contributions from subordinates were exacted as a form of tribute or enforced labor, whereas the prestations from members of the nobility took place in the context of alliance-building reciprocal "gift" exchanges.

Those feasts marking critical points on the agricultural calendar, in particular, were sufficiently regular to have been the key context in which tribute collection, communal agricultural labor, and amassing of chiefly surplus took place (see Cole 1913:111–120). It is probably not a coincidence that the largest and most protracted of the Bagobo feasts (the Gin Em feast) occurs just after the annual fall rice harvest, when the granaries of subordinate chiefs and village commoners are full of available rice for large tribute exactions. There are parallels with the Makahiki festival and other chiefly agricultural rites of contact-period Hawaii (Earle 1977:225–226; Peebles and Kus 1977:425; also see Kirch, Chapter 6).

Ethnographic descriptions of these ritual events among the Tausug (the core cultural group of the Sulu sultanate), Bukidnon, and Bagobo of Mindanao indicate that a significant component of these events is the reinforcement of elite alliances (Claver 1985:74–75; Cole 1913:111–112; Kiefer 1972:26, 97). Alternately sponsored in their own districts by local chiefs and periodically by regional chieftains, these feasts appear to have been the primary opportunity for reciprocal gift exchanges between elites (involving exchange of imported porcelains, valuable metal gongs, gold jewelry and/or other prestige goods). Elite prestations occurring at any single feast represented links in intertwined chains of ongoing reciprocal exchange partnerships between kin-related and allied nobility, reflecting the unique state of specific social relationships at any one point in time. Analogies can be made with the alliance-based systems of prestige-good exchange recorded for other areas of island Southeast Asia (e.g., Beatty 1991; Volkman 1985) and Oceania (e.g., Gregory 1982; Rosman and Rubel 1978; Strathern 1971; also see Weissner, Chapter 4). Although a portion of the individual prestations are generally returned and new debt created through the host's prestige-enhancing feasting of all the attending celebrants, the host also acquires the obligation to make ceremonial contributions at future feasts sponsored by his exchange partners, ensuring the continuity of the exchange system. The social values transacted by these prestations include political cohesion through the circulation of resources and marriage partners, as well as the social prestige and political influence emanating from a wide network of exchange partners and sponsorship of lavish feasts (Beatty 1991:230).

Despite obligatory contributions from subordinates (exacted as a form of tribute) and from allied political leaders (framed in terms of alliance-building reciprocal gift exchanges), the Spanish chroniclers suggest that the feast sponsor bore the expensive burden of financing the feast (Boxer manuscript 1975:215; Chirino 1904:262–271; also see Claver 1985:27; De Raedt 1989:230; Prill-Brett 1989:30). Feast financing presumably depended heavily on stored resources accumulated over the long term by socially and politically prominent kin groups through their extensive marriage ties and exchange networks.

SOCIAL PRESTIGE OR "MERIT" AS A TRANSACTED VALUE
The prestige-enhancing aspects of these feasts in the Philippines are emphasized by Biernatzki's (1985) and Claver's (1985) ethnographic and historical work on the Bukidnon, a traditional chiefly society of northern Mindanao (also see Cole 1956:94–117). At ceremonial feasts marking the succession of a new chief or other politically significant events, the sponsoring chief typically invited as many chiefs from neighboring districts and regions as possible to participate in the lavish feast (Biernatzki 1985:36–37). The sponsoring of feasts was key to chiefly political strategies, since "the ease with which animals are procured, excellence in oratory, and the ability to feast guests and people sumptuously [were] qualities par excellence of a 'first-class' *datu* [chief]" (Claver 1985:86).

In his study of the feasting system amongst the Sagada Igorots and other groups of interior northern Luzon, Voss (1987:131) suggests that the prestige gained from sponsorship of such feasts came from the creation of social debt amongst the people attending the feast. In expending huge amounts of his

wealth in feeding the attendees at the feast, many of whom did not have the resources to reciprocate in kind, a feast's host expanded the number of people in an
asymmetrical relationship to him, as well as reinforced the "debt" of existing ties
of patronage. Voss notes that the prestige of an individual and of his immediate
kin group is gauged in terms of these accumulating debts or obligations that require the debtors to subsequently provide agricultural labor or other services, as
well as return prestations, when called on by the feast's sponsor. Spanish sources
suggest that sixteenth-century *datus* often invested their surplus wealth in aiding
other men to sponsor feasts associated with marriage rites or death rites, thus
tightening their grip on these individuals as core supporters in the *datu's* alliance
network (Alcina 1960b:76–77, 180–198).

Not only did the sponsoring chief or kin group increase their prestige in the region by providing the enormous supplies of food and status goods disbursed at
such a ritual event, but the occasion provided an opportunity for all the attending
datus (chiefs) and male kin-group leaders to attempt to improve their position
within a ranked political hierarchy of chiefly authority. Biernatzki (1985:36–37) describes this overt negotiation of power relations in the traditional "boasting contest" accompanying ceremonial feasts among the ethnographically known
Bukidnon chiefdoms of northern Mindanao. In these feasts, each *datu* in turn
climbed a ladder to a high ceremonial platform laid out with a lavish meal, at each
rung of the ladder reciting the genealogical history that supported his inherited
claim to chieftainship and elite status. However, he would also present an even
more protracted recital of his personal exploits in trading, raiding, and other
"wealth"-producing activities, attempting to out-boast other attending chiefs and
win a place at the highest-ranking ceremonial table. These public recitations and
symbolic movement of chiefs up the status ladder allowed the community to compare chiefly prowess and to rank the multiple district chiefs in terms of appropriate
levels of deference. At least one contact-period Spanish text refers to similar public
recitations of status-validating genealogies and heroic accounts of trading and raiding exploits as part of feasting ritual in the sixteenth century (e.g., Bobadilla
1990:332). Oral presentations of status-enhancing genealogies and personal achievements, allowing public assessment of the relative status, wealth, and power of attending chiefs, was associated with ceremonial feasting in other areas of Southeast
Asia and in Polynesia (Goldman 1970:522–536; Schnitger 1964; Volkman 1989).

Animals (most commonly carabao, pigs, chickens, and dogs), rice and other
plant foods, and alcohol beverages were offered for sacrifice in the ritual component of Philippine ceremonies. Both the quality and quantities of sacrificial offerings reflected the social rank, wealth, and political power base of the sponsoring
chief (Biernatzki 1985:36–37; Chirino 1904:269–270; Claver 1985:74; San Antonio
1990:335–336). As in other complex societies of Southeast Asia, the maintenance of

the social status quo or social mobility depended upon successful performance over a lifetime in ritual feasting events (as well as abilities in warfare, trading, and wealth acquisition; Beatty 1991; Kirsch 1973:26–27; Leach 1954:163). The carabao, as a draft animal with a slow reproductive rate, and the pig, appear to have been the most valued animals for both sacrifice and exchange in Philippine societies (Barton 1949:74–75; Biernatzki 1985:43; Claver 1985:74–75, 86; Dasmarinas 1958:429; Dozier 1966:84, 149, 194; Hart 1969:80, 88; Mendoza 1903:150; Prill-Brett 1989:1; Reid 1988:32–33; Scott 1984:196; Voss 1987:128).

Food delicacies were served to high-ranking guests on the sponsoring chief's collection of valuable imported mainland Asian porcelains and decorated earthenware (Pigafetta 1975:59; also see Biernatzki 1985:33; Cole 1913:88, 92). This was one of a number of occasions when chiefly household heirlooms were publicly displayed, and the lavishness of meal "presentation" on finely made plates and in delicate bowls (preferably imported porcelains) appears to have been a significant factor in determining the amount of social prestige accruing to a feast's sponsor (e.g., Alcina 1960b:133–136; Pigafetta 1975:59).

The importance of gaining prestige or "merit" through lavish feast sponsorship is echoed in ethnographic and historic accounts of other complex societies in the southern Philippines, such as the Manuvu, Tagbanua, and Magindanao (see Claver 1985:74; Cole 1913:111–120; Manuel 1973:196–197, 229–230, 266–267; C. Warren 1977:255–257). Prestige or "merit" translated into the expansion of political alliance networks that were at the core of political structure in Philippine societies, as examined in more detail below. The significance of ritual feasting in legitimating the political order has been a common emphasis in analyses of political economy in other complex societies (see Kirch, Chapter 6; Schmandt-Besserat, Chapter 14).

FOOD APPORTIONMENT AND SOCIAL RANKING

Although the amount and quality of food conferred prestige on the feast's sponsor, apportionment of the food reflected the social position of the feast's participants and their relationship to the sponsor. As noted by Voss (1987:128), "it is the system and the protocol of meat circulation which maintains and reproduces the structure of the relationship between community members." Foodstuffs were divided for consumption among participants in accordance with their kinship ties with the feast sponsor, their relative rank in the local and regional sociopolitical hierarchy, their history of exchange relations with the sponsoring social unit, and their perceived role in a chief's immediate alliance-building strategies (Biernatzki 1985:36; Pigafetta 1975:65–66; Plasencia 1903a:174; San Antonio 1990:313). As described by Voss for the Sagada Igorot, an ethnographically known group of the northern Luzon interior:

Meat is distributed according to strict protocol. The most senior old men, who conduct the ceremony, get the head and internal organs; other elderly relatives and *dap-
ay* mates (men's council or group of political authorities) get the belly and side fat;
close relatives are given parts of the hams; the ribs go to the middle distant relatives;
while the neck and back go to distant relatives. One close relative of a man who was
giving such a ritual told us that "it is better to get a small piece of the appropriate
status meat than a kilo from somewhere else." One could say that the symbolic representation of the social order is embodied in the pig and in these rituals. (1987:129)

The portions allocated to specific individuals and kin groups were carefully scrutinized and any perceived improprieties in meat distribution were openly criti-
cized by the feast attendees. As recounted by Voss:

One man I interviewed talked sarcastically about "those capitalistic old men who
capitalize on their age and prestige by showing up at all kinds of feast to demand
more than their share of meat." In such instances, bitter arguments can result between these old men—who feel they are getting their proper share—and those who
feel they are hogging too much of the pig. (1987:130)

Spanish sources suggest that the chief's immediate relatives and other elites with
whom he was strongly allied were commonly served the choicest meat dishes—
those consisting of carabao or domestic pig rather than smaller game animals
and, preferentially, the meatiest animal parts (e.g., the forelimbs and, secondarily,
the vertebrae and ribs; Pigafetta 1975:65–66; San Antonio 1990:313; Santa Ines
1648:78; also see Biernatzki 1985:36–37; Barton 1949:74–75; Prill-Brett 1989). Pig and
carabao skulls were also preferred body parts in some societies (Plasencia
1903b:191), probably for reasons other than meat quality. Gibson's (1986:158)
analysis of the symbolic aspects of animal partitioning among the Buid, a contemporary upland tribal group of Mindoro, suggests why the pig head might
have been preferred over even meatier animal parts. The head of the pig is
viewed by the Buid as the locus of the animal soul or vital spirit. Thus, by possessing this portion of the animal, the consumers are able to transfer the "vitality" or spiritual power of the animal to themselves to ward off the weakening
attacks of predatory spirits (Gibson 1986:157).

Food apportionment as the primary public measure of social status differentiation has been described in significant detail for complex societies engaging in ritual feasting on the Indonesian islands of Nias (Beatty 1991) and Sulawesi
(Volkman 1985). On Nias, slaughtered pigs were traditionally divided into carefully weighed meat portions, which were distributed according to recognized
rank in the social hierarchy, the history of prior exchange relations between the
host and guest, and kinship and co-residential ties between the host and guest
(Beatty 1991:224–225). Failure to receive the expected meat portion, in recognition

of rank and prior prestige payments, was considered a public affront that was frequently resolved through violent confrontation (Beatty 1991:225). In the Toraja highlands of Sulawesi, public meat divisions at feasts required specialists who could memorize the complicated "cutting histories" of hundreds of individuals—using criteria of age, genealogy, wealth, achievement, and temperament, in conjunction with the individual's past history and anticipated future of sponsoring and participating in feasts—to determine appropriate meat quantities and cuts (Volkman 1985:96–103). Perceived slights in meat apportionment could quickly escalate into a "meat fight" (Volkman 1985:100–101) in which wounded parties made inflammatory speeches around piles of carabao meat, frequently flinging meat and carabao excrement at the offending parties. Similarly, presentation of food delicacies at Polynesian feasts followed strict rules of allotment by social rank (Goldman 1970:501–502, 504, 508; Thomas 1990:97). In the Philippines, ritualized food distributions were occasions when social tensions over power differentials were overtly played out by individuals and larger factions. Those who played the feasting game well, particularly those who could engineer convincing public confrontations about their position in social and political hierarchies, were rewarded with upward mobility.

COMPETITIVE FEASTS OR "CHALLENGE FEASTS"

A significant issue is whether the Philippine feasts reported in contact period Spanish records and early ethnographic accounts represented what Beatty (1991:232–233) refers to as "challenge feasts" in Nias society. A "competitive" or "challenge" feast can be defined as one in which a primary goal was to achieve political domination through an ever-escalating cycle of feasting "one-upmanship" and public displays of generosity/hostility towards rival chiefs. The classic example of overtly competitive feasting is the so-called rivalry potlatch of Native Americans such as the Kwakiutl of the Northwest Coast. The primary objective in sponsoring a feast was to attempt to surpass the abilities of social peers and political rivals to amass, display, distribute and, in some cases, destroy property. The sponsor's performance resulted in immediate social antagonisms, social validation or humiliation, and political realignment for the participants (see Codere 1950; Drucker 1967).

However, recent anthropological analyses have questioned the emphasis on the socially combative nature of Northwest Coast feasting events and the overriding image of "warring with property" (e.g., Kan 1986; Miller 1984; Walens 1981). Instead, status differences are viewed as emerging subtly and gradually over the long-term process of prestige-good exchange relationships. This interpretive debate has recently entered analyses of the significance of feasting events for chiefly status rivalry in sociopolitically complex Southeast Asian societies. Nu-

merous authors cite the massive pig slaughters and ostentatious gifts of gold ornamentation as evidence of the strongly competitive ethos of Nias feasts
(Marschall 1976; Suzuki 1959; Schnitger 1964). However, other ethnographers
claim that overtly antagonistic "challenge" feasts were historically rare in Nias society, that most feasts had a highly reciprocal ethos in which enhanced status was
transitory, and that social "merit" and political legitimacy were gained only
slowly over the course of an individual's lifetime of ceremonial exchanges
(Beatty 1991; Slamet-Velsink 1995:130).

Some of this contention about the "competitive" nature of feasting events in
Southeast Asia and elsewhere derives from a lack of clarity in distinguishing feasting phenomena in which the social "merit" transacted is of a transitory and reciprocal nature, and feasting phenomena that attempt to accumulate permanent
wealth and to transform temporary status differentials into long-term and even
inheritable political power. Feasts that confer values of social "merit" but which
are not overtly "competitive," are characterized by cycles of balanced reciprocity,
in which surplus accumulation and status enhancement for any single individual
or kin group are transitory and eventually negated through the necessity of returning prestations to their partners in a feasting cycle. In "competitive" feasts,
there is an escalation of labor mobilization and surplus needed to finance future
feasts and the aim of translating feasting success into long-term political power
and economic profit (e.g., Friedman 1979).

Hayden (1994:25, 64) has suggested that competitive feasts aimed at creating
economic inequalities and negotiating political power differentials are primarily a
structural feature of what he refers to as "transegalitarian" or "Big Man" societies
such as those in New Guinea and other areas of Melanesia characterized by in-
stable (i.e., wholly achievement-based) criteria of social ranking and political succession. Hayden and others (e.g., Clark and Blake 1994; Friedman and Rowlands
1978; Rosman and Rubel 1978) argue that competitive feasting is one of a number
of evolving strategies among "big-men" or "aggrandizers" for transforming transitory, achievement-based political authority and differential wealth into the inheritable political power and wealth, which are key to the emergence of
chiefdom-level societies. Hayden suggests that the need for competitive feasts is
largely obviated in chiefdom-level societies, since the competition for political
succession and economic surplus has been resolved in the emergence of inheritable chieftainship and enforceable tribute systems maintaining permanent labor
pools and stored wealth (1994:64). In other words, political authority and the right
to economic surplus is no longer a matter to be negotiated in contexts of social
interaction such as competitive feasting, but rather a largely inalienable, ideologically reinforced "fact" of ascribed chieftainship. According to this view, "feasts"
in chiefdom-level societies should primarily consist of ritual events exclusively

controlled by chiefly leaders and they should be characterized by (1) a more uniform scale and regular periodicity, (2) a strong schism between elite and commoner modes of participation, and (3) a primary emphasis on ideological
reinforcement of existing political power hierarchies, ritual potency of the chief,
and a sense of community solidarity and economic well-being within the polity.
Hayden concludes:

> Some forms of competitive feasts probably continued to be used among the lower-
> level elites in chiefdoms as criteria for promotion to positions of power and to in-
> crease the value of elite children, but they do not appear to be broadly based feasts
> with obligatory interest payments geared to attract supporters such as found in
> transegalitarian communities. (1994:64)

However, there is ethnohistoric evidence to support the idea that feasting in
many Philippine societies was overtly competitive, with chiefs attempting to up
the ante of displayed wealth and lavish food giveaways with each successive
round of ceremonial sponsorship (Anon. 1990b:110–111; Boxer manuscript
1975:215; Chirino 1904:262–271; Colin 1906:75; also see Keesing 1962:165, 190; Scott
1982:192, 196). This competitive element is exemplified by the ethnographic accounts of feasting in the Bukidnon chiefdoms of central Mindanao. Public recitations extolling the hereditary superiority and grand achievements of the feast's
chiefly host were accompanied by attempts to sicken the guests by providing
prodigious amounts of food (particularly meat) that had to be consumed on the
spot (Biernatzki 1985; Claver 1985; Cole 1956). As Claver (1985:74, 86) notes, Bukidnon chiefs were continually striving to become the region's most socially esteemed and politically influential *datu* by "providing food for the most people
and for the longest time" (1985:74). One Bukidnon *datu* is claimed to have
achieved the almost insurmountable feat of slaughtering more than 70 buffalo
and 180 chickens for a multiweek feast. That rival chiefs were overtly challenged
by chiefly sponsorship of a particularly elaborate feast, and that this social rivalry
could evolve quickly into social hostilities among elite participants, is evidenced
by a number of Spanish accounts of "treacherous feasts," in which intense emotions of rivalry between the feast's sponsors and invited guests erupted into
armed battle (e.g., Anon. 1990a:79; Correa 1990:258–259; Pigafetta 1975:147).

At first glance, the Philippine case would seem to contradict Hayden's general
model of ritual feasting in chiefdoms. However, the political structures of Philippine polities and other complex societies in island Southeast Asia differ markedly
from the chiefdoms usually included in anthropological study of ceremonial
feasting. This divergent political structure appears to be connected to unique aspects of social organization, ecology, population dynamics, and labor use in these
small-scale Southeast Asian island societies. We will now turn to a discussion of

why ritual feasting is important not only in reinforcing, but also creating and reforming political and social hierarchies in Philippine chiefdoms.

THE POLITICS OF FEASTING IN SEGMENTARY OR "ALLIANCE-STRUCTURED" CHIEFDOMS

Southeast Asian complex societies have been variously described as "segmentary polities," "galactic polities," or "theater states" (Geertz 1980; Kiefer 1972; Tambiah 1976; Winzeler 1981). These societies were typically decentralized, had weakly integrated political hierarchies, and were particularly vulnerable to short-term cycles of alternating coalescence and disintegration. Political authority traditionally relied, not on control over fixed territorial bases or well-defined unilineal descent groups, but on cultivating ties of personal loyalty and expanding one's power base through frequent and elaborate gift-giving and ceremonialism (Wolters 1982:6–15).

Recent work on comparative political structures by Blanton (Blanton et al. 1996) and Feinman (1995) has suggested that these ubiquitous features of Southeast Asia polities are not extraordinary in state-level and chiefly societies, but instead represent an extreme emphasis on "network" strategies of political power relations and political economy, a strategy for maintaining rulership that is practiced to a lesser or greater degree in many complex societies. Blanton and Feinman have contrasted "corporate-based" and "network-based" or "exclusionary" power strategies as differing, but not mutually exclusive, ways of achieving political dominance in complex societies. They suggest that these strategies are part of the political dynamics in all complex societies, but political actors in a particular society and historical context may emphasize one mode of control more than the other.

In the exclusionary or network power strategy, political actors try to create personal networks of political dominance through the strategic distribution of portable wealth items and symbolic capital (such as ritual potency and religious knowledge). Alliances are typically created and maintained outside local groups through "prestational events" (Blanton et al. 1996:4), involving exchanges of marriage partners, prestige goods, food, esoteric knowledge, and labor. Often these prestational events occur in the context of ritual feasting. Individuals who can most successfully translate the exchanges of foodstuffs, prestige goods, labor, and other resources into patronage over a large network of allies and followers, gain political preeminence in the community. However, as noted by Blanton and Feinman, in societies where a network strategy is the predominant mode in the political economy, leadership is generally highly conflictive, unstable, and prone to relatively short cycles of expansion and collapse.

Several factors may have been significant in creating the highly fragmented political landscape, the relatively weak integration between vertically allied leaders, and the highly personalized nature of political power relations characteristic of Southeast Asian polities. A number of historians and archaeologists have pointed to the fragmented geography and diverse environments of Southeast Asia as promoting diffuse centers of political power and frustrating attempts at large-scale political integration (Andaya 1992:405; Geertz 1973:331–338; Reid 1992:460–463; Winzeler 1981:462). In addition, most of precolonial Southeast Asia (with the possible exception of Bali, Java, and parts of Vietnam) had exceedingly low population densities relative to land and resources (Reid 1988:11–18; 1992:460–463). Anthony Reid estimates an overall average of 5.5 persons/km^2 for the region in A.D. 1600, less than a fifth of that of India and China and roughly half that of Europe (Reid 1988:11–18, 1992:460–463). The Philippines and Borneo were the least densely populated parts of Southeast Asia at the time of European contact (see Junker 1999 for a more detailed discussion of population dynamics).

Relatively low population levels, combined with an economic emphasis on swidden cropping rather than intensive permanent agriculture, an abundance of unoccupied fertile land, and a seemingly inexhaustible supply of wood and bamboo for easily rebuilding settlements, meant that many island Southeast Asian populations were inherently mobile and not particularly concerned with control of land as a political and economic commodity (Hall 1992:187; Reid 1983:157; Winzeler 1981:462). An obvious conclusion is that shortages of labor relative to land engendered a political system in which a ruler's power base was measured in terms of the size of the labor force bound to him through extensive alliance networks, rather than fixed geographic territories. Thus, competition between political leaders (and between rulers and would-be rulers) focused on commanding labor rather than commandeering land. This may explain the enormously strong emphasis in island Southeast Asian complex societies on alliance-building activities such as gifting of prestige goods, the creation of extensive marriage ties, ritualized feasting, and religious pageantry aimed at social cohesion.

The strongly competitive nature of these critical alliance-building activities is undoubtedly related to the frailty of hereditary rights to political leadership. In most ethnographically and historically known complex societies of Southeast Asia, kinship is generally reckoned bilaterally, corporate descent groups are lacking, postmarital residence is bilocal or neolocal, and rank and wealth are inherited along both the maternal and paternal lines (Hall 1985:110–111; Reid 1988:147; Winzeler 1976:628). In the Philippines, as in many Southeast Asian complex societies (e.g., Andaya 1992:409, 419; Reid 1988:152), polygamy was the cultural norm amongst rulers and other nobility (Saleeby 1905; Scott 1994), producing multiple heirs and further exacerbating conflicts over inheritance of the chieftainship. Adding to the chaos of chiefly succession was a pronounced ideology of warrior prestige that allowed men who were successful raiders and slave-takers to accumulate the material base for chieftainship (Junker 1999). In many island South-east Asian societies, ambitious warriors were frequently able to garner significant wealth and establish independent power bases through their close association with elite patrons (Hall 1992:260) and ultimately threaten the latter's hegemony (Reid 1988:167).

In Philippine chiefdoms cognatic descent rules, and the widespread practice of polygamy and demographic factors created an emphasis on coalition-building rather than territorially based political power. Lasting political control was prob-lematic and the achievement-based dimension of political authority continued to be important. A chief's social status and sphere of political authority were not fixed through inheritance, but were instead continually renegotiated through material exchanges that took place within the arena of ritual feasting. The cre-ation of social debt among a wide range of participants in a particularly lavish feast enlarged the sponsor's alliance network, which could be called upon for raiding, trading, and other wealth-generating activities. Although most of the historic and ethnographic descriptions of ritual feasts do not provide enough de-tail to determine precisely which segment of society was most involved in the competitive aspects of feasting, it is likely that competitive one-upmanship was most fierce among lower-ranking chiefs and ambitious warriors rather than the chiefly paramounts.

ARCHAEOLOGICAL EVIDENCE FOR COMPETITIVE FEASTING IN THE PREHISPANIC PHILIPPINES

The preceding discussion on the politics of feasting in traditional Philippine chiefdoms has largely focused on structural dynamics and not the long-term evo-lution of these feasting systems, which often requires the use of archaeological evidence. The presence of some type of ceremonial feasting system has been in-ferred for a number of complex societies on the basis of archaeological evidence alone, in the absence of any ethnographic or historic sources. Evidence for differ-ential access to certain ritual foods or high-quality subsistence commodities, and particularly their concentration in elite habitation contexts or in association with ceremonial structures, is one approach in identifying ritual feasting activities in the archaeological record (e.g., Crabtree 1990; J. Fox 1996; Kim 1994; Marcus and Flannery 1996:115–116; Pohl 1994; Welch and Scarry 1995). In addition, archaeolo-gists have inferred ritual feasting from the nature of ceramic assemblages found at settlements. Some archaeologists have noted larger-than-normal cooking and serving vessels at prominent regional centers, suggesting large-scale food or drink preparation (e.g., Blitz 1993; Dietler 1989, 1990). Archaeologists have also suggested that ceremonial feasting can be recognized by the presence of ceramic assemblages that consist of elaborate and aesthetically superior serving bowls, cups, and plates, assemblages that vary significantly from mundane household food preparation and serving assemblages (e.g., Clark and Blake 1994; Welch and Scarry 1995). Representations of what appear to be ceremonial events painted on pottery, molded on metal artifacts, painted in murals, or carved into stone stelae have also been interpreted by archaeologists as depictions of politically charged ritual feasting (e.g., Gero 1992; Higham 1996:133, 151–158). Despite the richness of ethnographic and historic references to ritual feasting as part of traditional political and social dynamics in premodern Southeast Asia and China, there has been limited archaeological research on this phenomenon (e.g., De Veyra 1986; Higham 1996; Junker, Mudar, and Schwaller 1994; Kim 1994; Mudar 1997).

In terms of material evidence for ritual feasting in the Philippines, access to feasting foods and feasting paraphernalia was highly correlated with a household's social rank, with the most elaborate feasts sponsored by and participated in by high-ranking chiefs. Furthermore, these sacrificial ritual feasts are reported to have taken place within or directly adjacent to the sponsoring chief's residence (Bobadilla 1990:334; Morga 1903:303–304; Pigafetta 1975:65; Plasencia 1903b:186; Santa Ines 1990:78; also see Barton 1949:73–75; Cole 1913:65–67, 111–120; Manuel 1973:246–255). This is true of even mortuary rites, since burials were traditionally placed under contemporaneously occupied residences in many contact-period Philippine complex societies (Junker 1993b). In other regions of island Southeast Asia, early historic accounts suggest that ceremonial feasts took place at special locales with "megalithic" monuments (including menhirs, dolmens, and circular arrangements of stones; Slamet-Velsink 1995:113). Although the archaeological record of megaliths on Borneo, the Malay Peninsula, and many island locales in between is extensive, their association with ritual feasting in precolonial complex societies has not been examined and, in fact, their cultural associations and chronology are poorly known.

At ritual feasts in the Philippines, guests were served on the sponsoring elite's household collection of finely made earthenware and imported porcelain plates and bowls (Alcina 1960b:129–130; Pigafetta 1975:65), a ritually and socially significant ceramic assemblage that was distinct from "everyday" domestic wares. Ethnographic and ethnoarchaeological studies of domestic activities and trash disposal patterns in traditional lowland Philippine households (De la Torre and Mudar 1982; Hart 1958; Nurge 1965:20–21) indicate that faunal debris, other subsistence remains, and broken serving dishes were routinely swept to the edges of the house yard or under the pile houses to form concentrated middens. Over time, archaeologically recognizable midden deposits and trash concentration areas were formed that are spatially contiguous with associated domestic structures. Thus, elite households that regularly sponsored large-scale feasting events would be expected to contain significantly larger numbers of porcelain and high-quality earthenware serving dishes, as well as remnants of feasting foods, in contrast to households that rarely sponsored feasts or sponsored these events on a smaller scale.

At the outset, we should note that very little archaeological research in the Philippines has been devoted to the specific issue of ritual feasting, and to reconstructing chiefly political economies in general. Twelfth- to sixteenth-century Tanjay and fourteenth- to sixteenth-century Cebu are the only prehispanic chiefly centers where archaeological research has been carried out at the household level and where evidence relevant to evolution of ritual feasting has been recorded. Therefore, much of what we have to say here about the material evidence is sketchy at best and in need of corroboration by archaeological investigations at a wider range of prehispanic sites.

ANIMAL SACRIFICE AND MEAT DISTRIBUTION
IN PHILIPPINE FEASTING

Excavations of pile houses at the coastal chiefly center of Tanjay have yielded archaeological evidence for distinct elite and non-elite residential zones, marked by differences in house size and densities of "prestige goods" (foreign porcelains, fancy earthenware, and metal goods). Although these household wealth differentials are found in occupation phases dated back to the twelfth to fourteenth centuries A.D., they became even more pronounced and complexly graded at the site in the fifteenth and sixteenth centuries, as foreign porcelains and other exotics flowed into the settlement in increasingly higher volumes and local production of prestige goods expanded (see Junker 1993a and Junker, Mudar, and Schwaller 1994). Excavations at Tanjay have yielded a large sample of animal bone from middens and trash pits within the two distinct residential sectors, which have been analyzed for status-related differences in daily meat consumption and differential access to ritual foods (Junker, Mudar, and Schwaller 1994; Mudar 1997). Archaeological faunal assemblages have also been analyzed from several excavation locales at Cebu, spanning the fourteenth and sixteenth centuries (Mudar 1997; Nishimura 1992), although the complexities of the site make it much more difficult to separate out factors of socioeconomic status, ecological change, and Spanish impact on faunal use than at Tanjay (Mudar 1997:96).

At Tanjay, the faunal assemblages recovered from both the early second millennium A.D. Santiago phase and the fifteenth- and sixteenth-century Osmena phase contained a number of demonstrably domesticated species, including *Bubalus bubalus* (carabao, or water buffalo), *Gallus gallus* (chicken), *Sus scrofa* (pig), and *Canis familiaris* (dog). Wild tropical forest fauna included Philippine spotted deer *(Cervus alfredi)*, monkey *(Macaca fascularius)*, civet cat (*Viverra* sp.), fruit bat, and various reptiles. Marine fauna (fish, turtles, and rays) complete the household subsistence assemblages (see Junker, Mudar, and Schwaller 1994 and Mudar 1997 for quantitative data). A similar range of species characterized the Cebu faunal assemblages (Mudar 1997). Quantitative comparison of the faunal assemblages from the two residential zones at Tanjay indicates that the inhabitants of the large, stockaded house-compounds with relatively high densities of "prestige goods" derived a significantly greater proportion of their subsistence from domestic species (see Fig. 10.2). The inhabitants of the small, unstockaded house-compounds included only two species of small- to medium-sized domestic animals in their diet (pig and chicken) but yielded a wider range of wild species such as monkey, civet cat, and turtle. The elite households in both cultural phases had a significantly higher percentage of water buffalo in their diets, as measured by the Minimum Number of Individuals (MNI), raw bone weights, and percentage by weight of the total faunal assemblage. Similarly, large mammals, including water buffalo and pig, were found in significantly higher densities at what Nishimura (1992) has identified (on the basis of foreign trade goods) as the highest-status residential locale in sixteenth-century Cebu. Historic sources cited earlier suggest that water buffalo, pig, and other large mammals were preferred feasting foods that were not consumed on a regular daily basis in the contact-period Philippines.

There is also some evidence to suggest that inhabitants of the elite residential zones at Tanjay and Cebu had greater access to meatier and culturally preferred animal parts. This pattern may reflect ritual-associated redistribution practices that accorded the best meat cuts to chiefs and their kinsmen at ceremonial feasts. Ethnohistoric sources detailed earlier suggest that relatively meaty limb bones were highly prized in meat distributions in the Philippines, as were the skulls of water buffalo and pig for their symbolic value during associated ritual activities.

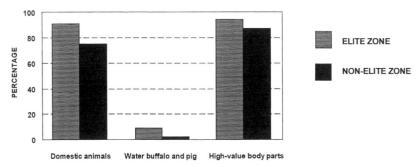

Figure 10.2. Comparisons of the percentages by weight of domestic (vs. wild) animals, water buffalo and pig (vs. smaller animals), and high-value parts (long bones and crania vs. rib bones and neck bones) in household middens of elite and non-elite residences dated to the fifteenth and sixteenth centuries at Tanjay.

Whereas both residential areas at fifteenth- and sixteenth-century Tanjay showed a preference for long bones and skulls compared to "low-value" body parts, the presumed elite households had a significantly higher percentage by weight of the prized long-bone meat cuts (see Fig. 10.2). Mudar (1997) found a strikingly similar percentage of meaty long bones in elite habitation zones at fifteenth- and sixteenth-century Cebu (64 percent by weight of the medium and large mammal bones). Surprisingly, the percentage by weight of water buffalo and pig skull fragments in the fifteenth- and sixteenth-century habitation levels at Tanjay was higher for the non-elite residential zone. Thus, whereas the meaty long-bone cuts were preferentially distributed in elite households at Tanjay, ceremonial display of animal heads was more frequently taking place in the non-elite sector during this period.

At Tanjay, we see changes over time in household access to high-quality protein and particularly ceremonial feasting foods such as water buffalo and pig. Comparison of faunal assemblages from Santiago phase (ca. 1100–1400) and Osmena phase (ca. 1400–1600) occupation levels suggests an overall increase in the consumption of water buffalo and domestic pig within the settlement as a whole in the fifteenth and sixteenth centuries. Mudar (1997) and Nishimura (1992) note a similar increase in the use of pig and water buffalo in the diet in the late fifteenth to early sixteenth centuries at Cebu. A possible interpretation is that domestic pig herds and water buffalo stocks were increasing as stored forms of wealth in Philippine lowland societies such as Tanjay and Cebu. They were then being consumed in the context of inflationary competitive feasts sponsored by chiefs and other "wealthy" individuals, a feasting system that required escalating inputs of sacrificial meat. At Tanjay, it is in the "non-elite" Osmena Park residential zone that we see a particularly striking increase in the consumption of water buffalo, and it is also in this non-elite sector that we see increasing numbers of water buffalo and pig skulls, presumably for ceremonial status display. One possible interpretation of this patterning is that participation in the feasting system became more widespread among non-elite as well as elite sponsors in fifteenth- and sixteenth-century Tanjay, with escalating competition amongst individuals outside the hereditary elite for wealth, status, and political power.

THE DISTRIBUTION OF RICE AS A STATUS FOOD

Early Spanish sources indicate that root crops such as yams and taro were the staple foods of the bulk of the population, except in Philippine regions such as the Luzon cordillera, the upper Cotabato River plain, the Tagalog area around Manila, and the Bicol peninsula where artificial terracing and the construction of substantial-sized irrigation systems made wet rice production possible on a large scale (Scott 1994:181). The Spanish writer Francisco Alcina (1960a:88–93, 133–136; 1960b:121) emphasizes that rice was considered a high status food in comparison to tubers in most areas of the Philippines lacking broad floodplains, and it was an important prestige food to be served at ceremonial feasts.

Recent paleoethnobotanical work by Mary Gunn (1997) on plant material from fifteenth- and sixteenth-century habitation contexts at Tanjay is consistent with historical references to rice as a high-status food and particularly a ritual feasting food. In a study of plant macrofossils from hearths and middens, she found that rice was significantly more prevalent in the presumed elite habitation zone in comparison to the non-elite residential zone. However, the prevalence of rice relative to root crops as dietary components cannot be directly assessed, since root crops are virtually absent from the both the plant macrofossil and pollen records. In addition, few identifiable plant remains were recovered from pre–fifteenth-century habitation contexts. Therefore, we cannot presently say whether rice consumption increased over time at chiefly centers such as Tanjay as a function of expanding ritual feasting activity. Unfortunately, with the exception of palynological investigations of early rice origins, there have been few archaeological projects in the Philippines in which plant material has been collected and analyzed.

THE SERVING ASSEMBLAGE IN PHILIPPINE FEASTING

Early Spanish accounts indicate that Philippine elites presented high-status meats and other food delicacies on their impressive array of Chinese, Siamese, and Annamese trade porcelains (Fig. 10.3), along with some locally made decorated and pedestaled earthenware. Possession of these ritual feasting wares was essential to a kin group's ability to participate in the feasting cycle. In addition, competitive aspects of the ceremonial feasting system would have encouraged potential sponsors of feasts to seek new avenues of production and trade for obtaining an increasingly impressive array of food-serving vessels. In the cases of Iron Age Europe and Formative period Mesoamerica, archaeologists have suggested that competition for access to foreign trade vessels was tied to expanding demands for elaborate feasting and drinking paraphernalia (and possibly exotic foods and drinks; e.g., Clark and Blake 1994; Dietler 1989, 1990).

In his detailed analysis of imported porcelains from the Cebu excavations, Masao Nishimura (1992) showed that the bulk of the imported porcelains coming into the Cebu chiefdom's maritime trade port in the fifteenth and sixteenth centuries were forms that we might label as "plates" and "bowls," that is, food-serving dishes (Fig. 10.4). Nishimura suggests that Philippine elite of this period are focusing their trade demands somewhat narrowly on those porcelain wares,

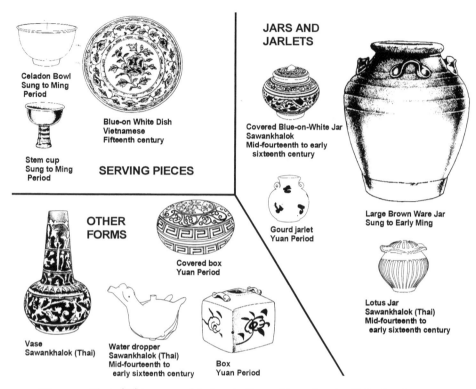

Figure 10.3. Typical Chinese porcelain "serving" assemblages found at Philippine sites dated to the eleventh through sixteenth centuries.

which functioned in displaying food and drink at ritual feasts. Consistent with Nishimura's study of the Cebu porcelain forms, fifteenth- and sixteenth-century porcelains recovered from the smaller chiefly center of Tanjay show a strong bias towards "bowl" and "plate" forms (Fig. 10.4), suggesting that household porcelains may have been used primarily in serving ritual foods at ceremonial events. Burial assemblages with Late Ming porcelain also tend to concentrate on a highly standardized range of plates and bowls, which may have contained ritual foods, and are less likely to yield the more diverse porcelain jars, ewers, figurines, and boxes of the Tang, Sung, Yuan, and Early Ming period cemeteries (e.g., R. Fox 1959, 1964, 1967; Hutterer 1973; Legaspi 1974; Nishimura 1988; Peralta and Salazar 1974). Quantitative comparisons of the frequency of porcelain forms from the largest of these cemeteries, the Calatagan burial sites (R. Fox 1959), confirm the qualitative observations of archaeologists working at other burial sites that cups, jars, covered boxes, and figurines are very rare as imported grave accompaniments (Fig. 10.4). However, porcelain bowls are more

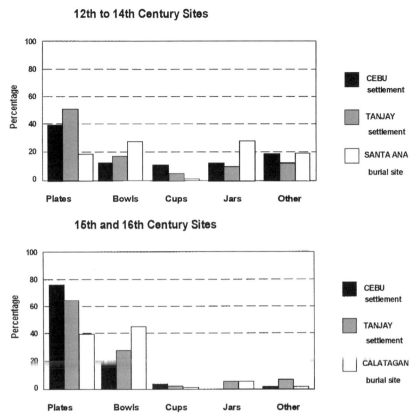

Figure 10.4. Percentages of porcelain forms by weight in excavations of Tanjay and Cebu, and percentage of porcelain forms by quantity (whole vessels) at cemeteries, dated to the twelfth to fourteenth centuries and fifteenth to sixteenth centuries A.D.

common than the porcelain plates that dominate habitation sites. This pattern may represent slight differences in the content of ritual feasting and mortuary assemblages, or may simply reflect the higher breakage rates of plates as they are used in consumption rituals (see DeBoer and Lathrap 1979 for a discussion of the archaeological implications of differential breakage rates in household assemblages).

At Tanjay, where we have a relatively long occupation sequence, there is archaeological evidence that the demand for porcelain as feasting paraphernalia was expanding over time. The density of foreign porcelains in habitation deposits increased more than twofold in the fifteenth and sixteenth centuries over the preceding twelfth- to fourteenth-century levels of occupation (Junker 1994). As shown in Figure 10.4, porcelain imports derived from trash pits and other domestic contexts at Tanjay are less restricted in their range of functional types in this earlier phase of foreign trade, with a comparatively high proportion of non-serving pieces such as jars, ewers, figurines, and boxes. Unfortunately, Tanjay is the only habitation site where we have quantitative information on imported porcelain assemblages prior to the fifteenth century. However, the large eleventh- to fourteenth-century cemetery of Santa Ana (near modern Manila) yielded even larger volumes of porcelains that would not fit the category of serving pieces (including jars of various sizes and forms, figurines, and lidded boxes; Locsin and Locsin 1967). The diversity of foreign porcelain assemblages at both settlement and burial sites supports the observation that local preferences for feasting wares had not strongly affected the import market yet in this period.

At Tanjay, statistical analyses show that though porcelain was heavily concentrated in the elite habitation zone with large houses in the twelfth- to fourteenth-century Santiago phase, it was more diffusely scattered in both elite and non-elite habitation zones by the fifteenth and sixteenth centuries (Fig. 10.5). By the later phase, foreign porcelains may have been available to a significantly larger portion of the Tanjay population, including those outside the chiefly class who could at-

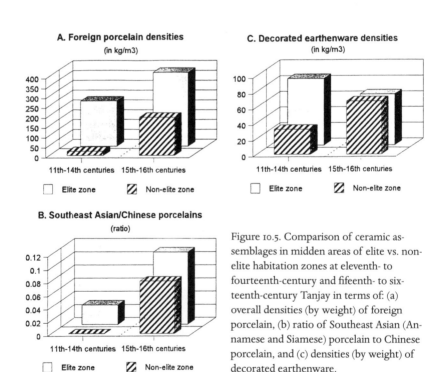

Figure 10.5. Comparison of ceramic assemblages in midden areas of elite vs. non-elite habitation zones at eleventh- to fourteenth-century and fifteenth- to sixteenth-century Tanjay in terms of: (a) overall densities (by weight) of foreign porcelain, (b) ratio of Southeast Asian (Annamese and Siamese) porcelain to Chinese porcelain, and (c) densities (by weight) of decorated earthenware.

tempt to improve their social rank by acquiring the porcelains necessary for criti-cal alliance exchanges and for sponsoring feasting events. The non-elite and elite porcelain assemblages have almost identical proportions of bowl and plate forms versus nonserving vessels. However, at both Tanjay and Cebu, areas of the site with lower-ranking households (as measured by other criteria such as house size and access to other prestige goods) tended to have a high percentage of low *qual-ity* foreign porcelains (e.g., poorly made Sawankholok wares or Siamese and An-namese copies of Chinese forms) and/or locally made "fancy" earthenware mimicking Chinese styles (Fig. 10.5). Thus, non-elites sponsoring this type of feasting event emulated the choices of elites, when possible, in acquiring a presti-gious porcelain assemblage. Because they did not generally have the resources to acquire the quantity and quality of porcelains available to elites, they substituted aesthetically inferior Siamese or Annamese porcelains and locally made deco-rated earthenware in their ritual food displays.

The long-accepted explanation for the beginnings of Chinese mass production of poorer-quality porcelains for Philippine export and the rise of competing mainland Southeast Asian export porcelain manufacturers in the fifteenth cen-tury focuses on changing Chinese production modes and trade policies, rather than transformations in Philippine trade demands. Robert Fox (1964, 1967) sug-gested that the advent of direct Chinese bulk shipping (rather than reliance on in-termediary Malay traders), the loss of revenue to expanding Chinese and Annamese kilns, and the resulting establishment of large-scale export-focused kiln sites in southern China, led to the loss of many delicately made jarlet forms and the proliferation of compact, mass-produced types coming into Philippine chiefly centers, particularly plate and bowls. An alternative interpretation ties this shift in foreign trade volume and assemblage content to the expansion of a com-petitive feasting system in Philippine chiefdoms, increasing the demand for prestige-enhancing foreign serving assemblages. The wider distribution of these Late Ming mass-produced bowls and plates within the households of populations of varying social rank at Cebu and Tanjay may indicate an expanded scale and broadening participation in the competitive feasting system, hence creating a massive demand for foreign serving vessels of varying quality and status value.

A significant issue in the evolution of ritual feasting systems in the Philippines is whether the elaborately pedestaled and footed earthenware bowls and plates found at Philippine sites traditionally dated to the "Metal Age" (ca. 1000 B.C.–A.D. 800; Fig. 10.6) might have functioned in feasting activities prior to the foreign porcelain trade. There are several problems with the archaeological evidence that make it difficult to assess whether decorated earthenware pottery was used in these kind of commensal rituals during the prehistoric period. First, the vast ma-jority of Metal Age sites recorded by archaeologists are described as burial locales

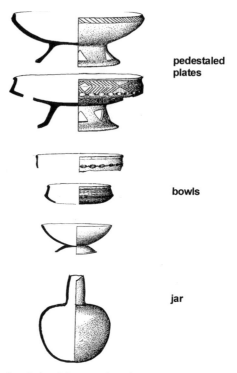

pedestaled
plates

bowls

jar

Figure 10.6. Characteristic pedestaled and decorated earthenware "serving assemblages" from Philippine sites of Iron Age and later date (from Solheim 1964).

with no clear habitation features (Solheim 1964; Tenazas 1974; Dizon 1996) in which jars, lidded pots, funerary boxes, and anthropomorphic forms dominate. Although there is a general impression amongst archaeologists who have excavated presumed Metal Age settlements that decorated plates and bowls may be more common than in mortuary contexts (Dizon 1987; Junker 1993a; Mascunana 1986; Solheim 1964), none of these sites yielded adequate samples of pottery sherds to quantitatively assess differences in household versus burial assemblages. Secondly, there are serious problems with site chronologies prior to the historic period. Many archaeologists have assumed that earthenware bowls, plates, and jars with elaborately incised, impressed, stamped, and appliqué decoration are almost exclusively "pre-porcelain" or "Metal Age" in date (Fox 1964, 1967; Solheim 1964), a chronological assignment that has been little tested through secure dating methods. The assumption is that maritime trade for the aesthetically superior foreign porcelains virtually replaced the local fine earthenware industry as prestige goods.

However, a recent restudy of supposed "Metal Age" earthenware by Gunn and Graves (1996) has demonstrated that stylistic analysis and seriation methods used to assign consistently early dates to decorated earthenware complexes such as the Kalanay wares may have been methodologically flawed. Excavations at Tanjay, Cebu, and other locales (Junker 1993c; Nishimura 1992; Spoehr 1973) suggest that indigenous production of slipped and decorated earthenware, particularly forms associated with food serving, persisted and even expanded throughout the period of foreign porcelain trade. Like the rising popularity of less costly foreign imports, the steady and even increased local production of decorated earthenware vessels in the fifteenth and sixteenth centuries may be related to wider participation in, and sponsorship of, status feasts by lower-ranking individuals who had limited access to the more valued foreign porcelains as serving pieces. Because of the chronological uncertainties and problems of context with most of the Philippine decorated earthenware, it is not currently possible to suggest, on the basis of pottery assemblages, that ritualized feasting was a component of chiefly political economies prior to the late first-millennium advent of foreign trade.

THE EVOLUTION OF THE FEASTING SYSTEM

The archaeological evidence from the Philippines suggests that overtly competitive feasting may have become increasingly key to status competition and political alliance building in the fifteenth- and sixteenth-century chiefdoms. Faunal assemblages at chiefly centers such as Cebu and Tanjay show a differential distribution of water buffalo and pig, known historically as important feasting foods, to what are identified as probable elite households by the early second millennium A.D. In addition, meaty body parts (particularly limb bones) of large mammals are found in higher frequencies in these elite habitation contexts where ceremonial meat divisions likely took place. However, the fifteenth and sixteenth centuries see both an increase in the use of these high-status feasting foods within the chiefly centers as a whole and increased availability of these prestige-enhancing foods to inhabitants of non-elite residential zones. Serving assemblages also show an increasing lavishness of material display and wider distribution of feasting paraphernalia in the two centuries prior to Spanish contact.

These trends may be interpreted in terms of escalating status competition and expanding scale of social participation in the feasting system. Unlike many chiefdoms where feasting systems have been studied, prehispanic Philippine chiefdoms had a political structure consisting of unstable alliance networks that were maintained through continual material exchanges. In terms of political economy, Philippine chiefdoms emphasized "wealth finance" (circulation of prestige goods) rather than "staple finance" (investment in agricultural intensification and tribute mobilization; D'Altroy and Earle 1985; Earle 1997). In a chiefly society where political power was traditionally decentralized, where chiefly coalitions lacked the stable core of territorial lineage groups, and where chiefs vied for control of scarce labor, the circulation of prestige goods at ritual feasts were key to the expansion of political patronage networks. I argue that, even as paramount chieftaincies of significant scale emerged, ceremonial feasts became increasingly important arenas for political and social competition, particularly amongst local chiefs, lesser elites, and upwardly mobile commoners who were filling the lower tiers of increasingly complex political hierarchies.

The expansion of ritual feasting systems appears to be linked to the development of foreign trade and the greater possibilities it offered for alliance-building wealth circulation. Jonathan Friedman has developed an evolutionary scenario that ties initial growth of a competitive feasting system to foreign trade wealth, and eventually led to the evolution of societies with more permanent hereditary stratification. Using the Kachin of Burma as an ethnographic example, Friedman (1979) noted that foreign contacts with an adjacent more complex society (the Shan kingdoms) would provide certain Kachin lineages advantage over initially equal-ranked lineages in sponsoring ritual feasts. This is due to the inflow of high-status Shan wives and lowland prestige goods to Kachin lineages strategically located for interaction and trade. Through their greater control of foreign wealth, Kachin chiefs could hold more elaborately financed feasts, as well as attract further lucrative marriage ties, thus creating asymmetrical alliances with other lineages through their greater control of wealth. In Friedman's model, economic advantage and social prestige could then be translated into supernaturally reinforced superiority of the wealthy lineage, since success in sponsoring ritual feasts is conferred through successfully placating powerful ancestral spirits. Eventually the enhanced ritual potency of this elite lineage might engender a quasi-historical linkage to these ancestral deities, creating an ideological justification for a hereditary elite class.

An influx of exotic forms of feasting foods and/or feasting paraphernalia can also result in spiraling inputs in the feasting system by already competing elites and, in some cases, emulation of elite status behavior by non-elites using now-devalued local goods. In an analysis of ceremonial feasting among the Chin, a Tibeto-Burman people of the Indian-Burmese border, Lehman (1989) suggests that the availability of external sources of wealth can set off an inflationary cycle in an already socially competitive feasting system. Once foreign serving vessels and exchangeable goods enter the feasting system as prestige symbols of exceptionally high value, other feast-givers must obtain similar exotic goods and/or inflate their distributions of now-devalued locally manufactured goods to maintain their relative ranking in the feasting system. In addition, the feasting system often expands the diversity of social groups participating in status display, as the availability of exotic prestige goods creates a two-tiered system of value in which local luxury goods are more widely available for lower-ranking groups to engage in elite-emulating ceremonial feasts.

In the Philippines, foreign porcelain trade reaches its peak in the few centuries before Spanish contact, at a time when many Philippine chiefdoms grew in scale and manifested more complexly tiered systems of social stratification. The foreign porcelains coming into the Philippines in increasing volume in the Ming period have a narrower range of highly standardized forms compared to earlier periods, emphasizing the plates, bowls, and other serving pieces associated with ritual food presentations. We may suggest that chiefs who competed favorably for control of foreign trade through strategic coastal locations, through sponsored "trade missions" to the Chinese court, and through the development of attractive port facilities gained an advantage in the sponsoring elaborate feasts and circulating the prestige goods necessary to consolidating political power. Chiefs with restricted access to foreign feasting assemblages and local "men of renown" who hoped to parlay military prowess and charisma into political sway probably augmented their small porcelain assemblages with large volumes of "second rate" decorated earthenware that allowed them to emulate the more elaborate feasts of the trade-controlling paramounts. The presence of poorer-quality foreign porcelains, decorated earthenware, and pig and water buffalo skulls outside the wealthiest residential zone at fifteenth- and sixteenth-century Tanjay may reflect high-intensity status competition amongst lower-tier leaders to build their own patronage and alliance networks.

The development of competitive feasting systems is likely to be tied to changes in other aspects of chiefly political economies as Philippine chiefdoms became more complex in the centuries before European contact. An escalating scale, widening social participation, and expanding competitive focus in feasting should be evident in changing subsistence production choices (e.g., a greater emphasis on raising large pig herds) and in changing strategies for surplus mobilization (e.g., agricultural intensification, wider tribute networks). Faunal assemblages from household middens suggest that residents of chiefly centers such as Tanjay and Cebu increasingly concentrated their economic efforts on raising large pig herds and water buffalo, which were the primary status foods in ritual feasting. Geomorphological evidence for accelerating alluviation around the coastal center of Tanjay (e.g., Schwab 1983) and decreasing numbers of tropical forest species in faunal assemblages at both Tanjay and Cebu (Mudar 1997) are indirect evidence for expanded land clearance for agriculture in the fifteenth and sixteenth centuries. We noted that intensified rice production may be particularly associated with expanding surplus in elite households, since rice is an important ritual food distributed in competitive feasting events. However, archaeological and historical evidence suggest that Philippine chiefs never made large-scale investments in irrigation systems or other forms of intensification typical of Polynesian chiefdoms and mainland Southeast Asian polities emphasizing "staple finance" of rulership (Junker 1999).

In the Marquesas, Thomas (1990:87–108) has suggested that a spiraling system of competitive feasting is associated with increased interpolity raiding and warfare, as chiefs vied for exotic resources and especially foreign captives to use in status-enhancing sacrificial rites. In the Philippines, feasting is similarly linked with slave-raiding and head-taking, since human sacrifice was a common component of feasts associated with chiefly mortuary rites, chiefly succession, annual agricultural ceremonies (such as the Gin Em feast amongst the Bagabo), and perhaps other ceremonial occasions (Chirino 1904:303–305; Cole 1913; Keesing 1962:189; Junker 1993b; Scott 1991:51). Warren (1985) has suggested that the tremendous escalation of maritime slave-raiding by the Ilanun (specialized sea-raiders supported by the still-independent Sulu sultanate) in the seventeenth through nineteenth centuries was related to an expanding demand for "foreign" captives to trade for ritual sacrifices in the Philippines and Borneo. Although escalating competition for status in feasting may have precipitated increased raiding to obtain sacrificial victims and other expendable resources, chiefly feasts also served to mediate social conflict between competing groups and create at least temporary social solidarity. This is most overtly manifested in "peace pact" or "blood oath" ceremonies carried out at some ritual feasts, marking the cessation of hostilities and newly formed alliances between formerly warring social units or polities (e.g., Keesing 1962:274; Kiefer 1972; Loarca 1903:160–163; Pigafetta 1975:56, 77, 79; Scott 1982:190).

In archaeologically known cases, such as Iron Age Europe, the Mississippian chiefdoms, and Formative period Mesoamerica, there often appears to be a strong correspondence between archaeological indicators for intensive elite feasting activities and material evidence for escalating interpolity conflict (e.g., Blitz 1993; Dietler 1989, 1990; Marcus and Flannery 1996:120). Both historic sources and archaeological evidence point to an upsurge in the scale and intensity of interpolity conflict among Philippine chiefdoms in the two centuries just prior to Spanish contact (Junker 1997, 1999). Although Chinese accounts of the eleventh through fourteenth centuries describe Philippine coastal ports that are nonfortified and readily accessible by traders, the early Spaniards emphasize the widespread use of both home fortresses (generally wooden stockade-and-ditch complexes) and interior refuge locales. Historic sources also point to the rapid adoption of foreign military technologies (particularly Chinese-style iron cannons, swivel guns, and bronze helmets) and to the development of a professional warrior class (*maharlika* in Tagalog-speaking chiefdoms) with distinctive emblems some time after the fourteenth century (also see Scott 1994).

Archaeological investigations of coastal trading settlements and cemeteries support ethnohistoric analysis in suggesting expanding interpolity conflict in the fifteenth and sixteenth centuries. Archaeological remnants of fortification at coastal centers and refuge locales are almost invariably late in date (Dizon and Santiago 1994; Junker 1997). Analysis of skeletal remains from burials shows a striking increase in the incidence of violent death and the use of decapitated heads as burial accompaniments in the fifteenth and sixteenth centuries (Junker 1993b, 1997). Male burials in fifteenth- and sixteenth-century deposits at Tanjay, Calatagan, and other sites (Fox 1959; Junker, Gunn, and Santos 1996) begin to exhibit standardized "emblems" of warrior status, including filed and gold-pegged teeth, animal-tooth jewelry, trophy heads, and bronze and iron weaponry. Finally, evidence for expanded metals production at coastal chiefly centers such as Cebu and Tanjay (Junker 1999), and the appearance of foreign artillery at Manila and Sulu (Scott 1994) suggest that control of metal weaponry becomes increasingly important at this time. The relationship between military power and ideological power is always complex in chiefdom-level societies (Earle 1997). In the Philippines, competitive aspects of ceremonial feasting may have precipitated raiding as a strategy for obtaining status-enhancing resources, whereas socially integrative aspects of ceremonial feasting served to diffuse social tension and mediate disputes between factions.

Figure 10.7 is a schematic presentation of inferred changes in political structure, social stratification, agricultural production, foreign trade volumes, systems of specialist production, the intensity of warfare, and the scale and frequency of ritual feasting in Philippine chiefdoms in the two millennia prior to European contact. Unfortunately, our understanding of processes of sociopolitical evolution in the Philippines is based on limited ethnohistoric analysis and archaeological study of very few of these prehispanic polities. What is clear is that the ritual feasting system, and particularly the social exchanges involved in its operation, was increasingly critical to Philippine chiefly political economies, which emphasized alliance-building through the circulation of prestige goods. Any study of long-term political processes in the prehispanic Philippines must necessarily focus on the evolution of ritual feasting systems.

Phase	Political Structure	Social Strata	Agricultural Intensification	Foreign Trade	Specialized Production	Warfare/ Slave raids	Ritual Feasting
			increased →	increased →	increased →	increased →	increased →
A.D. 1500 LATE PORCELAIN PERIOD	3-level hierarchy	CHIEFS NOBILITY COMMONERS SLAVES	increased forest clearance / increased labor capture in warfare	LATE MING / EARLY MING	specialist production of domestic goods (standardized ceramics)	fortification iron weapons production warrior insignia violent deaths in burials	increased water buffalo and pig consumption / more specialized porcelain assemblages
A.D. 1000 EARLY PORCELAIN PERIOD	paramount chief, local chiefs, village headmen	complex status differences in burials		SUNG / TANG	fancy earthenwares and iron production (standardized designs)		
A.D. 500	2-level hierarchy	simple status differences in burials		first porcelains			
A.D. 0 IRON AGE	local chiefs, village headmen			EARLY IRON AGE TRADE			
500 B.C.	?	?			possible fancy earthenware and iron production by specialists		?

Figure 10.7. Schematic model of the relationship between changing sociopolitical organization, agricultural intensification, increasing foreign trade, specialized production, increased warfare, and expanded ritual feasting in Philippine chiefdoms over the two millennia prior to European contact.

ACKNOWLEDGMENTS

The archaeological fieldwork in the Philippines that provided much of the empirical support for my analysis of ritual feasting was sponsored over a number of field seasons by the Fulbright Foundation, the Social Science Research Council, the Wenner-Gren Foundation, Vanderbilt University Research Council, the Mellon Foundation, and the National Geographic Society. I am grateful to Karl Hutterer, Mary Gunn, Karen Mudar, Marla Schwaller, Masao Nishimura, Eusebio Dizon, Angel Bautista, Wilfredo Ronquillo, and countless others for assisting in or facilitating my investigations of the animal and plant remains and ceramics at Tanjay. My interpretations of the Southeast Asian historic and archaeological evidence, as well as the more general analysis of the role of ritual feasting in chiefly political economies, benefited enormously from discussions with Brian Hayden, Michael Dietler, Polly Weissner, Patrick Kirch, and other contributors to this volume. I also appreciate the comments of historian colleagues at Brigham Young University (including Susan Rugh, Lee Butler, Tom Alexander, Jenny Pulsipher, Michael Murphy, David Wright, Ignacio Garcia, David Montgomery, and many others) when I presented a version of this paper at the faculty seminar.

REFERENCES

Alcina, F. I.

1960a Historia de las Islas e Indios de las Bisayas, Book 3, Part 3. In *The Muñoz*
[1688] *Text of Alcina's History of the Bisayan Islands,* edited by Paul Lietz. Chicago: University of Chicago, Philippine Studies Program.

1960b Historia de las Islas e Indios de las Bisayas, Book 3, Part 4. In *The Muñoz*
[1688] *Text of Alcina's History of the Bisayan Islands,* edited by Paul Lietz. Chicago: University of Chicago, Philippine Studies Program.

Andaya, B.

1992 Political Development between the Sixteenth and Eighteenth Centuries. In *The Cambridge History of Southeast Asia, Volume 1: From Early Times to c. 1800,* edited by N. Tarling, pp. 402–459. Cambridge: Cambridge University Press.

Anonymous

1990a Relation of the Voyage to Manila. In *Documentary Sources of Philippine History*
[1570] *Vol. 2,* edited by G. Zaide, pp. 59–85. Manila: National Bookstore.

1990b Relation of the Conquest of Manila and Other Islands. In *Documentary*
[1572] *Sources of Philippine History, Vol. 2,* edited by G. Zaide, pp. 93–115. Manila: National Bookstore.

Barton, R. F.

1949 *The Kalingas.* Chicago: University of Chicago Press.

Beatty, A.

1991 Ovasa: Feasts of Merit in Nias. *Bijdragen: Tot de Taal-, Land- en Volkenkunde*
147:216–235.

Biernatzki, W. E.

1985 Bukidnon Datuship in the Upper Pulangi River Valley. In *Bukidnon Politics and Religion,* edited by A. Guzman and E. Pacheco, pp. 15–49. Institute for Philippine Culture, Papers No. 11. Quezon City: Ateneo de Manila Press.

Blanton, R., G. Feinman, S. Kowalewski, and P. Peregrine

1996 A Dual-Processual Theory for the Evolution of Mesoamerican Civilization. *Current Anthropology* 37 (1): 1–14.

Blitz, J.

1993 Big Pots for Big Shots: Feasting and Storage in a Mississippian Community. *American Antiquity* 58:80–96.

Bobadilla, D. de

1990 Relation of the Philippine Islands. In *Documentary Sources of Philippine History*
[1640] *Vol. 4,* edited by G. Zaide, pp. 329–343. Manila: National Bookstore.

Boxer manuscript

1975 The Manners, Customs, and Beliefs of the Philippine Inhabitants of Long
[1590] Ago. In *The Philippines at the Spanish Contact,* edited and translated by F. L. Jocano, pp. 188–235. Manila: MCS Publishing.

Chirino, P.

1904 Relación de las Islas Filipinas. In *The Philippines, 1493–1898, Vol. 12,* edited
[1604] by E. Blair and J. Robertson. Cleveland: Arthur H. Clark.

Clark, J. E., and M. Blake
1994   The Power of Prestige: Competitive Generosity and the Emergence of Rank
        Societies in Lowland Mesoamerica. In *Factional Competition in the New World*,
        edited by E. Brumfiel and J. Fox, pp. 17–30. Cambridge: Cambridge University
        Press.
Claver, F.
1985   Dinawit Ogil: High Datu of Namnam. In *Bukidnon Politics and Religion*, ed-
        ited by A. Guzman and E. Pacheco, pp. 51–114. Institute for Philippine Cul-
        ture, Papers No. 11. Quezon City: Ateneo de Manila Press.
Codere, H.
1950   *Fighting with Property.* American Ethnological Society, Monograph No. 18,
        Washington, D.C.
Cole, F. C.
1913   *Wild Tribes of the Davao District.* Publication No. 162, Anthropology Series 13,
        No. 1. Chicago: Field Museum of Natural History.
1956   *The Bukidnon of Mindanao.* Chicago: Chicago Natural History Museum Press.
Colin, F.
1906   Labor Evangelica, Ministerios Apostolicos de los Obreros de la Compania de
[1660] Jesus, Fundacion y Progressos de su Provincia en las Islas Filipinas. In *The
        Philippines, 1493–1898, Vol. 40*, edited by E. Blair and J. Robertson, pp. 37–48.
        Cleveland: Arthur H. Clark.
1975   Native Races and Their Customs: Of the Origin of the Nations and Peoples
[1660] Who Inhabit These Islands. In *The Philippines at the Spanish Contact*, edited
        and translated by F. Landa Jocano, pp. 147–187. Manila: MCS Press.
Correa, G.
1990   Lendas da India. In *Documentary Sources of Philippine History, Vol. 1*, edited by
[1563] G. Zaide, pp. 251–264. Manila: National Bookstore.
Crabtree, P.
1990   Zooarchaeology and Complex Societies: Some Uses of Faunal Analysis for
        the Study of Trade, Social Status, and Ethnicity. In *Advances in Archaeological
        Method and Theory, Vol. 2*, edited by M. Schiffer, pp. 155–205. Tucson: Univer-
        sity of Arizona Press.
D'Altroy, T., and T. Earle
1985   State Finance, Wealth Finance, and Storage in the Inka Political Economy.
        Current Anthropology 26:187–206.
Dasmarinas, G. P.
1958   The Manners, Customs, and Beliefs of the Philippine Inhabitants of Long
[1590] Ago. Translated by C. Quirino and M. García. *Philippine Journal of Science*
        87:389–445.
De la Torre, A., and K. Mudar
1982   The Becino Site: An Exercise in Ethnoarchaeology. In *Houses Built on Scattered
        Poles: Prehistory and Ecology in Negros Oriental, Philippines*, edited by K. Hut-
        terer and W. Macdonald, pp. 117–146. Cebu City, Philippines: University of
        San Carlos Press.

DeBoer, W., and D. Lathrap
  1979   The Making and Breaking of Shipibo-Conibo Ceramics. In *Ethnoarchaeology: Implications of Ethnography for Archaeology*, edited by C. Kramer, pp. 102–138. New York: Columbia University Press.
DeMarais, E., L. J. Castillo, and T. K. Earle
  1996   Ideology, Materialization, and Power Strategies. *Current Anthropology* 37:15–31.
De Raedt, J.
  1989   Kalinga Sacrifice. University of the Philippines Cordillera Studies Center, Baguio, Philippines.
De Veyra, E.
  1986   Pigs and Rituals on Bohol Island, Philippines. In *Southeast Asian Archaeology 1986*, edited by I. Glover. Oxford: BAR Publications in Anthropology.
Dietler, M.
  1989   Greeks, Etruscans, and Thirsty Barbarians: Early Iron Age Interaction in the Rhone Basin of France. In *Centre and Periphery: Comparative Studies in Archaeology*, edited by T. Champion, pp. 127–141. London: Unwin Hyman.
  1990   Driven by Drink: The Role of Drinking in the Political Economy and the Case of Early Iron Age France. *Journal of Anthropological Archaeology* 9:352–406.
Dizon, E.
  1987   An Iron Age in the Philippines? A Critical Examination. Ph.D. dissertation, University of Pennsylvania.
  1996   The Anthropomorphic Pottery from Ayub Cave, Pinol, Maitum, South Cotabato, Mindanao, Philippines *Bulletin of the Indo-Pacific Prehistory Association* 14:186–196.
Dizon, E., and R. Santiago
  1994   Preliminary Report on the Archaeological Explorations in Batan, Sabtang, and Ivuhos Islands, Batanes Province, Northern Philippines. Unpublished report submitted to the Philippine National Museum, Division of Archaeology.
Dozier, E. P.
  1966   *Mountain Arbiters: The Changing Life of a Philippine Hill People.* Tucson: University of Arizona Press.
Drucker, P.
  1967   The Potlatch. In *Tribal and Peasant Economies*, edited by G. Dalton. New York: Natural History Press.
Earle, T. K.
  1977   A Reappraisal of Redistribution: Complex Hawaiian Chiefdoms. In *Exchange Systems in Prehistory*, edited by T. K. Earle and J. Ericson, pp. 213–229. New York: Academic Press.
  1997   *How Chiefs Come to Power: The Political Economy in Prehistory.* Stanford: Stanford University Press.
Feinman, G.
  1995   The Emergence of Inequality: Focus on Strategies and Processes. In *Foundations of Social Inequality*, edited by T. D. Price and G. Feinman, pp. 255–279. New York: Plenum.

Fox, J. G.
    1996   Playing with Power: Ballcourts and Political Ritual in Southern Mesoamer-
            ica. *Current Anthropology* 37 (3): 483–510.
Fox, R.
    1959   The Calatagan Excavations: Two Fifteenth Century Burial Sites in Batangas,
            Philippines. *Philippine Studies* 7:325–390.
    1964   Chinese Pottery in the Philippines. In *Chinese Participation in Philippine Cul-
            ture and Economy,* edited by S. Liao, pp. 96–115. Manila: Liao.
    1967   The Archaeological Record of Chinese Influences in the Philippines. *Philip-
            pine Studies* 15 (1): 41–62.
Friedman, J.
    1979   *System, Structure, and Contradiction in the Evolution of "Asiatic" Social Forma-
            tions.* Copenhagen: National Museum Press.
Friedman, J., and M. Rowlands
    1978   Notes towards an Epigenetic Model of the Evolution of "Civilization." In
            The Evolution of Social Systems, edited by J. Friedman and M. Rowlands,
            pp. 201–276. Pittsburgh: University of Pittsburgh Press.
Geertz, C.
    1973   *The Interpretation of Culture.* New York: Basic Books.
    1980   *Negara: The Theatre State in Nineteeth-Century Bali.* Princeton: Princeton Uni-
            versity Press.
Gero, J.
    1992   Feasts and Females: Gender Ideology and Political Meals in the Andes. *Nor-
            wegian Archaeological Review* 25 (1): 15–30.
Gibson, T.
    1986   *Sacrifice and Sharing in the Philippine Highlands.* London School of Economics
            Monographs in Social Anthropology No. 37. London: The Athlone Press.
Goldman, I.
    1970   *Ancient Polynesia Society.* Chicago: University of Chicago Press.
Gregory, C. A.
    1982   *Gifts and Commodities.* London: Academic Press.
Gunn, M. M.
    1997   The Development of Social Networks: Subsistence Production and Ex-
            change Between the Sixth and Sixteenth Centuries A.D. in the Tanjay Region,
            Negros Oriental, Philippines. Ph.D. dissertation, University of Hawaii.
Hall, K.
    1985   *Maritime Trade and State Development in Early Southeast Asia.* Honolulu: Uni-
            versity of Hawaii Press.
    1992   Economic History of Early Southeast Asia. In *The Cambridge History of South-
            east Asia. Volume 1. From Early Times to c. 1800,* edited by N. Tarling, pp. 183–275.
            Cambridge: Cambridge University Press.
Hart, D. V.
    1958   *The Cebuano Filipino Dwelling in Caticugan: Its Construction and Cultural Aspects.*

Southeast Asian Studies Cultural Reports Series, No. 7. New Haven: Yale University Press.

1969   *Bisayan Filipino and Malayan Humoral Pathologies: Folk Medicine and Ethnohistory in Southeast Asia.* Ithaca: Cornell University Press.

Hayden, B.

1994   Pathways to Power: Principles for Creating Socioeconomic Inequalities. In *Foundations of Social Inequality,* edited by T. D. Price and G. Feinman, pp. 15–86. New York: Plenum.

Higham, C.

1996   *The Bronze Age of Southeast Asia.* Cambridge: Cambridge University Press.

Hutterer, K. L.

1973   *An Archaeological Picture of Prehispanic Cebuano Community.* Cebu City, Philippines: University of San Carlos Press.

1977   Prehistoric Trade and the Evolution of Philippine Societies: A Reconsideration. In *Economic Exchange and Social Interaction in Southeast Asia: Perspectives From Prehistory,* edited by K. L. Hutterer, pp. 177–196. Michigan Papers on South and Southeast Asia No. 13. Ann Arbor: University of Michigan Center for South and Southeast Asian Studies.

Jocano, F. L.

1975   *Philippine Prehistory.* Quezon City, Philippines: Garcia.

Junker, L. L.

1993a   Archaeological Excavations at the Late First Millennium and Early Second Millennium A.D. Settlement of Tanjay, Negros Oriental. Household Organization, Chiefly Production and Social Ranking. *Philippine Quarterly of Culture and Society* 21 (2): 146–225.

1993b   Archaeological Excavations at the 12th–16th Century Settlement of Tanjay, Negros Oriental: The Burial Evidence for Social Status Symboling, Headtaking, and Inter-Polity Raiding. *Philippine Quarterly of Culture and Society* 21 (1): 39–82.

1993c   Craft Goods Specialization and Prestige Goods Exchange in Philippine Chiefdoms of the Fifteenth and Sixteenth Centuries. *Asian Perspectives* 32 (1): 1–35.

1994   Trade Competition, Conflict, and Political Transformations in Sixth- to Sixteenth-Century Philippine Chiefdoms. *Asian Perspectives* 33 (2): 229–260.

1997   Slave-Raiding and Warfare in Philippine Maritime Trading Chiefdoms. Paper presented at the Annual Meeting of the Society for American Archaeology, Nashville, Tennessee.

1998   Integrating History and Archaeology in the Study of Contact Period Philippine Chiefdoms. *International Journal of Historical Archaeology* 2 (4): 291–320.

1999   *Raiding, Trading, and Feasting: The Political Economy of Philippine Chiefdoms.* Honolulu: University of Hawaii Press.

Junker, L. L., M. Gunn, and M. J. Santos

1996   The Tanjay Archaeological Project: A Preliminary Report on the 1994 and 1995 Field Seasons. *Convergence* 2 (2): 30–68.

Junker, L. L., K. Mudar, and M. Schwaller
    1994   Social Stratification, Household Wealth, and Competitive Feasting in 15th–16th Century Philippine Chiefdoms. *Research in Economic Anthropology* 15:307–358.

Kan, S.
    1986   The Nineteenth Century Tlingit Potlatch: A New Perspective. *American Ethnologist* 13:191–212.

Keesing, F.
    1962   *The Ethnohistory of Northern Luzon.* Palo Alto: Stanford University Press.

Kiefer, T.
    1972   *The Tausug: Violence and Law in a Philippine Moslem Society.* New York: Holt, Rinehart and Winston.

Kim, S.
    1994   Burials, Pigs, and Political Prestige in Neolithic China. *Current Anthropology* 35 (2): 119–141.

Kirsch, A. T.
    1973   Feasting and Social Oscillation: A Working Paper on Religion and Society in Upland Southeast Asia. Cornell University, Dept. of Asian Studies, Southeast Asian Data Paper No. 92, Ithaca, New York.

Leach, E. R.
    1965   *Political Systems of Highland Burma.* Boston: Beacon Press.

Legaspi, A.
    1974   *Bolinao: A Fourteenth–Fifteenth Century Burial Site.* Manila: National Museum of the Philippines Publications No. 7.

Lehman, F. K.
    1989   Internal Inflationary Pressures in the Prestige Economy of the Feast of Merit Complex: The Chin and Kachin Cases from Upper Burma. In *Ritual, Power, and Economy: Upland-Lowland Contrasts in Mainland Southeast Asia,* edited by S. Russell, pp. 89–101. DeKalb, Ill.: Northern Illinois University Center for Southeast Asian Studies Occasional Paper No. 14.

Loarca, M. de.
    1903   Relacíon de las Islas Filipinas. In *The Philippines, 1493–1898, Vol. 5,* edited by
    [1582]   E. Blair and J. Robertson,pp. 32–187. Cleveland: Arthur H. Clark.

Locsin, L., and C. Locsin
    1967   *Oriental Ceramics Discovered in the Philippines.* Tokyo: Rutland.

Manuel, E. A.
    1973   *Manuvu Social Organization.* Quezon City, Philippines: University of the Philippines Press.

Marcus, J., and K. V. Flannery
    1996   *Zapotec Civilization.* New York: Thames and Hudson.

Marschall, W.
    1976   *Der Berg des Herrn der Erde.* Munich: Deutscher Taschenbuch Verlag.

Mascunana, R.
    1986   The Bacong Artifacts in the Silliman Anthropological Museum Collection: A Morphological Analysis of Displayed Material Culture. In *Artifacts from the*

Visayan Communities: A Study of Extinct and Extant Culture, edited by R. Cadelina and J. Perez, pp. 1–200. Dumaguete City, Philippines: Silliman University Press.

Mendoza, J. G.

1903   History of the Great Kingdom of China. In *The Philippines, 1493–1898, Vol. 6,*
[1586]   edited and translated by E. Blair and J. Robertson, pp. 85–153. Cleveland: Arthur H. Clark.

Miller, J.

1984   Feasting with the Southern Tsimshian. In *The Tsimshian: Images of the Past, Views for the Present,* edited by M. Seguin, pp. 37–39. Vancouver: University of British Columbia.

Morga, A.

1903   Sucesos de las Islas Filipinas. In *The Philippine Islands, 1493–1803, Vol. 16,*
[1609]   edited by E. Blair and J. Robertson. Cleveland: Arthur H. Clark.

Mudar, K.

1997   Patterns of Animal Utilization in the Holocene of the Philippines: A Comparison of Faunal Samples from Four Archaeological Sites. *Asian Perspectives* 36 (1): 67–105.

Nishimura, M.

1988   Long Distance Trade and the Development of Complex Societies in the Prehistory of the Central Philippines—The Cebu Archaeological Project: Basic Concepts and First Results. *Philippine Quarterly of Culture and Society* 16:107–157.

1992   Long Distance Trade and the Development of Complex Societies in the Prehistory of the Central Philippines: The Cebu Central Settlement Case. Ph.D. dissertation, University of Michigan.

Nurge, E.

1965   *Life in a Leyte Village.* Seattle: University of Washington Press.

Peebles, C., and S. Kus

1977   Some Archaeological Correlates of Ranked Societies. *American Antiquity* 42:421–448.

Peralta, J., and L. A. Salazar

1974   *Pre-Spanish Manila: A Reconstruction of the Pre-History of Manila.* Manila: National Historical Commission.

Pérez, D.

1951   Relación de los Indios Zambales de la Playa Honda: Su Sitio, Sus Costumbres.
[1680]   In *Un Héroe Dominicano Mantanes en Filipinas,* edited by Honorio Muñoz. Manila: Santander.

Pigafetta, A.

1975   First Voyage Around the World. In *The Philippines at the Spanish Contact,*
[1521]   edited and translated by F. L. Jocano, pp. 44–80. Quezon City: Garcia Publications.

Plasencia, J. de

1903a   Las Costumbres de los Indios Tagalogs de Filipinas. In *The Philippine Islands,*
[1589]   *1493–1803, Vol. 7,* edited by E. Blair and J. Robertson, pp. 173–185. Cleveland: Arthur H. Clark.

1903b Instrucción de las Costumbres que Antiguamente Tenían los Naturales
[1589] de las Pampanga en Sus Pleitos. In *The Philippine Islands, 1493–1803, Vol. 7*, edited by E. Blair and J. Robertson, pp. 185–196. Cleveland: Arthur H. Clark.

Pohl, M.
1994 The Economics and Politics of Maya Meat Eating. In *The Economic Anthropology of the State*, edited by E. Brumfiel, pp. 119–148. Monographs in Economic Anthropology, No. 11. Lanham: University Press of America.

Powers, W. K., and M. Powers
1984 Metaphysical Aspects of an Oglala Food System. In *Food in the Social Order*, edited by M. Douglas, pp. 40–96. New York: Russell Sage Foundation.

Prill-Brett, J.
1989 The Bontok Chuno Feast in the Context of Modernization. University of the Philippines, Cordillera Studies Center Working Paper No. 12, Baguio, Philippines.

Reid, A.
1983 "Closed" and "Open" Slave Systems in Pre-Colonial Southeast Asia. In *Slavery, Bondage, and Dependency in Southeast Asia*, edited by A. Reid, pp. 156–181. New York: St. Martin's Press.

1988 *Southeast Asia in the Age of Commerce 1450–1680, Vol 1: The Lands Below the Winds*. New Haven: Yale University Press.

1992 Economic and Social Change, c. 1400–1800. In *The Cambridge History of Southeast Asia. Volume 1. From Early Times to c. 1800*, edited by N. Tarling. Cambridge: Cambridge University Press.

1993 Introduction: A Time and a Place. In *Southeast Asia in the Early Modern Era*, edited by A. Reid, pp. 1–22. Ithaca: Cornell University Press.

Rosman, A., and P. Rubel
1978 Exchange as Structure, or Why Doesn't Everyone Eat His Own Pigs? *Research in Economic Anthropology* 1:105–130.

Saleeby, N. M.
1905 *Studies in Moro History, Law, and Religion*. Bureau of Printing, U.S. Department of the Interior, Ethnological Survey Publications, Vol. 4, Part 1, Manila.

San Antonio, F.
1990 Cronicas de la Apostólica Provincia de San Gregorio de Religiosos
[1738] Descalzados de N.S.P.S. Francisco de las Philipinas, China, Japón, etc. In *Documentary Sources of Philippine History, Vol. 5*, edited and translated by G. Zaide, pp. 299–341. Manila: National Bookstore.

Sánchez, M.
1617 *Bocabulario de la Lengua Bisaya*. Manila: National Archives.

Santa Ines, F. de
1990 Cronica de la Provincia de San Gregorio Magno de China, Japón, etc. In
[1676] *Documentary Sources of Philippine History, Vol. 5*, edited and translated by G. Zaide, pp. 67–92. Manila: National Bookstore.

Schnitger, F. M.

    1964   *Forgotten Kingdoms in Sumatra*. Leiden: Brill.

Schwab, A. M.

    1983   The Geomorphology and Archaeological Geology of the Bais Anthropological Project, Negros Oriental, Philippines. M.A. thesis, Department of Geology, University of Michigan.

Scott, W. H.

    1982   *The Discovery of the Igorots: Spanish Contacts with the Pagans of Northern Luzon.* Quezon City, Philippines: New Day Publications.

    1984   *Prehispanic Source Material for the Study of Philippine History.* Quezon City, Philippines: New Day Publications.

    1991   *Slavery in the Spanish Philippines.* Manila: De la Salle University Press.

    1994   *Barangay: Sixteenth Century Philippine Culture and Society.* Quezon City: Ateneo de Manila Press.

Slamet-Velsink, I.

    1995   *Emerging Hierarchies: Processes of Stratification and Early State Formation in the Indonesian Archipelago: Prehistory and the Ethnographic Present.* Leiden: Koninkluk Instituut Voor Taal-, Land- en Volkenkunde Press.

Solheim, W. G.

    1964   *The Archaeology of the Central Philippines: A Study Chiefly of the Iron Age and Its Relationships.* Manila: Philippine Bureau of Printing.

Spoehr, A.

    1973   *Zamboanga and Sulu: An Archaeological Approach to Ethnic Diversity.* Pittsburgh: University of Pittsburgh, Ethnology Monograph No. 1.

Strathern, M.

    1971   *The Rope of Moka.* Cambridge: Cambridge University Press.

Suzuki, P.

    1959   *The Religious System and Culture of Nias, Indonesia.* The Hague: Exelsior Press.

Tambiah, S.

    1976   *World Conqueror and World Renouncer: A Study in Religion and Polity in Thailand Against an Historical Background.* Cambridge: Cambridge University Press.

Tenazas, R.

    1974   A Progress Report on the Magsuhot Excavations in Bacong, Negros Oriental, Summer 1974. *Philippine Quarterly of Culture and Society* 2:133–155.

Thomas, N.

    1990   *Marquesan Societies: Inequality and Political Transformation in Eastern Polynesia.* Oxford: Clarendon Press.

Volkman, T.

    1985   *Feasts of Honor: Ritual and Change in the Toraja Highlands.* Urbana, Ill.: University of Illinois Press, Illinois Studies in Anthropology, No. 16.

Voss, J.

    1987   The Politics of Pork and Rituals of Rice: Redistributive Feasting and Commodity Circulation in Northern Luzon, the Philippines. In *Beyond the New*

Economic Anthropology, edited by J. Clammer, pp. 121–141. New York: St. Martin's Press.

Walens, S.

1981   *Feasting with Cannibals: An Essay in Kwakiutl Cosmology.* Princeton: Princeton University Press.

Warren, C.

1977   Palawan. In *Insular Southeast Asia: Ethnographic Section 4: The Philippines*, edited by F. Lebar, pp. 229–290. New Haven: HRAF Publications.

Warren, J. F.

1985   *The Sulu Zone, 1768–1898: The Dynamics of External Trade, Slavery, and Ethnicity in the Transformation of a Southeast Asian Maritime State.* 2nd edition. Quezon City, Philippines: New Day Publications.

Welch, P., and M. Scarry

1995   Status-Related Variation in Foodways in the Moundville Chiefdom. *American Antiquity* 60 (3): 397–419.

Winzeler, R.

1976   Ecology, Culture, Social Organization, and State Formation in Southeast Asia. *Current Anthropology* 17:623–640.

1981   The Study of the Southeast Asian State. In *The Study of the State*, edited by H. Claessen and P. Skalnik, pp. 455–467. The Hague: Mouton.

Wolters, O. W.

1982   *History, Culture, and Region in Southeast Asian Perspectives.* Singapore: Institute of Southeast Asian Studies.

11

FEASTING AND THE EMERGENCE
OF PLATFORM MOUND CEREMONIALISM
IN EASTERN NORTH AMERICA

Vernon James Knight

Freestanding platform mounds are a prominent feature of certain prehistoric sites in the southeastern United States belonging to the period roughly between 100 B.C. and 700 A.D. These Woodland period mounds are the earliest examples of the platform type found in the cultural chronology of the southeastern region. In the interest of exploring the variability within this category, my discussion is focused upon a subset of these early mounds that I believe has relevance to the topic of this volume.

It has been known for some time that, despite similarities of form, earlier Woodland period platform mounds of the Southeast exhibit fundamental differences from the later and far better known late prehistoric platform mounds of the same region. Generally, the late prehistoric Mississippian earthworks, dating to approximately A.D. 1000–1550, are typified by the occurrence of summit buildings of various kinds. These occur in the context of chiefdom-type societies. As to their ancestry, their immediate prototype, it appears, is found in the slightly earlier platform mounds of the Coles Creek culture of the Lower Mississippi Valley (ca. A.D. 700–1200). Excavated examples of Coles Creek platform mounds at the Greenhouse and Morgan sites in Louisiana possess large, circular buildings on their summits, which are arguably elite residences (Ford 1951; Fuller and Fuller 1987). By contrast, those Woodland platform mounds that predate A.D. 700 seldom exhibit summit buildings. The majority belonging to this earlier period of transegalitarian societies were not lived on, and seem to be associated with altogether different kinds of summit activity, at least partly of a ritual nature (Knight 1990; Mainfort and Walling 1992; Jefferies 1994; Lindauer and Blitz 1997; Kohler 1997).

Despite this chronological shift in summit use, the mounds themselves show important commonalities in their formal characteristics through time. These commonalities include rounded quadrilateral contours, multistage construction, and intentional use of contrasting fills. Specifically for the Mississippian case I have argued that, in attempting to understand mounds-as-artifacts, summit use ought to be decoupled from mound building per se, and that mound-building activity is best considered in itself as a repetitive ritual process. Some years ago I developed an interpretive model using ethnographic analogy, drawing from the languages, mythology, religious beliefs, and ritual practices of historic southeastern Indians, wherein Mississippian mounds were conceived by their builders as earth icons, the "navels of the earth" as the Chickasaw called them, periodically reburied in a purificatory process of world renewal (Knight 1981, 1986, 1991). If this model has merit, the continuity of formal characteristics I have mentioned suggests that the analogy might be extended with equal plausibility to pre-Mississippian platform mounds. Fundamentally, from that point of view, the entire history of platform mound building in the Southeast may be seen as a conservative, long-term complex of world-renewal ritual. I will return to this point further on.

The known distribution of pre-Mississippian and pre–Coles Creek freestanding platform mounds is shown in Figure 11.1. This map is accompanied by a table (Table 11.1) giving the site names and basic references. Although there is uncertainty about the dating of some of these examples, particularly those excavated early in the twentieth century, other potential claimants are excluded for shortage of evidence. Despite this uncertainty there is no longer any question that the platform mound building tradition in the Southeast extends back in time to the Middle Woodland period and that such constructions were very much a part of southeastern Hopewellian and post-Hopewellian landscapes.

There is one seeming "hot spot" in the distribution: Northwest Florida and the adjacent Chattahoochee River Valley on the northern Gulf Coastal Plain was an early center of such activity. Otherwise, the remainder are rather widely spread out. The settings differ as well, expressing something of a duality. Some sites, such as Marksville, Florence, and Pinson, possess large mounds within essentially vacant ceremonial centers, sometimes enclosed by earthen embankments. Elsewhere, in contrast, platform mounds lie at the margins of permanently occupied settlements. It is intriguing that among the latter are some of the earliest well-defined nucleated *villages,* as contrasted to seasonal *base camps,* in the Southeast. It is the examples tangent to permanent villages rather than those at vacant centers that have special importance to the goals of the present paper.

As Richard Jefferies noted in his recent summary of this phenomenon, "The characteristics of the Woodland platform mound surfaces suggest not only that activities differed from those proposed for Mississippian platform mounds, but that a great deal of variability existed among the [Woodland] mounds themselves" (1994:83). This variability is indeed worthy of close attention (Knight 1990:172). For example, excavated summit surfaces at the Ingomar and Pinson sites (Rafferty 1990; Mainfort and Walling 1989) are in character quite unlike those reported elsewhere. Data are still scarce, however, and the temptation to overgeneralize is better resisted.

Nonetheless, despite this variability there is at least one identifiable pattern of mound-summit configuration that, at least to me, stands out from the rest and therefore commands attention. A good way to introduce this pattern is by quoting from William Sears's first encounter with it. Of his excavation of Mound B at the Kolomoki site in southwest Georgia in 1952, the veteran southeastern archaeologist writes as follows.

> This was the most unusual mound it has ever been the writer's misfortune to encounter. As a result of a trench cut into it in the first season's work, it was hypothesized that this small structure, fifty feet in diameter and not over five feet high, represented the remains of a collapsed earth covered lodge. It would be difficult to have been more in error. . . . It rapidly became obvious that Mound B consisted of a collection of post holes. Very large posts, twenty-four to thirty inches in diameter, were erected successively in this small area. . . . Later posts often cut through the remains of earlier ones, so that in only a few instances were complete outlines produced. (Sears 1956:10–11)

Sears goes on to describe post-insertion ramps leading down into the postholes from one side, and he provides a sketch showing how these post-insertion ramps must have been used. It is rather obvious that his bewilderment resulted from expectations derived from a literature on Mississippian mounds that almost invariably possessed clear structure patterns; in finding multiple postholes Sears was accustomed to looking for intelligible patterns that would belong to definite

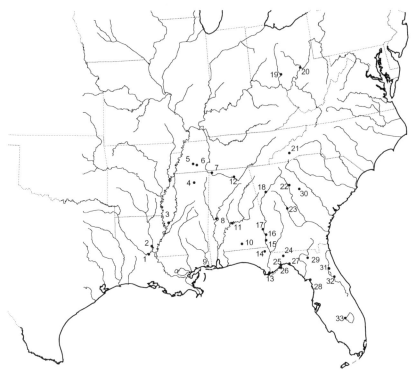

Figure 11.1. Truncated mounds in the eastern United States, 100 B.C.–700 A.D.

buildings. Here there were none; just a surface resembling Swiss cheese from the repetitive emplacement of large posts.

The McKeithen site in northern Florida is closely related to Kolomoki in its material culture. It was excavated by Jerald Milanich and his colleagues and thoroughly reported in 1984. Like Mound B at Kolomoki, Mound A at McKeithen also possesses a platform mound surface prominently marked by randomly situated, large postholes having overlapping post-insertion ramps (Figure 11.2). Associated with this surface were other pits showing a complex intrusion sequence indicative of frequent reuse, numerous small fire pits, a central hearth, two deposits of red ochre, and two refuse deposits containing hundreds of potsherds and pieces of deer bone (Milanich et al. 1984:94–105). McKeithen Mound A is situated at one side of a permanent village that, like the village area at Kolomoki, takes the form of a ring-shaped midden and additional mounds. At McKeithen the other mounds consisted of a conical burial mound and a second platform mound supporting a small building, the latter perhaps the earliest clearly documented domiciliary use of a platform mound in the eastern United States.

TABLE 11.1
Truncated Mounds in the Eastern United States, 100 B.C.–700 A.D.

Map No.	Site Name	No. Truncated Mounds	References
1	Marksville	3*	Fowke 1928; Vescelius 1957; Toth 1974
2	Troyville	1	Walker 1936
3	Leist	1*	Phillips 1970
4	Ingomar	1	Rafferty 1987, 1990
5	Johnston	2	Kwas and Mainfort 1986
6	Pinson	5	Mainfort 1988; Mainfort and Walling 1983
7	Florence	1	Boudreaux and Johnson 1998
8	Forkland	1	Shogren 1989
9	Graveline	1	Greenwell 1984
10	Mitchell	1	Sears n.d.
11	Durant Bend	1	Nance 1976
12	Walling	1	Knight 1990
13	Pierce	2*	Moore 1902
14	Waddells Mill Pond	1	Anonymous 1974b; Brose 1979
15	Kolomoki	5	Sears 1951a, 1951b, 1953, 1956
16	Mandeville	1	Kellar et al. 1962
17	Shorter	1	Kurjack 1975
18	Annawakee Creek	1	Dickens 1975
19	Cinth up	1	Sherrone 1929; McMichael 1964
20	Marietta Works	1	Squier and Davis 1848; McMichael 1964
21	Garden Creek	1	Keel 1972, 1976
22	Cold Springs	1	Jefferies 1994
23	Swift Creek	1	Kelly and Smith 1975; Jefferies 1994
24	Block-Sterns	1	Jones, Penton, and Tesar 1998
25	Hall	1*	Moore 1902
26	Yent	1	Moore 1902
27	Aucilla River	1	Moore 1902
28	Crystal River	2	Bullen 1953
29	McKeithen	2	Milanich et al. 1984
30	Fortson	1	Williams 1992; Williams and Harris 1998
31	Murphy Island	1*	Moore 1896
32	Tick Island	1*	Moore 1894
33	Fort Center	10*	Sears 1982

*One or more mounds circular or elliptical in plan.

In these particulars of site structure and configuration of Mound A, the Mc-Keithen site is strongly reminiscent of the situation at the Walling site in the Tennessee Valley of northern Alabama. The platform mound at Walling (Site Ma°50) was excavated by the author and reported in 1990. At Walling there is once again a Middle Woodland village marked by a ring-shaped midden, with a low platform

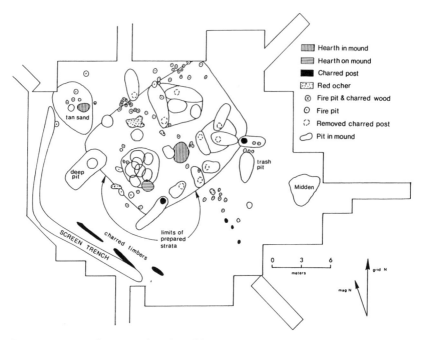

Figure 11.2. McKeithen Mound A, plan of features. From Milanich et al. 1984; reprinted with the permission of the University Press of Florida.

mound standing tangent to it. On the opposite side of the village site from the platform mound, lying at a distance, are two burial mounds, one of which has been excavated and establishes a connection between the habitation area and the Copena mortuary complex (Webb and DeJarnette 1942).

On the second stage of the Walling platform mound (Fig. 11.3), labeled Fill No. 2, were found three massive postholes with diameters of approximately one meter, all provided with post-insertion ramps. One of these monumental posts had, in addition, a separate post-extraction ramp. On the same mound summit were found dozens of additional, randomly scattered postholes of various sizes and fill characteristics. Posts frequently intruded into other posts and pit features, showing intermittent reuse of the surface. Some of the larger postholes had peculiar funnel-shaped profiles, with wide pits at the top transitioning into a vertical-sided posthole at the bottom. Such features are plausibly interpreted as post-extraction pits dug around the base of previously implanted large posts to facilitate their removal. Together with these posts were ash-laden surface hearths, small pits, and concentrations of surface midden yielding potsherds, stone tools, and abundant animal bone.

Large, funnel-shaped postholes and posts with post-insertion ramps are dupli-

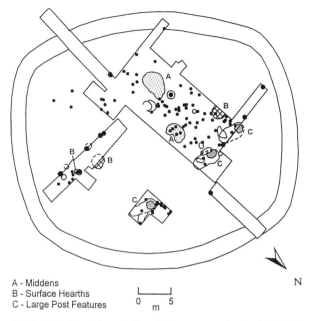

A - Middens
B - Surface Hearths
C - Large Post Features

N

0   m   5

Figure 11.3. Walling Platform Mound, plan of features associated with Fill No. 2. After Knight 1990.

cated at Mound A of the Cold Springs site in northern Georgia, excavated by Suzanne Fish and reported by Richard Jefferies (1994). Mound A is a low platform mound at the northern end of a village of Swift Creek affiliation. Fish and Jefferies estimated that this village possessed approximately eight off-mound dwellings (Fish and Jefferies 1986). A smaller, second mound located to the southwest of Mound A had, at least in part, a mortuary function as indicated by a cremation containing a fragmentary copper ear spool. In Mound A, the multistage platform mound at Cold Springs, a portion of the surface of Floor 3 was exposed (Fig. 11.4), revealing over 100 postholes, many quite large and set as much as one meter deep. The arrangement of posts was once again seemingly random. Among the large postholes, Jefferies describes and illustrates obvious post-insertion ramps, and other large posts appear to have post-extraction pits as found at Walling (Fig. 11.5). Other features of this mound stage included small pits and surface areas mottled with charcoal. Although Jefferies concludes that the Floor 3 surface "remained exposed for a long time and was the scene of much activity," he also concluded from the paucity of artifacts that this surface was not used for ordinary domestic activity (1994:80).

Yet another, similar situation is Mound No. 2 at the Garden Creek site in western North Carolina, reported by Bennie Keel in 1972 (see also Keel 1976). This is

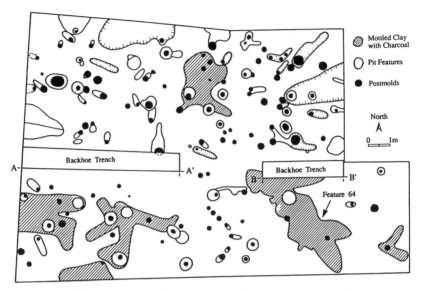

Figure 11.4. Cold Springs, plan of features associated with Floor 3. From Jefferies 1994 (in *Ocmulgee Archaeology: 1936–1986*, edited by David J. Hally [Athens: University of Georgia Press]).

another low mound situated on the margin of a Woodland village site (designated Hw 8). At least the first two mound stages at Garden Creek No. 2 are attributed to the Middle Woodland Connestee phase. Of most interest in this thoroughly excavated case is the well-preserved summit of the primary mound (Fig. 11.6). This surface is riddled with hundreds of postholes of various sizes, many intruding into others and indicating a protracted period of use. Despite Keel's assertion that these postholes must indicate the presence of a structure, he was unable to demonstrate any definite structure outline. Indeed, to judge from his map, postholes appear to be haphazardly distributed across the surface. Keel classifies three features as "large post holes." The largest of these, with a diameter of 88 centimeters and a depth of 149 centimeters, has a characteristic funnel-shaped orifice, in common with certain large posts at Walling and Cold Springs, that in my view is probably a post-extraction pit. Other features of the primary mound surface were a large, central burned area covered with ash, surface hearths, ceremonial deposits of stones, small refuse-filled pits, and a deposit of dark midden soil placed on one side of the mound which yielded over five hundred potsherds. Animal bone was not well preserved and no special analysis was made of the primary mound fauna, although general field observations indicate deer as the main species encountered in these deposits (Keel 1976:78–85, 149).

These five mounds—Kolomoki Mound B, McKeithen Mound A, the platform

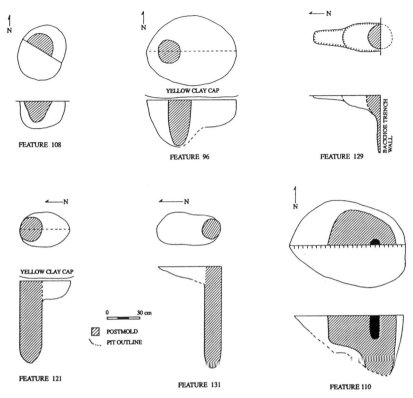

Figure 11.5. Cold Springs, cross-sections of large postholes. From Jefferies 1994 (in *Ocmulgee Archaeology: 1936–1986*, edited by David J. Hally [Athens: University of Georgia Press]).

mound at Walling, Cold Springs Mound A, and Garden Creek Mound No. 2—are sufficient to illustrate the existence of a unitary phenomenon. The primary signature of this phenomenon is the presence of dense, irregular scatters of postholes of various sizes, some of which are large and are equipped with post-insertion ramps, extraction ramps, or extraction pits. The abundance of these postholes, plus the evidence of intrusion sequences, points to repeated reuse of these surfaces over a substantial period of time. Conspicuously absent are posthole alignments or configurations that would indicate the presence of roofed architecture. In general, this evidence is perhaps best denominated as *scaffolding behavior*, repeated cycles of erection and subsequent dismantling of scaffolds, racks, and isolated poles on platform mound summits. Moreover, this activity seems to manifest itself at at least two different scales or modes. On the one hand, we have evidence of scaffolds or racks employing vertical posts of ordinary diameter, but on the other we have postholes that qualify as monumental. The latter were footings for large, upright log poles, presumably of a height com-

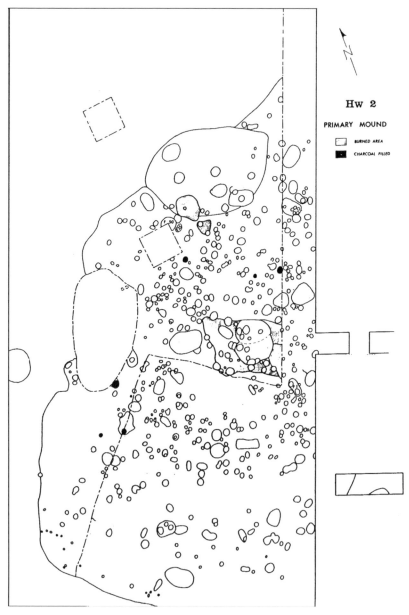

Hw 2

PRIMARY MOUND

□ BURNED AREA

■ CHARCOAL FILLED

Figure 11.6. Garden Creek Mound No. 2, plan of features associated with the primary mound. From *Cherokee Archaeology* by Bennie C. Keel, published 1976 by the University of Tennessee Press.

mensurate to their girth, requiring special procedures and facilities to put up and take down. Uprights of this sort were meant to impress.

Associated features on the mound summits include small pits, surface hearths, and middens. Hearths and dense midden deposits, in particular, are strongly indicative of food preparation and consumption. Exotic raw materials, products of long-distance exchange, and special-use pottery are also found in a number of these contexts, pointing to some sort of ceremonial use. In this connection, the Walling platform mound and Garden Creek Mound No. 2 both exhibit specific Hopewellian-related artifacts in their respective mound assemblages. Table 11.2 summarizes the associations so far discussed (see also Knight 1990:170–172).

The fact that these mounds all stand within the boundaries of small permanent settlements is significant. Access does not seem to be restricted in any important way, and whatever activities occurred on them probably would have been in full view of villagers residing only a few meters away. (A possible exception is presented by evidence for a curving, pine post screening wall found on the southwest side of McKeithen Mound A [Milanich et al. 1984:97–98], but this screen seems ill-placed to impede either view or access. Summit activities would still have been perfectly visible from the vantage point of the village's central plaza.) Owen Lindauer and John Blitz (1997) believe that public access is one of the chief variables that distinguish such Woodland platform mounds from their later, Mississippian counterparts. To use their terminology, whereas Woodland platform mounds were principally communal, *integrative* facilities, Mississippian mounds emphasized social *differentiation.*

In summary, minor variations aside, these mounds reveal a patterned combination of behaviors. As I interpret them, these involve intermittent, repetitive activity involving manipulation of exotic artifacts, caching of goods in small pits, food preparation and consumption, frequent scaffolding of objects unknown, and monumental display of poles. All of this occurred on low, earthen stages, periodically renewed and connected symbolically with world renewal.

Up to now I have sidestepped any acknowledgment of previous models of the uses of these mounds. Jerald Milanich and his colleagues argued that McKeithen Mound A was a charnel structure, on which the remains of the honored dead were reduced to bones, later to be collected, bundled, and removed for final interment in the nearby burial mound, Mound C. In this interpretation the pits on the summit of Mound A were for maceration. Milanich conjectures that the adjacent large posts held aloft pottery sculptures that functioned as charnel "guardians" (Milanich et al. 1984:99–100). What makes this argument particularly compelling is the adduced complementarity of three contemporaneous mounds in the McKeithen village. Mound C, the burial mound, contained numerous bundle burials in various states of decomposition; these remains clearly require a

TABLE 11.2

Associations of Certain Woodland Platform Mounds

	Dense Posthole Scatters	Large Postholes	Post-Insertion/ Extraction Ramps	Post- Extraction Pits	Small Pits	Surface Hearths	Middens	Exotics or Special Ceramics	Mound at Edge of Village
Kolomoki Mound B	x	x	x						x
McKeithen Mound A		x	x		x	x	x	x	x
Walling Mound Ma°50	x	x	x	x	x	x	x	x	x
Cold Springs Mound A	x	x	x	x	x	x			x
Garden Creek No. 2	x	x		x	x	x	x	x	x

charnel structure, which is supplied by Mound A, accounting for the full mortuary program. Richard Jefferies, in discussing the Cold Springs earthworks, pointed to similarities between the monumental postholes in Cold Springs Mound A and McKeithen Mound A. Noting that at Cold Springs, adjacent Mound B contained at least one human cremation, he cautiously invoked Milanich's McKeithen model as an analog (Jefferies 1994:78–80). Bennie Keel, in contrast, interpreted the primary and secondary mound summits of Garden Creek No. 2 as each supporting "some type of building" in the manner of later Mississippian platform mounds. This interpretation was based on the presence of an irregular burned area which he felt was a structure floor, in addition to the ubiquity of postholes, which, as noted previously, failed to resolve into any definite structure pattern (Keel 1976:78–86, 156).

Turning again to the Walling platform mound, I have previously argued for a nonmortuary and also nonresidential use. Postholes on the second mound stage at Walling were numerous, as at Garden Creek No. 2, but were not necessarily part of any building. As to any potential function as a charnel structure, neither burials nor human bone scraps were found anywhere in association with the Walling platform mound (except for obvious Mississippian intrusive burials, which is also the case for Garden Creek No. 2), despite reasonable bone preservation. This observation is in fact true of all five of the examples discussed; in no case are burials or scraps of human bone reported in association with the Middle Woodland platforms, even for McKeithen Mound A which has been so strongly asserted to be a charnel platform. Certainly there are other Woodland platform mound sites that *have* yielded human remains, the most prominent example of which, perhaps, is Kolomoki Mound D, which is assuredly a mortuary monument. But in general, mortuary use is *not* a prominent feature among the freestanding examples.

For Walling, I suggested that "the faunal and botanical data, taken together with other signs of 'kitchen' activity such as midden accumulations, broken pots, and surface hearths, ultimately support a scenario of communal food preparation and consumption—i.e., feasting—taking place at intervals on the summit" of the second mound stage. I also highlighted the presence of exotic chert debitage on the mound summit, along with evidence for the use of copper-covered artifacts, claiming that one aspect of mound use was the manufacture of goods for ritual display and exchange. This evidence, I concluded, "agree[s] with a broader picture of gift-giving and gift receiving in the context of feasting as a primary social mechanism in Hopewellian exchange" (Knight 1990:160–161).

It remains to discuss any direct evidence at these mounds for communal feasting in the most telling form: that of faunal and ethnobotanical data. Unfortunately, published reports for Kolomoki Mound B, Cold Springs Mound A, and

Garden Creek No. 2 do not provide us with detailed data of this sort. However, for McKeithen Mound A, we are fortunate to have an analysis of the faunal remains coming primarily from the two midden deposits on the edge of the platform (carried out by Arlene Fradkin and reported in Milanich et al. 1984:102). Bone was only moderately well preserved. Much of the bone, however, was identifiable and this sample was restricted largely to that of a single species, the white-tailed deer, the only exceptions being tiny amounts of duck, fish, and rabbit. As to specific skeletal elements of the deer bone, "the elements are overwhelmingly from the haunches of deer . . . Whoever was eating deer on the Mound A platform mound was receiving almost solely the haunches. Presumably the deer were butchered elsewhere" (Milanich et al. 1984:102).

For the Walling platform mound, an ethnobotanical analysis of flotation samples was made by Margaret Scarry and two separate analyses of the faunal remains were made by John Worth and Gweneth Duncan. Of the botanical remains Scarry (1990) says that the assemblage is an unusually diverse one, despite the small size of the samples. Some cultivated plants are present in small amounts including maize (stalk and cupule fragments), cucurbits, sunflower, chenopod, maygrass, and little barley. Besides these, Scarry reports a surprising diversity of seeds from gathered wild greens and fruits, including plants that are generally uncommon in archaeological deposits in this region. Nutshell remains, ordinarily the most abundant component of botanical assemblages for this period, are relatively scarce. Scarry proposed that this unusual species composition is the result of seasonality of use.

> Feasts (or offerings) prepared in the summer might contain a high proportion of early garden products and fruit, while a fall or winter feast might include nuts and fall-ripening grains. The Walling assemblage as a whole contains few nut remains, a varied assortment of seeds from summer-ripening fruits, and comparatively abundant grains of maygrass—an early summer crop. If season of deposit is a factor, then most remains are derived from summer activities. (Scarry 1990:127)

Thus, although the plant food assemblage is relatively unusual, much of this peculiarity is plausibly accounted for by the season of use. Moreover, the assemblage does not particularly bespeak of feasting; among the foodstuffs nothing is so overrepresented as to suggest large-scale consumption, nor indeed do fruits and greens seem especially well suited for bulk accumulation.

The faunal remains from the Walling platform mound tell a somewhat different story. The species list is remarkably lacking in diversity, as the faunal assemblage is overwhelmed by bones of the white-tailed deer. Using formulas relating bone weight to total biomass, Worth discovered that deer accounted for over 90 percent of the total meat weight in contexts related to the second mound stage summit, distantly followed by remains of beaver. In contrast to faunal remains re-covered from the premound midden, those from the mound summit showed no evidence of gnawing by rodents or dogs. About one-third of the deer bone was, however, burned; most of these specimens came from the vicinity of a surface hearth. A study of bone elements revealed that heavy meat-bearing body parts were overrepresented, mirroring the findings at McKeithen Mound A. Finally, the ageable specimens revealed an unusually high frequency of adult deer. Worth concludes that "the high proportion of deer in the total sample, and the possibil-ity that the meat-bearing portions of older deer may dominate the sample, sug-gests that the Walling site may in fact reflect Hopewellian ceremonial activity, including the redistribution of meat through ceremonial feasting" (Worth 1990:143). Duncan's (1990) analysis of separate faunal samples, primarily from the upper mound stages at Walling, concurs with Worth's conclusion. It thus appears that deer meat was being processed elsewhere and mobilized to the mound area for roasting and consumption. It is unfortunate that the data are not available to test the obvious question of whether these findings are generalizable to the other sites herein reviewed.

Most of the postholes contributing to what I have called *scaffolding behavior* on the Walling platform mound and elsewhere are not associated with surface hearths. Such scaffolds, then, are mostly not racks for drying or roasting meat like the ones depicted in the De Bry engravings of the sixteenth century Timu-cua (Lorant 1946:83; Fig. 11.7). However, it may be not too much of a leap to sug-gest that they might have served as racks for the collection and perhaps conspicuous display of dried meat in the days prior to small-scale feasts. We have here an alternative model to those which would invoke either mortuary practices on the one hand, or mounds-as-substructures on the other, as the central use-pat-terns of these Woodland mound summits.

I agree with Lindauer and Blitz (1997) that these uses of Woodland platform mounds were essentially communal. Access was apparently unrestricted within small village communities. In our data the individual is evidently submerged, suggesting that the main locus of interaction was between kin groups or com-munities serving as hosts. It is perhaps important for comparative purposes to re-view our evidence for the scale of this activity.

One point of reference is the size of the attached villages. Six or seven con-temporaneous houses have been estimated for the village size at Walling (Knight 1990:8), and eight for Cold Springs (Jefferies 1994:80), suggesting permanent vil-lage populations perhaps in the range of 30–60 inhabitants for these sites. Kohler (in Milanich et al. 1984:89), using rates of sherd deposition, estimated the maxi-mum population of McKeithen at slightly over 100. Kolomoki is by far the largest of the communities reviewed here. Based on the size of the Kolomoki phase

Figure 11.7. Timucuan method of smoking meat on a scaffold, sixteenth-century Florida. Engraving by Theodore De Bry, after a painting by Jacques le Moyne de Morgues. From Lorant 1946.

midden as reported by Sears (1956), a resident population in the low hundreds would be a reasonable guess. On the question of whether such villages hosted supracommunity festivals as well as gatherings at the level of the local community, current consensus weighs in favor of region-wide involvement (Walthall 1985; Knight 1990; Milanich et al. 1984; Smith 1986), particularly in view of the strong evidence for external exchange at many of these sites. If so, the size of the largest gatherings might considerably exceed the population of the host village.

There are other limiting factors on the potential scale of feasting at these sites. One is the small absolute size of the facilities I have been describing, possessing use-surfaces between 17–34 m in diameter. Notably, Kolomoki's Mound B, although it is at the largest site, has the smallest use-surface in the sample. A second limiting factor is that systems of food production were only weakly developed in these societies. Despite the use of some cultigens in a gardening complex, the main source of carbohydrates was still wild gathered plants, while domesticated animals other than dogs were absent. Venison, evidently the preferred food in the mound contexts, is not particularly suited to storage or bulk accumulation in advance of a major feast, even when dried. As a hunted product, supplies would have been limited at any given time. Moreover, if there is a correlation between the size of social gatherings and the size of associated cooking vessels, it is my impression that average vessel size in these mound deposits does not exceed that from ordinary domestic contexts. Standard cooking vessels at the Walling mound are small, short jars with orifice diameters of about 15–20 cm. I must say, however, that the kinds of studies necessary to confirm such impressions have not been done at any of the sites. All these factors considered, it is possible to envision supracommunity festivals hosting no more than 100–200 participants at most of these sites; perhaps they were smaller. Gatherings at Kolomoki, a larger center, conceivably could have been at a somewhat grander scale, although that site lies within a sparsely populated region and its scaffolding facilities, as shown by Mound B, were quite small.

A principal function of feasting in these societies may have been the establishment and preservation of intervillage alliances. A security advantage would thus be conferred to the community that could routinely host festivals; it is no accident that the period in question in the Southeast is one in which evidence of strife or warfare is depressed. However, if the nexus of feasting was indeed between neighboring communities, it was not entirely reciprocal and symmetrical. Most contemporary settlements within a given region lacked platform mounds, suggesting that host groups who could muster the labor to erect one thereby gained a measure of prestige that could be translated as a source of political influence for individual village headmen.

As I have previously emphasized for the Walling site, feasting seems to have provided a context for the manufacture and giving of gifts, especially nonlocal, finely crafted high-prestige items that would ultimately become concentrated in burial mounds as mortuary offerings. Clearly some communities, and some individuals, profited from such traffic more than did others.

In their level of sociopolitical organization these societies were transegalitarian, which is to say "those between chiefdoms and true egalitarian societies as represented by generalized hunter/gatherers" (Chapter 2). In the Southeast, successful community leaders of the Woodland era have routinely been compared to Big Men as described ethnographically in Oceania (e.g., Milanich et al. 1984; Smith 1986). That such individuals enjoyed special advantages including access to exotic craft goods and even retainer burials is clearly shown in the Mound D and Mound E burials at Kolomoki (Sears 1953, 1956). They also had privileged access to special foods, as is shown by the individual centrally buried in the summit of McKeithen Mound B. Isotopic analysis of skeletal remains has shown that of the McKeithen individuals tested, this person alone routinely consumed maize (Milanich 1997). Maize, an introduced tropical cultigen, is rare in the Southeast at this time level and may have been cultivated in small quantities in the vicinity of ceremonial centers for special use (Scarry 1993).

In sum, sites discussed in this paper exhibit at least some of the archaeological signatures of feasting outlined by Hayden (Chapter 2). There is growing evidence that communal consumption of food was an important social process among Woodland societies of the southeastern United States. One of the things that seems important here is that we find it connected in the present instance with a specific kind of ritual activity, one having to do with platform mound building and, as I perceive it, world-renewal ceremony. Recently Robert Hall (1997) has made the claim that aspects of historic world-renewal symbolism in the Plains and Eastern Woodlands can be linked to the material remains of Middle Woodland cultures, and mound building in particular. Hall in fact suggests that the whole complex Woodland burial mound tradition and interregional Hopewellian exchange of goods is best thought of in terms of a combination of elements of world-renewal and reincarnation ceremony as practiced historically. This is certainly a provocative model that has the potential to explicate much of what we know about the Middle Woodland cultural climax.

The thrust of the present paper is to suggest, however, that in parts of the Woodland Southeast, burial-mound ceremonialism was segregated from a second kind of ceremonialism. This second kind centered on world renewal and feasting, emphasizing community integration, very similar in type to the Green Corn ceremonialism practiced throughout the Eastern Woodlands in the historic era. Green Corn ceremonialism was, and in several cases still is, a major Native American Indian ritual associated with the ripening of corn. It was (and is) performed within a consecrated ceremonial area that is a world symbol, renewed by the sweeping or the addition of earth (Witthoft 1949). It is ironic, therefore, to consider how often historic Green Corn ceremonialism has been invoked—awkwardly—as a model for Mississippian ritual practices, whereas in fact the historic Green Corn practices, with their emphatically communal ethic, may be much more closely akin to decidedly *pre-Mississippian* forms of ritual expression.

REFERENCES

Anonymous
  1974   Early Swift Creek Indian Mound. *Archives and History News* 4:2. Tallahassee: Florida Division of Archives, History, and Records Management.
Boudreaux, Edmond A., and Hunter B. Johnson
  1998   Test Excavations at the Florence Mound in Northern Alabama. Report submitted to the Alabama Historical Commission and the City of Florence, Alabama. Tuscaloosa: University of Alabama Department of Anthropology.

Brose, David S.
  1979   An Interpretation of the Hopewellian Traits in Florida. In *Hopewell Archaeology: The Chillicothe Conference*, edited by David S. Brose and N'omi Greber, pp. 141–149. Kent, Ohio: Kent State University Press.

Bullen, Ripley P.
  1953   The Famous Crystal River Site. *The Florida Anthropologist* 6:9–37.

Dickens, Roy S.
  1975   A Processual Approach to Mississippian Origins in the Georgia Piedmont. *Southeastern Archaeological Conference Bulletin* 18:31–42.

Duncan, Gweneth A.
  1990   A Supplemental Vertebrate Faunal Analysis of the Walling Site (Ma°50). In *Excavation of the Truncated Mound at the Walling Site: Middle Woodland Culture and Copena in the Tennessee Valley*, by V. J. Knight Jr., pp. 144–152. Report of Investigations 56. Alabama Museum of Natural History, Division of Archaeology, University of Alabama, Tuscaloosa.

Ford, James A.
  1951   *Greenhouse: A Troyville-Coles Creek Period Mound Site in Avoyelles Parish, Louisiana*. Anthropological Papers 44, Part 1. New York: American Museum of Natural History.

Fowke, Gerard
  1928   Archaeological Investigations—II. *Forty-Fourth Annual Report of the Bureau of American Ethnology*, pp. 399–436. Washington, D.C.

Fuller, Richard S., and Dianne Silvia Fuller
  1987   *Excavations at Morgan: A Coles Creek Mound Complex in Coastal Louisiana*. Bulletin 11. Cambridge: Lower Mississippi Survey, Peabody Museum, Harvard University.

Greenwell, Dale
  1984   The Mississippi Gulf Coast. In *Perspectives on Gulf Coast Prehistory*, edited by Dave D. Davis, pp. 125–155. Gainesville: University of Florida Press.

Hall, Robert L.
  1997   *An Archaeology of the Soul: North American Indian Belief and Ritual*. Urbana: University of Illinois Press.

Jefferies, Richard W.
  1994   The Swift Creek Site and Woodland Platform Mounds in the Southeastern United States. In *Ocmulgee Archaeology: 1936–1986*, edited by David J. Hally, pp. 71–83. Athens: University of Georgia Press.

Jones, B. Calvin, Daniel T. Penton, and Louis D. Tesar
  1998   1973 and 1994 Excavations at the Block-Sterns Site, Leon County, Florida. In *A World Engraved: Archaeology of the Swift Creek Culture*, edited by Mark Williams and Daniel T. Elliot, pp. 222–246. Tuscaloosa: University of Alabama Press.

Keel, Bennie C.
  1972   Woodland Phases of the Appalachian Summit. Ph.D. dissertation, Department of Anthropology, Washington State University, Pullman.

1976   *Cherokee Archaeology: A Study of the Appalachian Summit.* Knoxville: University of Tennessee Press.

Kellar, J. H., A. R. Kelly, and E. V. McMichael

1962   The Mandeville Site in Southwest Georgia. *American Antiquity* 28:338–355.

Kelly, Arthur R., and Betty A. Smith

1975   The Swift Creek Site, 9Bi3, Macon, Georgia. Ms. on file, National Park Service, Southeastern Archaeological Center, Tallahassee, Florida.

Knight, Vernon James, Jr.

1981   Mississippian Ritual. Unpublished Ph.D. dissertation, Department of Anthropology, University of Florida, Gainesville.

1986   The Institutional Organization of Mississippian Religion. *American Antiquity* 51:675–687.

1989   Symbolism of Mississippian Mounds. In *Powhatan's Mantle: Indians in the Colonial Southeast,* edited by P. H. Wood, G. A. Waselkov, and M. T. Hatley, pp. 279–291. Lincoln: University of Nebraska Press.

1990   *Excavation of the Truncated Mound at the Walling Site: Middle Woodland Culture and Copena in the Tennessee Valley.* Report of Investigations 56. Alabama Museum of Natural History, Division of Archaeology, University of Alabama, Tuscaloosa.

Kohler, Timothy A.

1997   Public Architecture and Power in Pre-Columbian North America. Paper presented at the symposium, "Power, Monuments, and Civilization," Nara, Japan, December.

Kurjack, Edward B.

1975   Archaeological Investigations in the Walter F. George Basin. In *Archaeological Salvage in the Walter F. George Basin of the Chattahoochee River in Alabama,* edited by D. L. DeJarnette, pp. 87–198. Tuscaloosa: University of Alabama Press.

Kwas, Mary L., and Robert C. Mainfort

1986   The Johnson Site: Precursor to Pinson Mounds? *Tennessee Anthropologist* 11:29–41.

Lindauer, Owen, and John H. Blitz

1997   Higher Ground: The Archaeology of North American Platform Mounds. *Journal of Archaeological Research* 5:169–207.

Lorant, Stefan, ed.

1946   *The New World: The First Pictures of America.* New York: Duell, Sloan, and Pearce.

Mainfort, Robert C., Jr.

1988   Middle Woodland Ceremonialism at Pinson Mounds, Tennessee. *American Antiquity* 53:158–173.

Mainfort, Robert C., Jr., and Richard Walling

1983   Excavations at Pinson Mounds: Ozier Mound. *Midcontinental Journal of Archaeology* 17:112–136.

McMichael, Edward V.

1964   Veracruz, the Crystal River Complex, and the Hopewellian Climax. In

Hopewellian Studies, edited by Joseph R. Caldwell and Robert L. Hall, pp. 124–132. Springfield: Illinois State Museum.

Milanich, J. T.

1997   Preface. In *Archaeology of Northern Florida, A.D. 200–900: The McKeithen Weeden Island Culture*, by J. T. Milanich, A. S. Cordell, V. J. Knight Jr., T. A. Kohler, and B. J. Sigler-Lavelle. Gainesville: University Press of Florida.

Milanich, J. T., A. S. Cordell, V. J. Knight Jr., T. A. Kohler, and B. J. Sigler-Lavelle

1984   *McKeithen Weeden Island, the Culture of Northern Florida, A.D. 200–900*. Orlando, Florida: Academic Press.

Moore, Clarence B.

1894   Certain Sand Mounds on the St. Johns River, Florida. *Journal of the Academy of Natural Sciences of Philadelphia* 10:130–246.

1896   Certain River Mounds of Duvall County, Florida. *Journal of the Academy of Natural Sciences of Philadelphia* 10:449–516.

1902   Certain Aboriginal Remains of the Northwest Florida Coast. Part 2. *Journal of the Academy of Natural Sciences of Philadelphia* 12 (2): 125–335.

Nance, C. Roger

1976   *The Archaeological Sequence at Durant Bend, Dallas County, Alabama*. Special Publication 2. Orange Beach: Alabama Archaeological Society.

Phillips, Philip

1970   *Archaeological Survey in the Lower Yazoo Basin, Mississippi: 1949–1955*. Papers of the Peabody Museum of American Archaeology 60. Cambridge: Harvard University

Rafferty, Janet

1987   The Ingomar Mounds Site: Internal Structure and Chronology. *Midcontinental Journal of Archaeology* 12:147–173.

1990   Test Excavations at Ingomar Mounds, Mississippi. *Southeastern Archaeology* 9:93–102.

Scarry, C. Margaret

1990   Plant Remains from the Walling Truncated Mound: Evidence for Middle Woodland Horticultural Activities. In *Excavation of the Truncated Mound at the Walling Site: Middle Woodland Culture and Copena in the Tennessee Valley*, by V. J. Knight Jr., pp. 115–129. Report of Investigations 56. Alabama Museum of Natural History, Division of Archaeology, University of Alabama, Tuscaloosa.

1993   Variability in Mississippian Crop Production Strategies. In *Foraging and Farming in the Eastern Woodlands*, edited by C. M. Scarry, pp. 78–90. Gainesville: University Presses of Florida.

Sears, William H.

n.d.   An Investigation of Prehistoric Processes on the Gulf Coastal Plain. Final report submitted to the National Science Foundation. On file, Florida Museum of Natural History, Gainesville.

1951a   *Excavations at Kolomoki, Season I*. University of Georgia Series in Anthropology, No. 2. Athens.

1951b *Excavations at Kolomoki, Season II, Mound E.* University of Georgia Series in Anthropology, No. 3. Athens.

1953   *Excavations at Kolomoki, Seasons III and IV, Mound D.* University of Georgia Series in Anthropology, No. 4. Athens: University of Georgia Press.

1956   *Excavations at Kolomoki: Final Report.* University of Georgia Series in Anthropology, No. 5. Athens: University of Georgia Press.

1982   *Fort Center: An Archaeological Site in the Lake Okeechobee Basin.* Gainesville: University Presses of Florida.

Shetrone, Henry C.

1925   Exploration of the Ginther Mound. The Miessee Mound. *Ohio Archaeological and Historical Quarterly* 34:154–168.

Shogren, Michael G.

1989   *A Limited Testing Program at Four Mound Sites in Greene County, Alabama.* De Soto Working Paper 11. Alabama De Soto Commission. Alabama Museum of Natural History, University of Alabama, Tuscaloosa.

Smith, Bruce D.

1986   Archaeology of the Southeastern United States: From Dalton to de Soto, 10500–500 B.P. *Advances in World Archaeology* 5:1–92.

Squier, E. G., and E. H. Davis

1848   *Ancient Monuments of the Mississippi Valley.* Smithsonian Contributions to Knowledge 1. Washington, D.C.: Smithsonian Institution.

Toth, Alan

1974   *Archaeology and Ceramics at the Marksville Site.* Anthropological Papers 56. Ann Arbor: University of Michigan Museum of Anthropology.

Vescelius, Gary S.

1957   Mound 2 at Marksville. *American Antiquity* 22:416–420.

Walker, Winslow M.

1936   *The Troyville Mounds, Catahoula Parish, Louisiana.* Bulletin 133. Washington, D.C.: Bureau of American Ethnology.

Walthall, John A.

1985   Early Hopewellian Ceremonial Encampments in the South Appalachian Highlands. In *Structure and Process in Southeastern Archaeology,* edited by R. S. Dickens Jr. and H. T. Ward, pp. 243–262. Tuscaloosa: University of Alabama Press.

Webb, William S., and David L. DeJarnette

1942   *An Archaeological Survey of Pickwick Basin in the Adjacent Portions of the States of Alabama, Mississippi, and Tennessee.* Bulletin 129. Washington, D.C.: Bureau of American Ethnology.

Williams, Mark

1992   *Archaeological Investigations of Fortson Mound, Wilkes County, Georgia.* Lamar Institute Publication 3. Watkinsville, Georgia: Lamar Institute.

Williams, Mark, and Jennifer F. Harris

1998   Shrines of the Prehistoric South: Patterning in Middle Woodland Mound

Distribution. In *A World Engraved: Archaeology of the Swift Creek Culture,* edited by Mark Williams and Daniel T. Elliot, pp. 36–47. Tuscaloosa: University of Alabama Press.

Witthoft, John

1949   *Green Corn Ceremonialism in the Eastern Woodlands.* Occasional Contributions 13. Ann Arbor: University of Michigan Museum of Anthropology.

Worth, John

1990   Vertebrate Faunal Analysis for the Walling Site (Ma°50), 1986 Excavations. In *Excavation of the Truncated Mound at the Walling Site: Middle Woodland Culture and Copena in the Tennessee Valley,* by V. J. Knight Jr., pp. 129–144. Report of Investigations 56. Tuscaloosa: Alabama Museum of Natural History, Division of Archaeology, University of Alabama.

12

A CASE OF RITUAL FEASTING
AT THE CAHOKIA SITE

Lucretia S. Kelly

The site of Cahokia is an early Mississippian (A.D. 1050–1350) center located in the American Bottom region of the central Mississippi River floodplain, just east of St. Louis on the northern edge of Mississippian development. The Mississippian cultural tradition (A.D. 1000–1500) extends spatially over portions of the Midwest and Southeast United States (Fig. 12.1) including societies that display distinctive ceramic technology, platform mounds, intensification of agricultural crops, and ranked sociopolitical systems. Cahokia is the largest Mississippian site, with over 100 mounds, and represents the most complex of all Mississippian communities (Emerson 1995; Fowler 1974, 1975, 1978, 1989; Mehrer 1988, 1995; Milner 1990, 1998; Pauketat 1991, 1994).

During the past two decades, much has been written about the nature and

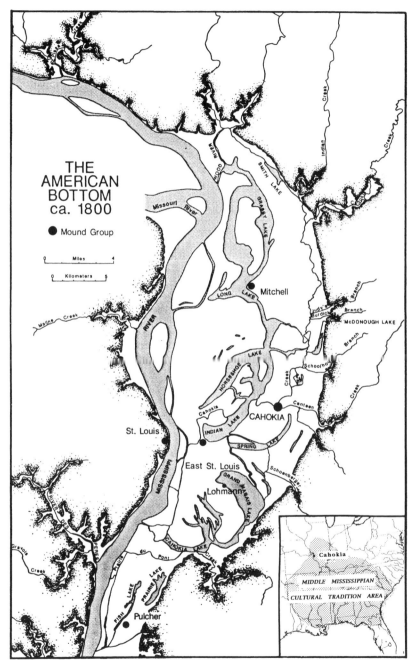

Figure 12.1. The American Bottom region, with inset showing the extent of the Middle Mississippian cultural tradition.

form(s) of political economy associated with Mississippian societies (see Muller 1997 for a discussion). Two dichotomous schools of thought about its structure and function have recently been articulated and termed the "top-down" and "bottom-up" perspectives (Pauketat 1997b; Saitta 1994). In this chapter, I approach Cahokia's early economy from an empirical perspective, emphasizing the analysis of fauna and other classes of material recovered from a large pit at Cahokia designated sub-Mound 51. The faunal assemblage, in particular, provides very specific information on ritual feasting activity. I suggest that investigation of ritual feasting and its integration into the larger body of existing literature about sociopolitical mechanisms can provide finer resolution to questions concerning Cahokia's political economy early in its florescence as a mound center.

CAHOKIA'S SETTLEMENT SYSTEM AND POLITICAL ECONOMY

During the 1970s and 1980s, a large number of sites in the American Bottom were excavated as part of the FAI-270 highway project (Bareis and Porter 1984). Results of these excavations include a highly refined regional chronology (Bareis and Porter 1984; Fig. 12.2), and a better understanding of changes in the regional set-

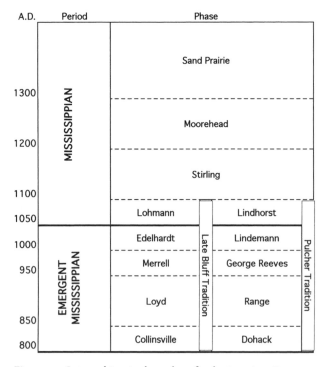

Figure 12.2. Late prehistoric chronology for the American Bottom.

tlement pattern between A.D. 800 and 1100. During the Emergent Mississippian (A.D. 800–1050), regional population aggregated into large nucleated villages (J. Kelly 1992). Beginnings of social ranking appear at this time, and form the roots of Cahokia's future complexity (J. Kelly 1990, 1992; Pauketat 1994).

The initial Mississippian episode (the Lohmann phase, A.D. 1050–1100) is designated by major and rather rapid changes in the regional landscape. Emergent Mississippian populations that were aggregated in large nucleated villages either disperse to small farmsteads and civic/ceremonial nodes, or coalesce into mound centers (Emerson 1995; J. Kelly 1992; Mehrer 1995; Pauketat 1991). At Cahokia itself, there is a five- to tenfold population increase (Pauketat and Lopinot 1997), and status differentiation is evident (Fowler 1989; Pauketat 1994). The creation of the site's plan (Fowler 1973, 1989; J. Kelly 1996, 1997) is centered upon Monks Mound, the Grand Plaza (Holley, Dalan, and Smith 1993; Pauketat and Rees 1996), and several flanking plazas (Fig. 12.3). The Grand Plaza was demarcated as an important area of the site by major earthmoving public-works projects. Recent archaeological investigations in this area have revealed that a meter of clayey deposits overlying a ridge and swale topography were stripped and used for borrow, possibly for the initial construction of Monks Mound (the site's largest mound) to the north. This area was then reclaimed by filling in the swales and raising the plaza to about its premodified level to form a clean and level surface (Dalan 1997; Dalan et al. 1994). This provided a large centralized space to accommodate ritual activities attended by the Cahokia population (Dalan 1997).

There is now fundamental agreement that the Mississippian settlement pattern in the northern American Bottom was hierarchical and that Cahokia was at its center. Other smaller mound centers (with either multiple or single mounds) and numerous nonmound communities that may have served several functions complete a proposed three-tiered settlement hierarchy (Emerson 1995, Finney 1993, Mehrer 1995, Milner 1990). Emerson (1995) believes the lowest tier of nonmound communities can be differentiated from each other by how they may have functioned in the overall regional settlement system. He has identified nodal centers that served specialized political, religious, and economic functions.

Members of the two schools of thought on the development of political economy at Cahokia disagree about how the small farmstead/hamlet entities of the third settlement tier were tied (if at all) to Cahokia or to the smaller mound centers (e.g., about how much regional control Cahokia actually had). Advocates of the top-down perspective (Emerson 1997; Pauketat 1994) view Cahokia's political economy from the theoretical stance of agency. They think that the three-tiered settlement hierarchy was a manifestation and explicit creation of the Cahokia ruling class (Emerson 1997). Elites in the countryside were responsible for production and mobilization of foodstuffs to support the central elite at Cahokia. In

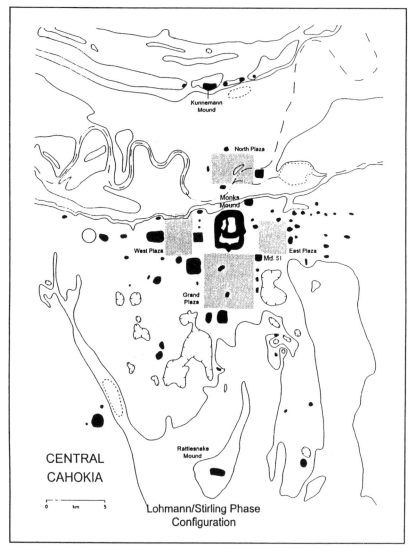

Figure 12.3. Site plan of central Cahokia showing Monks Mound, the Grand Plaza, and flanking plazas.

effect, the Cahokia elite were not leaving the procurement of their subsistence to chance (Emerson 1997).

Those with the bottom-up perspective (Mehrer 1995; Milner 1990, 1998; Muller 1997) view Cahokia's economy from an environmental and functionalist standpoint. They believe the Cahokia settlement system to have been somewhat decentralized and loosely structured. They argue that Cahokia elites would have had only limited, direct influence over the hinterland communities, which are viewed as autonomous, self-sufficient units. However, it is also argued that surplus produced by these farmsteads would have been sent to Cahokia as tribute, but, perhaps on a periodic basis, and may have been a means by which leaders augmented their positions and expanded and reinforced patron/client relationships (Milner 1990, 1998).

SOCIAL AND POLITICAL DIMENSIONS OF FOOD

Tribute or tributary systems are usually considered inherent to chiefdoms such as those of the Mississippian Southeast (Anderson 1994; Carneiro 1981; DePratter 1991; Service 1962; Steponaitis 1978), but, tribute can encompass a variety of items including food, prestige or exotic goods, and labor. In this paper I examine food and its political and social dimensions within a tributary system. The term *tribute,* however, means different things to different people. For instance:

> At one end of the scale we have the complete and equitable reassignment of a village's harvest back to its producers by a chief who is merely a temporary and benign custodian of it [a bottom-up perspective]. At the other end [a top-down perspective] there is enforced appropriation of a part of a society's food supply by a powerful ruler for his own benefit and that of a small ruling elite. (Carneiro 1981:59–60)

Because of the range of meanings, Muller (1997:14) argues that the term should not be used, especially in reference to prestate societies, and instead prefers the use of *prestation.* But, "tribute" is commonly used in the literature as a catchall term for the general mobilization of goods and labor by the elite (Blitz 1993). It can encompass a number of provisioning strategies including gift-giving, ritual feasting, or a collected tax. The term is useful as long as its meaning is defined.

Various models of tribute collection and redistribution have been outlined for Mississippian societies (see Steponaitis 1978; Welch 1991). However, they do not offer much information about what mechanisms governed collections and redistribution (if any). For instance, was tribute collected on a regular basis, was it a type of usury tax (paid for use of land or hunting territories), was it collected for the exclusive use of the elite, or did collected stores of produce serve as insurance against hard times (risk management)? The way one thinks about tribute is usually dependent upon the chiefdom model that one embraces.

However, by using empirical evidence in conjunction with theoretical models, we may be able to identify some of the mechanisms involved in tributary systems or food mobilization, and thus gain a better understanding of the construction of social relations within a society (*sensu* Dietler 1996). The most direct evidence would be the food remains themselves, that is, faunal and floral materials. It is only recently that zooarchaeological and archaeobotanical data have been used to directly address such social issues (see Blitz 1993; Jackson and Scott 1995; Welch and Scarry 1995).

Fortunately, large-scale archaeological excavations, undertaken as part of the massive highway projects mentioned earlier, have generated an enormous amount of zooarchaeological and archaeobotanical data for the American Bottom (Johannessen 1984, 1988, 1993; L. Kelly and Cross 1984; L. Kelly 1997b; Lopinot 1991, 1992, 1994; Rindos and Johannessen 1991; Simon and Parker 1995). This extraordinary biological database can be used to address the role played by the higher-ranked segment of Cahokia's population in food provisioning and possible tributary systems. Was the chiefly class just a temporary caretaker of a village's harvest, holding it for the benefit of all society, or was it coercively appropriating food for the exclusive benefit of the elite? In other words, by examining the way one segment of the population relates to another in the provisioning of food, can we gain a better understanding of the articulation of social relations among the various social segments? To examine alternative hypotheses about tribute at Cahokia, one must take into account several factors regarding the nature of the archaeological evidence, and how food items might fit into a tributary system.

FOOD AS TRIBUTE

For instance, consider fresh meat from game animals (e.g., deer). Unlike domestic animals in other areas of the world, deer may not have made good, regular sources of tribute (Zeder 1996). Acquisition of hunted wild game is unpredictable, especially during certain times of the year. Fresh meat would also be difficult to transport long distances and to stockpile for future use because of spoilage problems (Jackson and Scott 1995). On the other hand, dried meat and skins probably did enter into a tributary system (Zeder 1996). We know these were common tribute items ethnohistorically in the Southeast (Clayton, Knight, and Moore 1993), but animal products in these forms would be almost impossible to detect archaeologically.

It has been argued (Blitz 1993) that maize and other native grain crops may have been difficult to control or redistribute by the elite unless or until they were centrally stockpiled or stored in large quantities. Ethnohistorical information indicates that large granaries were controlled by the chiefs in the Southeast (Clayton, Knight, and Moore 1993; Barker 1992; Smith and Hally 1992). Above-ground granaries are difficult to identify archaeologically, but those that have been recognized at Cahokia are located in domestic or residential areas. They are interpreted as having been communal resources rather than having been under chiefly

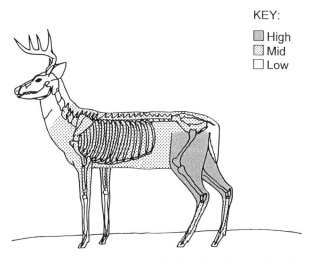

KEY:
▨ High
▥ Mid
☐ Low

Figure 12.4. Portions of deer belonging to the high, mid, and low Food Utility Index (FUI) categories. Reprinted from *Cahokia: Domination and Ideology in the Mississippian World*, edited by T. R. Pauketat and T. E. Emerson, by permission of the University of Nebraska Press, copyright University of Nebraska Press (1997).

control (Collins 1990, 1997; Fritz and Johannessen 1996; Lopinot 1994). It has also been documented ethnohistorically, however, that chiefs' granaries were sometimes located in areas nearer the producers (Smith and Hally 1992) than the chiefs' residences. Therefore, interpreting control solely on location may be problematical (Muller 1997).

ARCHAEOLOGICAL EVIDENCE

For the American Bottom and Cahokia, differential access to animal resources based on status has been investigated by the employment of two different types of faunal studies: taxonomic diversity and body-part distribution of deer, the largest vertebrate species recovered in any abundance from Cahokia (L. Kelly 1997b). Deer body-part studies, particularly those made on assemblages from Cahokia, indicate a flow of meaty portions of deer into the site (L. Kelly 1979, 1997b). However, the studies of faunal assemblages from outlying communities do not yet provide the data necessary to determine whether they were furnishing deer meat to Cahokia. Faunal assemblages from these sites are small, and it is difficult to distinguish faunal refuse resulting from daily subsistence from that resulting from butchering animals to be used as tribute.

Plant products such as shelled maize appear to have been a very important component of tribute ethnohistorically (Clayton, Knight, and Moore 1993; Smith and Hally 1992) and theoretically should be visible in the archaeological record.

However, archaeobotanical evidence for tribute from the American Bottom tends to be equivocal (Lopinot 1997; Pauketat 1997a). The data do not exhibit strong differences among site types and locations, but rather they indicate that the same varieties of crops were grown and eaten in all parts of the region (Lopinot 1997).

There is evidence of agricultural intensification for a suite of native cultigens (knotweed, chenopod, maygrass) and maize (Fritz and Johannessen 1996; Lopinot 1994) in the Emergent Mississippian to Mississippian. And, there is some indication of a decrease in maize kernel-to-cob ratios from the Emergent Mississippian to Mississippian (Lopinot 1994). This has been interpreted as movement of shelled maize from outlying, producing communities to Cahokia (e.g., tribute; Emerson 1995; Esarey and Pauketat 1992; Pauketat 1994). Fritz and Johannessen (1996), however, do not think there is convincing evidence that shelled maize was being consumed in greater quantities by higher-ranked social groups. In fact, stable carbon isotope studies run on high-status, Lohmann-phase burials in Mound 72 at Cahokia indicate high-ranking personages may not have eaten as much corn as other Mississippians (Buikstra, Rose, and Milner 1994).

Because the database for the American Bottom area is so large, Fritz (personal communication, 1998) dismisses the argument that preservational problems associated with archaeobotanical materials may obscure the fact that maize and/or cultivated native crops were part of a tributary system of foodstuffs being utilized differentially along class lines. Fritz and Johannessen (1996) do not see evidence for chiefly manipulation or centralized political control of agricultural surplus, especially maize. There is evidence, however, that other kinds of plants—such as tobacco and red cedar—may have had more restricted use by ritual specialists (Fritz and Johannessen 1996; Lopinot 1994; Lopinot and Woods 1993).

The above discussion demonstrates that the zooarchaeological and the archaeobotanical evidence from the American Bottom are somewhat equivocal when used to examine broad questions concerning food tribute. If the focus is narrowed, however, it may be possible to identify tribute or food-provisioning mechanisms that are more visible in the archaeological record. This, in turn, may help elucidate broader questions regarding the articulation of social relations. Recent analysis of material from the sub-Mound 51 pit is providing strong evidence for large public events held during Cahokia's development that may be linked to one such mechanism: ritual feasting.

THE CAHOKIA EXAMPLE: SUB-MOUND 51

An extraordinary assemblage of cultural material was recovered in the late 1960s from a large, prehistoric borrow pit, revealed under Mound 51 when that mound was removed by the owner for fill (Chmurny 1973). It is located 175 m to the southeast of Monks Mound, the site's largest mound, and is on the northeast edge of the Grand Plaza (Fig. 12.3). The dirt removed from this borrow pit was presumably used in the construction of nearby mounds, possibly even in the early stages of Monks Mound, and for the leveling of the Grand Plaza. After the pit ceased functioning as a borrow pit, it was left open for several months before being rapidly filled (possibly within one to three years) by a sequence of at least seven distinct depositional episodes or zones (Fig. 12.5; Chmurny 1973; Pauketat 1997b). Mound 51 was subsequently built in two stages on this reclaimed surface (Chmurny 1973).

Salvage excavations of the sub-mound pit were conducted between 1966 and 1970 (Bareis 1975). Because only a portion of the pit was excavated, its exact shape and horizontal dimensions are unknown, but excavations did indicate a minimum north-south dimension of 53 m, a width of more than 20 m, and a depth of 3 m. Five 3-by-3 m units were excavated between 1966 and 1968. The first unit, dug in 1966, was not excavated by cultural zone but by arbitrary levels. The four additional units, excavated in 1967 and 1968, were dug by cultural strata. One of the four units was only partially excavated (Pauketat 1997b).

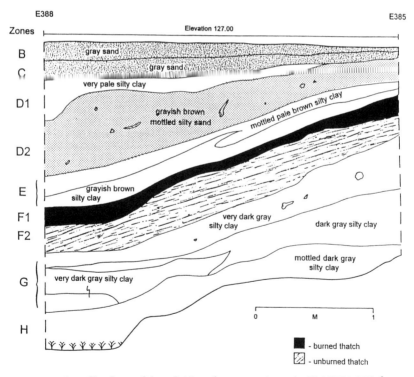

Figure 12.5. A profile of one of the sub-Mound 51 excavation units (S53 E385–388) showing the various zones.

The preservation of organic materials from this pit is unparalleled for this area of the Midwest U.S., with a portion of the plant remains being preserved in an uncarbonized state. Optimum preservational conditions resulted from an anaerobic environment created by the rapid burial of the deposits, which were subsequently sealed beneath the mound. William Chmurny analyzed a large sample of the organic material recovered from the 1966 and 1967 excavation seasons for his 1973 dissertation. More recently, very fine-grained analyses of additional samples were undertaken as part of Timothy Pauketat's Early Cahokia Project.[1]

Though it is important to interpret the data from this pit in its entirety (i.e., from all classes of material), in this paper I focus on the faunal remains. A full accounting of the various analyses performed by all the participants of this project has not yet been made, but preliminary results have been presented.[2]

FAUNAL ANALYSES: CAHOKIA AND THE AMERICAN BOTTOM

In order to interpret the faunal assemblage from sub-Mound 51, one must compare it to faunal patterns of general subsistence for the American Bottom during Emergent Mississippian and early Mississippian periods. Faunal data from American Bottom sites indicate that Emergent Mississippian populations were self-sufficient, relying on faunal resources in proximity to their settlements to meet their animal-protein requirements (Kelly and Cross 1984). They were apparently directing their faunal exploitation away from the procurement of large animals, such as deer, to smaller animals such as marsh birds, medium-sized mammals, and fish (L. Kelly 1990, 1997b). This localized exploitation pattern is also present at Cahokia. However, there is a major difference in deer body-part distribution[3] for the Emergent Mississippian occupations at Cahokia. Elements representing the higher-utility[4] portions of the deer are represented in much higher proportions than they are at other Emergent Mississippian sites (L. Kelly 1997b). The Cahokia percentages indicate that complete deer carcasses were not brought to the site. This may be a reflection of Cahokia's distance (4–5 km) from the uplands adjacent to the American Bottom where deer would be most abundant.[5] Because of this distance, I proposed that only the higher-utility portions of the deer were transported to Cahokia (L. Kelly 1979).

A rather dramatic shift in faunal composition is observed at Cahokia during the initial Mississippian, Lohmann phase and is interpreted as resulting from political and social changes. The relative quantity of mammals jumps from about 10 percent NISP (number of identified specimens) in the Emergent Mississippian, Edelhardt phase to about 67 percent NISP in the Mississippian, Lohmann phase. The main reason for this increase is the concomitant increase in deer remains (6 percent NISP to 63 percent NISP; Fig. 12.6). Fish remains decrease from 77 percent to 10 percent NISP and bird remains gradually increase (L. Kelly 1997b).

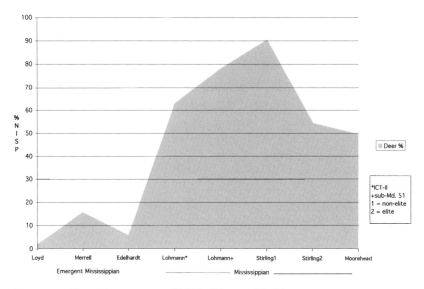

Figure 12.6. Change in percentage of NISP of deer at Cahokia.

Deer body-part representation does not change greatly, however. Deer were apparently still being procured at a distance from the site, but deer meat was seemingly making up a larger portion of the faunal diet. A possible explanation for this increase in venison is discussed below.

Unfortunately, the bulk of the faunal data from both the Emergent Mississippian and Lohmann phases at Cahokia are from non-elite domestic contexts. No Lohmann phase assemblages from purely elite contexts are yet known. There are assemblages from the subsequent Stirling phase (A.D. 1100–1200), however, that may represent elite subsistence refuse (L. Kelly 1997b). These indicate that deer may have been distributed along class lines with the higher-status segment of the population receiving more hindquarters; but it cannot be determined whether this was also the case in the earlier Lohmann phase.

SUB-MOUND 51 FAUNAL ASSEMBLAGE

Before analysis of the material recovered from the sub-Mound 51 pit was undertaken, it was postulated that it represented elite subsistence and craft-production refuse (Pauketat et al. 1993). However, my immediate impression of the sub-Mound 51 faunal assemblage was that it was very different from Mississippian assemblages elsewhere in the American Bottom and from Cahokia itself, and that impression was confirmed by subsequent study.

I have examined a faunal sample not studied by Chmurny that was recovered from the 1967 and 1968 excavations. Only well-provenienced remains in my sample were identified. As noted above, part of the faunal debris recovered from the 1966 and 1967 excavation seasons was analyzed by William Chmurny for his 1973 dissertation. As far as can be determined, no overlap exists in the materials included in the present study and those of Chmurny.

In his dissertation, Chmurny reported the faunal material as a single unit, rather than by depositional zones. He did this because different sample sizes were recovered, and because he was addressing ecological questions rather than social issues, so keeping the material separated by zone was not thought to be necessary. Some notes and tables not presented in his dissertation included information by zone, but he does not provide provenience data other than zone designations nor is the excavation year given. I do not know what criteria he may have used to determine zone designations for the 1966 material. Hence, I report his findings by zone, but cannot verify the accuracy of that information.

For the present discussion, I present data from only one zone—D2—(Fig. 12.5) a very rich provenience unit in the upper half of the pit. Faunal remains were recovered from all zones of the sub-mound pit (Fig. 12.7) in varying amounts, but the majority of sub-Mound 51 faunal remains (D2 NISP=8666) was recovered from zone D2 (Fig. 12.7). This zone also yielded an array of Lohmann phase exotics and craft goods, in addition to items that can best be termed "sumptuary," such as crystals, exotic arrowheads, axehead debitage, and sherds from engraved and painted vessels (Pauketat 1997b). Unusual or unique faunal remains that can be placed in this sumptuary category include a drilled alligator tooth (the most

zones	D2		G		H		F	
assemblage	K	C	K	C	K	C	K	C
Mammals								
NISP	1553	2847	583	638	215	250	295	392
# taxa	3	5	3	5	2	2	1	3
% NISP deer	99.7	99.2	99.5	98.6	98.6	99.6	100.0	99.0
Birds								
NISP	206	1363	25	363	30	109	2	327
# taxa	5	19	4	14	7	11	1	8
Fish								
NISP	873	1549	261	1359	27	152	2	1037
# taxa	9	9	7	7	4	5	1	8
Reptile								
NISP	-	1						
# taxa	-	1						
Not ident.								
NISP	274	-	175	-	44	-	25	-

K = Kelly's Assemblage
C = Chmurny's Assemblage

Figure 12.7. Summary of faunal materials from sub-Mound 51 pit.

unusual faunal item in zone D2), a bone harpoon, a bone earspool, and marine shell beads and spoons. Bone harpoons and marine shell beads were also part of the display of exotic goods recovered from an elite Lohmann phase burial in Mound 72.

The deer bone stood out immediately from all other assemblages that I have studied. It made up 99.7 percent (NISP=1253/1257) of the identified mammalian remains in the assemblage I identified (Fig. 12.7). Elements with low structural densities—vertebrae, innominates, and scapulae—that are fragmentary or nonexistent in many assemblages, were found relatively whole in sub-Mound 51. About 72 percent of such elements recovered from zone D2 are half or more than half complete. Many elements with unfused epiphyses were recovered in such close association with their epiphyses that they can be readily refitted. There are a number of deer bones from my zone D2 sample that appear to articulate, particularly sections of thoracic and lumbar vertebrae. Chmurny (1973) noted similar articulations in his assemblage. A number of bones from the forelimb are whole or nearly so, including two radii, two humeri, and three ulnae. The femora and tibiae do have broken shafts, but they have not been shattered. Long bone fragments are not abundant. Chmurny (1973) suggests the breakage of the hindlimb long bones in his sample is a product of butchering rather than of marrow extraction, and I believe this to be true for my sample as well.

It should be noted that FUIs (Food Utility Index) for the sub-Mound 51 deer are figured on percentage of minimum numbers of skeletal elements (MNE). Skeletal element here is a complete element, and, where applicable, rights and lefts are summed. I calculated deer FUIs for Chmurny's data, even though I am not completely confident about his zone designations. The MNE calculations may not be entirely accurate either, because I used the data tables Chmurny constructed rather than visual observations of the bones themselves. But even with these potential problems, the results are remarkable. The deer FUIs calculated from Chmurny's data were almost identical to those for the assemblages that I studied. Each zone is similar regardless of the size of the sample. This indicates that the cuts of meat or portions of deer utilized were consistent throughout the deposit.

The articulation and completeness of many bones probably reflect the manner in which the meat was brought to the area, and the way it was prepared for consumption. Primary butchering debris, such as skull fragments and the lower limb bones of metapodials, phalanges, and carpals, are almost nonexistent in the assemblage I analyzed, except for several carpals. These appear to articulate with one of the radii and may have been riders on a forelimb. Chmurny's assemblage does contain a few loose teeth, phalanges, and metapodials, but they represent only 3 percent of his zone D2 MNEs. It seems reasonable to conclude that the meat was brought to the area in large or bulk cuts after having been initially butchered elsewhere.

On the basis of large numbers of blowfly pupal remains and flesh-eating bee-tles recovered from the sub-mound pit (Elias and Pauketat 1997), it appears at least some of the bones were deposited in the pit with raw, soft tissue still adher-ing to them. These insects feed almost exclusively on decaying flesh and are un-likely to colonize cooked meat. This suggests that the meat was cut from the bones prior to cooking. Cutting meat from the bone prior to cooking would not seem to be an efficient way to maximize the amount of meat prepared and may suggest that meat was plentiful. Another indication that meat was in good supply is that most of the bones were not processed for the recovery of marrow or bone grease. The easiest method of cooking meat removed from the bone would be boiling, possibly in stews. It is also possible that the meat being stripped from the bones was dried for future use. In either case, the bones would be left relatively intact when deposited.

The bird and fish components of the present D2 assemblage are also unique in comparison to other Cahokia and American Bottom assemblages. In contrast to the mammals, they differ in several ways from the assemblage Chmurny ana-lyzed. His assemblages were much larger and the birds were more varied (Fig. 12.7). Only five taxa of birds were identified from my zone D2 assemblage (Fig. 12.8). This is quite low when compared to other assemblages at Cahokia or in the American Bottom—usually twice as many are identified—whether from elite or non-elite contexts. The other unusual aspect is that over half my zone D2 bird re-mains represent swan, a bird not frequently recovered, but there are no wings represented among the swan elements present. Chmurny's assemblage also con-

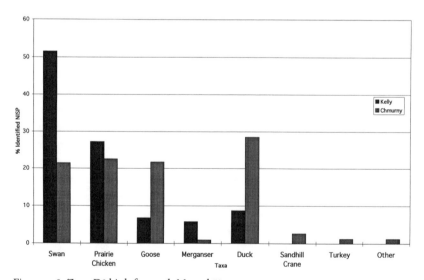

Figure 12.8. Zone D2 birds from sub-Mound 51.

tained a large number of swan elements, representing 21 percent of his identifiable bird NISP. But he does not report wing elements for this assemblage. Hence, it appears that the swans were being processed, at least in part, for their wings.

The other avian taxa I identified from zone D2 include Canada goose, common merganser, mallard, and prairie chicken. Prairie chicken remains at 28 percent make up a relatively large proportion of the total. Chmurny's assemblage contained 22.5 percent prairie chicken (Fig. 12.8). Prairie chicken remains recovered from Mississippian occupations at Cahokia have been previously identified only from later Stirling phase, elite contexts. They were also noted in non-elite residential contexts at Cahokia during the Emergent Mississippian, however. It is possible these birds increased in value for some reason or acquired some symbolic meaning, making them attainable only by the elite segment of the population during the Mississippian.

Goose and mallard are represented by low percentages in my assemblage (15 percent combined). However, for Chmurny's D2 assemblage, ducks and geese make up almost 50 percent of the identified NISP (Fig. 12.8). His sample contained nine other taxa of duck besides mallard, and includes pintail, gadwall, green- and blue-winged teals, shoveler, woodduck, redhead, ring-necked or lesser scaup, and ruddy duck. Other taxa identified include coot, sandhill crane, turkey, and perching birds.

It is difficult to evaluate the differences in sample sizes and number of taxa present between the bird assemblages in the present analysis and those of Chmurny's. They could be due to significant depositional variation within the zones, or could be a result of postexcavation factors such as mixing of materials from various zones that may be reflected in Chmurny's sample. Nevertheless, swan and prairie chicken make up the majority of avian remains from both assemblages.

Fish assemblages from American Bottom sites are typically large and quite varied, with as many as twenty-five or more taxa represented. In contrast, the sub-Mound 51 zone D2 assemblage I examined (Fig. 12.7) is small (NISP=873), has relatively few taxa (nine), and is represented by large individuals. This in part may be because I analyzed only material recovered from hand excavation. It is possible that small fish bone was missed, creating a bias toward larger fish remains. I examined bulk samples that were recently dry fine-screened in the paleoethnobotany lab at Washington University, however, and although some small fish bones were observed, they were not abundant, and in fact they could represent the stomach contents of some of the larger fish.

The assemblage I studied consisted mostly of buffalo sucker (79 percent), followed by gar (Fig. 12.9). The remaining taxa identified from zone D2 include members of the catfish family, freshwater drum, and bass. Chmurny reports a

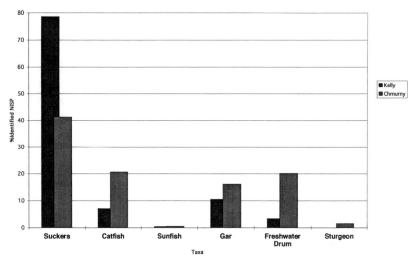

Figure 12.9. Zone D2 fish from sub-Mound 51.

lower percentage of suckers than I found, but they still represent the most abundant family. He noted higher percentages of bullheads, gar, and freshwater drum, and also reported sturgeon. More taxa of fish from the sub-Mound 51 deposits represent large river fish than backwater slough varieties. The latter are generally more common in fish assemblages from the American Bottom, including Cahokia.

There were no reptile or amphibian remains in any of the sub-mound pit assemblages I analyzed. The drilled alligator tooth was the only reptile remain Chmurny reports for zone D2.

INTERPRETATION OF THE SUB-MOUND 51 ASSEMBLAGE

The faunal remains recovered from the sub-Mound 51 pit, especially those from zone D2, differ in significant ways from other Cahokia assemblages that are interpreted as household refuse, elite or non-elite. Most of us involved in the analysis of the sub-mound material now agree that the contents were the product of large-scale Cahokian events (Fritz 1997; L. Kelly 1997a; Pauketat 1997b). The sumptuary items of crystals, exotic arrowheads, axehead debitage, and sherds from engraved and painted vessels, listed earlier, reinforce the interpretation that elite personages were associated with the represented activities. But non-elite participation is indicated as well by the presence of domestic cooking vessels (Pauketat 1997b) and the domestic variety of subsistence plants (Fritz 1997). What is believed to be represented here are public ritual and feasting activities attended by all segments of the community.

The faunal refuse from sub-Mound 51 has many of the signatures proposed by others as representing feasting. There is a relatively low taxonomic diversity; it contains high-yielding meat species from all classes represented; bulk cuts of meat can be identified, as well as bulk cooking, probably by boiling; little butchering debris is present (Jackson and Scott 1995). Bones are not completely broken or disarticulated, and bones are present in great quantities in a single deposit (Hayden 1996) that was laid down in a short period of time.

The contents of this pit are perceived to be, in large part, the result of feasting preparation rather than its aftermath. The material discarded in the pit may be derived from a staging area where the different ingredients for a ritual feast were being gathered, prepared, or manufactured. For example, the faunal remains indicate that deer meat was being stripped from the bones. The wings of swans were being disarticulated, removed, and perhaps curated for future use. Large fish were being filleted. The manufacture of quartz crystal arrowheads, basalt axe-heads, and exotic chert tools also appears to be taking place in the area as evidenced from the recovered quartz crystal, basalt, and chert debitage. In addition, there is evidence that paints and pigments were being mixed and painted onto ceramic vessels after they had been fired (Pauketat 1997b). A large number of un-carbonized squash seeds may be the result of the preparation or cleaning out of the squash fruits. Fritz reports that squash seeds in some of the bulk samples she examined were "stuck together and covered with material as if they represented the contents of fruits that had been scooped out and discarded, the way most of us treat jack-o-lantern seeds" (1997:5).

Chiefly involvement appears to be evident in the acquisition of some of the animals represented. The consistent body-part representation for deer in this pit indicates that the portion of the deer brought to the area was prescribed. This may suggest that hunters attached to the hosting group, or members of the hosting group themselves, procured the meat (see DuPratz in Swanton 1911). This suggestion may be further strengthened by the fact that basically only one kind of mammal is present in the deposit. A variety of mammals and a more random sample of deer parts would be expected if commoners brought in portions of their hunt.

Seeman (1979), in his study of Ohio Hopewell ritual feasting, hypothesizes that meat, particularly venison, was a vital resource in maize farming societies in the Eastern Woodlands. As such, it may have been ritually regulated. Applying Seeman's argument to the American Bottom, one might conclude that, as a result of crop intensification and increased population, the demand for tillable and habitable floodplain land may have diminished prime habitat areas for deer and other wildlife, or at least pushed them farther away from Cahokia.[6] This may have increased the value of deer meat in particular, and enhanced its procurement and consumption in ritual contexts. Helms believes hunting can be equated with long-distance trade and skilled craft activities. Hunting is a "strongly ritualized activity involving acquisitional and transformative dealings with outside powers (e.g., supernatural masters of animals) and since success in hunting frequently is taken as evidence of supernatural approval and support," it is often associated with the elite (Helms 1992:189). Chiefly ritualization of deer hunting could possibly account, in part, for the large increase in deer remains at Cahokia at the beginning of the Mississippian.

Historically, ritual was also involved with the serving of deer. For instance, the Menomini (Douglas 1976) used red cedar to render parts of the deer safe to eat. Without the ritual precaution, the deer would remain supernaturally charged. High frequencies of red cedar branchlets along with moderate amounts of tobacco seeds were recovered from zone D2 of the sub-Mound 51 pit (Fritz 1997). There are also numerous ethnographic references to tobacco being used for purification in ritual contexts.

It is probable that the birds represented in this pit were eaten, but it is more likely that they were primarily used for their feathers. Birds were imbued with symbolism, being representations of the Upper World in Southeastern Indian cosmology (Hudson 1976; Jackson and Scott 1995; Swanton 1946). Skins and feathers of birds, such as mallards, cranes, herons, owls, hawks, were used for ornamental clothing and headdresses, as well as used in ceremony (Swanton 1946). Swan feathers seem to have been particularly important in the ritual aspect of feasting, as ethnohistorically documented. As an example, during the Winnebago Thunderbird feast, the host scatters swan feathers in the lodge and wears them on his head (Radin 1990). Swan feathers have also been mentioned as important in Southeast Indian culture, and in many instances they were associated with persons of rank (DuPratz 1972; Swanton 1946). For instance, in an account by Adair of a Chickasaw green corn ceremony (DePratter 1991:62), he describes the rekindling of the sacred fire. The priest selected special wood chips and used a fire drill to start the fire. The flame was fanned by a swan's wing. DePratter believes when chiefdoms were still in existence, it would have been the chiefs who would have rekindled the fire because of their descent from the sun.

Unlike the mammals, a variety of bird species is represented in the sub-Mound 51 pit, especially in Chmurny's assemblage. This may indicate that the types of birds furnished for the feast were not prescribed, different segments of the population may have procured them, or a variety of symbolic meanings were attached to a wide range of bird species.

Fish are not generally considered to be animals of as high value as hunted animals (Kent 1989), but this would vary regionally (for instance, fish were highly valued in Northwest Coast societies). Rees (1997) found fish were rated highly enough to be given as tribute ethnohistorically in the central Mississippi river valley region of the interior Southeast. Larger fish (Scott and Jackson 1995) and those difficult to capture may have had increased value. In the sub-Mound 51 pit, the remains of larger-sized river fish that are more difficult to catch were recovered in much higher quantities than the smaller, more easily obtainable backwater slough varieties.

Seeman (1979) claims meat was the principal food consumed at mortuary feasts in Hopewell times. Unfortunately, ethnohistoric accounts of feasts in the Southeast generally do not state what foods were served. It would seem logical that different foods might be served at different feasts depending on the season of the year the feast was held (see DuPratz 1972 for description of monthly feasts held among the Natchez). Deer would have been the primary source of meat at the feast(s) represented by the sub-Mound 51 faunal assemblage. The season of the year represented by the faunal remains in this pit can only be suggested at this time. Tooth eruption cannot be used, because no skulls or mandibles were recovered, and epiphyseal fusion cannot give the fine-grained information needed (Purdue 1983). The availability of deer was at its peak in the fall and early winter (September–December; Rue 1997; B. Smith 1975). Swans and other waterfowl would be at their peak abundance during the spring migrations in March and fall migrations in October–November (Bent 1962). The fall swan migration and prime deer-hunting season would have coincided. The bones were deposited during warm weather because large numbers of insects were also recovered. Based on this information, it is most likely that the feasting activity represented by the faunal remains from zone D2 of sub-Mound 51 took place in the early fall before the weather turned cold. Late summer and fall would correspond to the time Swanton (1946:256) indicates the greatest feasts and ceremonies were held in the Southeast. These would include feasts of the first fruits and would be a time when the maximum amount of food would be available.

The extraordinary preservation of materials from the sub-Mound 51 pit has allowed a rare opportunity to recover many ingredients resulting from a large public gathering at Cahokia. The contents and context of this pit provide one of the most unequivocal data sets for ritual feasting recovered from a Mississippian site. The faunal remains indicate that food played a very important part in the event(s) represented, and that many of the animals were used because of the symbolic meaning they carried. This may also be true for the other material classes recovered.[7] The pit contents seem to reflect events orchestrated by hosts of elevated social status to convey particular messages to the attendees, including commoners.

FEASTING: A MECHANISM OF TRIBUTE
AND SOCIAL INTEGRATION

Ritual and feasting have a long history in the Eastern Woodlands, dating back to at least the Middle Woodland period (100 B.C.–300 A.D.; Blitz 1993; Seeman 1979; Styles and Purdue 1991). Blitz (1993) has very effectively demonstrated how both ritual and feasting were manifested in Mississippian chiefdoms to the south of Cahokia, but feasts have not been emphasized in sociopolitical development at Cahokia (Emerson 1997; J. Kelly 1996). The sub-Mound 51 material allows us to focus our attention on the role large, public ritual feasting events may have played in Cahokia's history.

Ritual feasting can be considered a mechanism by which food was mobilized to the main center (DePratter 1991), and it adds a new dimension to discussions of tribute. It must be understood, however, that feasts were not the only mechanism involved in food tribute, and the functions of feasts go far beyond food mobilization.

It has been shown that the feast represented by the sub-Mound 51 material was a public event with both commoners and higher-ranked individuals in attendance. This would indicate that the chiefs as hosts were (re)distributing food to the populace, rather than being the sole beneficiary of it. It is also evident that at least some of the foods (e.g., deer) were furnished or prescribed by the chiefly class. Whether the distribution or "sharing" of the food was equitable cannot be determined. Because chiefs were hosting the event(s), based on the location of the pit, and may have been determining what was being served, it could not be termed a purely "potluck" affair (Muller 1997). Therefore, this form of tribute collection would seem to fall somewhere between the two ends of the tributary scale—equitable reassignment, and enforced appropriation of food—and, thus, between the perspectives expressed by proponents of the top-down and bottom-up schools of Mississippian political economy. Obviously, both schools of thought could incorporate feasts into their formulations. There were most likely a multitude of different feasting events, big and small, taking place throughout year in the Cahokia region. For this discussion, only the large public-type feast represented by the empirical evidence from sub-Mound 51 is considered.

Feasts of this type would have solved several of the problems previously mentioned in regards to food being part of a tributary system. They would have afforded a reason to transship large quantities of food to the center in a short period of time. This would solve the spoilage problem for meat. If grain was not to be stored for long periods of time, granaries may not have been built, at least ones that could be detected archaeologically. To mobilize the labor force for the collection and preparation of the amount of food necessary to feed a large public gathering, superior managerial ability as dictated by tradition would be needed by the hosts. The feast would therefore serve as a means for the hosting individual or group to gain (or maintain) prestige by displaying managerial skills and economic superiority. Thus, large, public ritual feasts such as that represented by sub-Mound 51, served functions besides food mobilization that define broader social articulations within the developing Cahokian society.

Feasts would also be a venue whereby individuals or groups sanctified their positions within the population at large by establishing their connections to gods or ancestors (Dietler 1996; Friedman 1984). Social change could be achieved through the ritual and ideological realm by consensus, a feature of kin-based societies such as Cahokia (Blitz 1993). The top and bottom segments of society, as well as those residing at the mound centers and at outlying communities, were linked by kinship ties, a point often forgotten when political economy is discussed. As noted by Knight (1990:19), commoners and nobles were tied together by kinship in webs of rights and obligations. Kinship rights and obligations could be, at least partially, operationalized through ritual feasts.

The spatial layout of Mississippian Cahokia reflects the way in which the society was organized socially, politically, and ideologically. It is an elaboration or embellishment of principles that extend back to the Emergent Mississippian, when the beginnings of social ranking can be seen (J. Kelly 1990). The early plan for Cahokia utilized the cardinal directions and incorporated the principles of centrality, quadrilateralism, and dualism that were so important to the Mississippian worldview (J. Kelly 1996). The construction of Monks Mound and the central ritual spaces (plazas) flanked by smaller mounds is closely linked with the ideology of the dominant social group. It is argued that leading kinsmen, to sanctify their elevated social and ideological position, co-opted a long-standing sacred symbol, the mound, by placing their structures on top of them (Knight 1986; Steponaitis 1986:386). The public plazas next to these mounds served as focal points or arenas for public gatherings including chief-sponsored ritual and feasting activity (Blitz 1993; Smith and Williams 1994). The deep-rooted sacredness of these areas can be observed in the maintenance of these areas over many generations.

The labor needed for mound building could have been effectively mobilized through feasts. The mounds at Cahokia were enlarged on a continuous and seemingly periodic basis (Knight 1986; Pauketat 1993), and therefore may not have required a large, centrally coordinated labor force (Dietler 1996; Lindauer and Blitz 1997; Muller 1997). Mound enlargement was probably accomplished in connection with rites of renewal and intensification and chiefly succession (Blitz 1993; Knight 1986). Labor for large-scale projects, such as the leveling of the Grand Plaza, may also have been coordinated through feasts. The resulting monument or sacred space, beyond having immense cultural significance, would be "a conspicuous advertisement of the scale of labor capable of being mobilized" (Dietler 1996:105).

Through ritual and competitive feasting (Hayden 1990, 1996), ranks of social inequity within Mississippian Cahokia may have been formalized. One lineage of the American Bottom population may have been able, over time, to accumulate symbolic capital and social credit (Dietler 1996) substantial enough for it to affect the behavior of the rest of the population (Drennan 1993). Blitz argues that ritual acts can support the status quo or can serve as a force for social change. "Individuals do not merely react to the social idiom of ritual but continually create, alter, reinterpret, or manipulate its information content with dramatic results" (Blitz 1993:23). This would have been a noncoercive but very effective way of establishing who was in charge and why, and a means by which all could participate and benefit. In this latter respect, ritual feasts would have a socially integrating effect by promoting community solidarity and achieving a more homogenous form of Cahokian Mississippian.

CONCLUSION

The sub-Mound 51 material provides the best evidence to date for the occurrence of large ritual feasts at Cahokia. Quantities of deer bone representing uniform bulk cuts of meat in conjunction with sumptuary items of crystals, engraved and painted pottery sherds, finely made chert projectiles, and axehead debris composed part of the debris recovered from the pit located within the sacred precinct of the site. These materials indicate elite involvement, if not actual hosting, of a major feasting event. But, the sheer volume of debris along with domestic cooking vessels and common plants indicate the attendance of the general populace. The ritual activity that accompanied the feast included the use of swans, tobacco, red cedar, and squash.

The specific event cannot be determined, but it appears to have occurred in the late summer or early fall. Historically, within the southeastern United States, feasts and ceremonies connected with food harvesting and world renewal such as the widespread Green Corn Ceremony (Swanton 1946; Witthoft 1949) were held at this time of the year. The sub-Mound 51 material represents only one type of communal ceremonial event. It is presumed that many types of large community-based and smaller household rituals and feasts would have taken place at Cahokia and the surrounding region. It is important that other examples are identified archaeologically. Different types should have different archaeological signatures (see Jackson and Scott 1995).

The roles of large ritual feasts in early Cahokian society may not be able to be specifically ascertained based on current data and methods, but several possibilities can be offered based on our knowledge of how feasts functioned ethnohistorically in the southeastern United States and ethnographically in other parts of the world. It can be hypothesized that at Cahokia, large feasting events, such as that represented by the sub-Mound 51 material, were a means to integrate the Cahokia community or region. Evidence suggests they were more than a "potluck" gathering of the general populace (*sensu* Milner and Muller). Large public feasting events likely provided articulation and coordination between the center and outlying communities and between the various ranked segments of the population. It appears Cahokia and its hinterland were not totally autonomous nor was the hinterland directly dominated by Cahokia at this time.

It can be further postulated that highly ranked individuals may have been attempting to solidify their more favorable and influential roles within a prescribed social order through the hosting of large, conspicuous ritual feasts. Whether conscious negotiation of a new Cahokian political order (*sensu* Pauketat 1997b) was taking place is difficult to determine. However over time, the more prominent Cahokian lineages that had been able to accrue a large amount of social credit and capital (*sensu* Dietler 1996) from past ritual, feasting events may have been able to advantageously mobilize the growing Lohmann phase population for mound building, plaza leveling, and the provisioning of large quantities of food, thus effecting changes and elevating the Cahokian sociopolitical system to a more complex level. A continued effort to identify and study remains from other feasting events should allow this interpretation of political economy and social relations at Cahokia to be refined.

Discussions of ritual activity for the American Bottom region have recently become more frequent (Emerson 1997; Kelly 1996), however, because evidence for large ritual feasts has not been previously identified at Cahokia, the role of such socioreligious activity has not been a major component of the sociopolitical models proposed for the site. The sub-Mound 51 material now provides evidence for a mechanism, ritual feasting, that helps explain some of the dynamics associated with the sociopolitical system of early Cahokia. It draws our attention away from the extremes previously characterized as the top-down and bottom-up models, to a more central position and one more in line with the community-based manner in which many Native American societies functioned historically. Rituals and feasts have been and still are an integral part of Native American society.

ACKNOWLEDGMENTS

I would like to thank Tim Pauketat, University of Illinois, for including me in his NSF-funded Early Cahokia Project. The opportunity to study a faunal assemblage such as that from sub-Mound 51 is a zooarchaeologist's dream. I would like to thank Karli White and Terry Martin of the Illinois State Museum for giving me access to the comparative osteology collections in order to identify some of the specimens. I would like to acknowledge the Cahokia Mounds Museum Society for providing support for part of the sub-Mound 51 faunal analysis. John Kelly graciously gave of his time to draft two of the figures. Several people, including Fiona Marshall, Gayle Fritz, Patty Jo Watson, David Browman, and John Kelly, all of Washington University, read and gave constructive criticisms of various drafts of this paper. I would also like to thank the anonymous reviews for their helpful suggestions. I am, however, solely responsible for any mistakes or inaccuracies.

NOTES

1. Support for the sub-Mound 51 portion of Tim Pauketat's Early Cahokia Project was provided by National Science Foundation (SBR-9305404). Support was also provided to the author for further faunal analysis of the sub-Mound 51 remains by the Cahokia Mounds Museum Society.

2. Preliminary analytical results were presented at the 54th Southeastern Conference in Baton Rouge, LA, Nov. 5–8, 1997 in a symposium entitled "New Evidence of Early Cahokian Provisions and Rituals" and a co-authored journal article is forthcoming.

3. The study of body-part distribution must be undertaken cautiously. Many factors, cultural and noncultural, can play roles in what body parts form an assemblage (Klein 1989; Lyman 1984; Marshall and Pilgrim 1991). Noncultural taphonomic factors such as weathering, trampling, and animal gnawing do not appear to have significantly affected the composition of the Cahokia assemblages, however. The consistent pattern at Cahokia throughout its occupational history is a high proportion of those parts of the deer that have low structural density (i.e., are thin and fragile such as scapulae) and a very low proportion of some bones (e.g., metapodials) with high structural density, a pattern that is not density-mediated. Therefore, a cultural explanation is more likely for most of the assemblages' compositions.

4. As a convenient way of illustrating the relationship between food utility and deer body part distribution, I have employed Purdue's (Purdue, Styles, and Masulis 1989) adjusted Food Utility Index (FUI) categories of high, mid, and low. These are based on Metcalfe and Jones's (1988) continuous FUI variable but emphasize the extremes of the FUI spectrum where human behavior may be less variable. Figure 12.4 illustrates which portions of the deer are considered to belong to the low, mid, and high FUI categories.

5. Deer would not have been overly abundant in the floodplain near Cahokia because of lack of preferred habitat. The area around Cahokia was mostly wetlands and prairie (Lopinot 1991; White et al. 1984). The highest density of deer would have occurred in the bluff edge zone and the adjacent uplands that contained an extensive oak/hickory woodland zone (Halls 1984; B. Smith 1975).

6. It could be argued, however, that the increasing land under crop cultivation would increase edge habitats that might attract more deer.

7. Because several types of squashes are represented by many seeds (>3,000) throughout the sub-Mound 51 deposit, Fritz (1997) believes squash may have been a ritually significant plant. This evidence lends support to an earlier interpretation (Emerson 1982; Prentice 1986) that squash (cucurbits) may have had particular significance in fertility-related rituals. This earlier interpretation is based on a Mississippian, Stirling phase figurine recovered from the BBB Motor site. This figurine depicts a woman

kneeling on the back of a serpent with a hoe embedded in its back. The tail of the serpent splits into squash vines and fruits identified as *Cucurbita argyrosperma* (Fritz 1994) that climb the woman's back.

REFERENCES

Anderson, D. G.
  1994   *The Savannah River Chiefdoms: Political Change in the Late Prehistoric Southeast.* Tuscaloosa: University of Alabama Press.
Bareis, C. J.
  1975   Report of 1971 University of Illinois-Urbana Excavations at the Cahokia Site. In *Cahokia Archaeology: Field Reports,* pp. 9–11. Papers in Anthropology No. 3. Springfield: Illinois State Museum.
Bareis, C. J., and J. W. Porter, eds.
  1984   *American Bottom Archaeology.* Urbana: University of Illinois Press.
Barker, A. W.
  1992   Powhatan's Pursestrings: On the Meaning of Surplus in a Seventeenth Century Algonkian Chiefdom. In *Lords of the Southeast: Social Inequity and the Native Elites of Southeastern North America,* edited by A. W. Barker and T. R. Pauketat, pp. 61–80. Archaeological Papers No 5. Washington, D.C.: American Anthropological Association.
Barker, A. W., and T. R. Pauketat, eds.
  1992   *Lords of the Southeast: Social Inequity and the Native Elites of Southeastern North America.* Archaeological Papers Papers No 5. Washington, D.C.: American Anthropological Association.
Bent, A.
  1962   *Life Histories of North American Wild Fowl,* Part II. New York: Dover Publications.
Blitz, J.
  1993   *Ancient Chiefdoms of the Tombigbee.* Tuscaloosa: University of Alabama Press.
Buikstra, J. E., J. C. Rose, and G. R. Milner
  1994   A Carbon Isotope Perspective on Dietary Variation in Late Prehistoric Western Illinois. In *Agricultural Origins and Development in the Midcontinent,* edited by W. Green, pp. 155–170. Report No. 19. Iowa City: Office of the State Archaeologist.
Carniero, R. L.
  1981   The Chiefdom: Precursor to the State. In *The Transition to Statehood in the New World,* edited by G. D. Jones and R. R. Kautz, pp. 37–79. Cambridge: Cambridge University Press.
Chmurny, W. W.
  1973   The Ecology of the Middle Mississippian Occupation of the American Bottom. Unpublished Ph.D. dissertation, Department of Anthropology, University of Illinois, Champaign-Urbana.

Clayton, L. A., V. J. Knight Jr., and E. C. Moore, eds.

1993 *The De Soto Chronicles: The Expedition of Hernando De Soto to North America in 1539–1543.* Tuscaloosa: University of Alabama Press.

Collins, J. M.

1990 *The Archaeology of the Cahokia Mounds ICT-II: Site Structure.* Illinois Cultural Resources Study 10. Springfield: Illinois Historic Preservation Agency.

1997 Cahokia Settlement and Social Structures as Viewed from the ICT-II. In *Cahokia: Domination and Ideology in the Mississippian World,* edited by T. R. Pauketat and T. E. Emerson, pp. 124–140. Lincoln: University of Nebraska Press.

Dalan, R. A.

1997 The Construction of Mississippian Cahokia. In *Cahokia: Domination and Ideology in the Mississippian World,* edited by T. R. Pauketat and T. E. Emerson, pp. 89–102. Lincoln: University of Nebraska Press.

Dalan, R. A., W. Watters Jr., G. R. Holley, and W. I. Woods

1994 Sixth Annual Cahokia Mounds Field School: Understanding Mound Construction. Office of Contract Archaeology, Southern Illinois University at Edwardsville. Submitted to Illinois Historic Preservation Agency, Springfield.

DePratter, C. B.

1991 *Late Prehistoric and Early Historic Chiefdoms in the Southeastern United States.* New York: Garland Press.

Dietler, M.

1996 Feasts and Commensal Politics in the Political Economy: Food, Power, and Status in Prehistoric Europe. In *Food and the Status Quest: An Interdisciplinary Perspective,* edited by P. Wiessner and W. Schiefenhövel, pp. 87–126. Oxford: Berghahn Books.

Douglas, J. G.

1976 Collins: A Late Woodland Ceremonial Complex in the Woodfordian Northeast. Unpublished Ph.D. dissertation, Department of Anthropology, University of Illinois, Champaign-Urbana.

Drennan, R.

1983 Ritual and Development at the Early Village Level. In *The Cloud People: The Divergent Evolution of the Zapotec and Mixtec Civilizations,* edited by K. V. Flannery and J. Marcus, pp. 46–50. New York: Academic Press.

Du Pratz, L. P.

1972 *The History of Louisiana or of the Western Parts of Virginia and Carolina: Con-*
[1754] *taining a Description of the Countries that Lie on both Sides of the River Mississippi: With an Account of the Settlements, Inhabitants, Soil, Climate, and Products.* Reprint. Baton Rouge: Claitor's Publishing Division.

Elias, S., and T. R. Pauketat

1997 The Paleoentomology of Cahokia's Sub-mound 51 Pit. Paper presented at the 54th Southeastern Archaeological Conference, Baton, Rouge, LA.

Emerson, T. E.
1982   *Mississippian Stone Images in Illinois.* Circular No. 6. Urbana: Illinois Archaeological Survey.
1995   Settlement, Symbolism, and Hegemony in the Cahokian Countryside. Unpublished Ph.D. dissertation, Department of Anthropology, University of Wisconsin, Madison.
1997   *Cahokia and the Archaeology of Power.* Tuscaloosa: University of Alabama Press.

Esarey, D., and T. R. Pauketat
1992   *The Lohmann Site: An Early Mississippian Center in the American Bottom.* Urbana: University of Illinois Press.

Finney, F. A.
1993   Spatially Isolated Structures in the Cahokia Locality: Short-term Residences or Special Purposes Shelters? In *Highways to the Past: Essays in Honor of Charles J. Bareis,* edited by T. E. Emerson, A. Fortier, and D. McElrath, pp. 381–392. Illinois Archaeology, Volume 5 (1 and 2). Urbana: Illinois Archaeological Society.

Fowler, M. L.
1973   The Cahokia Site. In *Explorations into Cahokia Archaeology,* edited by M. L. Fowler, pp. 1–30. Illinois Archaeological Survey Bulletin 7, Urbana.
1974   *Cahokia: Ancient Capital of the Midwest.* Addison-Wesley Module in Anthropology, No. 48.
1975   A Pre-Columbian Urban Center on the Mississippi. *Scientific American* 233 (2): 92–101.
1978   Cahokia and the American Bottom: Settlement Archaeology. In *Mississippian Settlement Patterns,* edited by B. D. Smith, pp. 455–478. New York: Academic Press.
1989   *The Cahokia Atlas: A Historical Atlas of Cahokia Archaeology.* Studies in Illinois Archaeology No. 6. Springfield: Illinois Historic Preservation Agency.

Friedman, J.
1984   Tribes, States, and Transformations. In *Marxist Analyses and Social Anthropology,* edited by M. Bloch, pp. 161–202. London: Tavistock.

Fritz, G. J.
1994   Precolumbian *Cucurbita argyrosperma* ssp. *argyrosperma* (Cucurbitaceae) in the Eastern Woodlands of North America. *Economic Botany* 48 (3): 280–292.
1997   Special Plants from Early Cahokia: Deposits from Sub-Mound 51. Paper presented at the 54th Southeastern Archaeological Conference, Baton Rouge, LA.

Fritz, G. J., and S. Johannessen
1996   Social Differentiation in the American Bottom: Late Prehistoric Plant Remains from Household, Communal, and Ceremonial Contexts. Paper presented at the 61st Annual Meeting of the Society for American Archaeology, New Orleans.

Halls, L. K., ed.
1984   *White-tailed Deer Ecology and Management.* Harrisburg, Pa.: Stackpole Books.
Hayden, B.
1990   Nimrods, Piscators, Pluckers, and Planters: The Emergence of Food Production. *Journal of Anthropological Archaeology* 9:31–69.
1996   Feasting in Prehistoric and Traditional Societies. In *Food and the Status Quest: An Interdisciplinary Perspective,* edited by P. Wiessner and W. Schiefenhövel, pp. 127–148. Oxford: Berghahn Books.
Helms, M. W.
1992   Political Lords and Political Ideology in Southeastern Chiefdoms: Comments and Observations. In *Lords of the Southeast: Social Inequity and the Native Elites of Southeastern North America,* edited by A. W. Barker and T. R. Pauketat, pp. 185–194. Archaeological Papers of the American Anthropological Association No. 5.
Holley, G. R., R. A. Dalan, and P. A. Smith
1993   Investigations in the Cahokia Site Grand Plaza. *American Antiquity* 58:306–318.
Hudson, C.
1976   *The Southeastern Indians.* Knoxville: University of Tennessee Press.
Jackson, H. E., and S. Scott
1995   The Faunal Record of the Southeastern Elite: The Implications of Economy, Social Relations, and Ideology. *Southeastern Archaeology* 14 (2): 103–119.
Johannessen, S.
1984   Paleoethnobotany. In *American Bottom Archaeology,* edited by C. J. Bareis and J. W. Porter, pp. 197–214. Urbana: University of Illinois Press.
1988   Plant Remains and Culture Change: Are Paleoethnobotanical Data Better than We Think? In *Current Paleoethnobotany,* edited by C. A. Hastorf and V. S. Popper, pp. 145–166. Chicago: University of Chicago Press.
1993   Food, Dishes, and Society in the Mississippi Valley. In *Foraging and Farming in the Eastern Woodlands,* edited by C. M. Scarry, pp. 182–205. Gainesville: University Press of Florida.
Kelly, J. E.
1990   The Emergence of Mississippian Culture in the American Bottom Region. In *The Mississippian Emergence,* edited by B. D. Smith, pp. 113–152. Washington, D.C.: Smithsonian Institution Press.
1992   The Impact of Maize on the Development of Nucleated Settlements: An American Bottom Example. In *Late Prehistoric Agriculture: Observations from the Midwest,* edited by W. I. Woods, pp. 167–197. Studies in Illinois Archaeology No. 8. Springfield: Illinois Historic Preservation Agency.
1996   Redefining Cahokia: Principles and Elements of Community Organization. *The Wisconsin Archeologist* 77 (3/4): 97–119.
1997   Stirling Phase Sociopolitical Activity at East St. Louis and Cahokia. In *Cahokia: Domination and Ideology in the Mississippian World,* edited by T. R. Pauketat and T. E. Emerson, pp. 141–166. Lincoln: University of Nebraska Press.

Kelly, L. S.

1979　Animal Resource Exploitation by Early Cahokia Populations on the Merrell Tract. Circular 4, Illinois Archaeological Survey, Department of Anthropology, University of Illinois, Urbana.

1990　Range Phase Faunal Analysis. In *The Range Site 2: The Emergent Mississippian Dohack and Range Phase Occupations,* by J. E. Kelly, S. J. Ozuk, and J. A. Williams. American Bottom Archaeology, FAI-270 Site Report 20. Urbana: University of Illinois Press.

1997a　Lohmann Phase Faunal Provisioning at the Cahokia Site. Paper presented at the 54th Southeastern Archaeological Conference, Baton Rouge, LA.

1997b　Patterns of Faunal Exploitation at Cahokia. In *Cahokia: Domination and Ideology in the Mississippian World,* edited by T. R. Pauketat and T. E. Emerson, pp. 69–88. Lincoln: University of Nebraska Press.

Kelly, L. S., and P. G. Cross

1984　Zooarchaeology. In *American Bottom Archaeology,* edited by C. J. Bareis and J. W. Porter, pp. 215–232. Urbana: University of Illinois Press.

Kent, S.

1989　Cross-cultural Perceptions of Farmers as Hunters and the Value of Meat. In *Farmers as Hunters: The Implications of Sedentism,* edited by S. Kent, pp. 1–17. Cambridge: Cambridge University Press.

Klein, R. G.

1989　Why Does Skeletal Part Representation Differ between Smaller and Larger Bovids at Klasies River Mouth and Other Archaeological Sites? *Journal of Archaeological Science* 6:363–381.

Knight, V. J., Jr.

1986　The Institutional Organization of Mississippian Religion. *American Antiquity* 51 (4): 675–687.

1990　Social Organization and the Evolution of Hierarchy in Southeastern Chiefdoms. *Journal of Anthropological Research* 40 (1): 1–23.

Lindauer, O., and J. H. Blitz

1997　Higher Ground: The Archaeology of North American Platform Mounds. *Journal of Archaeological Research* 5 (2): 169–207.

Lopinot, N. H.

1991　Archaeobotanical Remains. In *The Archaeology of the Cahokia Mounds ICT-II: Biological Remains,* by N. H. Lopinot, L. S. Kelly, G. R. Milner, and R. Paine. Illinois Cultural Resources Study 13. Springfield: Illinois Historic Preservation Agency.

1992　Spatial and Temporal Variability in Mississippian Subsistence: The Archaeobotanical Record. In *Late Prehistoric Agriculture Observation from the Midwest,* edited by W. I. Woods, pp. 44–94. Studies in Illinois Archaeology No. 8. Springfield: Illinois Historic Preservation Agency.

1994　A New Crop of Data on the Cahokian Polity. In *Agricultural Origins and Development in the Midcontinent,* edited by W. Green, pp. 127–154. Report No. 19, Office of the State Archaeologist, University of Iowa, Iowa City.

1997   Cahokian Food Production Reconsidered. In *Cahokia: Domination and Ideology in the Mississippian World*, edited by T. R. Pauketat and T. E. Emerson, pp. 52–68. Lincoln: University of Nebraska Press.

Lopinot, N. H., and W. I. Woods

1993   Wood Overexploitation and the Collapse of Cahokia. In *Foraging and Farming in the Eastern Woodlands*, edited by C. M. Scarry, pp. 206–231. Gainesville: University Press of Florida.

Lyman, R. L.

1984   Bone Density and Differential Survivorship of Fossil Classes. *Journal of Anthropological Archaeology* 3:259–299.

Marshall, F., and T. Pilgrim

1991   Meat versus Within-bone Nutrients: Another Look at the Meaning of Body Part Representation in Archaeological Sites. *Journal of Archaeological Science* 18:149–163.

Mehrer, M. W.

1988   The Settlement Pattern and Social Power of Cahokia's Hinterland Households. Unpublished Ph.D. dissertation, Department of Anthropology, University of Illinois, Champaign-Urbana.

1995   *Cahokia's Countryside: Household Archaeology, Settlement Patterns, and Social Power.* DeKalb: Northern Illinois University Press.

Metcalfe, D., and K. T. Jones

1988   A Reconsideration of Animal Body Part Indices. *American Antiquity* 53 (3): 486–504.

Milner, G. R.

1990   The Late Prehistoric Cahokia Cultural System of the Mississippi River Valley: Foundations, Florescence, and Fragmentation. *Journal of World Prehistory* 4 (1): 1–43.

1998   *The Cahokia Chiefdom: The Archaeology of a Mississippian Society.* Washington, D.C.: Smithsonian Institution Press.

Muller, J.

1997   *Mississippian Political Economy.* New York: Plenum.

Pauketat, T. R.

1991   The Dynamics of Pre-State Political Centralization in the North American Midcontinent. Unpublished Ph.D. dissertation, Department of Anthropology, University of Michigan, Ann Arbor.

1993   *Temples for Cahokia's Lords: Preston Holder's 1955–1956 Excavations of the Kunnemann Mound.* Memoirs No. 26. Ann Arbor: University of Michigan Museum of Anthropology.

1994   *The Ascent of Chiefs: Cahokia and Mississippian Politics in Native North America.* Tuscaloosa: University of Alabama Press.

1997a   Cahokian Political Economy. In *Cahokia: Domination and Ideology in the Mississippian World*, edited by T. R. Pauketat and T. E. Emerson, pp. 30–51. Lincoln: University of Nebraska Press.

1997b   New Evidence of Early Cahokian Provisions and Rituals. Paper presented at the 54th Southeastern Archaeological Conference, Baton Rouge, LA.

Pauketat, T. R., G. J. Fritz, L. S. Kelly, and N. H. Lopinot

1993   Early Cahokia: A New Research Project in the American Bottom. Paper presented at the 1993 Midwest Archaeological Conference, Milwaukee, WI.

Pauketat, T. R., and N. H. Lopinot

1997   Cahokian Population Dynamics. In *Cahokia: Domination and Ideology in the Mississippian World*, edited by T. R. Pauketat and T. E. Emerson, pp. 103–123. Lincoln: University of Nebraska Press.

Pauketat, T. R., and M. A. Rees

1996   Early Cahokia Project 1994 Excavations at Mound 49, Cahokia (11-S-34-2), Early Cahokia Project Papers, No. 2. Submitted to the Illinois Historic Preservation Agency, Springfield.

Prentice, G.

1986   An Analysis of the Symbolism Expressed by the Birger Figurine. *American Antiquity* 51:239–266.

Purdue, J. R.

1983   Epiphyseal Closure in White-tailed Deer. *Journal of Wildlife Management* 47 (4): 1207–1213.

Purdue, J. R., B. W. Styles, and M. C. Masulis

1989   Faunal Remains and White-tail Deer Exploitation from a Late Woodland Upland Encampment: The Boschert Site (23SC609), St. Charles County, Missouri. *Midcontinental Journal of Archaeology* 14 (2): 146–163.

Radin, P.

1990   *The Winnebago Tribe*. Lincoln: University of Nebraska Press.

Rees, M. A.

1997   Coercion, Tribute, and Chiefly Authority: The Regional Development of Mississippian Political Culture. *Southeastern Archaeology* 16 (2): 113–133.

Rindos, D., and S. Johannessen

1991   Human-Plant Interactions and Culture Change in the American Bottom. In *Cahokia and the Hinterlands: Middle Mississippian Cultures of the Midwest*, edited by T. E. Emerson and R. B. Lewis, pp. 35–45. Urbana: University of Illinois Press.

Rue, L. L.

1997   *The Deer of North America*. New York: Lyons and Burford.

Saitta, D. J.

1994   Agency, Class, and Archaeological Interpretation. *Journal of Anthropological Archaeology* 13:201–227.

Seeman, M. F.

1979   Feasting with the Dead: Ohio Hopewell Charnel House Ritual as a Context for Redistribution. In *Hopewell Archaeology: The Chillicothe Conference*, edited by D. S. Brose and N. Greber, pp. 39–46. Kent, Ohio: Kent State University Press.

Service, E. R.

1962   *Primitive Social Organization: An Evolutionary Perspective.* New York: Random House.

Simon, M., and K. Parker

1995   Detours and Divergences on the Pathway of Prehistoric Plant Exploitation. Paper presented at the 60th Annual Meeting of the Society for American Archaeology, Minneapolis, Minnesota.

Smith, B. D.

1975   *Middle Mississippi Exploitation of Animal Populations.* Anthropology Papers No. 57. Ann Arbor: University of Michigan Museum of Anthropology.

Smith, M. T., and D. J. Hally

1992   Chiefly Behavior: Evidence from Sixteenth Century Spanish Accounts. In *Lords of the Southeast: Social Inequity and the Native Elites of Southeastern North America,* edited by A. W. Barker and T. R. Pauketat, pp. 99–110. Archaeological Papers No 5. Washington, D.C.: American Anthropological Association.

Smith, M. T., and M. Williams

1994   Mississippian Mound Refuse Disposal Patterns and Implications for Archaeological Research. *Southeastern Archaeology* 13 (1): 27–35.

Steponaitis, V. P.

1978   Location Theory and Complex Chiefdoms: A Mississippian Example. In *Mississippian Settlement Patterns,* edited by B. D. Smith, pp. 417–453. New York: Academic Press.

1986   Prehistoric Archaeology in the Southeastern United States, 1970–1985. *Annual Reviews of Anthropology* 15:363–404.

Styles, B. W., and J. R. Purdue

1991   Ritual and Secular Use of Fauna by Middle Woodland Peoples in Western Illinois. In *Beamers, Bobwhites, and Bluepoints: Tributes to the Career of Paul W. Parmalee,* edited by J. R. Purdue, W. E. Klippel, and B. W. Styles, pp. 421–436. Illinois State Museum Scientific Papers, Vol. XXIII and The University of Tennessee, Department of Anthropology Report of Investigations No. 52. Springfield: Illinois State Museum.

Swanton, J. R.

1911   *Indian Tribes of the Lower Mississippi Valley and Adjacent Coast of the Gulf of Mexico.* Bulletin 43. Washington, D.C.: Bureau of American Ethnology.

1946   *Indians of the Southeastern United States.* Bulletin 137. Washington, D.C.: Bureau of American Ethnology.

Welch, P. D.

1991   *Moundville's Economy.* Tuscaloosa: University of Alabama Press.

Welch, P. D., and C. M. Scarry

1995   Status Related Variation in Foodways in the Moundville Chiefdom. *American Antiquity* 60 (3): 397–419.

White, W. P., S. Johannessen, P. G. Cross, and L. S. Kelly

1984   Environmental Setting. In *American Bottom Archaeology,* edited by C. J. Bareis and J. W. Porter, pp. 15–33. Urbana: University of Illinois Press.

Witthoft, J.
    1949   *Green Corn Ceremonialism in the Eastern Woodlands.* Occasional Contributions
            No. 13. Ann Arbor: University of Michigan Museum of Anthropology.
Zeder, M.
    1996   Zooarchaeological Approaches to Complexity: A View from the Old World.
            Paper presented at the 53rd Annual Meeting of the Southeastern Archaeolog-
            ical Conference, Birmingham, Alabama.

13

FEASTING ON THE PERIPHERY

THE PRODUCTION OF RITUAL FEASTING AND VILLAGE
FESTIVALS AT THE CERÉN SITE, EL SALVADOR

Linda A. Brown

And they [the sixteenth-century Yucatec Maya] often spend on one banquet what they have
earned by trading and bargaining many days. And they have two ways of celebrating these
feasts: the first, which is that of the nobles and of the principal people, obliges each one of the
invited guests to give another similar feast. And to each guest they give a roasted fowl, bread
and drink of cacao in abundance; and at the end of the repast, they were accustomed to give a
manta [cloth] to each to wear, and a little stand and vessel, as beautiful as possible. And if one
of the guests should die, his household or his relations are obliged to repay the invitation. The
second way of giving feasts was used among kinfolk when they marry their children or celebrate the memory of the deeds of their ancestors, and this does not oblige the guests to give
a feast in return, except if a hundred persons have invited an Indian to a feast, he also invites
them all when he gives a banquet or marries his children. They have strong friendship and
they remember for a long time these invitations, although they are far apart from one another.

Bishop Diego de Landa (Tozzer 1941:92)

In the Maya region, feasting was a pivotal component of rituals for the elite and
non-elite alike. As noted by Bishop Diego de Landa, elite Maya rulers engaged in
a form of competitive feasting and gift-giving with strict understandings for repayment. Social obligations were so embedded in sixteenth-century Maya elite
consumption rituals that the debts acquired during feasts did not end with death
but would be inherited by surviving kin (Tozzer 1941:92).

But in addition to the competitive feasting of the elite, Landa mentioned feasting among the commoners, or "kinfolk," associated with ancestor veneration
and life-cycle celebrations. Many of these feasts occurred in conjunction with ritual activities, such as dancing with animal headdresses, bloodletting, animal sacrifice, carving new idols, and displays of ideologically charged icons, which took

place during public religious performances at community festivals (e.g., Tozzer 1941).

In this chapter I explore this second type of feast, that of the "kinfolk," focusing on the archaeological correlates of ritual feasting at the site of Cerén, El Salvador. The Cerén site, located in the Zapotitán Valley, was a flourishing Middle Classic period agricultural community located on the southern Maya periphery (Sheets 1992a; Fig. 13.1). Around A.D. 590 a volcanic vent, located only 600 meters from the site, opened up beneath the nearby Rio Sucio and buried the community under 6 meters of ash (Sheets 1992a). The suddenness of the eruption precipitated a catastrophic abandonment of the community leaving virtually complete artifact assemblages in their context of use or storage, in addition to preserving fragile earthen architecture and organic artifacts. The unique mode of abandonment and subsequent extraordinary preservation of the site provides archaeologists with a rare glimpse of rural village life, including material remains that can be interpreted as functioning in the production of community festivals and ritual feasting. The archaeological signature suggesting participation in village feasting at Cerén adds important new criteria to the archaeological identification of feasts, one of the major themes of this volume.

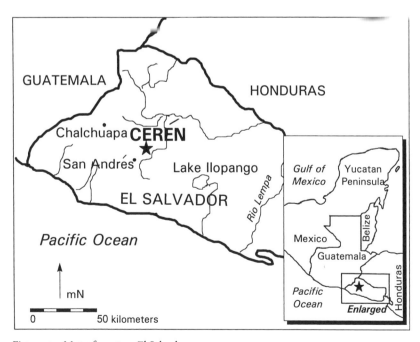

Figure 13.1. Map of western El Salvador.

Material correlates of feasting inferred from the Cerén data include many of the expected categories as proposed by Hayden (1995,1998, Chapter 2) including: (1) a specialized permanent facility, known as Structure 10, that was used for food storage, food preparation during feasts, and as a storage house for ritual paraphernalia between events; (2) a cleared area around the exterior of the building interpreted as a gathering space for food consumption and ritual performances; (3) an artifact assemblage indicative of large-scale food preparation and storage; and (4) ritual items that included a deer-skull headdress with other likely components of a ceremonial dance costume.

In this chapter, my objective is to examine the archaeological signature of ritual feasting. First the archaeological evidence of feasting at Cerén is examined and data suggesting that one household may have been linked with feasting are presented. Then I turn to ethnographic accounts to begin to generate possible expectations for the archaeological recognition of ritual feasting in Maya rural village communities. Finally, building on the growing body of research into ancestor veneration and the built environment in the Maya area (e.g., McAnany 1995), I propose that we may be able to recognize rural lineage feasts from distinct types of remains in the archaeological record.

A few terms should be defined at the outset. In using the term *feast,* I refer to the communal consumption of food and drink in a context that differs from that of daily household food consumption practices. By the term *ritual feasting,* I mean that social network in which communal food and alcohol consumption co-occurs with a series of requisite ritual performances. Finally, in using the term *festival,* I refer to the period of time, usually several days, which is set apart for open public celebrations, including ritual feasting, ceremonial performances, and other forms of entertainment.

THE CERÉN SITE
THE ENVIRONMENT
The Cerén site is located in the Zapotitán Valley of west-central El Salvador at an elevation of 450 meters (1,500 feet) above sea level. The site is situated along the western terrace of the Rio Sucio, the main river of the valley. Today the Zapotitán Valley, an intermontane basin that covers an area of approximately 182 square kilometers, is extremely fertile and productive agricultural land. But the Zapotitán Valley was not always an advantageous environment.

Around A.D. 260, the southern Maya periphery underwent a regional disaster when the massive eruption of the Ilopango volcano, in central El Salvador, spewed tephra over millions of square kilometers (Hart and Steen-McIntyre 1983). As a result of this eruption, the Zapotitán Valley was virtually depopulated and evidence suggests that it took two centuries before the soil recovered and people resettled the valley (Sheets 1983:287). Based on survey data (Black 1983), we know that by the sixth century people had migrated back into the valley and the area was emerging as a "complex stratified society, with hierarchical settlement system" complete with occupational specialists controlling obsidian industries at San Andrés, the primary regional center (Sheets 1983:290). It was during this reoccupation that the agricultural village of Cerén was founded.

Attempting to reconstruct population estimates for the Cerén community is particularly challenging as most structures remain buried under 6 meters of volcanic ash. Currently, ten structures have been excavated and an additional seven structures have been identified by test pits (Fig. 13.2). Data gathered from ground penetrating radar studies suggest that at least eighteen more structures, yet to be verified in test excavations, may remain buried (Conyers 1995). Based on these data, Sheets (personal communication, 1998) estimates that the ancient Cerén community consisted of at least 150 individuals.

Although estimating the size of the population is problematic, we do know that Cerén residents settled on top of a very thin, yet extremely productive soil. Residents exploited and grew numerous plant species including maize, beans, squash, manioc, maguey, cacao, and chili, as well as a number of medicinal and/or ceremonial plants (Lentz et al. 1996). Additionally community members kept and tended ducks, raised domesticated dogs, and exploited wild fauna such as white-tailed deer, peccary, and freshwater turtles (Brown, in press).

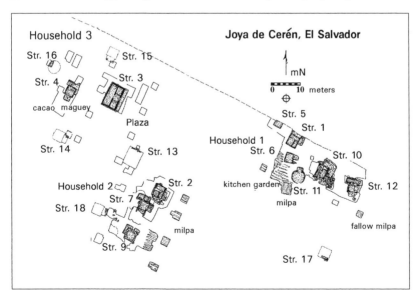

Figure 13.2. Site map for Cerén, El Salvador.

EXCAVATIONS AT THE CERÉN SITE

Payson Sheets (principal investigator) has conducted archaeological investigations at the site since 1978, with a hiatus between 1980 to 1989 during the height of the El Salvador civil war (Sheets 1992a). Excavations resumed in 1989, and in the following years portions of four household clusters and associated extramural areas, three ceremonial structures, a civic building, a midden, and various agricultural areas were excavated.

Of the household clusters excavated to date, Household 1 is the best known (Beaudry-Corbett, Simmons, and Tucker, in press). It consists of three separate buildings—a kitchen (Structure 11), a storeroom (Structure 6), a domicile (Structure 1)—as well as a covered open work area (Structure 5), cleared extramural activity areas around the compound, and agricultural zones.

Structure 10 is located immediately to the east of Household 1. This building was excavated during the 1992 and 1993 Cerén field seasons under the supervision of Andrea Gerstle (1992, 1993). The following section on Structure 10, except where otherwise noted, is a condensed version of Brown and Gerstle (in press) and two preliminary reports (Gerstle 1992, 1993).

STRUCTURE 10

The archaeological evidence suggests that Structure 10 was used as a headquarters for the production of community festivals that included ritual feasting. Structure 10 is a thatched-roof wattle-and-daub building that was oriented approximately 23 degrees east of north (Fig. 13.3). The superstructure was constructed on a square clay platform 3.7 meters on a side and has two rooms, an east (front) room and a west (back) room. The only entranceway into the building was through a wooden pole door that faced west toward the Household 1 compound. Unlike other buildings excavated at the site, walled corridors were erected outside and along the north and east sides of the superstructure and the corridors were covered with a thatch roof. Moreover, Structure 10 does not follow the dominant 30 degrees east of north alignment used in domestic buildings at the site.

Structure 10 was divided into several functionally distinct activity areas. The north exterior corridor was utilized for food preparation as indicated by the presence of two hearths, a *metate* and *mano* (grinding and hand stone), bone and antler corn huskers with empty ears of corn discarded just outside the entranceway, food-serving vessels, and a number of large cooking and storage vessels, one of which was found resting on one of the hearths.

The east corridor was utilized primarily for ceramic vessel storage. The southern portion of the corridor remains unexcavated under several fallen walls; however, the excavated northern portion was packed with at least seventeen medium

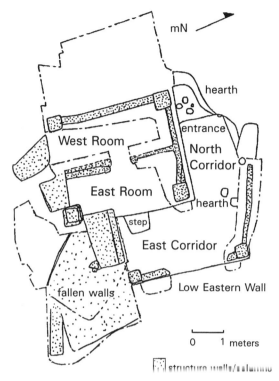

Figure 13.3. Plan view of Structure 10 at Cerén, El Salvador.

to large storage jars, serving vessels, and several painted gourds (Beaubien and Lundberg 1993; Beaudry-Corbett 1993).

A half-height wall forms part of the exterior wall of the east corridor directly abutting the food-preparation area (Fig. 13.4). This low wall is interpreted as a food-dispensing area and likely functioned as a pass-through for food and drink to festival participants gathered outside of the building (Gerstle 1993). This interpretation is supported by the observation that the ground to the north and east of Structure 10 was highly compacted, flattened, and smoothed, suggesting an area of high foot traffic (Simmons and Villalobos 1993). Additionally, this area was relatively free of artifacts and plants suggesting a well-maintained area that was regularly swept clean. Presumably, this cleared hard packed surface was where participants gathered for ceremonial celebrations that included outdoor feasting.

Moving inside Structure 10, the east room is notable for both the wall treatment and the kinds of artifacts present. It was the sole painted room in the building, with the eastern face of the dividing wall, cornices, and door pilasters painted red and the lowermost portion of the pilasters accented with white. This

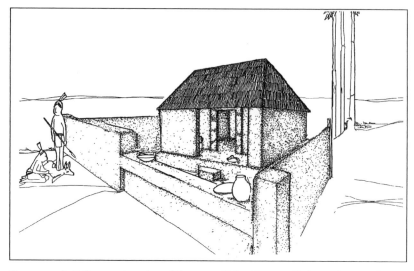

Figure 13.4. Artist's reconstruction of Structure 10 (roof over walled corridors not depicted). Modified from an illustration by Karen Kievit.

room was used for the storage of ceremonial and unique artifacts. Ritual items included a deer-skull headdress, which was painted red, in association with other components of a possible dance costume—including a matched set of bone beads, bone ornaments, and deer scapulae. The headdress—formed from the cranium minus the mandible of an adult white-tailed deer stag *(Odocoileus virginianus)*, was in storage on a high shelf. It was recovered with bits of twine still wrapped around the antler bases. Presumably the twine was used to secure the headdress on the wearer.

A large jar with an appliquéd caiman head effigy and another large jar containing squash seeds were recovered *in situ* on the east room floor. The caiman effigy jar was full of achiote seeds, used by various contemporary Maya as food color, and by the Lacandon Maya to produce a red paint symbolic of human blood (Coe 1994; McGee 1990; Tozzer 1907). Additionally, twenty ears of corn were stored in an elevated context in this room. Apparently, the corn was stored shucked as no remnant of husks remained.

In contrast with the special-use items stored in the east room, the west room was used for the storage of utilitarian vessels, including a large jar full of beans. The pattern of the storage of ceremonial artifacts in the east room is consistent with practices of contemporary Maya in Zinacantán who place household altars and associated ceremonial paraphernalia along the east wall of their homes, the wall toward the direction of the rising sun (Vogt 1976).

A few other notable patterns in the artifact assemblage should be mentioned here. Structure 10 contained relatively few serving vessels, with only five ceramic serving vessels and two painted gourds, a number less than some of the domestic structures at the site (Beaudry-Corbett 1993). Instead of serving vessels, Structure 10 contained the highest number of large utilitarian food storage jars of any Cerén building excavated to date (Beaudry-Corbett 1992, 1993).

STRUCTURE 10 AND DEER CEREMONIALISM
In addition to feasting, festivals at Cerén may have involved the display of white-tailed deer artifacts. The presence of the deer headdress in storage suggests that the white-tailed deer stag was associated with ceremonial activities at Structure 10 and the headdress may have been part of a dance costume used at village festivals. Mary Pohl (1981) argued that the white-tailed deer stag was a prominent pre-Columbian deity who played a significant role in ritual. Specifically, Pohl argued, the white-tailed deer was associated with the *cuch* ceremony that linked community leaders with agricultural fertility, the sun, rain, economic prosperity, the cyclic nature of time, death, renewal, and rebirth.

LINKAGES BETWEEN HOUSEHOLD 1
AND FEASTING AT STRUCTURE 10
One of the questions posed in this volume (see Clarke, Chapter 5, and Hayden, Chapter 2) concerns how archaeologists might identify households that regularly sponsored feasts from remains found in the archaeological record. At Cerén, the archaeological evidence suggests that Household 1 was involved in the processing of consumable goods for public feasting at Structure 10 (Beaudry-Corbett, in press; Beaudry-Corbett, Simmons, and Tucker, 1998; Brown and Gerstle, in press). This relationship is inferred from numerous lines of material remains, which are reviewed below.

Physical Proximity and Building Modifications
Evidence linking Household 1 with Structure 10 is implied from building proximity (Beaudry-Corbett, Simmons, and Tucker, in press) and the orientation of structure entranceways, with inferred foot-traffic patterns (Simmons and Villalobos 1993). Structure 10 is located only 5 meters to the east of Household 1. The only access into Structure 10 is through a wooden pole door that faces west, directly toward Household 1. Meanwhile, the entrance to the Household 1 storeroom faces east toward Structure 10 (Beaudry-Corbett, Simmons, and Tucker, in press). This is notable because all other entranceways into Cerén domestic storerooms open to the north, toward the household domicile. Presumably this would have facilitated the flow of people and goods between Structure 10 and Household 1's storeroom.

Groundstone

Only one *metate* was recovered inside of Structure 10. A single *metate* hardly seems sufficient for the amount of grinding necessary for the scale of food preparation as inferred from the size of the large pot resting on the nearby hearth. In contrast, a total of five complete *metates* and five curated *metate* fragments were recovered from Household 1 (Fig. 13.5). Four *metates* were in use positions, mounted on forked sticks or on the kitchen floor, whereas one was in temporary storage resting a pair of forked sticks that presumably it would be mounted on during use (Beaudry and Tucker 1989; Mobley Tanaka 1990). The number of complete *metates* in use or temporary storage at Household 1 suggests that women were grinding more maize than would be necessary for household consumption alone. It is conceivable that a surplus of maize could have been produced for household life-cycle celebrations. However, the evidence of large-scale food preparation in Structure 10 would suggest that the Household 1 compound was used for labor-intensive food grinding associated with public feasts.

This interpretation is further supported by use-wear analyses. Only one *metate*, located on the floor of the kitchen (Structure 11), showed evidence of

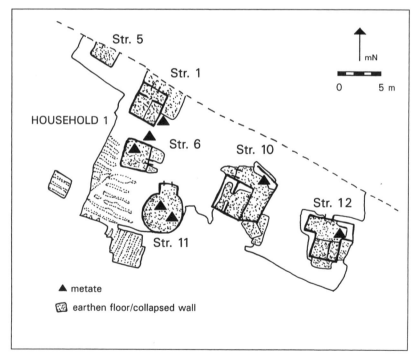

Figure 13.5. Household 1, Structure 10, and Structure 12 showing positions of complete *metates* in use contexts or temporary storage.

heavy use-wear suggesting that it was the main *metate* used daily by this household (Sheets 1990, 1992b). The other four complete *metates* exhibited minimal wear, suggestive of short-term or periodic use, a material expectation for *metates* used occasionally for feasts. Interestingly, not all *metates* had matching *manos* (hand stones), as only three *manos* were found (Sheets 1992b).

Faunal Remains and Blood Residue Analysis

In addition to grinding, Household 1 appears to have been the location of meat processing. Although a sample of obsidian blades from all site contexts was tested for organic residues, thus far only tools from Household 1 indicate the presence of animal protein. Two obsidian blades in Household 1, from the kitchen and storeroom respectively, tested positive to artiodactyla (deer or peccary) antiserum by immunoelectrophoresis whereas two blades discarded outside of Household 1 tested positive to *Canidae* (domesticated dog, fox, coyote, wolf; Newman 1993). The presence of deer and dog faunal remains recovered from storage and discard contexts at this household would suggest that these were the species being processed here (Brown in press). A duck was recovered *in situ* tied to a pole wall inside of the Household 1 storeroom, once again a deviation from other Cerén contexts as this is the only household to have a live animal tethered inside. It should be kept in mind that currently only ten structures have been fully excavated at the site; thus the sample size is quite small. However, given the available data this pattern suggests that this household was the locus of more meat processing compared with other households excavated thus far. It is conceivable that Household 1 members processed meat for feasting activities at Structure 10.

Frequency and Type of Ceramic Vessels

The ceramic assemblage further supports the interpretation of a relationship between Household 1 members and feasting at Structure 10. Household 1 had more large jars without handles than did other Cerén households, a pattern interpreted as related to a household's need for long-term food storage (Beaudry-Corbett, in press). Furthermore, Household 1 had more utilitarian bowls with handles than other households suggesting a greater need for transferring and transporting a higher volume of consumable goods (Beaudry-Corbett, in press). Beaudry-Corbett (in press) argued that Household 1's greater need for long-term food storage, as well as for transferring and transporting a higher volume of consumable goods than other households, could reflect a role in feasting at Structure 10.

Ceramic Compositional Analyses

In addition to the amount and types of vessels recovered from Household 1, compositional analyses suggest further linkages between this household and Structure 10. Beaudry-Corbett (in press) identified two imported red wares in the Cerén assemblage. One originated from within the Zapotitán Valley, close to the main civic-ceremonial center, San Andrés; the other was produced close to the site of Chalchuapa, approximately 40 kilometers from Cerén. Notably all imported red ware identified at Cerén to date was found exclusively in either Household 1 or the two ceremonial buildings, Structures 10 and 12. Interestingly, although the ceramics originating from Chalchuapa consisted of both utilitarian jars and food serving vessels, red wares produced within the Zapotitán Valley close to the site San Andrés, the civic-ceremonial core, consisted exclusively of polychrome food-serving vessels (Beaudry-Corbett, in press).

SUMMARY

Based on the archaeological evidence, a number of inferences concerning the structure of festivals at Cerén can be proposed. Cerén festivals included ritual feasting in the context of deer ceremonialism. The limited space inside Structure 10, in addition to the well-trodden and well-maintained exterior ground surface, suggest that festivals were public events and food consumption occurred in open outdoor areas.

The Household 1 compound may have been used periodically for food preparation prior to and during feasts at Structure 10. The restricted distribution of obsidian blades testing positive to animal blood residue suggests that meat was processed here. Additionally, the number of functional *metates* recovered in Household 1 suggests that this household was the locus of more food grinding than would be necessary solely for household consumption. Women living in Household 1 likely assisted with labor-intensive grinding for feasts prepared at Structure 10. However, the presence of worn *metates*, without matching *manos*, suggests that some women living in other households brought their own *manos* to this compound to assist in grinding (Sheets 1997 personal communication). Thus, responsibility for food preparation for feasts seems to have involved a small group of women living in and beyond the immediate household.

The use of household space for the preparation of ritual feasts associated with nearby ceremonial buildings has parallels among the contemporary Maya. In the Guatemalan village of Santiago Atitlán, *cofradía* members stage festivals that include feasting. The *cofradía* building, a specialized ceremonial structure that houses the corporately owned sacra of the sodality and serves as the site for festivals, is always located within the domestic household compound of the highest-ranking male and female *cofradía* members. Prior to a festival, a small work party of women gather at the household of the highest-ranking members to begin preparing food for ceremonial feasts (Fig. 13.6). *Metates* used periodically for festivals are moved from storage locations, washed, and then set up

Figure 13.6. Women's work group using household space to grind corn for a ritual feast at a nearby *cofradía* building in Santiago Atitlán, Guatemala. (Photo by the author)

in use contexts, generally on the ground under an outdoor roofed area close to the kitchen. While a few women tend to the food cooking over hearths, the majority of the women are involved in various labor-intensive food preparation activities such as grinding corn or preparing tamales. Thus, for several days prior to a festival and for the duration of the festivities, the household compound is converted into a semipublic work area for the organized female labor needed to produce feasts associated with festivals at the nearby ceremonial building. It is conceivable that the Household 1 compound at Cerén may have functioned in a similar way in the time immediately before and during festivals at Structure 10.

Returning to Cerén, festival foods included corn, beans, and squash, as indicated by empty corn cobs discarded outside of Structure 10, the husked corn cobs stored in an elevated context inside the building, and the large jar of beans and squash seeds stored in Structure 10. Corn, beans, and squash also are found in domestic contexts at the site and probably were consumed daily. But in addition to these everyday provisions, some more unique food items are present, including deer, dog, and a large number of achiote seeds, which probably do represent special festival foods. Early Colonial accounts note that meat commonly was consumed in the context of public ritual feasting (e.g., de Palacio 1985; Tozzer 1941). The faunal evidence from the Household 1 compound suggests that meat consumption at Cerén likely followed a similar pattern.

Estimated vessel capacities for cooking and serving vessels make it possible to approximate the size of feasts at Structure 10. An extremely large cooking pot with a capacity of 56,429 cc was recovered *in situ,* resting directly on one of the Structure 10 hearths (Beaudry-Corbett 1993). Currently, vessel capacities of approximately one third of all Cerén ceramic individual serving vessels have been directly measured (Stacy Barber, personal communication, 1998), allowing for preliminary inferences of the maximum number of individuals this pot could serve. Assuming that they were completely filled, Cerén individual ceramic serving vessels could hold a mean of 885 cc, or approximately 3.5 cups of food. Thus, at maximum capacity, the large cooking pot could have served up to 64 individual servings or approximately one half the 150 individuals that Sheets (personal communication, 1998) estimates may have lived in the village. Another similar extremely large cooking vessel was recovered beside the hearth in the kitchen of Household 1 and if it were used simultaneously it would raise the number that could be served to 128 individuals. Although preliminary, estimates of Cerén festival crowd size based on maximum capacities of cooking vessels, then, would suggest that some feasts at Structure 10 were open to the entire community.

Feasts at Cerén were frequent enough for hosts to construct, and continuously maintain, a specialized building solely dedicated to feasting activity and the storage of ritual paraphernalia. The association of two permanent building types, ritual architecture in close proximity to a residential compound, suggests that the relationship between Household 1 members with activities at Structure 10 was institutionalized. This interpretation is further supported by a series of building modifications to both Structure 10 and Household 1 suggesting some time-depth to existence of these buildings.

In addition to linking Household 1 with feasting at Structure 10, interpretations based on ceramic compositional analyses also link Household 1 members with social networks beyond the immediate community (Beaudry-Corbett, in press). The restricted distribution of imported ceramics within the village suggests that Household 1 members, in their role as producers of ritual feasting and festivals, had greater access to extravillage social relations, apparently a social network not available to all community members (Beaudry-Corbett, in press).

RURAL FEASTING IN THE MAYA AREA: ETHNOGRAPHIC SOURCES AND ARCHAEOLOGICAL INFERENCES

Ethnohistoric sources note that at the time of Contact, Maya lineages maintained permanent lineage houses or small temples (Fox and Cook 1996). Although lineage houses no longer exist in the Maya area, there is evidence that suggests that the modern Maya fiesta system (specifically *cofradías*), a syncretistic Catholic/Maya institution involved in the production of village festivals including ritual feasting, subsumed some of their functions (Cook 1981). An examination of the material correlates associated with contemporary Maya village festivals might elucidate features potentially useful for the archaeological identification of rural feasting spaces.

SPECIALIZED FEASTING SPACES

In general, two types of physical spaces were noted by ethnographers: those marked by permanent dedicated ceremonial buildings, and open-air feasting spaces usually in association with permanent structures.

Permanent Dedicated Ceremonial Buildings

Ethnographic references frequently stated that rural ceremonial facilities were constructed similarly to domestic buildings. Thompson noted of Cehach Maya villages that "specialized temple buildings seem to be absent; instead, as among the Lacandon, a hut of normal residential type, although perhaps a little larger, serves the religious needs of the village" (1970:76). Likewise, among the Xpichil and Xyatil Maya of Quintana Roo, Shattuck (1933) noted that ceremonial huts were constructed of similar material and size as the family hut.

The Lacandon Maya (McGee 1990) have a sacred hut that is shared by several related families. Interestingly, these structures are associated with accompanying sacred cook huts: "The sacred hut has its own fire and its own utensils, which are exclusively used for the celebration of religious observations. To bring any food into the domestic hut renders it unfit to be offered to the gods" (Tozzer 1907:91–92). Ceremonial kitchen huts were utilized by the ritual sponsor's wife, who prepared tamales and food offerings in these locations (McGee 1990). The use of separate kitchens, artifacts, and features for the preparation of ceremonial food may reflect the concept of ritual purity (Thompson and Thompson 1955; Tozzer 1907).

Among the Chorti Maya of Guatemala, Wisdom (1940:384–386) noted the presence of two types of specialized permanent facilities utilized in the production of festivals: ceremonial houses and *cofradía* houses. Both the ceremonial house and the *cofradía* house functioned as storage areas for corporately owned ritual paraphernalia, as well as for food preparation and dispensing during communal feasting. Ceremonial houses were common features of rural settlements whereas *cofradía* houses were associated with the more populated towns.

Ceremonial houses, constructed and maintained by the communal labor of members of the community, were said to be communally owned by all members of the *aldea* (rural settlement; Wisdom 1940:281). These rural ceremonial structures were the loci for ritual feasting and rites for rainmaking, agricultural fertility, and Day of the Dead celebrations.

> Most of the larger *aldeas* have a ceremonial house, the construction of which is like that of any other house, consisting usually of a sleeping-house and kitchen. The former is actually the ceremonial house, while the latter is used by the women for cooking food during ceremonies. (Wisdom 1940:384)

> [After the ceremony] the Indians then return to the ceremonial house, where feasting, drinking, and dancing go on through the night. A large group of women prepare tamales, *atol* [maize gruel], *chilate*, tortillas, meats, and coffee, using the sacred water for this purpose. (Wisdom 1940:438–439)

Cofradía houses were located in more populated settlements. In addition to serving as the locus of festivals, the *cofradía* house was the temporary residence of the *mayordomo* (native religious official) and his family during his year of service in office.

> The cofradia is found only in the pueblos and is used in connection with festivals. The *mayordomos* live in it during their period of service at the church and use it as a storage house for the festival paraphernalia. On festival days the Indians bring their contributions of maize to this house and the women grind it and cook it into foods, especially *chilate* and tortillas, which are often given gratis to those who attend the festival. The house is usually built at the edge of the pueblo, near some important trail which leads to large outlying *aldeas*. It is built like any other house but it is much larger. (Wisdom 1940:385)

Open-Air Feasting Spaces Associated with Ceremonial Structures

Although descriptions of buildings used for feasting were scant in the literature, the use of outdoor space in association with feasting was even less frequently reported by ethnographers. However, Wisdom (1940) noted that the cleared space outside of the ceremonial house was used for several types of activities related to the production of festivals.

> Indians from all over the *municipio* [township] gather in the open space surrounding the house, bringing large quantities of chicken tamales, *cacao*, *chilate*, *atol*, fruits, and *chicha* [fermented sugarcane drink]. Each family contributes a peso or two until about one hundred are collected. The money and food are given to the leader as

payment for performing the ceremony. Each family brings additional food which is cooked by the women in the ceremonial house kitchen and eaten by everyone.

The land upon which any ceremonial house . . . sits is considered a sacred spot and is not to be used for any secular purpose. The ceremonial house has a large space around it, kept clear of vegetation by communal *aldea* labor, where the Indians congregate during ceremonies. (Wisdom 1940:426)

Meanwhile, at the larger *cofradía* house the open exterior space also was used for food preparation and consumption:

A group of fifty women, appointed by the *mayordomos*, are busy at the cofradia making *chilate*, *atol*, coffee, and tortillas in the large ovens and fireplaces in the cofradia courtyard. Long benchlike tables are covered with gourd bowls filled with the *chilate*, which all the Indians drink free of charge. (Wisdom 1940:449–450)

It [the *cofradía* house] is built like any other house but it is much larger and has a large courtyard, since on important festivals many hundreds of Indians congregate around it. In the courtyard stands a clay oven, used for boiling *chilate* served to Indians on festival days. (Wisdom 1940:385)

SOCIAL GROUPS THAT SPONSOR FEASTS
The Archaeological Signature of Lineage Spaces

As seen in this volume, it is possible to recognize the material correlates of various types of feasts from remains in the archaeological record. Moreover, those households that regularly engaged in feasts are expected to have an artifact assemblage indicative of this role. Among the contemporary Maya, rural households occupied by lineage heads (Hayden and Cannon 1984:178), as well as *cofradía* leaders, have more large fiesta pots and *metates* than other households, reflecting participation in lineage or sodality feasts during fiestas. The question arises as to whether it would be possible to identify the type of social group (lineage versus sodality) that sponsored feasts from remains found in the archaeological record. In the Maya area, it may be possible to identify lineage-sponsored feasts when they occur in a specialized context, such as a lineage house or shrine, by combining the expectations of feasting with the material correlates proposed for demarcating sacred lineage space (McAnany 1995). McAnany argued that one of the ways in which lineage groups demarcated sacred space had a strong material component that left a distinct archaeological signature.

[Ancestors] were venerated by name because particular resource rights and obligations were inherited through them by their descendants. This is precisely why ancestors "slept" within the construction mass of residential compounds—to insure the chain of continuity in resources transmitted between generations . . . Burial of ancestors often marks the termination of the use of an older structure and the commencement of the construction of a new one. *Over time, these places of the ancestors often become sacralized locales at which ritual structures such as temples or shrines com-*

pletely replace domestic structures. I have cited one such sequence from K'axob, but the pattern is ubiquitous throughout the lowlands of Mesoamerica. (McAnany 1995:161; emphasis added)

Although many archaeological household compounds in the Maya area are likely to have burials under domestic platforms, those representing the practice of demarcating sacred space for lineage ancestors showed a fundamental change in building function (e.g., a domestic space that was transformed into a specialized ritual locale; McAnany 1995). This pattern is dramatically illustrated in the main acropolis at Copan, where elite members of the founding lineage were buried under floors of their domestic compounds. These underwent impressive building renovations until eventually the entire domestic compound was literally entombed within a large temple known as Structure 16 (Stuart 1997).

The transformation of domestic space into a sacred lineage house is not unique to the Maya area. For example, Kirch (Chapter 6) noted that ritual feasting in the village of Tikopia, Polynesia, also occurred at lineage and clan temples that historically functioned as residences for ancestors. After years of domestic use and the subsequent burial of ancestors within them, some residential buildings were transformed into "holy houses" used for ritual feasting.

Assuming that such a change in building function could be inferred from remains in the archaeological record, then domestic structures displaying a similar life history, in conjunction with the material correlates of feasting, may enable us to infer ritual feasting revolving around a lineage organization.

Social Groups and Feasting at Structure 10

Returning to Cerén, can we infer anything about the social unit that sponsored feasts at Structure 10? As suggested earlier, the Household 1 compound appears to have been used periodically for large-scale food preparation. Similarly, the ceramic assemblage and architectural orientation suggest linkages between Household 1 members and Structure 10. That this linkage may reflect a lineage activity is suggested by the particular history of building modifications at Structure 10.

As mentioned earlier, at the time of the eruption Structure 10 had undergone at least three building modifications. With the exception of building alignment, a point to which I will return below, the original structure and architectural features followed the same building plan as domiciles at the site: a two-room superstructure constructed on a elevated square platform and a centrally placed door in the interior wall that allowed access into the back room where the "sleeping" bench was located. At some point, Structure 10 underwent a series of renovations. A low clay floor was constructed around the east and north sides of the superstructure, walls were erected restricting access, and this area was roofed. A kitchen was placed in the north corridor. A new doorway was built in the north wall of the corridor to be later moved to the west wall opening toward Household 1. The sleeping bench was obliterated and buried during a renovation in which the entire floor level of the back room was raised.

The conservation ethic at Cerén prevents excavating into the floors of structures, thus precluding an important source of data from subfloor burials and caches to fully test this hypothesis. However, the above-ground architectural pattern suggests that Structure 10 was a domestic residence that, at some point in its life history, underwent modifications to become a ceremonial locale that perhaps was a rural lineage house. If this interpretation is correct, then the deviation in the Structure 10 building alignment would suggest that original occupants of Structure 10 held a distinctive status in the community.

CONCLUSIONS

A number of features potentially useful for the archaeological identification of spaces used for Maya village feasting can be inferred from ethnographic, ethnohistoric, and archaeological evidence from Cerén. Although rural Maya ceremonial houses often have a similar architectural plan and scale as domestic compounds, they should have more hearths or other cooking features than expected for domestic use. Those areas used for large-scale food preparation might have features that facilitate the distribution of food serving, such as the low service wall. If ceremonial houses are the same size as domestic compounds, then they should be associated with open exterior spaces that are used by groups gathered for feasting and ritual performance. Areas used for ceremonial gatherings may be regularly maintained and kept clear of trash and debris. Moreover, cleared ceremonial gathering areas are expected to have a hard-packed ground surface indicative of an area of heavy foot traffic.

Households or groups involved in sponsoring festivals may reside in buildings located in close proximity to the specialized ceremonial structures. The architecture may be designed to facilitate the movement of people and goods between the living quarters of the hosts and the specialized ceremonial structure and associated cooking features. Areas used for the large-scale food processing should have a higher frequency of food-preparation artifacts, especially those heavy, difficult-to-transport items such as *metates,* than expected in domestic household assemblages. Moreover, *manos* and *metates* used only periodically for preparation of feasting foods may show evidence of lighter use-wear when compared with those used in daily household food preparation.

Ethnohistoric, ethnographic, and archaeological sources suggest that Maya feasts often occurred in the context of lineage celebrations that honored the ancestors. Combining the material correlates of lineage ceremonial buildings with those associated with feasting may allow us to infer lineage-sponsored feasts from the archaeological record, specifically when these feasts occur in specialized lineage houses.

So what were the advantages to those involved in sponsoring ritual feasting and festivals at Cerén? A range of benefits, from functional equilibrium to more competitive interest-theory models, have been proposed for participation in the contemporary Maya fiesta system (e.g., Camara 1952; Cancian 1965; Carrasco 1961; Chance and Taylor 1985; Collier 1979; Farris 1984; Hayden and Gargett 1990; Nash 1958; Vogt 1969; Wolf 1959). Interestingly, ritual feasting among contemporary agriculturalists in Asia suggests that both models may have heuristic value (Ahern 1973; Freedman 1958, 1970). For example, in some Asian villages permanent ceremonial lineage halls are used for ritual activities including feasts. In addition to this utilitarian function, ceremonial halls take on a symbolic role and stand as visible icons of the economic strength of a lineage as the "hall requires for its building and its maintenance and for the upkeep of its rites that it be endowed; hence a hall is a mark of riches" (Freedman 1970:168). As lineages constantly assess themselves by comparing their halls with those owned by other lineages in the village, the material trappings of feasts as well as the actual lineage-feasting event have strong boundary-marking potential (Ahern 1973:112). Both promote within-group solidarity as well as being a means to compete with other lineages and engage in self-aggrandizing behaviors (Ahern 1973). A similar observation was made by Clarke (see Chapter 5) concerning the feasting practices of the rural Akha in Northern Thailand.

Whether feasting at Cerén followed a similar trajectory is unknown. However, if the interpretation that Household 1 members sponsored feasts at Structure 10 is correct, then the archaeological evidence does suggest a possible benefit. Rather than the accumulation of a disproportionate amount of material goods, inferences based on the ceramic assemblage suggest that Household 1 participated in a geographically broader social network that did other households excavated to date (Beaudry-Corbett, in press). Scholars have argued that extended social networks created by consumption rituals are risk-reducing strategies that, during times of crisis, can be accessed to provide critical support and information to participants (Douglas and Isherwood 1996:xxii). The sponsorship of feasting at Structure 10 may have provided a similar advantage to Household 1 members.

In a broader perspective, feasting was likely an activity for forming alliances in the Zapotitán Valley. The restricted distribution of polychrome serving vessels produced close to San Andrés, which were found only in Household 1 and the two ceremonial buildings to the east, suggests that Household 1 members may have been more closely linked to the civic-ceremonial center than other households excavated to date (Beaudry-Corbett, in press). Feasting may have been a social arena used in alliance formation linking the civic-ceremonial center to more rural settlements throughout the valley. If so, then perhaps the gifting of food-serving vessels, vessels that function in both utilitarian and symbolic realms of consumption rituals, were tangible reminders of the social relations and obligations embedded in participation in those networks.

ACKNOWLEDGMENTS

I would like to thank Brian Hayden and Michael Dietler for inviting me to participate in the SAA symposium and subsequent volume. Thanks go to Payson Sheets who generously allowed me use of the Cerén data and to Marilyn Beaudry-Corbett for use of her ceramic analyses. I also thank Payson Sheets, Barbara Voorhies, and Harriet "Rae" Beaubien for valuable comments on earlier drafts.

REFERENCES

Ahern, E. M.

> 1973   The Cult of the Dead in a Chinese Village. Stanford: Stanford University Press.

Beaubien, H. F., and H. Lundberg

> 1993   Artifact Conservation during the 1993 Field Season. In Cerén Project 1993 Preliminary Report, edited by P. Sheets and S. Simmons, pp. 164–172. Boulder: University of Colorado.

Beaudry, M., and D. Tucker

> 1989   Household 1 Area Excavations. In A Preliminary Report: Cerén Project 1989, edited by P. Sheets and B. McKee, pp. 29–40. Boulder: University of Colorado.

Beaudry-Corbett, M. P.

> 1992   Ceramic Analysis, Joya de Cerén: 1992 Season. In 1992 Investigations at the Cerén Site, El Salvador: A Preliminary Report, edited by P. Sheets and K. Kievit, pp. 82–95. Boulder: University of Colorado.

> 1993   Ceramic Analysis, Joya de Cerén: 1993 Season. In Cerén Project 1993 Preliminary Report, edited by P. Sheets and S. Simmons, pp. 138–151. Boulder: University of Colorado.

> in press   Ceramics. In Before the Volcano Erupted: The Ancient Cerén Village in Central America, edited by P. D. Sheets. Austin: University of Texas Press.

Beaudry-Corbett, M. P., S. E. Simmons, and D. B. Tucker

> in press   Household 1. In Before the Volcano Erupted: The Ancient Cerén Village in Central America, edited by P. D. Sheets. Austin: University of Texas Press.

Black, K. D.

> 1983   The Zapotitán Valley Archaeological Survey. In Archaeology and Volcanism in Central America: The Zapotitán Valley of El Salvador, edited by P. Sheets, pp. 62–97. Austin: University of Texas Press.

Brown, L. A.

> in press   Household and Village Animal Use at Cerén. In Before the Volcano Erupted: The Ancient Cerén Village in Central America, edited by P. D. Sheets. Austin: University of Texas Press.

Brown, L. A., and A. Gerstle

> in press   Structure 10: The Production of Village Festivals. In Before the Volcano Erupted: The Ancient Cerén Village in Central America, edited by P. D. Sheets. Austin: University of Texas Press.

Camara, F.

1952   Religious and Political Organization. In *Heritage of the Conquest,* edited by S. Tax, pp. 142–173. Free Press, Glencoe, Illinois.

Cancian, F.

1965   *Economics and Prestige in a Maya Community.* Stanford: Stanford University Press.

Carlsen, R.

1997   *The War for the Heart and Soul of a Highland Maya Town.* Austin: University of Texas Press.

Carrasco, P.

1961   The Civil-Religious Hierarchy in Mesoamerican Communities: Pre-Spanish Background and Colonial Development. *American Anthropologist* 63:483–497.

Chance, J., and W. Taylor

1985   Cofradías and Cargo: An Historical Perspective on the Mesoamerican Civil-Religious Hierarchy. *American Ethnologist* 12:1–26.

Coe, S. D.

1994   *America's First Cuisines.* Austin: University of Texas Press.

Collier, J. F.

1979   Stratification and Dispute Handling in Two Highland Chiapas Communities. *American Ethnologist* 6:305–328.

Conyers, L.

1995   Paleogeography of the Cerén Site, El Salvador. Ph.D. dissertation, University of Colorado. Ann Arbor: University Microfilms.

Cook, G. W.

1981   Supernaturalism, Cosmos and Cosmogony in Quichean Expressive Culture. Ph.D. dissertation, State University of New York. Ann Arbor: University Microfilms.

de Palacio, D. G.

1985   *Letter to the King of Spain: Being a Description of the Ancient Provinces of Guaza-capan, Izalco, Cuscatlan, and Chiquimula, in the Audiencia of Guatemala, with an Account of the Languages, Customs, and Religion of Their Aboriginal Inhabitants, and a Description of the Ruins of Copan.* Translated by Ephraim Squier. Culver City, Cal.: Labyrinthos.

Douglas, M., and B. Isherwood

1996   *The World of Goods: Towards an Anthropology of Consumption.* New York: Routledge.

Farris, N. M.

1984   *Maya Society under Colonial Rule.* Princeton: Princeton University Press.

Fox, J., and G. Cook

1996   Constructing Maya Communities: Ethnography for Archaeology. *Current Anthropology* 37 (5): 811–830.

Freedman, M.

1958   *Lineage Organization in Southeastern China.* London: Athlone.

1970   Ritual Aspects of Chinese Kinship and Marriage. In *Family and Kinship in Chinese Society,* edited by M. Freedman, pp. 163–187. Stanford: Stanford University Press.

Gerstle, A. I.

1992   1992 Excavations at Structure 10, Joya de Cerén. In *1992 Investigations at the Cerén Site, El Salvador: A Preliminary Report,* edited by P. Sheets and K. Kievit, pp. 30–54. Boulder: University of Colorado.

1993   1993 Excavations at Structure 10, Joya de Cerén. In *Cerén Project 1993 Preliminary Report,* edited by P. Sheets and S. Simmons, pp. 46–90. Boulder: University of Colorado.

Hart, W. J. E., and V. Steen-McIntyre

1983   Tierra Blanc Joven Tephra from the A.D. 260 Eruption of Ilopango Caldera. In *Archaeology and Volcanism in Central America: The Zapotitán Valley of El Salvador,* edited by P. Sheets. Austin: University of Texas Press.

Hayden, B.

1995   Pathways to Power: Principles for Creating Socioeconomic Inequalities. In *Foundations of Social Inequality,* edited by T. D. Price and G. Feinman, pp. 15–86. Fundamental Issues in Archaeology, G. Feinman and T. D. Price, general editors. New York: Plenum.

1998   Fabulous Feasts: A Prolegomenon to the Archaeological and Theoretical Importance of Feasting. Paper presented at the Society for American Archaeology Annual Meeting, Seattle.

Hayden, B., and A. Cannon

1984   *The Structure of Material Systems: Ethnoarchaeology in the Maya Highlands.* SAA Papers No. 3. Washington, D.C.: Society for American Archaeology.

Hayden, B., and R. Gargett

1990   Big Man, Big Heart? A Mesoamerican View of the Emergence of Complex Society. *Ancient Mesoamerica* 1:3–20.

Lentz, D. L., M. P. Beaudry-Corbett, M. L. Reyna de Aquilar, and L. Kaplan

1996   Foodstuffs, Forests, Fields, and Shelter: A Paleoethnobotanical Analysis of Vessel Content From the Cerén Site, El Salvador. *Latin American Antiquity* 7 (3): 247–262.

McAnany, P.

1995   *Living with the Ancestors: Kinship to Kingship in Ancient Maya Society.* Austin: University of Texas Press.

McGee, R. J.

1990   *Life, Ritual, and Religion among the Lacandon Maya.* Belmont, Cal.: Wadsworth Publishing Company.

Mobley Tanaka, J.

1990   1990 Excavations in Operation 1, Cerén El Salvador. In *1990 Investigations at the Cerén Site, El Salvador,* edited by P. Sheets and B. McKee, pp. 36–47. Boulder: University of Colorado.

Nash, M.

1958   Political Relations in Guatemala. *Social and Economic Studies* 7:65–75.

Newman, M.

1993   Organic Residues on Obsidian Blades. In *Cerén Project 1993 Preliminary Report,* edited by P. Sheets and S. Simmons, pp. 182–184. Boulder: University of Colorado.

Pohl, M.

1981   Ritual Continuity and Transformation in Mesoamerica: Reconstructing the Ancient Maya Cuch Ceremony. *American Antiquity* 46 (3): 513–529.

Sheets, P. D.

1990   Chipped Stone, Cerén, 1990 Season. In *1990 Investigations at the Cerén Site, El Salvador: A Preliminary Report,* edited by P. Sheets and B. McKee, pp. 176–181. Boulder: University of Colorado.

1992a   *The Cerén Site: A Prehistoric Village Buried in Volcanic Ash in Central America.* Case Studies in Archaeology Series. Fort Worth, Tex.: Harcourt Brace & Company.

1992b   Chipped Stone and Ground Stone Artifacts from Joya de Cerén, 1991–92. In *1992 Investigations at the Cerén Site, El Salvador: A Preliminary Report,* edited by P. Sheets and K. Kievit, pp. 86–104. Boulder: University of Colorado.

Sheets, P. D., ed.

1983   *Archaeology and Volcanism in Central America: The Zapotitán Valley of El Salvador.* Austin: University of Texas Press.

Simmons, S. and S. Villalobos

1993   Landscape Archaeology in Operation 8 between Household 1 and the Structure 10 Patio. In *Cerén Project 1993 Preliminary Report,* edited by P. Sheets and S. Simmons, pp. 31–45. Boulder: University of Colorado.

Stuart, G. E.

1997   The Royal Crypts of Copan. *National Geographic* 192:68–93.

Thompson, D., and J. E. S. Thompson

1955   A Noble's Residence and its Dependencies at Mayapan. *Carnegie Institution of Washington, Current Reports* 2 (25): 225–251.

Thompson, J. E. S.

1970   *Maya History and Religion.* Norman: University of Oklahoma Press.

Tozzer, A. M.

1907   *A Comparative Study of the Mayas and the Lacandones.* New York: Macmillan.

1941   *Landa's relación de las cosas de Yucatan.* Translated by Alfred Tozzer. Cambridge: Peabody Museum of Archaeology and Ethnology, Harvard University.

Vogt, E. Z.

1969   *Zinacantan: A Maya Community in the Highlands of Chiapas.* Cambridge: Harvard University Press.

1976   *Tortillas for the Gods: A Symbolic Analysis of Zinacanteco Rituals.* Cambridge: Harvard University Press.

Wisdom, C.

1940   *The Chorti Indians of Guatemala.* Chicago: University of Chicago Press.

Wolf, E.

1959   *Sons of Shaking Earth.* Chicago: University of Chicago Press.

14

FEASTING IN THE ANCIENT NEAR EAST

Denise Schmandt-Besserat

In the ancient Near East, the feast was a leitmotif in art (Collon 1992; Pinnock 1994) and cuneiform texts (Bottéro 1994). Images carved in stone illustrate banquets of 4,500 years ago and economic tablets record the movement of goods they occasioned. In this paper, I draw information from both art and texts to assess the role of feasting in Sumer in the third millennium B.C. I argue that the feast was a significant factor in the Mesopotamian redistribution economy. I also contend that the economic function of feasting was maximized by the fact that festivals were religious and sociopolitical events.

THE MESOPOTAMIAN CITY STATES

Before starting my discussion on the feast, I summarize briefly the sociopolitical and economic conditions of Mesopotamia in the third millennium B.C. Situated in present-day southern Iraq, the country of Sumer was a low alluvial plain, made of silt and lacking the most elementary raw materials such as stone, metal, or even timber wood. As it is today, it was cursed in summer by a scorching heat and would have been a barren desert if not watered by two rivers, the Tigris and Euphrates. It is along the banks of the Euphrates, the less unpredictable of the two rivers, that the Sumerians first settled. They transformed the dry silt by irrigation and drained swamps into rich fertile soils. They could thus engage in farming. They specialized in the cultivation of dates and barley, as well as the raising of sheep and cattle.

The population was clustered where irrigation was possible along the river and the canals. The first settlements were villages, but around 3500 B.C. the first cities, such as Uruk and Girsu, appeared in the south. The process spread to the north and along the Tigris with the rise of Nippur, Kish, Shuruppak, and Khafaje. Each city with its surrounding villages was separated from the next by long stretches of swamps and desert. The hinterland was a desert where nomadic tribes were probably roaming. This geographic situation, in which each settlement was confined to relative isolation, favored the development of small political units called city-states. In the third millennium, individual city-states may have had populations of 5,000 to 10,000 people.

The political leadership of the city-states was first in the hands of high priests of the powerful Mesopotamian temple. However, by 2900 B.C., a king ruled from a royal palace, built next to the sacred temple area. The king's main function was to build and keep in good repair the temples of the gods, to plan, oversee and maintain the irrigation system and the defensive fortification wall surrounding the city. He was also in charge of raising and supplying the army, including costly metal armaments. Finally, we may assume that the king and his queen played an important ceremonial role, in particular, during the monthly festivals, which, I will argue, generated the capital to support the royal endeavors.

FEASTING IN ART

The famous "Standard of Ur," which features the most detailed image of a Near Eastern feast, illustrates the Sumerian king hosting a banquet (Moorey 1982:98–102; Fig. 14.1). The panel, inlaid with shell, limestone, and lapis lazuli, shows the ruler as the largest figure of the top register, and sporting a kilt with multiple tiers of fringes. The six guests facing him are identical in size, wear the same garment with a single fringe, sit on similar wooden stools, make the same gesture, and hold similar cups. A harpist and a singer entertain the elegant assembly while attentive servants are busy helping. Below, nineteen offering bearers, organized in five delegations led by ushers, stand in a long line stretching over two registers. Unlike the stereotyped banquet guests, the gift bearers have

Figure 14.1. Standard of Ur. After Denise Schmandt-Besserat, *Before Writing*, p. 173, fig. 104 (Austin: University of Texas Press, 1992).

individual features and assume different positions. Sumerians with shaven heads and wearing fringed kilts lead the procession. Some of them pull or push a cow, one escorts a small flock of goats and rams while another carries bundles of fish. Foreigners follow wearing skirts overlapping in front. They are depicted with curly hair, bearded or clean-shaven, and occasionally with a headdress. One of the men brings a kid in his arms, another leads a team of asses, still others carry heavy loads of goods on their backs or shoulders. The procession advances towards the right indicating that it is proceeding toward the banquet hall in order to parade the goods before the king. The occasion for the feast is no doubt a military victory since the opposite side of the standard shows the king inspecting prisoners in the aftermath of a battle. The inlaid panel therefore discloses that a Mesopotamian victory feast was attended by males (military leaders?), drinking and music was involved, and it included a procession of local offering bearers followed by the display of booty or tribute from foreign countries. The fact that similar inlaid standards excavated at Mari, Syria, also combined banqueting with an exhibition of goods (Parrot 1953:figs. 64–66 and 70–72) confirms that the two scenes belonged together as two episodes of a victory feast. It is noteworthy that more space and attention is devoted to the display of merchandise suggesting that the parade of goods was deemed the more significant of the two.

About twenty carved stone plaques excavated in the Sumerian city of Nippur (Fig. 14.2) in sites of the Diyala Valley (Fig. 14.3) and Elam, depict a more popular feast where music and competitive sports, such as wrestling, were taking place (Boese 1971:Pl. X:2; Fig. 14.4). Humans and sometimes deities wearing horned headdresses (Boese 1971:Pl. XVIII:8–11; Fig. 14.2) are shown banqueting on the upper register. As on the standard, the guests sit on wooden stools and usually hold cups. Here, however, females are present. Servants and musicians are of either sex (Boese 1971:Pl. I:2; III:2; XVII:1). More importantly, the king faces a woman of equal size and therefore of equal status—most likely the queen (Boese 1971:Pl. I:1; III:3; etc.; Fig. 14.3). On the lower registers, individuals are pictured leading bulls, goats, and kids on the hoof, hauling jars, carrying on their heads piles of goods or trays loaded with merchandise, while still others are holding rings of precious metal or bundles of fish (Boese 1971:Pl. I:2; III:1; V:2; IX:1; XVI:2, 3; XVII:1). It is conceivable that the chariot with a team of four onagers, sometimes depicted on the last register, was also a prized offering (Pallis 1926:155). The carved plaques therefore concur with the standard for suggesting that feasting in the ancient Near East meant not only banqueting but also gift giving.

The glyptic artists competed in virtuosity to depict feasts on the minuscule field of cylinder seals (Collon 1992; Fig. 14.5). Here food was served. Meat haunches and bowls filled with prepared dishes were displayed on high chests (Amiet 1980:Pl. 90:1182–1188). Beer, kept in tall jars, was sipped with metal straws

Figure 14.2 (top). Perforated plaque from Nippur. After Johannes Boese, *Altmesopotamische Weihplatten*, Pl. XVIII:1 (Berlin: Walter de Gruyter, 1971). Figure 14.3 (bottom). Perforated plaque from Khafaje. After Johannes Boese, *Altmesopotamische Weihplatten*, Pl. IX:1 (Berlin: Walter de Gruyter, 1971).

Figure 14.4. Perforated plaque from Khafaje. After Johannes Boese, *Altmesopotamische Weihplatten*, Pl. X:2 (Berlin: Walter de Gruyter, 1971).

(Amiet 1980:Pl. 90:1183, 1186–1187). As on the perforated plaques, the banquet guests were human or sometimes divine (Amiet 1980:Pl. 92:1218–1221; Fig. 14.6). They could include both sexes (Amiet 1980:Pl. 90:1181–1184) or be exclusively males or females (Amiet 1980:Pl. 90:1192). Dancing took place to the tune of harpists, flutists, and clappers (Amiet 1980:Pl. 90:1193–1194). Offering bearers are shown bringing fish, a kid, or a large jar (Amiet 1980:Pl. 90:1187, 1190–1191; Pl. 92:1218).

In sum, feasting was a popular motif of Mesopotamian art. It is noteworthy that the monuments focused only on the economic aspect of the feast and never pictured the religious rituals that certainly took place during the festivals (Postgate

Figure 14.5. Seal impressions from Ur. After Pierre Amiet, *La Glyptique Mésopotamienne Archaïque*, Pl. 90:1190–1191 (Paris: Editions du Centre National de la Recherche Scientifique, 1980).

Figure 14.6. Seal impression from unknown site. After Pierre Amiet, *La Glyptique Méso-potamienne Archaïque*, Pl. 92:1218 (Paris: Editions du Centre National de la Recherche Scientifique, 1980).

1992:123–124). Instead they glorify banqueting and the parade of goods. This suggests that, in the ancient Near East, the importance of festivals was collecting as well as consuming victuals. In fact, seen through art, the delivery of offerings may be regarded as the most significant aspect of feasting. This seems very similar to the chiefly feasting systems described by Kirch (Chapter 6) and Junker (Chapter 10).

FEASTING IN THE TEXTS

Feasts were also a frequent topic of mythological (Vanstiphout 1992:9–21), royal (Postgate 1992:146–147), and economic texts, such as those excavated at Girsu (Rosengarten 1960a:249–302). The cuneiform tablets complement the information provided by art with the advantage that the texts spell out the purpose of the celebrations, their location, duration, and frequency. Moreover, the economic tablets record the movement of goods that took place during the festivals and the individuals involved.

The texts, as the art monuments, refer to multiple types of feasts. Some marked special events such as the king's investiture, military victories, alliances with neighboring countries (Bottéro 1994:11) and the inauguration of a temple or a palace (Sauren 1970). However, Mesopotamian life revolved around monthly festivals celebrating the multiple gods of the pantheon (Cohen 1996:14). For example, twice a year the people of Girsu honored the goddess Nanshe by a feast lasting up to seven days (Cohen1993:45). The two feasts celebrating the god Ningirsu were four days long (Rosengarten 1960a:262) and that of his consort, the goddess Bau, was two days (Rosengarten 1960b:39).

The tablets elucidate various features of the banquet images. For example, they make it clear why deities were among the banqueters. According to the texts, the feasts marked the days when the deities descended from heaven to be worshipped. Since mankind was created to provide for their upkeep, the gods and goddesses expected not only rituals, but also a banquet and lavish offerings (Oppenheim 1964:187–193). At her feasts, Nanshe was given silver crowns, vessels of stone and of precious metal, and goods including animals on the hoof (Cohen 1993:46). Other gods received meat, fish, flour, beer, oil, special dairy dishes, and dates in quantities according to their rank in the pantheon (Rosengarten 1960b:40).

The texts also clarify the prominent place given to the queen in the stone reliefs by revealing her role as the intermediary between people and gods. The household servants, herders, and farmers brought her offerings of small cattle, bread, and beer, which she was in charge of sacrificing to the pantheon on their behalf (Cohen 1993:37). She also organized pilgrimages to attend the festivities honoring Nanshe in the various cities of the state (Cohen 1993:44–45).

We gather from the texts that the culmination of the religious festivals was a sacrificial meal shared by the gods, the royal family, the priesthood, and the citizenry (Pallis 1926:173). As pictured in art, the events involved drinking, toasting, and merry making. The names of the two yearly Nanshe and Ningirsu festivals, "the feast of barley eating" (She-ku) and "the feast of malt eating" (Bulug-ku), leave no doubt that the feasts were the occasion for massive consumption. The fabulous quantities of food involved are disclosed in an inscription of Ur-Nanshe, king of Lagash, ca. 2500 B.C., who boasted of the 70 *guru* (equivalent to 30,800 kiloliters) of barley consumed at the inauguration of the temple of Ningirsu (Cooper 1986:29). In turn, the feast of Ur Nanshe presages the extravagant banquet offered by the Assyrian king Assurnasirpal II for the inauguration of his palace of Nimrud in 879 B.C. The 69,574 guests were then entertained at the expense of 300 oxen, 1,000 calves, 15,000 sheep, 1,000 lambs, 500 deer, 500 gazelles, 10,000 eggs, 10,000 loaves of bread, 10,000 jars of beer, 10,000 skins of wine, 10,000 measures of chick pea, and so on (Finet 1992:31–35).

That collecting goods was an essential part of the feast comes out loud and clear in the tablets as it does in art. The stone carvings illustrating endless processions of worshippers, bringing a kid in their arms, pushing animals on the hoof, hauling jars, or carrying trays and loads of goods are echoed by the innumerable lists of offerings compiled by the palace administration. The tablets stipulate several types of gifts. Some, specially earmarked for the banquet (Nig-ku-da, literally "with" the meal), were offered by the priesthood, high officials, and palace employees. They consisted of fish, meat, a certain milk dish or cheese, particular types of breads, and beer. Second, goods including animals, bread, and beer were brought to the palace by household servants, the palace farmers, and herders to be sacrificed to the gods by the queen (Rosengarten 1960b:44). Finally, the most significant contributions were the so-called offerings for the feast provided by professional guilds, such as that of the fishermen, who brought baskets of various kinds of fish and turtles as well as jars of fish oil (Rosengarten 1960a:255–256). Individuals also contributed offerings for the feast. Servants of the princes, high administrators, and foremen brought one animal. For example, a certain Ur-Lama is recorded as delivering a kid for "the feast of barley eating" and the same for "the feast of malt eating" (Rosengarten 1960a:256). However—*noblesse oblige*—the priest of Nanshe and his wife, are listed as each offering three animals or respectively, one sheep and two lambs, and one sheep, one kid, and one lamb (Rosengarten 1960b:41). The other high priests and their wives gave exactly the same. For the feast of Bau, the contribution of the Priest of Nanshe and his colleagues changed to one sheep, one kid, strong beer, black beer, loaves of bread, bunches of vegetables, dates, and roasted barley (Rosengarten 1960b:39). As illustrated in art, the most frequent offerings reported in the texts were animals on the hoof, fish, and other victuals. But the contributions were not limited to edibles. Some texts from Umma and Ur list considerable deliveries of bundles of reeds, and firewood (Limet 1970:67).

Although the texts reveal in amazingly specific details the monthly feast offerings a certain Ur-Lama paid some four thousand years ago, they fail to disclose the big picture. For instance, the records are not complete enough to evaluate the amount of revenues generated by banquet gifts, compared to those derived from other palace resources, such as landholdings. It is also unclear what percentage of the offerings was consumed at the feast and how much was levied by the palace.

The most significant information revealed by the economic texts is that the same offerings were repeated over and over again. Month after month, the sea fishermen delivered the same amounts of their catch—namely some 120 fish and 10 kg per fisherman; the administrators and foremen brought a kid; and the priests invariably contributed three animals for Nanshe and two with other foods and drinks for Bau. This strongly suggests that the "offerings for the feast" were strictly regulated, mandatory contributions (Rosengarten 1960b:49). In our own vocabulary they were monthly taxes.

THE FEAST AS A RELIGIOUS EVENT

The texts make it clear that the monthly festivals established a calendar stipulating the days of the month when goods were to be delivered at the palace or the temple. The feast, however, did far more than providing a rhythm for giving. The fact that the festivals were religious made giving an awesome obligation.

The religion of the Sumerians was greatly influenced by their land. The deities of their pantheon were natural powers on whose mercy they depended for their daily sustenance. Major gods were Enki, the god of fresh water, Enlil, that of the wind, and Utu, the sun. Inanna was the goddess of the storehouse and primarily a fertility deity. Each city stood under the special protection of a patron god and was responsible for catering to every possible need of that deity—who, like humans, required food, drink, and shelter.

The temple perpetrated the idea that mankind had been created in order to provide the pantheon with its upkeep (Lambert 1993:197–198). Each household was therefore expected to produce more goods than what it required for its own needs and surrender the surplus to the gods as "gifts." The matter was urgent because the deities were capable of doing evil as well as good. They were loving gods, when satisfied with the care they received from their city, but wrathful when displeased. They could in a whim generate favorable rains, produce plentiful harvests, multiply the animals of the herds, and bring prosperity to families. Just as well, they could send famine, turn fields and orchards into barren wasteland, plague flocks or people with diseases, and unleash devastating storms. Each individual, therefore, had the awesome responsibility of fulfilling the expectations of the powerful deities. Each household was to avoid irritating the pantheon by failing to attend the rituals and to provide quality goods in enough quantities. Each individual held in his hands the welfare and the doom of the city. Giving plentifully was not a matter of choice: it was a stern obligation.

THE FEAST AS A SOCIOPOLITICAL EVENT

The feast was not only religious, it was an important social and political event. There can be no doubt that Sumerian festivals, like feasts all over the world, attracted crowds from far and near for the pageantry, music, and drama. City dwellers and villagers flocked to view the king and his court in their ceremonial paraphernalia and to hear the high priests utter sacred words while performing sacred gestures. More importantly, the presence of the gods at the sacrificial meal brought the entire community together. Finally, as depicted in art, after the rituals were over, it was time for merry making. Music, dance, and competitive games gave everyone a chance to display elegance, beauty, grace, strength, and dexterity in front of all. The feast was a place to see and be seen.

The royal family was the focal point of the feast. We may assume that they stood out from the crowds by wearing lavish ceremonial regalia. Most importantly, the king and the queen played a key role in the ritual. As shown on the Standard of Ur, the king presided over the procession of offerings. As represented on the plaques, the royal couple hosted banquets. Finally, the texts spell out the active part played by the queen in collecting offerings and making sacrifices. We may infer that in all these various circumstances the king and the queen occupied positions of honor segregated from the rest of the community. For instance, the standard of Ur presents the king seated on one side, facing the guests. The festivals thus singled out the royal family, highlighting the importance of monarchy. The feast reinforced the king and the queen's prestige and authority. By the same token, the actual presence of the king to review the parade of gifts, and that of the queen to receive the offerings, further increased the pressure for giving.

The procession of worshippers bringing gifts, glorified in art, certainly was a main attraction of the feast. We would like to know whether it was compulsory or voluntary to show publicly the offerings presented to the gods. Was each head of household obliged to parade his contribution in view of the king and the entire community? Or, was the procession a special honor reserved for the bearers of unusually priced products? In any case, one can well imagine that the public exhibition of offerings created an extraordinary social pressure—because in Sumer, as elsewhere, the human virtue most admired was generosity, and the vice most despised, stinginess. Those who brought the most lavish gifts were praised and admired, whereas those who supplied little were ridiculed and chastised. The competitiveness of giving is well illustrated by a wisdom composition featuring the heated dialogue between Enten and Emesh, personifying Winter and Summer, arguing the worth of their respective banquet gifts. The text amounts to a battle of words between the two protagonists boasting about the value of their respective offerings. Enten claimed that the lambs, kids, cattle, honey, and wine he gave were far superior to the bountiful harvests brought by Emesh, and vice versa (Vanstiphout 1992:14–15). At the feast, citizens sought approval from the gods, but also prestige in the community.

Texts and art are mute concerning the consequences of failing to attend the feast and to bring offerings. Martial coercion is not discussed or depicted, except in a series of early fourth-millennium seals showing the priest-king presiding over the beating of prisoners (Schmandt-Besserat 1992:180–181). It is conceivable that in the third millennium B.C., ideological coercion was put to work for people to bring the most lavish gifts in the greatest quantity. Failing to partake was probably deemed such a profound insult to the gods and the community that, as a rule, it did not occur. Otherwise, society deals efficiently with delinquents with a gamut of punishment ranging from ridicule to ostracism. The festivals were the time when fame and shame were created.

CONCLUSION

The combined information derived from the art and economic texts of the ancient Near East suggests that, in the third millennium B.C., the religious, social, and political aspects of feasting were manipulated to amass palace wealth. (1) The feasts honored deities and therefore giving was obligatory. Failing to provide for the gods spelled divine rage, famine, epidemics, and doom for the community. (2) The procession of offerings was a social event when, in the midst of pageantry, before the entire citizenry, worshippers rivaled each other in presenting the most generous gift. (3) The queen, acting as intermediary between the people and the pantheon, gave the palace economic control. Finally, the king was the central figure of the ceremonies and the ultimate recipient of the offerings. The delivery of "gifts to the gods" set in motion the wheels of the Mesopotamian redistribution economy. The contributions forced each household to produce a surplus. Of course, all the monthly deliveries of animals and merchandise were not consumed at the feast, but increased the palace herds and granaries until their redistribution (Rosengarten 1960a:44). In Mesopotamia the feast was a fulcrum of the state redistribution economy.

ACKNOWLEDGMENT

Research assistance by Ines Rivera is gratefully acknowledged.

REFERENCES

Amiet, Pierre
　　1980　　*La glyptique Mésopotamienne archaïque.* Paris: Editions du Centre National de la Recherche Scientifique.

Boese, Johannes
　　1971　　*Altmesopotamische Weihplatten.* Berlin: Walter de Gruyter.

Bottéro, Jean
　　1994　　Boisson, banquet, et vie sociale en Mésopotamie. In *Drinking in Ancient Societies,* edited by Lucio Milano, pp. 3–13. Padova: Sargon srl.

Cohen, Mark E.
　　1996　　The Sun, the Moon, and the City of Ur. In *Religion and Politics in the Ancient Near East,* edited by Adele Berlin, pp. 7–20. Bethesda: University Press of Maryland.
　　1993　　*The Cultic Calendars of the Ancient Near East.* Bethesda: CDL Press.

Collon, Dominique
　　1992　　Banquets in the Art of the Ancient Near East. In *Banquets d'Orient,* edited by R. Gyselen, pp. 23–30. Res Orientales Vol. IV, Groupe pour l'Etude de la Civilisation du Moyen-Orient: Bures S/Y.

Cooper, Jerrold S.
　　1986　　*Sumerian and Akkadian Royal Inscriptions,* Vol. 1. New Haven: The American Oriental Society.

Finet, André
　　1992　　Le Banquet de Kalah offert par le Roi d'Assyrie Ashurnasirpal II (883–859). In *Banquets d'Orient,* edited by R. Gyselen, pp. 31–43. Res Orientales Vol. IV, Groupe pour l'Etude de la Civilisation du Moyen-Orient: Bures S/Y.

Lambert, W. G.
　　1993　　Donations of Food and Drink to the Gods in Ancient Mesopotamia. In *Ritual and Sacrifice in the Ancient Near East,* edited by J. Quaegebeur, pp. 191–201. Leuven: Uitgeverij Peeters en Departement Oriëntalistiek.

Limet, H.
    1970   L'organisation de quelques fêtes mensuelles á l'époque néo-Sumérienne. In *Actes de la XVIIe Rencontre Assyriologique Internationale,* edited by André Finet, pp. 59–74. Ham-sur-Heure: Comité Belge de recherches en Mésopotamie.

Moorey, P. R. S.
    1982   *Ur 'of the Chaldees': A Revised and Updated Version of Sir Leonard Woolley's Excavations at Ur.* Ithaca: Cornell University Press.

Oppenheim, A. Leo
    1964   *Ancient Mesopotamia.* Chicago: University of Chicago Press.

Pallis, Svend Aage
    1926   *The Babylonian Akitu Festival.* Copenhagen: Bianco Lunos Bogtrykkeri.

Parrot, André
    1953   *Mari.* Collection des Ides Photographiques, vol. 7. Neuchatel: Edition des Ides et Calendes.

Pinnock, Frances
    1994   Considerations on the 'Banquet Theme,' in the Figurative art of Mesopotamia and Syria. In *Drinking in Ancient Societies,* edited by Lucio Milano, pp. 15–26. Padova: Sargon srl.

Postgate, J. N.
    1992   *Early Mesopotamia.* London: Routledge.

Rosengarten, Yvonne
    1960a   *Le Concept Sumérien de Consommation dans la Vie Economique et Religieuse.* Paris: Editions E. de Boccard.
    1960b   *Le Régime des Offrandes dans la Société Sumérienne.* Paris: Editions E. de Boccard.

Sauren, H.
    1970   Les fêtes néo-sumériennes et leur périodicité. In *Actes de la XVIIe Rencontre Assyriologique Internationale,* edited by André Finet, pp. 11–29. Ham-sur-Heure: Comité Belge de recherches en Mésopotamie.

Schmandt-Besserat, Denise
    1992   *Before Writing.* Austin: University of Texas Press.

Vanstiphout, H. L. J.
    1992   The Banquet Scene in the Mesopotamian Debate Poems. In *Banquets d'Orient,* edited by R. Gyselen, pp. 9–21. Res Orientales Vol. IV, Groupe pour l'Etude de la Civilisation du Moyen-Orient: Bures S/Y.

15

GARBAGE AND THE MODERN AMERICAN FEAST

Douglas C. Wilson and William L. Rathje

In the last several decades, home entertaining in America has evolved dramatically from a matter of rules and regimens into a very personal, freewheeling affair.

Martha Stewart (1982:12)

The Crystal Ballroom in Portland, Oregon, operated between 1914 and 1968, hosting a diverse cross-section of American music and dance, from Dixieland jazz, waltzes, and "old time" traditional (square) dancing to soul music and psychedelic light shows. Historian Tim Hills's (1997) monograph on the ballroom documents that in the late 1950s and early 1960s, the operators augmented their revenues by leasing out the hall for Gypsy celebrations, including Feasts of the Dead. Attempts by Hills in the 1990s to interview participants at these mid-twentieth-century feasts were stymied by the Gypsy community's secretive and exclusionary nature, and their inherent mobility (Timothy Hills 1998, personal communication). The only reports on these Gypsy feasts are recollections by the operators of the Ballroom, who described the "vibrant attire," bouquets of flowers, tall candles, unfamiliar music, and exotic dance steps. What was most clearly remembered, however, was the massive cleanup afterwards, with gallons of spilled beer and pounds of roast lamb, pork, chicken bones, and waste scraps that had been casually discarded on the floor. One operator went to the trouble of taping cardboard over the entire dance floor prior to the Gypsy feasts to facilitate the subsequent cleanup.

In discussing feasting in industrialized societies, and the United States in particular, the Gypsy celebrations at the Crystal Ballroom are important anecdotes because they illustrate the difficulty in characterizing an "American" feasting behavior. The broad ranges of ethnic groups and economic classes that make up the United States participate in an equally daunting array of feasting activities, and it is difficult, even for those who live within the culture, to understand the full range of extant feasting behaviors. The Gypsy feasts also illustrate the problem of ethnographic-respondent recall and reporting, especially when the feast organizers and participants are unwilling to be interviewed. This bias in informant interviews, which has been discussed at length elsewhere (e.g., Ritenbaugh and Harrison 1984; Sechrest 1979; Webb et al. 1966), underscores the importance of the archaeological examination of feasting behavior, since the study of material objects is not subject to the same biases as traditional ethnographic techniques (Rathje 1995; Rathje and Murphy 1992:53–78).

In this chapter, we espouse a materials-based approach to the study of the American feast. We argue that the social and economic processes that have led to the widespread availability of specialty foods, the mass-production of low-cost commercial goods, and the shrinking size and increased financial independence of households in urban and suburban settings, have democratized, downsized, and fragmented the American feast. We suggest that many of the functions of American feasts have fallen away with their formal attributes, leaving "parties" that function primarily as solidarity feasts.

TYPES OF AMERICAN FEASTS

In attempting to discriminate between the many types of feasts in the United States, it is first appropriate to segregate those feasts held in and by the household from those given by larger social groups in nonhousehold settings. Although one might expect that this distinction has something to do with the number of feast participants or the size of the feast, this is not always the case. Some household gatherings can include hundreds of guests, whereas some business feasts include only a handful of people. Sometimes the only distinguishing feature of a household-level feast is its setting in a residence.

Inspection of a range of twentieth-century "American" cookbooks and entertaining guides suggests a variety of idealized "emic" types of household celebrations. Biddle and Blom's (1937), *The Book of Table Setting*, for example, details those times when "significant" table settings are appropriate, including family birthdays, Washington's Birthday, Lincoln's Birthday, Easter, Election Day, Valentine's Day, Independence Day, New Year's Day, St. Patrick's Day, April Fools Day, Memorial Day, Columbus Day, and wedding anniversaries. Berolzheimer's (1963:55–59) *The American Woman's Cookbook* identifies menus for "special occasions," including (in order), a St. Patrick's Day Luncheon, three varieties of Thanksgiving dinner, two varieties of Christmas dinner, four wedding menus, afternoon tea, afternoon or evening refreshments, a children's party, a school reception, a bridge party supper, a men's card party, and a cocktail party. Likewise, Meta Given's (1952:1573, 1576–1579) *Modern Encyclopedia of Cooking*, identifies two types of wedding breakfast, a wedding tea, a wedding dinner or supper, three types of Thanksgiving dinner, two types of Christmas dinner, two types of New Year's Day dinner, three menus for showers, two types of Easter menu, two types of Fourth of July menu, a Washington's Birthday luncheon, a Christmas luncheon, a "Hallowe'en" party, a birthday luncheon or dinner party, an after-skating, skiing or football "get-together," and an after-school Valentine's Day party. Other holidays not mentioned in these mid-twentieth-century guides include Martin Luther King's Day, Veterans Day, and Presidents' Day. The generic nature of most twentieth-century cookbook and entertaining guides is reflected in the fact that no non-Christian religious occasions are mentioned.

Cocktail parties are perhaps the most American of feasts, but as a type they are hard to define. Martha Stewart's (1982:30–61) menus for cocktail parties range from small gatherings of 6–8 people to a "large extenuated bash" of 200. Susan Roane's (1988:133) business guide, *How to Work a Room: A Guide to Successfully Managing the Mingling,* suggests that there are three types of cocktail parties: social, business, and fundraisers. Social cocktail parties often have a theme, based on a holiday or event, such as an engagement, housewarming, or holiday. Business cocktail parties include no-host receptions at conferences and business socials, including company picnics and the infamous year-end office party.

Sally Quinn (1997), who provides a unique insight into feasting behaviors in Washington D.C., describes a variety of functions, including (1) political parties, where information and ideas can be exchanged in an informal setting, (2) economic parties, which are designed to meet new contacts and reconnect with old ones, and (3) parties that are given for a person or to celebrate an event, such as a book signing.

Another set of American feasts, for which there are no guides, are those related to institutionalized settings, including campus fraternity and sorority parties, and payday and "leave" binges at logging camps, military posts, and other work-related settlements. Alcohol-dominated parties, related to pathological drinking behavior, also include those conducted by youths in areas hidden from parental and local authorities. "Raves" and other youth parties are poorly documented and only partly understood. Although Staski (1984) has detailed the potential for historical archaeology to address alcohol-consumption behavior, rarely have archaeologists considered their bottles of liquor, ale, beer, and wine as a possible reflection of feasting behavior.

Other American feasting types include dances and balls, bar mitzvahs, and funerals. Tourist entertainment feasts, such as Hawaiian luaus or "medieval banquets," are feast types specifically designed for tourist consumption (literally).

FIVE TUCSON FEASTING CASES

Though idealized American feasting types can be identified in the menus and entertaining guides that have flourished in the late twentieth century, they cannot alone predict how feasts in America are actually held, including how feasting materials are purchased, prepared, used, consumed, and wasted. In this section, we examine feasting refuse in modern Tucson, Arizona, discussing some of the variability in the material remains of these feasts and what they generally reveal about feasting in the United States. Our focus is narrowed to the household-level feast and limited to the distinctions in feasting that are visible archaeologically and that can be studied in a material sense. In our discussion, below, we treat American feasting in a more general context, extrapolating the patterns seen in the Tucson households to other social groups.

Over the years we have discerned many differences between the reported perceptions and understanding of a particular behavior and the material realities that represent the consequences of that behavior. Through taking an archaeological, rather than ethnographic or sociological approach to American feasting, we hope to provide information that is of practical value to archaeologists and that will contrast with our own, imperfect, understanding of feasting in industrialized societies (see Rathje 1995; Rathje and Murphy 1992:53–78).

Household garbage in Tucson, Arizona, is picked up twice a week. Since 1972, sanitation workers in Tucson have systematically gathered samples of household garbage left at the curbside and delivered them to student volunteers and research archaeologists of the University of Arizona's Garbage Project. The unit of cultural deposition for this study, therefore, is the individual household pickup, representing all the refuse placed at the curb for collection on a particular pickup day. Because we focus on the household pickup, our analysis is limited to those behaviors that occur within the household, and excludes those feasts that take place in restaurants, meeting halls, ballrooms, and elsewhere outside the household.

Residues from two different time periods were examined for evidence of feasting behavior: the Fall 1991 sample and the combined Spring and Fall 1994 sample.

Each pickup sampled during these two periods was painstakingly pored over by University of Arizona student researchers, documenting each specific item in the garbage. The goal of the present analysis is to identify the material remains of a small sample of Tucson feasts, and to detail those material associations for the types and quantities of foods, beverages, tobacco, and other material items used and discarded, the types of special serving vessels, the presence of conspicuous waste of food, and any evidence for the number and composition of people present. Based on the material remains, we also attempt to make some inferences on the likely organizers and contributors to the feast, the likely purpose of the feast, aspects of material redistribution, and other important elements of feasting behavior. Although we rely almost entirely on the material record to guide our interpretations, we acknowledge that we are participants in the culture we are studying and shamelessly employ our unique knowledge and experiences, and also an understanding of the American feasting calendar, to help in our interpretations.

The Fall 1991 sample comprised 65 pickups collected at various times between September 27 and December 5. Project archaeologists recorded more than 8,000 individual items. Four of the sample pickups were collected on December 2, the Monday after the November 28 Thanksgiving holiday. Two of these pickups contained good evidence for Thanksgiving feasting behavior. The first feasting type we discuss, then, is perhaps the most traditional of all the secular holidays of the United States. Both pickups were collected from a census tract of middle-class, predominantly Anglo-American families on the east side of Tucson.

CASE ONE: THANKSGIVING

A picture of the Thanksgiving feast associated with Sample C45-120291 (which we refer to as Case One) emerges from the close examination of the material items. Noting that any of these material objects could be found in any household pickup, it is the association of items, the high frequency of items, the diversity of items, and the date of deposition, that provides the best evidence for feasting behavior. Artifacts believed to originate from the Thanksgiving feast are listed in Table 15.1. In the practice of American historical archaeology, we have included the particulars of brand names and container sizes, along with frequency and type distinctions. This provides a clear material-culture context for the artifacts and an associational framework for the comparative study of feasting behavior in historical archaeology. Other students of material culture interested in identifying feasting behavior also may find it useful.

As discussed in the introductory chapter, one distinguishing attribute of feasting behavior is the preparation and serving of special foods. Not surprisingly,

TABLE 15.1
Artifacts Related to a Thanksgiving Feast in Sample C45-120291

Type	Material	Brand	Size	Description	No.
Food	plastic	Sager Crest		turkey wrapper	1
Food	faunal			turkey bones	17
Food	botanical		48 g	potato peel	
Food	plastic			preprepared potato wrapper	2
Food	paper	Kingston	7 oz.	macaroni and cheese wrapper	1
Food	ferrous can	Cablecar	20 oz.	peach can	1
Food	ferrous can	Kingston	10 oz.	sweet pea can	1
Food	plastic	Rainbow	48 oz.	bread wrapper	1
Food	paper/ferrous	Pillsbury	8 oz.	biscuit mix box	1
Food	faunal/botanical		350 g	"slop"	
Snack food	paper	Fritos	3 oz.	corn tortilla chip wrapper	1
Snack food	plastic	Saguaro	1 oz.	potato chip wrapper	1
Snack food	plastic	Tootsie Roll	5 lb	candy wrapper	1
Snack food	paper	Brachs		chocolate candy wrapper	1
Snack food	paper	Lifesavers		hard candy wrapper	1
Snack food	paper	Topps	1 oz.	bubble gum wrapper	1
Snack food	paper	Starburst		fruit chew candy wrapper	2
Snack food	paper	Kit Kat	2 oz.	chocolate candy wrapper	1
Food preparation/serving	aluminum			foil sheets	7
Food preparation/serving	textile			kitchen towel	1
Food preparation/serving	textile/plastic			table cloth	1
Food preparation/serving	plastic			trays	4
Food preparation/serving	paper			plates	38
Food preparation/serving	plastic			cups	3
Food preparation/serving	paper			paper towel roll	2
Food preparation/serving	plastic	Bounty		paper towel wrapper	1
Nonalcoholic beverages	aluminum	Pepsi	12 fl. oz.	soda can	1
Alcoholic beverages	aluminum	Old Milwaukee	12 fl. oz.	"light" lager beer can	3
Alcoholic beverages	aluminum	Hamms	12 fl. oz.	"light" lager beer can	3
Alcoholic beverages	aluminum	Budweiser	12 fl. oz.	"light" lager beer can	1
Alcoholic beverages	paper	Old Milwaukee	12-pack	lager beer label	1
Beverage related	plastic			six-pack ring	1
Other	plastic	Crystal Ice		ice bag	1
Tobacco	textile/paper	Marlboro		filter tip	149
Tobacco	textile/paper	Marlboro Lights		filter tip	18
Tobacco	textile/paper	Kool Lights		filter tip	10
Tobacco	textile/paper	Winston		filter tip	12
Tobacco	textile/paper	Viceroy		filter tip	1
Tobacco	paper/plastic	Doral Lights		pack	1
Tobacco	paper	Winston		carton	1

roasted turkey is one of the more archaeologically visible correlates of Thanks-giving feasting in the United States. For example, Dickens and Bowen (1980:51–53) used the relative frequency of turkey bones from a 1910 refuse deposit, associated with a "working class" neighborhood in Atlanta, Georgia, as one means to infer early-twentieth-century Thanksgiving and Christmas holiday behavior.

As shown in Table 15.1, the most obvious food items related to the Case One feast include a plastic "Sager Crest" turkey wrapper and 17 turkey bones. The bones found in this single pickup represent over one-quarter (27 percent) of the poultry bones (n=64) and 16 percent of the total bones (n=109) documented dur-ing the Fall analysis. As in the Dickens and Bowen (1980) study, the frequency of turkey items in Case One provides a strong indication of holiday feasting behav-ior. Other food items that may be related to the feast (Table 15.1) include various fresh and packaged food items, including 350 grams of mixed and unidentifiable food debris (classified as "slop" by the Garbage Project researchers). Snack foods are well represented, including both chips and candy.

There are several materials in the Case One pickup related to the preparation and serving of the Thanksgiving feast. These include aluminum foil sheets, plas-tic trays, and 38 paper plates, suggesting that at least part of the feast was served on disposable dinnerware. Evidence for beverage use at the feast is dominated by alcoholic beverages, with at least three types of low- to moderate-cost American lager beers. Tobacco consumption is represented by 190 filter tips from five differ-ent brands of cigarettes. These filters represent over 14 percent of all the cigarette butts recorded in the Fall 1991 sample of pickups. The quantity and diversity of cigarettes recorded in the Case One pickup provide good evidence that this Thanksgiving feast included an extended-family or suprahousehold gathering, with perhaps as many as six different smokers.

The image that emerges from Case One is of an extended family gathering with a traditional turkey dinner, notable alcohol consumption, the use of dispos-able paper plates, and a smoke-filled environment. Although some foods were apparently prepared from scratch, such as the turkey, many were purchased preprepared from the grocery store. There is no evidence for the use of expen-sive or exotic materials and much of the serving materials are cheap disposables.

CASE TWO: THANKSGIVING

Sample D45-120291 (Case Two) also contained good evidence for a Thanksgiving feast, but one that differs somewhat from that documented in Case One. For the sake of brevity, we have not listed in detail the materials related to feasting, but merely describe their general characteristics and how they compare with Case One. Case Two contained plastic wraps from a "Honeysuckle" brand turkey and a four-pound "Foster Farms" duck, but only a single bone (obviously, there were leftovers). Other fresh and packaged feast-related food items include oysters, potatoes (peels), broccoli, corn-on-the-cob, rolls, and pumpkin bread. Materials related to cooking and serving include an aluminum pie tin, an aluminum plate, a ferrous metal bowl, eight plastic trays, five plastic dishes, a paper cup, a plastic cup, one ferrous metal fork, and two plastic spoons.

As with Case One, there is evidence for consumption of nonalcoholic beverages, including coffee and soda, but the majority of beverage materials are related to the consumption of alcohol, including 40-ounce glass bottles of inexpensive malt liquor and quart bottles of inexpensive lager beer. Tobacco products in Case Two are also represented, although in much lower numbers (n=43 filters and two packs) and varieties (n=3) than Case One. This suggests to us that there were relatively few smokers at the feast, and possibly a smaller group of feasters, perhaps only a single household.

The material discards from the two Tucson Thanksgiving feasts are quite different, even though they were held in the same year in the same neighborhood. Case Two contains fewer packaged items, more fresh foods, and probably was held for fewer people than the Case One feast. One common element in both, however, is the consumption of relatively large amounts of alcoholic beverages. Even in the 1990s, when the health effects of alcohol and the dangers of drunk driving have been well publicized, alcohol appears necessary to the success of many American feasts (see Quinn 1997:118).

CASE THREE: HALLOWEEN

The largest quantity of alcohol-related items found in a sample pickup from the Fall of 1991 is also closely associated with a typically American holiday. Four sample pickups were collected on November 5, which was the Tuesday pickup after a previous Thursday Halloween. Of the four, three contained evidence of participation in the Halloween celebration. Two of these contained a relatively diverse range of candy wrappers and some Halloween paraphernalia, including bags and balloons. In contrast, Sample D45-110591 (Case Three) contained no candy wrappers or food debris of any kind. Instead, the sample contained 92 cans of low- to average-cost lager beer in 12- and 16-ounce sizes, comprising three brands and five varieties, including two varieties of "light" beer. These represent 66 percent of all the beer artifacts recorded in the entire Fall 1991 sample. Tobacco smoking was represented by 37 filter tips and an empty pack, all representing a single brand of cigarettes. The remainder of the sample consisted of 9 paper grocery sacks.

According to Martha Stewart (1982:33) the ideal home bar for "entertaining" has 21 different types of hard liquor and liqueurs, 6 bottles of white wine, 3 bottles of red wine, a 6-pack of "light" beer, a 6-pack of "dark" beer, and a 6-pack of imported beer. It is likely that the home bars associated with the Case One to

Case Three samples fall short of this ideal. The dominance of inexpensive lager beers in the samples belies the fact that they are derived from a middle-income, Anglo-American neighborhood. In this case, as with many instances of American feasting behavior, the cultural norms dictated by entertainment guides, cookbooks, and advertising differ considerably from the actual behavior of American households.

CASE FOUR: PRESIDENTS' DAY

Turning to the 1994 sample, we find two other pickups associated with high alcohol consumption, each of which, however, represent very different expressions of feasting behavior. A total of 63 pickups was collected between February 15 and December 1, 1994, representing nearly 11,000 recorded items. The artifacts associated with feasting in Sample C7-022394 (Case Four) are listed in Table 15.2. As with the Case Three Halloween feast, many artifacts are associated with alcoholic beverages (n=33 cans and 3 cartons), representing 33 percent of all the recorded beer items in the 1994 sample. These containers, however, represent only a single variety of moderate-cost lager. As shown in Table 15.2, tobacco consumption is also well represented by 126 filter tips and 11 packs, together representing two brands and four varieties of cigarettes. As listed in Table 15.2, a trace

TABLE 15.2
Artifacts Related to a Presidents' Day Feast in Sample C7-022394

Type	Material	Brand	Size	Description	No.
Food	corrugated cardboard			pizza boxes	2
Food preparation/serving	paper	Dixie		plates	7
Food preparation/serving	plastic	Dart		plastic fork	1
Alcoholic beverages	paper	Budweiser	12-pack	lager beer can	3
Alcoholic beverages	aluminum	Budweiser	12 fl. oz.	lager beer can	33
Nonalcoholic beverages	glass	Seagrams	1 liter	ginger ale bottle	1
Nonalcoholic beverages	plastic	Coca Cola	20 fl. oz.	cola bottle	1
Tobacco	textile/paper	Marlboro		filter tip	92
Tobacco	textile/paper	Marlboro light		filter tip	23
Tobacco	textile/paper	Camel light		filter tip	10
Tobacco	textile/paper	Camel light menthol		filter tip	1
Tobacco	paper/plastic	Marlboro		pack	6
Tobacco	paper/plastic	Marlboro light		pack	2
Tobacco	paper/plastic	Camel Light		pack	3
Illicit drugs			trace	marijuana	1

of marijuana was also recorded. The pizza boxes provide the best evidence for foods consumed at the feast, although fast-food packaging found in the pickup (not listed) also could be related to the feasting activities. Serving items recorded in the sample include paper and plastic dinnerware.

Because there was only a single brand of beer, we initially thought that Case Four was associated with pathological alcohol consumption. A consideration of the date of the pickup, though, along with the amount and variety of cigarette butts, suggests that it is not. The sample was collected Wednesday, February 23, 1994, which closely followed the Presidents' Day holiday, on Monday, February 21. If these materials do represent pathological drinking, then this behavior is correlated with, and perhaps accentuated by, the holiday weekend. Holidays, such as paydays, are probably often an excuse for binge drinking. Many entertainment guides stress that there should be a defined purpose for a party. We hypothesize that in many American households, the excuse for feasting is that there is a surplus of cash, a day or two off work, and a thirst for ethyl alcohol.

CASE FIVE: MIDWEEK PARTY

Sample A7-031194 (Case Five) was collected on March 11, 1994, which was a Friday pickup not associated with any common United States holiday. The contents of Case Five are listed in Table 15.3. Alcoholic beverage artifacts are again dominated by beer containers, although a much greater variety of beers are present (seven brands), including more expensive imported Mexican lagers and specialty "craft-brewed" ales. Other alternative "malt beverages" are also present, and perhaps most interesting from a material-culture perspective, all of the containers are glass. The beer containers in this pickup represent 29 percent of all the beer items recorded in the 1994 sample. As with the other cases, nonalcoholic beverages are few in number.

Food items in Case Five are dominated by a variety of snack foods, including nuts, popcorn, and chips. The two plastic deli cups and three plastic containers may have held take-out party foods or snacks. Notably, there were no paper plates, cups, or silverware. The 60 grams of fresh lime waste are undoubtedly associated with the serving of the Mexican beer. There were no cigarette butts or other tobacco packaging.

Obviously, the materials recorded in Case Five contrast greatly with the Case Four Presidents' Day feast. A variety of higher-cost, imported beers are represented, and there is a selection of snacks and specialty foods. Smoking items are conspicuously absent. Based entirely on the types of artifacts present, it is very likely that the goals of the Case Five feast were considerably different from that of Case Four, especially in portraying status through beverage selection (a variety of more expensive imported and craft beers), food selection (snack foods), a feast-

TABLE 15.3

Artifacts Related to a Midweek Party in Sample A7-031194

Type	Material	Brand	Size	Description	No.
Food	paper	Wonder Roast		chicken wrapper	1
Food	faunal		504 g	chicken bones	
Food	botanical		60 g	lime	
Snack food	plastic	Laura Scudder		popcorn wrapper	2
Snack food	paper	Golden Valley	3 oz.	popcorn wrapper	1
Snack food	botanical		18 g	popcorn waste	
Snack food	plastic	Eagle	6 oz.	potato chip wrapper	1
Snack food	plastic	Reina	6 oz.	tortilla chip wrapper	1
Snack food	plastic	Penguina		hard candy wrapper	1
Alcoholic beverages	glass	Dos Equis	12 fl. oz.	lager beer bottle	11
Alcoholic beverages	glass	Corona	12 fl. oz.	lager beer bottle	8
Alcoholic beverages	glass	Amstel Light	12 fl. oz.	lager beer bottle	4
Alcoholic beverages	glass	Bohemia	12 fl. oz.	lager beer bottle	2
Alcoholic beverages	glass	Columbus	12 fl. oz.	lager beer bottle	1
Alcoholic beverages	glass	Bridgeport	12 fl. oz.	ale bottle	1
Alcoholic beverages	glass	McTarnahan's	12 fl. oz.	ale bottle	1
Alcoholic beverages	corrugated cardboard	Corona	12-pack	lager beer box	1
Alcoholic beverages	paper	Dos Equis	6-pack	lager beer label	1
Alcoholic beverages	paper	Winterfun	6-pack	beer label	1
Alcoholic beverages	glass	Zima	12 fl. oz.	malt beverage bottle	5
Alcoholic beverages	paper	Zima	6-pack	malt beverage label	1
Nonalcoholic beverages	aluminum	Pepsi Cola	12 fl. oz.	cola can	2
Nonalcoholic beverages	paper			coffee filters	2
Nonalcoholic beverages	botanical			coffee grounds	1

ing "etiquette" or a lifestyle that does not include tobacco consumption, and food service that does not employ disposable dinnerware.

DISCUSSION

This brief foray into feasting in modern Tucson, Arizona, provides some primary material data to discuss feasting behavior in the United States. Our first impression is that there are many feasts. The five cases of feasting, noted here, represent 4 percent of the 128 pickups for the combined Fall 1991 and Spring/Fall 1994 samples, and we have merely scratched the surface of the data, pulling out the most compelling examples. Even at 4 percent, it can be roughly estimated that feasts in Tucson are occurring at a rate of one per household every 100 days or so.

Second, certain types of foods, and most types of alcohol and tobacco products, are consumed at United States feasts in high frequencies compared with regular, everyday consumption of these items. Archaeologically, the material residues of feasting in Tucson skew the total frequencies of residues related to food and beverage use. Certain specialty items, such as fresh, whole turkey, are consumed predominantly during year-end holiday seasons. Because of the unique associations of materials and the diversity and high frequency of items, the residues of many modern feasts are probably archaeologically observable.

THE DEMOCRATIZATION OF THE AMERICAN FEAST

Another obvious characteristic of the five cases documented here is in the flexibility of expression of the feasting behavior. The particular choices of foods, beverages, and table settings, is based somewhat on tradition and "emic" prescriptions, but also clearly on choices dictated at the household level about what is appropriate for the guests. This observed flexibility is echoed in the twentieth-century entertaining guides. For example, Stewart notes that there are no longer rigorous prescriptions for social habits and rituals, but that "the growing body of experience in America—social as well as culinary—has fostered a new openness and respect for diversity" (1982:12). Biddle and Blom advise "As we may consider ourselves unhampered by the requisites of the formal dinner we may let our motto be: try anything" (1937:19).

There are a few bastions of formal feasting etiquette that remain. For example, The International Guild of Professional Butlers (1998), provides standards for service techniques over the Internet, including topics on "the Banquet," "the Formal Dinner," and "Entertaining." Quinn (1997:153–154) recommends that persons of "obvious rank or stature," such as the President of the United States, the secretary of state, a state's governor, or a city's mayor, should be given the seat of honor. However, in almost the same breath, she discourages seating guests "below the salt" and espouses the use of round tables to balance status differences and to treat all guests as if they were "celebrities." In America, the status differences of feasters appear to be kept well hidden.

It is also important to note that all of the items found in the Tucson refuse samples could be purchased from any grocery store in any town or city in the United States. In a sense, the United States has democratized feasting through making delicacies available to almost everyone year-round and through the mass-production of feasting paraphernalia, including low-cost china, decorations, and other elements of buffet and table settings. Only the most expensive, truly elite goods, are out of reach of most Americans. Although it is within the economic means for many households to pay $20 to $40 for a bottle of wine for a special occasion, there are only a few who will consume the most expensive products. Notably, the archaeological evidence for use of these extremely high-end products is exceedingly rare. They are simply not found in common grocery stores, or even in many specialty stores, and since such a small segment of the population is using them, they are archaeologically invisible. The notion of "saturation point" or decreasing marginal utility for white ceramics, considered by Spencer-Wood and Heberling (1987:60) is valuable in this regard. After attaining a certain level of value in feast foods and table settings, little is gained by additional expenditures, regardless of income and wealth. We would argue that in most American households this threshold has already been achieved.

The demise of formal, prescribed feasting rituals, such as the English tea ceremony and the formal dinner, is probably directly related to industrialization and the advent of mass-produced consumer goods in late-nineteenth- and twentieth-century America. This in turn has resulted in the flexibility that is a characteristic of the modern American feast. The *American Woman's Cook Book* identifies "the problem of the formal meal," suggesting that "elaborate meals are not justified from any point of view, social, physiological or economic, and that even the most formal meal must follow the rules of health" (Berolzheimer 1963:54).

Biddle and Blom (1937) noted the mid-twentieth-century economic processes that were changing the American feast: "Variety and change are not for the wealthy, the favored few, but for Everywoman." They suggest that the increased availability of mass-produced consumer goods resulted in "a change of glasses" being equal to the price of a movie, and the cost of a centerpiece bowl being equal to the cost of a pack of cigarettes. It is also clear that by the mid-twentieth century, there was a reemphasis away from the home production of feasting foods to the greater use of prepackaged substitutes. Feasting foods discussed in Jacqueline Williams (1996) *The Way We Ate: Pacific Northwest Cooking, 1843–1900*, are dominated by home-prepared cakes and sweet breads. In contrast, the 1954 *Cooked to Taste* cookbook of the Junior League of Portland provides a section entitled "The Cook Is at the Party" that lists meals that can be made in the morning, thereby releasing the "hostess" to enjoy her party.

Part of the trend away from formality is reflected in the abundance of disposable dinnerware noted in our Tucson feasts. Although entertainment guides discourage the use of paper and plastic plates, cups, and other disposable china and tableware, these are often used in lieu of ceramics, glass, and other durable items for a variety of American feasts. As early as 1964, the National Industrial Conference Board noted a downward trend in the United States production of ceramic products due partly to substitute products, including pressed glass and plastic materials. In the late twentieth century, paper and plastic disposable substitutes have become much more dominant. Franklin Associates (1998) estimates that the contribution of paper and plastic plates and cups in the municipal solid waste stream of the United States has risen from 0.3 percent by weight in 1960 to 0.9 percent in 1996.

This flexibility in feasting behavior is a characteristic of the United States and may be a characteristic of industrialized nations. Historical archaeologists have begun to track the material implications of the greater availability and lower costs of mass-produced ceramic tablewares and other consumer goods, and the decreasing reliance on home-processed and prepared foods reflected in late-nineteenth-century and early-twentieth-century refuse deposits (e.g., De Cunzo 1987:282; Purser 1992). The modern garbage data provides evidence for the newest and most disposable stage in the evolution of the American feast.

While the United States has democratized feasting, it also has downsized it. By downsizing, we mean both the size of the feasting group tends to be smaller and the percentage of material resources poured into the feast is much less. We hypothesize that feasts in America usually involve one or two extended families, say no more than 15 to 45 people. All of our examples, above, involved relatively low numbers of participants, usually one household, with perhaps no more than 6 to 12 additional people. As some papers in this volume illustrate, in nonindustrial societies, feasts often involve the best food and drink within the group's finances, and sometimes even beyond the group's finances. In contrast, American feasts have been streamlined, especially the larger ones, with standard menus, no seconds, and short serving times. We have routinized our fares. Even our largest and most grand "big man" feasts—the inauguration of the President of the United States, the annual meeting banquets for the strongest companies, and retirement dinners—cannot be termed food extravaganzas. Balls and socials, which were very popular in the late nineteenth and early twentieth centuries, have largely given way to cocktail parties and socializing in bars, taverns, and pubs. The roots of this shift in American feasting are undoubtedly related to the late-nineteenth- and early-twentieth-century shift from a largely agrarian society to one that is urban and suburban. Downsizing of the American family has led to the downsizing of the American feast.

FUNCTION AND FRAGMENTATION

Though it is possible that competitive feasting of the very wealthy in America may be to enhance status, secure positions, or to make alliances with business partners, the feasts of most Americans, as revealed in Tucson's garbage, are more closely tied to entertainment. Consider how many traditional religious and secular holidays in the United States have been corrupted, from honoring religious and traditional values to overt materialism. For many Americans, the original purposes of many of these feasting days, to celebrate social and economic mobility or to venerate a public figure or deity, has become another reason for a party. Drinking celebrations, such as St. Patrick's Day, or even Mardi Gras, are excellent examples. As Sally Quinn (1997:21) advises, "there are a thousand reasons to have a party or to entertain," but the one legitimate reason is to have a good time. As noted above, there are some practical benefits of the feast in industrialized societies. American feasts undoubtedly provide valuable settings for informal information exchange, yet because the size of households is small and the links with other relatives and friends are weak, they are probably qualitatively different from nonindustrial societies.

Perhaps the best illustration of how we differ from feasting in nonindustrial societies is how much feasting we do in restaurants (Fig. 15.1). Just try to get a dinner reservation on Christmas, Thanksgiving, or Easter! This also illustrates how the social value of feasting has been lost. By transporting them to restaurants, we have, in a sense, both emasculated and secularized feasts. Compare hundreds of

All of the trimmings.
None of the hassle.

This Thanksgiving, make a pilgrimage to our table
for a traditional feast without the traditional clean-up.

Figure 15.1. A Marriott hotel advertisement for a restaurant feast.

418

Enga (New Guinea) feast participants in and around a Kepele ancestral cult house (Wiessner, Chapter 4) with 200 Americans "feasting" in a restaurant. There is cohesion and integration in the United States because everyone knows the social rules for restaurant dining and everyone gets in and out in an orderly manner, but there is also tremendous luxury and individuality—anything can be ordered on the menu.

Perhaps the most striking element of the United States feast in restaurants, however, is fragmentation. There are numerous small social units that mingle in the same feasting hall, but do not acknowledge one another, do not know each other's background or where they are from. At the payment time, debts are not marked up in the social and political order, but each little social fragment presents a credit card and is gone with a full belly but no relationships left behind.

CONCLUSION

We are brought back to the Gypsy feasts at the Crystal Ballroom. The complexity of the American feasting system is daunting, and our generalities noted here cannot come close to characterizing the full range of feasts in the United States. We acknowledge that there are many feasts that still preserve religious and other important qualities, and like the Gypsy celebrations, they are difficult to approach using traditional methods. The archaeological evidence for feasting in the United States, however, is present in the abundant wastes discarded from feasting behavior. Through a materials-based approach, archaeologists and other anthropologists can begin to document systematically the variability in feasting in the United States and elsewhere, and begin to quantify and better specify our general statements about American feasting behavior.

REFERENCES

Berolzheimer, Ruth, ed.
  1963 *The American Woman's Cook Book*. Garden City, New York: Garden City Publishing.

Biddle, Dorothy, and Dorothea Blom
  1937 *The Book of Table Setting*. New York: Doubleday, Doran & Company.

De Cunzo, Lu Ann
  1987 Adapting to Factory and City: Illustrations from the Industrialization and Urbanization of Paterson, New Jersey. In *Consumer Choice in Historical Archaeology*, edited by Suzanne M. Spencer-Wood, pp. 261–295. New York: Plenum.

Dickens, Roy S., Jr., and William R. Bowen
  1980 Problems and Promises in Urban Historical Archaeology: The MARTA Project. *Historical Archaeology* 14:42–57.

Franklin Associates, Ltd.

1998   *Characterization of Municipal Solid Waste in the United States: 1997 Update.* Franklin Associates, Ltd., Prairie Village, Kansas. Submitted to the U.S. Environmental Protection Agency, Municipal and Industrial Solid Waste Division, Office of Solid Waste. Report No. EPA530-R-98-007. Copies available from the U.S. Environmental Protection Agency, Municipal and Industrial Solid Waste Division, Office of Solid Waste.

Given, Meta

1952   *Meta Given's Modern Encyclopedia of Cooking.* Chicago: J. G. Ferguson and Associates.

Hills, Tim

1997   *The Many Lives of the Crystal Ballroom.* Gresham, Ore.: Accuprint.

The International Guild of Professional Butlers

1998   The International Guild of Professional Butlers web page. Electronic document. http://www.butlersguild.com/201.htm

Junior League of Portland, Oregon

1954   *Cooked to Taste.* Portland, Ore.: The Junior League of Portland.

National Industrial Conference Board, Inc.

1964   *Stone, Clay, and Glass Products.* New York: National Industrial Conference Board.

Purser, Margaret

1992   Consumption as Communication in Nineteenth-Century Paradise Valley, Nevada. *Historical Archaeology* 26 (3): 105–116.

Quinn, Sally

1997   *The Party: A Guide to Adventurous Entertaining.* New York: Simon and Schuster.

Rathje, William L.

1995   Forever Separate Realities. In *Expanding Archaeology,* edited by James M. Skibo, William H. Walker, and Axel E. Nielsen, pp. 36–43. Salt Lake City: University of Utah Press.

Rathje, William L., and Cullen Murphy

1992   *Rubbish! The Archaeology of Garbage.* New York: HarperCollins.

Ritenbaugh, Cheryl K., and Gail G. Harrison

1984   Reactivity of Garbage Analysis. *American Behavioral Scientist* 28 (1): 51–70.

Roane, Susan

1988   *How to Work a Room: A Guide to Successfully Managing the Mingling.* New York: Shapolsky.

Sechrest, L., ed.

1979   *Unobtrusive Measures Today: New Directions for Methodology of Behavioral Science.* San Francisco: Josey-Bass.

Spencer-Wood, Suzanne M., and Scott D. Heberling

1987   Consumer Choices in White Ceramics: A Comparison of Eleven Early Nineteenth-Century Sites. In *Consumer Choice in Historical Archaeology,* edited by Suzanne M. Spencer-Wood, pp. 55–84. New York: Plenum.

Staski, Edward

1984   Just What Can a 19th Century Bottle Tell Us? *Historical Archaeology* 18 (1): 38–51.

Stewart, Martha

1982   *Entertaining.* New York: Clarkson N. Potter.

Webb, E. J., D. T. Campbell, R. D. Schwarts, and L. Sechrest

1966   *Unobtrusive Measures: Nonreactive Research in the Social Sciences.* Chicago: Aldine.

Williams, Jacqueline B.

1996   *The Way We Ate: Pacific Northwest Cooking, 1843–1900.* Pullman, Wash.: Washington State University Press.

Index

Page numbers followed by *f* refer to figures